Multicomputer Networks: Message-Based Parallel Processing

MIT Press Series in Scientific Computation
Dennis Gannon, editor

Multicomputer Networks: Message-Based Parallel Processing

Daniel A. Reed and Richard M. Fujimoto

The MIT Press
Cambridge, Massachusetts
London, England

Publisher's Note

This format is intended to reduce the cost of publishing certain works in book form and to shorten the gap between editorial preparation and final publication. Detailed editing and composition have been avoided by photographing the text of this book directly from the author's prepared copy.

Second printing, 1988

This book was printed and bound in the United States of America.

Library of Congress Cataloging-in-Publication Data

Reed, Daniel A.
  Multicomputer networks.

  (MIT Press series in scientific computation)
  Includes index.
  1. Computer networks. 2. Parallel processing
(Electronic computers) I. Fujimoto, Richard M.
II. Title. III. Series.
TK5105.5.R44 1987   004'.35   87-22833
ISBN 0-262-18129-0

To Andrea,
for her love and belief in my dreams

To Jan,
for her constant encouragement and devotion

Contents

Contents

Contents

Contents

Series Foreword

It is often the case that the periods of rapid evolution in the physical sciences occur when there is a timely confluence of technological advances and improved experimental techniques. Many physicists, computer scientists, chemists, biologists, and mathematicians have said that such a period of rapid change is now underway. We are currently undergoing a radical transformation in the way we view the boundaries of experimental science. It has become increasingly clear that the use of large-scale computation and mathematical modeling is now one of the most important tools in the scientific and engineering laboratory. We have passed the point where the computer is viewed as just a device for tabulating and correlating experimental data; we now regard it as a primary vehicle for testing theories for which no practical experimental apparatus can be built. NASA scientists speak of ''numerical'' wind tunnels, and physicists use supercomputers to see what happens during the birth of a universe.

The major technological change accompanying this new view of experimental science is a blossoming of new approaches to computer architecture and algorithm design. By exploiting the natural parallelism in scientific applications, new computer designs show the promise of being able to solve problems whose solutions were considered unreachable a few years ago. When coupled with the current biennial doubling of memory capacity, supercomputers are on their way to becoming the laboratories of much of modern science.

With the advent of fast, powerful microprocessors, a new branch of the computer industry has emerged. By using large numbers of these cheap processors, each connected to a large private memory, it is possible to build a computing system with very impressive potential performance. If the processors are connected to each other so that they can exchange messages in a reasonably efficient manner and if the programmer can decompose his computation into a large system of communicating processes, such a multicomputer network can be a powerful supercomputer.

Fujimoto and Reed have written the first comprehensive treatment of the architecture and performance modeling of this family of nonshared-memory MIMD computing systems. Their book begins with a survey of the basic architectural ideas behind the current generation of hypercube systems but quickly moves into the main contribution of the volume: a foundation for the analytical modeling and rigorous simulation of multicomputer networks. Along the way they give a treatment of the VLSI constraints on network nodes and a survey of the issues confronted in designing operating systems for multicomputer networks. The volume concludes with a detailed performance analysis of the current crop of commercial systems.

While it is very exciting to see a book on a topic of such great current interest to so many scientists, it is even more important to see a volume that can set the standard for analytical study of these systems. This volume is required reading not only for students wishing to learn about the current family of systems but also for the architects designing the next generation of hypercube machines.

Dennis B. Gannon

Preface

The recent appearance of powerful single-chip processors and inexpensive memory has renewed interest in the message passing paradigm for parallel computation. Much of this interest can be traced to the construction of the CalTech Cosmic Cube, a group of Intel 8086/8087 chips with associated memory connected as a D-dimensional **hypercube**.

Following the success of the Cosmic Cube, four companies (Intel, Ametek, Ncube, and Floating Point Systems) quickly began delivery of commercial hypercubes. These hypercube systems are but one member of a broader class of machines, called **multicomputer networks**, that consist of a large number of interconnected computing nodes that asynchronously cooperate via message passing to execute the tasks of parallel programs. Each network node, fabricated as a small number of VLSI chips, contains a processor, a local memory, and (optionally) a communication controller capable of routing messages without delaying the computation processor.

Multicomputer networks pose several important and challenging problems in network topology selection, communication hardware design, operating systems, fault tolerance, and algorithm design. This monograph summarizes recent results in each of these areas, with the following emphases.

● *Analytic Models of Interconnection Networks.* Although the hypercube topology has many attractive features, many other network interconnection topologies are not only possible, but are often preferable for certain algorithm classes. Chapter two analyzes the effectiveness of several metrics for topology evaluation and presents a new metric based on asymptotic bound analysis. The chapter concludes with a comparison of several proposed network topologies.

● *VLSI Constraints and Communication.* Whether each node of a multicomputer network is implemented as a single VLSI component or as a printed circuit board, packaging constraints limit the number of connections that can be made to the node, placing an upper bound on the total I/O bandwidth available for communication links. As more links are added to each node, less bandwidth is available for each one. However, increasing the number of links connected to each node will usually reduce the mean number of hops required to reach a particular destination. Chapter three examines the balance between link bandwidth and mean hop count as the number of links to each node varies.

● *Communication Paradigms and Hardware Support.* Because multicomputer networks are limited in extent to a few cabinets, rather than a geographic area, they require hardware, rather than software, support for message transport, routing, buffer management, and flow control. Chapter four evaluates design alternatives for each of these issues and presents one possible hardware realization.

- *Multicomputer Operating Systems.* There are two primary approaches to parallel processing and task scheduling on a multicomputer network. In the first, all parallel tasks in a computation are known *a priori* and are mapped onto the network nodes before the computation is initiated. The tasks remain on their assigned nodes throughout the entire computation. In the second, the mapping of tasks onto network nodes is done dynamically. Here, a parallel computation is defined by a dynamically created task precedence graph where new tasks are initiated and existing tasks terminate as the computation unfolds. Although static tasks can be scheduled at compile time by a single processor, dynamically created tasks must be assigned to network nodes by a distributed scheduling algorithm executing on the network. Chapter five summarizes approaches to the static scheduling problem, analyzes the feasibility of dynamic task scheduling, and reviews the current state of the art.

No examination of message passing systems would be complete without a discussion of potential application algorithms. Parallel discrete event simulation represents one extreme of the application spectrum where the task interaction pattern can be very irregular and change greatly over the program lifetime. At the opposite extreme, iterative partial differential equations (PDE) solvers typically iterate over a regular grid with nearest neighbor communication among parallel tasks.[1]

- *Applications: Distributed Simulation.* Simulation of complex systems imposes extraordinary computational requirements. War games with battlefield management, functional simulation of integrated circuits and Monte Carlo simulation of many particle systems often require hundreds or thousands of hours on the fastest computer systems that are currently available. Several approaches to discrete event simulation based on parallel execution and message passing paradigms have been developed. Chapter six surveys the state of the art in distributed simulation and discusses the performance ramifications for multicomputer networks.

- *Applications: Partial Differential Equations.* Existing hypercubes have already been widely used as testbeds for iterative, partial differential equations solvers. However, there are many ways to partition the iteration grid into parallel tasks. For example, on the Intel iPSC hypercube, domain partitioning by strips has been used even though strip

---

[1]More sophisticated PDE solvers exist, however, that exhibit complex, time dependent behavior.

partitions are provably non-optimal when data transfer is used as a metric. The reason: the high message startup costs on the iPSC favor minimization of message *count* rather than the amount of data transferred. Chapter seven analyzes the interaction of problem partitioning and architectural parameters and presents a performance model that identifies the appropriate partitioning for a given multicomputer network.

- *Commercial Hypercubes: A Performance Analysis.* Four hypercube families are now commercially available: the Intel iPSC, Ametek System/14, Ncube/ten, and FPS T Series. Moreover, several groups are actively constructing research prototypes, notably the JPL Mark-III at CalTech and NASA Jet Propulsion Laboratory. Chapter eight evaluates the hardware designs and system software of the four commercial hypercubes and the JPL Mark-III. In addition, chapter eight presents a comparative performance study using a set of processor and communication benchmarks.

Acknowledgments

We would be remiss not to acknowledge the colleagues and students whose insights, enthusiasm and suggestions shaped this work during its formative stages. In the early years, Herbert Schwetman and Carlo Séquin directed the dissertation research presented in chapters two, three and four. Their guidance was invaluable; we owe them a great debt.

Many of the benchmarks in chapter eight were conducted by Dirk Grunwald while visiting the NASA Jet Propulsion Laboratory. The evaluations of competing hypercube architectures and insights into their performance limitations are his. His eagerness to hypothesize and experiment embody the scientific spirit.

Members of the Concurrent Computation Project at CalTech/JPL, particularly John Fanslow and Herb Madan, cheerfully offered advice and provided access to the JPL Mark-III. Jack Dongarra provided access to the Intel iPSC at Argonne National Laboratory. David Poplawski and Brenda Helminen of Michigan Technological University graciously provided both the benchmark data and the FPS T Series example program discussed in chapter eight.

The students in the *Picasso* research group were a continual source of inspiration and delight. Without them this would not have been possible. To Dirk Grunwald, David Bradley, Bobby Nazief, Chong Kim and Balkrishna Ramkumar, our undying gratitude. Finally, students from the Computer Science Departments at the University of Utah and the University of Illinois at Urbana-Champaign provided many valuable comments on drafts of the text while they were used for classes.

During this writing Daniel Reed was supported in part by the National Science Foundation under grants NSF DCR 84-17948, NSF DCI 86-05082 and an NSF Presidential Young Investigator Award, and by the National Aeronautics and Space Administration under grants NASA NAG-1-613 and NASA NAG-1-595. Richard Fujimoto was supported by the Office of Naval Research under contract N00014-87-K-0184 and a University of Utah Research Grant. Both Dr. Reed and Dr. Fujimoto were also supported by Faculty Development Awards from International Business Machines.

Daniel A. Reed
Richard M. Fujimoto

July 1987

Multicomputer Networks: Message-Based Parallel Processing

1 Introduction

We do but learn today what our better advanced judgements will unteach us tomorrow.

Sir Thomas Browne

High speed computer design continues to be driven by the need to evaluate increasingly realistic models of natural phenomena. Many important problems in nuclear physics, weather prediction, oil exploration, and computer aided design require far more computational power than can be provided by the fastest computer systems currently available. For example, plasma confinement models used in controlled thermonuclear fusion research are simplified two-dimensional cross-sections of actual confinement chamber geometries. Estimates suggest that machines at least 100 times faster than today's supercomputers will be needed to evaluate realistic three-dimensional models.

Given the clear and pressing need for improved computer system performance, there are several means of achieving this end. In the simplest approach, current computer architectures are reimplemented using faster device technologies. Although this approach will always be exploited, physical, technological, and economic limitations make it incapable of providing all the needed computational power. Instead, *parallelism* must be exploited to obtain truly significant performance improvements.

In the spectrum of parallel processor designs, there are three primary demarcation points based on the number and complexity of the processors. At one extreme are simple, bit-serial processors. Although any one of these processors is of little value by itself, the aggregate computing power can be large when many are coupled together. This approach to parallel processing can be likened to a large colony of termites devouring a log. The most notable examples of this approach include the Goodyear Massively Parallel Processor (MPP) [Pott85] and the Thinking Machines Connection Machine that each use tens of thousands of 1-bit processing elements.

At the opposite extreme, machines such as the Cray X-MP use a small number of powerful processors. Each processor contains a sophisticated pipelined architecture and is built using the fastest available circuit technology. Continuing our analogy, this approach is similar to four woodsmen with chain saws.

The third, intermediate approach combines a large number of microprocessors. This is analogous to a small army of hungry beavers. Within the last ten years, several groups have advocated such an approach to parallel processing based on large networks of interconnected microcomputers [Jord78, Witt80, ArBG85, SeFu82, Fuji83, KuWR82, Seit85]. As proposed, the nodes of these **multicomputer networks** would contain a processor with some locally addressable memory, a communication controller capable of routing messages without delaying the processor, and a small number of connections to other nodes. Because multicomputer networks contain no shared memory, the cooperating tasks of a parallel algorithm must execute asynchronously on different nodes and communicate solely via message passing.

The development of multicomputer networks clearly depends on the recent appearance of powerful single-chip processors and inexpensive memory. Although the multicomputer network offers potentially enormous computational power at modest cost, many important questions must be resolved before multicomputer networks with performance exceeding today's supercomputers can be marketed. For example, multicomputer operating system software must adapt to communication transients and load imbalances; application programs must be partitioned into concurrently executing tasks and mapped onto the processor network. In this book, we examine several aspects of multicomputer networks, including hardware and software design issues, evaluations of existing multicomputer networks, and the design of parallel algorithms.

We begin this chapter by defining a multicomputer network and enumerating those characteristics that distinguish it from other parallel systems. Given this definition, we examine the spectrum of parallel systems designs and compare them to the multicomputer network. We conclude with an outline of the remainder of the book.

1.1. Multicomputer Networks: A Definition

A multicomputer network consists of hundreds or thousands of *nodes* connected in some fixed *topology*. As figure 1.1 shows, a multicomputer node minimally contains a microprocessor, local memory, and hardware support for internode communication.[1] Specific applications may dictate inclusion of specialized co-processors for floating point, graphics, or secondary storage operations. Ideally, each node would be directly connected to all other nodes. Unfortunately, packaging constraints and hardware costs

---

[1]The nodes of the Intel iPSC [Inte86a, Ratt85], a commercial multicomputer network, each contain an Intel 80286 microprocessor, an Intel 80287 floating point co-processor, 512K bytes of memory, and an Ethernet™ controller for each communication link.

limit the number of connections to a small number, typically ten or less. Because the node degree is limited, messages must often be routed through a sequence of intermediate nodes to reach their final destinations.

Given the interacting tasks of a parallel program, each multicomputer node must execute some number of those tasks; execute those operating system routines that manage system resources; and send and receive messages, both for the tasks resident on the node and for those tasks whose messages transit the node. Throughout this text we will examine important design issues related to each of these three functions.

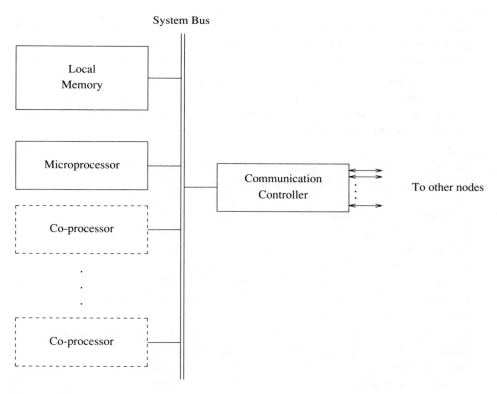

Figure 1.1
Multicomputer node

The key characteristics of a multicomputer network that distinguish it from other parallel processor organizations are:

- *Large numbers of processors.* Because microprocessors are inexpensive, easily packaged, and consume little power, it is economically feasible to design systems containing hundreds or thousands of processors. A multicomputer network of a few hundred nodes can have a peak performance exceeding that of today's supercomputers.

- *Asynchronous execution.* Each node executes independently of all other nodes. Synchronization between nodes relies on message passing primitives.

- *Message based communications.* In contrast to tightly coupled computer organizations such as the University of Illinois Cedar [KDLS86] and IBM RP3 [PBGH85] where processors communicate through shared memory, the nodes of a multicomputer network communicate solely via message passing.

- *Moderate communication overhead.* Communication delays are often measured in milliseconds in loosely coupled distributed systems such as a network of workstations. In contrast, delays in a well-designed multicomputer communication network should not exceed a few hundred microseconds.

- *Medium grained computation.* Any parallel program consists of a collection of cooperating "tasks." The "grain" of a computation denotes the size of these tasks and may be measured by the amount of computation between task interactions. The massive parallelism afforded by a multicomputer network encourages exploitation of parallelism by decomposing programs into many small tasks. However, an extremely *fine* computation granularity will be inefficient because communication and task swapping overheads will dominate. Balancing the desire for parallelism against these overheads leads one to conclude that multicomputer networks are best suited for medium grain computations whose lifetimes are significantly larger than a few arithmetic operations but smaller than the processes traditionally associated with sequential computer systems.

- *User implemented program decomposition.* Currently, application programs for multicomputer networks must be manually decomposed into concurrently executing tasks. Development of new programming languages, sophisticated compilers, and adaptive operating systems that can automatically exploit the parallelism provided by the multicomputer hardware is still nascent. The lack of adequate system software is currently the largest hindrance to parallel program development for multicomputer networks.

The appearance of any new computer system raises many design and performance issues; multicomputer networks are no exception. For example, what network topology should be used to interconnect the nodes? A network ill-suited to prevailing communication patterns results in message congestion and excessive communication delays. What communication paradigms should be used to transport messages through the network? Several mechanisms, including circuit switching, packet switching, datagrams, and virtual circuits have been proposed. What hardware support is required to implement these transport schemes? The tighter coupling of multicomputer nodes makes the software implementation of communications functions used on local area networks slow, inefficient, and inappropriate. How should the tasks of application programs be distributed across the network nodes? Static, *a priori* schemes are appropriate if the tasks are created before the computation begins, but dynamic schemes are necessary if tasks are created as the computation unfolds. How should the network detect and recover from component failures? Failures are inevitable in large multicomputer networks; the network must be robust enough to continue operation when portions are inoperative. Each of these issues will be discussed in greater detail in the chapters that follow.

1.2. A Parallel Computer Systems Comparison

As noted at the outset, the multicomputer network is but one point in a spectrum of highly parallel computers that have been proposed and developed to attack computation intensive application areas. With rare exception, these real and hypothetical parallel computer systems are restricted to a subset of the application domain. It is instructive to examine this architectural spectrum to understand the role of the multicomputer network and the types of applications for which it is best suited.

1.2.1. Pipelined Vector Processors

At one end of the architectural spectrum, high performance supercomputers such as the Cray X-MP and Fujitsu VP-200 [LuMM85] rely on high speed circuits and pipelined vector processing to achieve good performance. Pipelining divides an operation into a sequence of K simpler operations called *stages*. After an operand has been processed by the first stage of a pipeline, it can be processed by the second stage while the first stage accepts a second operand. In a K-stage pipeline, K operands or pairs of operands can be in the pipeline, each at a different stage. For example, floating point multiplication typically requires mantissa multiplication, exponent addition, and normalization. On the Cray X-MP, a *vector multiply* instruction sends two operands of a pair of vectors to the pipelined floating point multiplication unit each 8.5 nanoseconds. Each pipeline stage performs a portion of the multiplication algorithm. After the first pair of operands reaches the final pipeline stage, the pipeline is full, and a new result emerges each 8.5 nanoseconds.

Introducing a K-stage pipeline can, in principle, improve performance by a factor of K because K independent computations can proceed concurrently. However, pipelining is no panacea; the number of pipeline stages is limited by the number of logical partitions of the operation being pipelined and rarely exceeds ten. Moreover, realization of a K-fold performance improvement is dependent on keeping the pipeline filled. If the result of one computation in the pipeline is needed by a another computation just entering the pipeline, the latter must be delayed until the first result exits the pipeline. These data dependencies cause "bubbles" that propagate through the pipeline and limit the fraction of code amenable to vector processing. Finally, many pipelines impose a delay, i.e., a setup penalty, *before* the first operands of a vector operation can enter the first stage of the pipeline [Kogg81]. This penalty must be amortized over the length of the vector. If the penalty is high, and the vector is short, the performance gain will be substantially less than the pipeline's theoretical maximum.

Amdahl [Amda67] first formalized the relation between non-vectorizable code, pipeline setup penalty, and the maximum speedup S_p as

$$S_p = \frac{NKS}{(1-p)NKS + p\left[O + KS + S(N-1)\right]} \tag{1.1}$$

where N is the mean vector length, K is the number of pipeline stages, S is the delay through a single stage, p is the fraction of vectorizable code, and O is the pipeline setup penalty. The numerator of (1.1) is the time to perform N operations on a non-pipelined system whose functional units produce a result each KS time units. Similarly, the denominator reflects the weighted average of execution times for non-pipelined, i.e., non-vector, and pipelined operations. If either the vector length N is small, or the pipeline setup penalty O is large, (1.1) shows that a pipelined vector processor can be slower than a non-pipelined system. Only with long vectors is the pipelining overhead offset by parallelism. Finally, consider the effect of increasing the pipeline length K while all other parameters are fixed:

$$\lim_{K \to \infty} S_p = \frac{N}{N(1-p)+p} \approx \frac{1}{1-p}.$$

The maximum speedup is strikingly limited by the fraction of non-vectorizable code. Even with 90 percent vectorization ($p = 0.9$), a pipeline with an infinite number of stages is only ten times faster than a non-pipelined machine. Pipelined vector processors are best suited for applications requiring large amounts of structured numerical computation.

The logical constraint on the number of stages in a pipeline further reduces the maximum speedup. This limitation can be ameliorated through "chaining." With chaining, results from one pipeline are fed directly into another, increasing the effective pipeline length. As an example, the Cray X-MP chains the operation $aX + b$, where X and b are vectors and a is a scalar, by streaming the results of the scalar vector multiplication into the addition pipeline. Even with chaining and high speed circuits, the maximum speedup attainable via pipelining is limited to perhaps an order of magnitude.

Although the degree of parallelism exploited by pipelined vector processors is limited, this is offset by highly optimized functional unit designs based on the fastest available circuit technology. As a consequence, pipelined vector processors remain the fastest general purpose computers, even when the degree of vectorization is small.

Users of these pipelined vector processors typically develop programs in a sequential programming language, e.g., Fortran, or a sequential language with extensions to explicitly specify vector operations. Vectorizing compilers analyze the program and generate vector instructions.

Multicomputer networks differ from pipelined vector processors in several respects. Most importantly, multicomputer networks achieve their performance via parallelism rather than circuit speed. Thus, they offer potentially greater performance in application areas with high degrees of intrinsic parallelism. At present, the multicomputer network programmer must manually decompose the application program into interacting, parallel tasks. In fairness, programmers of vector processors must also restructure application code and insert compiler directives to maximize vectorization. Finally, multicomputer construction costs are substantially less than those for vector processors. This potential for high performance at a low cost is the principal factor motivating the design of multicomputer networks.

1.2.2. Shared Memory MIMD Multiprocessors

Not only has the appearance of inexpensive memory and powerful microprocessors stimulated multicomputer development, it also has lead to the development of commercial, microprocessor based, shared memory multiprocessors. Small scale systems typically contain a modest number of microprocessors connected to shared memory via a high speed bus.

Small scale multiprocessor systems are frequently used to increase throughput by running independent jobs concurrently. For example, one or more processors might be dedicated to time sharing while the remaining processors are used as compute servers for jobs that would otherwise degrade the response time of interactive users. The systems are well suited for "large grained" computations where an application can be decomposed into a small number of cooperating processes, each the size of a process in a conventional operating system.

1.2.2.1. The Sequent Balance 21000

The Sequent Balance 21000™ typifies the small scale, shared memory multiprocessor. Each of the thirty Balance 21000 processors is a 10 MHz National Semiconductor NS32032 microprocessor, and all processors are connected to shared memory by a shared bus with a 80 Mbyte/s (maximum) transfer rate. Each processor has an 8K byte, write-through cache and an 8K byte local memory; the latter contains a copy of selected read-only operating system data structures and code.

The Dynix™ operating system for the Balance 21000 is a variant of UC-Berkeley's 4.2BSD Unix™ with extensions for processor scheduling. Because Dynix schedules all processes from a common pool, a process may execute on different processors during successive time slices. However, as long as the number of active processes is less than the number of processors, each process will execute on a separate processor. To the time sharing user, the Balance 21000 appears as a standard Unix system, albeit with better interactive response time.

Parallel programs consist of a group of Unix processes that interact using a library of primitives for shared memory allocation and process synchronization. Shared memory is implemented by mapping a region of physical memory into the virtual address space of each process. Once mapped, shared memory can be allocated to specific variables as desired.

In summary, the Balance 21000 is a "standard" Unix system with minimal extensions for parallel programming. Consequently, many parallel operations are dominated by operating system overhead. The maximum number of processors is constrained by the bus interconnection, and the absolute performance is very small when compared with pipelined vector processors.

1.2.2.2. Large Scale Multiprocessors

Unlike small scale systems whose processors are connected via a fast bus, large multiprocessors contain hundreds or thousands of processors connected to memory modules via an interconnection network. Because a crossbar interconnection is prohibitively expensive, most proposed systems include a multistage switching network such as an Omega network whose hardware complexity is $O(N \log N)$ for an N processor system. Among the best known are the University of Illinois Cedar system [KDLS86], shown in figure 1.2, and the IBM RP3 [PBGH85]. The processor clusters of figure 1.2 each contain an Alliant FX/8,™ a commercial system whose eight

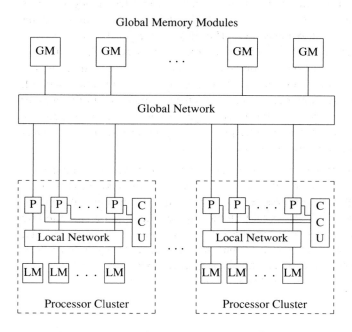

P: Processor
GM: Global Memory Module
LM: Local Memory Module
CCU: Cluster Control Unit

Figure 1.2
Cedar system architecture

processors are each pipelined vector processors. Data can reside in either the shared local memory of the cluster or the global memory shared by all clusters. A global Omega network [Lawr75] connects the clusters. Development plans call for a 16 cluster, 128 processor system by 1990.

The Cedar system is programmed using an extended Fortran. The compiler identifies parallel or vector code fragments and maps them onto one or more vector processors. Despite the compiler sophistication, careful program restructuring and data structure placement are necessary to maximize performance.

Despite the differences in programming paradigm between multicomputer networks and large scale multiprocessors, the latter are much closer in spirit to multicomputer networks than are pipelined vector processors. The most striking difference between multicomputer networks and shared memory multiprocessors is network latency. If memory is truly "shared," it must be possible to access any portion of memory within a few instruction cycles. This implies that the multiprocessor interconnection network must be faster[2] and correspondingly more expensive than a multicomputer interconnection network. This high performance, high cost interconnection network permits parallel tasks to interact much more frequently using the shared memory than is possible by passing messages on a multicomputer network.

On a shared memory system whose processors are connected to memory modules via a multistage interconnection network, all processors are equidistant, and network delay is minimized when the processors generate memory requests directed at random memory modules. In contrast, the nodes of a multicomputer network are separated by varying distances, and performance is maximized by minimizing the distance that messages must travel. As we shall see in chapter five, efficient strategies have been developed for mapping tasks onto processors in a multicomputer so that frequently communicating tasks are assigned to neighboring nodes.

1.2.3. SIMD Computers

Multiprocessors and multicomputers are MIMD (*Multiple Instruction, Multiple Data* stream) systems. Each processor in an MIMD computer contains a *control unit* that fetches and decodes instructions and an *execution unit* that executes these instructions. In contrast, an SIMD (*Single Instruction, Single Data* stream) computer contains a *single* control unit and multiple execution units.

Figure 1.3 depicts a typical SIMD machine architecture. Each execution unit or processing element (PE), together with its local memory, form a PEM. The key distinction between SIMD and MIMD computers is that all PEs in the SIMD system execute the same instruction at any given time.[3] This decoded instruction is broadcast by the control unit to all PEs.

Clearly, an MIMD system supports a more general computation model; the processors can operate autonomously. However, SIMD systems are potentially less

---

[2]On the IBM RP3 [PBGH85], the memory latency for a global memory reference is no more than twice that for a local memory reference. For an equivalent multicomputer network, the ratio of local memory access time to message transmission might be ten or even one hundred.

[3]However, some PEs can be *masked* or disabled during certain operations.

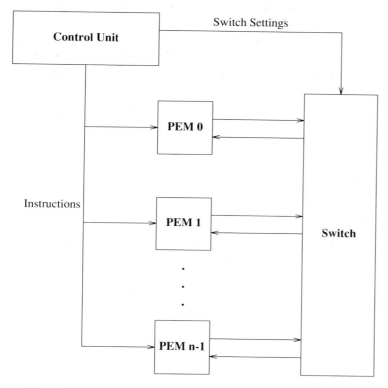

Figure 1.3
SIMD machine organization

expensive because the PEs do not require control units. Also, SIMD systems are more tightly coupled than asynchronous MIMD computers because all PEs execute synchronously in lock step with a global clock. If the program for an SIMD system is structured carefully, the results computed by one PE can be generated and transmitted to another PE at precisely the instant the results are needed by the second PE. Unlike MIMD systems, no queues or semaphores are needed to ensure proper synchronization between processors. Hence, SIMD systems are well suited for ''fine grained'' parallelism, e.g., concurrent execution of arithmetic operations.

SIMD systems are sometimes called *array processors* because, with appropriate PE floating point hardware, they can efficiently perform large matrix computations. Just as vector processors exploit the regularity of matrix computations via pipelining, SIMD systems distribute the matrix across processors and perform an arithmetic operation in each processor. Thus, SIMD systems are appropriate for many of the same applications as pipelined vector processors. In contrast with pipelined processors, SIMD systems offer greater parallelism because the number of PEs is much larger than the number of pipeline stages. However, SIMD systems perform poorly in applications that do not fit the SIMD model of computation or that contain significant portions of sequential code.

SIMD systems include the ILLIAC IV [BRKK68] with 64 PEs connected in a 2-dimensional square mesh, and more recently, the Thinking Machines Connection Machine™ with 64K 1-bit PEs connected in a pseudo-hypercube topology. SIMD systems have not been as widely accepted commercially as shared memory multiprocessors and pipelined vector processors, primarily because the special purpose nature of the SIMD architecture limits their applicability.

1.2.4. Systolic Arrays

Multicomputer networks, vector processors, and multiprocessors are general purpose parallel computers capable of executing a wide range of algorithms. In contrast, systolic arrays are special purpose computing structures designed specifically for a *single* algorithm, e.g., convolution or matrix multiplication [MeCo80, Kung82]. The simple processing elements of the array are each designed for a specific task, and the array is fabricated by tessellating the surface of a chip or silicon wafer with the interconnected processing elements. Typical interconnections include a linear array, the square mesh shown in figure 1.4, or a hexagonal mesh. Input data flow into the array from one or more edges and results exit via another edge. All processing elements execute synchronously and perform the following actions during each machine cycle:

(1)   Load input registers with results generated by neighboring processing elements or with externally provided data.

(2)   Compute new results using this newly received data.

(3)   Place these results in output registers.

The arrays are called systolic because data are rhythmically "pumped" through the array much as the heart pumps blood.

Because the processing element functionality and interconnection are hardwired, systolic arrays are special purpose, conceived as computational engines attached to a general purpose host computer. In recent years, several research groups have proposed generalizations of systolic arrays that permit either programmability or network reconfiguration. Among these, the Poker system [Snyd84] provides programmable

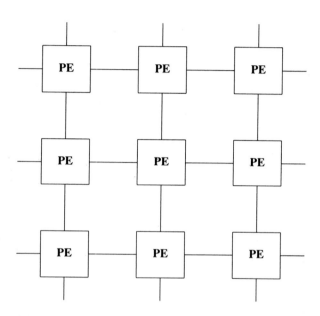

Figure 1.4
Systolic array

processing elements, each with a limited amount of local memory, and corridors of switches interspersed between rows and columns of processing elements. By changing the switch configurations, the connectivity of the systolic array can be changed. Despite this increase in flexibility, systolic arrays are best suited for algorithms whose phases require regular interconnection patterns.

1.2.5. Data Flow Computers

With few exceptions, conventional computer systems follow the von Neumann paradigm. The processor repeatedly fetches the instruction at the memory address specified by the program counter, decodes and executes the instruction, and increments the program counter. In this *control flow* approach, the sequence of executed instructions is but one possible serialization of the machine instructions. Not all instructions are dependent, and a dependency analysis of the machine code reveals that many instructions can be executed in parallel. Data flow computers are designed to execute these *data flow program graphs* [Denn80, ArKa81, Srin86]. The nodes of a data flow graph are computation and control constructs such as multiplication or conditional "if-then-else" instructions. Arcs pass *tokens* carrying data values between nodes. When a node has received tokens on each of its incoming arcs, its data dependencies have all been satisfied. It can then *fire*, i.e., absorb the input tokens, compute a result, and generate a token carrying the result value.

Figure 1.5 shows a block diagram of a typical data flow computer. The nodes of the data flow graph are contained in instruction cells. When all its input arguments arrive, an instruction cell is ready to execute. The node in the instruction cell is forwarded to the arbitration network, which sends the node to an idle processing element. The processing element evaluates the node, producing result tokens that are sent via the distribution network to waiting instruction cells.

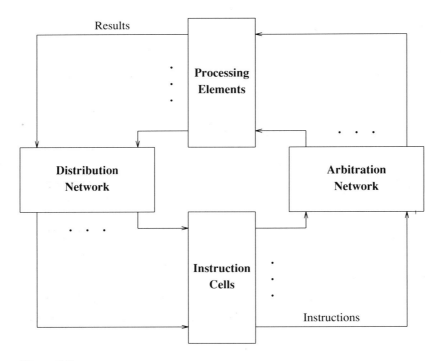

Figure 1.5
Data flow computer organization

The data flow architecture of figure 1.5 resembles a large, circular pipeline. For the processing elements to operate near peak efficiency, the arbitration and distribution networks must transport nodes and tokens efficiently. Moreover, the fine granularity of the computation, single instructions, implies that many processing elements are needed to achieve large speedups. Some research groups [GPKK82] have argued that the overhead of instruction level data flow is too high and that construction of a data flow computer containing a thousand or more simple processing elements serviced by fast interconnection networks is technologically and economically infeasible. As an alternative, graphs with computational complexity analogous to a subroutine reduce the potential parallelism but amortize the overhead over larger computational entities. These block data flow graphs could then be executed on either a shared memory multiprocessor or a multicomputer network.

1.2.6. Multicomputer Networks

Given a brief overview of the parallel computer architecture spectrum, the differences between multicomputer networks and other architectures now should be clear. Pipelined vector processors rely on the fastest available circuit technology; multiprocessor architectures such as the Cedar or RP3 systems contain many large, powerful processors and a fast interconnection network; and systolic arrays and data flow computers contain many, small arithmetic units. Multicomputer networks lie between these extremes, requiring neither exotic circuit technology, custom processor designs, nor thousands of processors. This reliance on standard parts and technology provides flexibility, familiarity, and extensibility.

Multicomputer networks are typically programmed using familiar sequential programming languages, augmented with message passing communication primitives. There is no shared memory, and given a judicious choice of interconnection network, a multicomputer network scales over a wide range of costs and performances. Multicomputer networks are intended as general purpose parallel computers that can provide speedups for a variety of numerical and non-numerical applications. As a penalty for generality, multicomputer networks, like shared memory multiprocessors, cannot provide the performance of special purpose machines designed for specific algorithms. As a penalty for the moderate price that results from using standard parts and conservative technology, multicomputer networks cannot provide the performance of pipelined vector processors on applications with low degrees of parallelism. The appeal of multicomputer networks and their commercial emergence are based on their effective exploitation of VLSI technology, the availability of high degrees of ''general purpose'' parallelism, and moderate price.

1.3. Multicomputer History

Although the commercial development of multicomputer systems is recent, the research and design history of multicomputer networks is rich and varied. To understand the architectural and software constraints imposed on commercial designs, it is necessary to examine the history of multicomputer research.

1.3.1. Early Projects

The introduction of the microprocessor in the early 1970's made inexpensive, but reasonably powerful, computation engines widely available. It was inevitable that multicomputer networks would soon follow. Early multicomputer networks include the Columbia Homogeneous Parallel Processor (CHoPP) [SuBa77], the Finite Element Machine at the NASA Langley Research Center [Jord78], MicroNet at the State University of New York at Stony Brook [Witt80], the X-Tree project at the University of California at Berkeley [SeFu82, Fuji83], and Zmob at the University of Maryland [KuWR82]. Each of the machines designed by these projects was based on a network node that contained a microprocessor for executing user and system code, local memory, and special purpose circuitry for internode communication.

CHoPP, among the earliest multicomputer network designs, was based on the hypercube topology,[4] and the nodes were multiprogrammed. The 36 nodes of the Finite Element Machine (FEM) were each connected to their eight nearest neighbors in a two-dimensional grid. This octagonal mesh reflected the communication pattern among the tasks of iterative finite element solvers [OrVo85]. The MicroNet project concentrated primarily on operating system design, task load balancing algorithms, and evaluation of network topologies. Communication protocols and hardware design were the emphases of the X-Tree project.[5] Finally, the Zmob project connected a group of Z80 microprocessors to a fast network and explored numerical algorithm design.

The breadth of multicomputer network design issues, including communication hardware, network topology evaluation, operating system software, and application algorithms forced most research projects to concentrate on a subset of these issues. Despite this limitation, the lessons learned were used to design today's commercial multicomputer networks.

---

[4]Described in §1.3.2.

[5]X-Tree was the name given to a binary tree, augmented with rings of links that connected nodes at each tree level. The additional connections were included to reduce communication traffic near the tree root.

1.3.2. The Hypercube Topology

Many multicomputer designs, both past and present, are based on the hypercube topology. Therefore, a brief digression is in order. The hypercube, also called the *binary n-cube*, is characterized by a single parameter called the hypercube *dimension*. This parameter determines both the number of nodes in the hypercube and the number of communication links connected to each node. An $n+1$ dimensional hypercube can be created by constructing two n-dimensional hypercubes and adding a link from each node in the first hypercube to its "twin" in the second. By definition, a 0-dimensional hypercube is a single node. Figure 1.6 shows the recursive creation of hypercubes from a single node.

An n-dimensional cube can be mapped onto an n-dimensional coordinate system. Assume only two points (labeled 0 and 1) lie *in each dimension*. The position of any

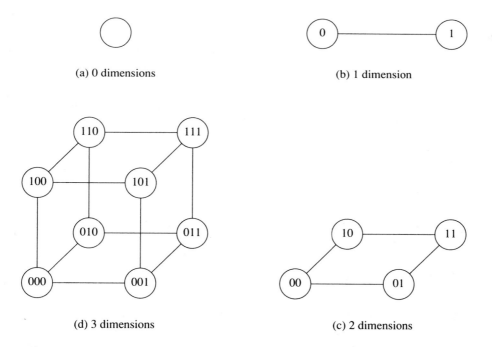

(a) 0 dimensions

(b) 1 dimension

(d) 3 dimensions

(c) 2 dimensions

Figure 1.6
Hypercube topology

node in an n-dimensional cube is a tuple of n binary digits, $(b_n, b_{n-1}, b_{n-2}, \cdots b_1)$. For example, the points in a two dimensional cube are denoted (00), (01), (10), and (11) as shown in figure 1.6. A link exists between two nodes of the hypercube if and only if the labels assigned to the two nodes are identical except in exactly one bit position. In the two dimensional case, a link exists between nodes (00) and (10) but not between nodes (10) and (01).

Clearly, an n-dimensional hypercube contains exactly 2^n nodes, each node of the hypercube has exactly n links to neighboring nodes, and a message from a node can reach any other node of the cube in at most n hops. The hypercube topology has been widely touted for connecting the nodes of a multicomputer network. Among the reasons are the following.

- The natural decomposition of many numerical algorithms creates tasks whose communication patterns match the hypercube topology.

- The hypercube provides a rich interconnection structure. Important topologies such as the ring and two dimensional mesh can be embedded in the hypercube topology. That is, these topologies can be obtained by simply removing appropriate hypercube links. Thus, ring or mesh algorithms can be executed efficiently on the hypercube because all communication is between neighboring nodes.

- Because crossing a hypercube communication link resolves one of the (at most) n bit differences between the addresses of a source and destination node, the maximum distance separating nodes grows logarithmically with the number of nodes.

- The message routing algorithm is simple. On receiving a message, a node need only compare its address with the message's destination address. If the addresses differ in bit position i, the message should be sent on the link corresponding to dimension i. If the addresses are identical, the destination has been reached. If there are multiple bit differences, any link corresponding to a bit difference can be used. These choices permit nodes to avoid congested areas by *adaptive routing*.

- The recursive definition of the topology simplifies packaging. A hardware module containing a k-dimensional hypercube can be used to construct hypercubes of larger dimension.

Despite its many advantages, the hypercube topology has one major liability: the number of connections to each node grows with the number of hypercube dimensions. When designing hardware, the maximum dimension must be fixed. Thus, a node building block with ten connections could be used to construct any hypercube with less than 1024 nodes. In addition to the design constraint, packaging technology limits the maximum number of connections per node. This limitation has not yet been reached, but it does constrain the maximum size system that can be designed.

1.3.3. The Cosmic Cube and Its Descendants

Although multicomputer networks have been the subject of research for many years, the recent explosion of interest can be traced to the construction of the Cosmic Cube [Seit85] at the California Institute of Technology. The 64 nodes of the Cosmic Cube were configured as a six-dimensional hypercube. Each node contained an Intel 8086 microprocessor, an Intel 8087 floating point co-processor, 128K bytes of random access memory (RAM), and 8K bytes of read only memory (ROM); the internode communication channels operated at 2 million bits per second. System software for the Cosmic Cube included a suite of subroutines for store-and-forward internode communication. The Cosmic Cube was designed primarily for large numerical problems in high-energy physics, astrophysics, quantum chemistry, fluid mechanics, structural mechanics, seismology, and computer science.

Following the success of the Cosmic Cube, four companies quickly began delivery of multicomputer networks configured as hypercubes.[6] Using existing chips, Intel developed the iPSC™[Ratt85], a hypercube of 32, 64, or 128 Intel 80286/80287 processor pairs configured as 5, 6, or 7 dimensional cubes. Processor interconnection in the Intel iPSC is via point-to-point Ethernets. As configuration options, Intel also provides memory expansion and vector processor boards. Ametek countered with the System/14,™ also based on the Intel 80286/80287 chip set.

Both the iPSC and System/14 designs use a conventional microprocessor coupled with additional logic to manage communication. In contrast, the Floating Point Systems T Series™ hypercube [GuHS86] is based on the Inmos Transputer.™ Following the Transputer lead, Ncube [HMSC86], developed a new VLSI chip containing hardware instructions for message passing. The Ncube/ten™ is a hypercube whose nodes each contain only seven chips, a processor and six memory chips.

1.4. Multicomputer Building Blocks

Many realized that a universal building block or "tinker toy" would greatly simplify multicomputer network design and construction. General purpose building blocks have been proposed, and in some cases implemented, for both the computation and communication aspects of a multicomputer network node. Two such building blocks, the Inmos Transputer and the torus routing chip, are discussed next. Design issues for a general purpose communication component will be discussed in chapter four.

---

[6]These and other hypercube architectures will be discussed in chapter eight.

1.4.1. The Inmos Transputer

Unlike other contemporary microprocessors, the Transputer was developed from the outset as a component for constructing large multicomputer networks [Whit85]. The IMS Transputer is a single chip containing a 32-bit processor, 2K bytes of memory, four bidirectional serial communication links, and interfaces to additional memory and I/O devices. The chip was designed so that a multicomputer node could be constructed with a minimal number of additional components.

The Transputer was designed specifically to support the Occam programming language [Inmo84]. However, the hardware can also support traditional programming languages. Occam is a simple, message-based language similar to Hoare's Communicating Sequential Processes (CSP) [Hoar78]. A parallel Occam program contains a collection of processes that execute concurrently and communicate through synchronous message passing primitives. A process invoking the send message primitive on a *channel* blocks until the receiving process invokes the receive primitive on the same channel.

Because the Transputer was designed with Occam in mind, message passing is supported in hardware, yielding a highly efficient implementation. The Transputer automatically suspends a process when it must wait for a message and begins executing another process. Process switching requires from 17 to 58 machine cycles, or from 850 to 2900 nanoseconds in a 20 MHz chip, depending on the priority of the processes being switched.

1.4.2. The Torus Routing Chip

Just as the Transputer is a building block processor for multicomputer networks, a general purpose switching component has also been studied by several researchers. One such component is the *torus routing chip* developed at the California Institute of Technology. The torus routing chip (TRC) supports message passing in a D-dimensional torus of width w, i.e., a D-dimensional cube with w nodes along each dimension [DaSe86]. The chip is intended primarily for two dimensional networks, but can support higher dimensions by building a cluster of routing chips at each node to achieve the necessary fanout.

The torus routing chip features cut-through message forwarding and deadlock free routing. Cut-through message passing, discussed in some detail in chapters three and four, allows a node to start forwarding the beginning of a message to the next node *before* the end of the message has arrived. In contrast, traditional store-and-forward message passing requires that the node receive the entire message before beginning to forward it.

Store-and-forward deadlock can occur in congested networks when each node in a cycle of nodes is waiting to forward a message to the next node in the cycle, but no free buffers exist. Such deadlocks can be avoided by controlling the *order* in which buffers are allocated so that no cyclic dependencies arise. In a communication network, this order is determined by the routing algorithm. Hence, it is possible to specify a deadlock free routing algorithm for certain topologies, notably the hypercube discussed earlier. It is possible to specify deadlock free routing algorithms for other important topologies such as tori of arbitrary dimension and width, cube-connected cycles, and shuffle exchange networks. Network topologies for multicomputer networks will be described and analyzed in chapter two.

For instance, deadlocks can be avoided in the hypercube if the routing uses a bitwise comparison of the current and destination node addresses in which the addresses are always scanned from, say, left to right to determine the link on which to forward the message. This avoids deadlock because higher dimension links are always demanded before lower dimension ones. As long as at least one buffer in each node is assigned to each dimension, i.e., each link in the hypercube, the ordering ensures that no deadlocks can occur.

The TRC uses a variation of this approach to achieve deadlock free routing in D-dimensional tori, a generalization of the hypercube. Assume that there are at least two buffers associated with each communication link in the network. The reason two buffers are required will become apparent shortly. Deadlock is avoided by assigning an integer tag to each buffer in the network, and designing the routing algorithm so that the sequence of tags on buffers used by each message forms a *strictly decreasing* sequence of values. This constraint ensures that cycles, and therefore deadlock, cannot occur. For example, the buffers in the hypercube for an outgoing link of dimension i may be assigned a tag of i. The "left-to-right scan" routing algorithm just described will result in each message using buffers with successively lower tags.

This approach can be extended to the torus of width w. Each node in the torus is assigned an n-digit, radix w address where the ith digit represents the position of the node in the ith dimension. This corresponds to a simple concatenation of the components of the Cartesian coordinate position of the node. An example of the node numbering scheme for a dimension two, width three, torus is shown in figure 1.7. The tag assigned to each buffer contains three fields concatenated to form a single integer:

(1)   The high order (leftmost) field is the dimension of the corresponding link.

(2)   The next field is a single bit. There is at least one buffer on each link where this bit is set, and at least one where it is cleared.

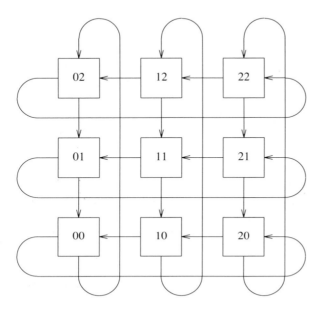

Figure 1.7
Dimension Two, Width Three, Torus.

(3)   The third field is the node address where the buffer resides. This occupies the least significant bit positions of the tag.

Deadlock free routing is obtained by giving priority to higher dimension links, much like the routing scheme just described for the hypercube. More precisely, each node compares the current node number with the destination node number by scanning the addresses digit by digit, left to right, until corresponding digits do not match. The message must be routed along the dimension corresponding to these differing digits. Using the same rationale as for the hypercube, cycles among buffers corresponding to links on *different* dimensions are avoided. However, a cycle may still occur among links within the *same* dimension. As we shall see in a moment, two buffers are required on each link to avoid deadlock within a dimension.

Suppose we were to assign each buffer a tag which is identical to the number of the node where that buffer resides. No deadlock could occur if we could ensure that the series of nodes visited by each message forms a decreasing sequence of node numbers. This is not always possible when routing along a single dimension of the torus however. For example, this condition is violated in the torus of figure 1.7 whenever a message traverses one of the "wraparound" connections. To remedy this situation, we partition the buffers on each link into two classes: a *high* class and a *low* class. Buffers in the low class are assigned a tag whose second field is zero, and the third is the number of the node. Buffers in the high class are assigned a tag with the second field set to one. This guarantees that among buffers in the same dimension, buffers in the high class always have a higher buffer tag than buffers in the low class. Within each class an ordering based on the node number prevails.

This new buffer tagging scheme allows deadlock free routing *within* a dimension. The sequence of nodes through which each message passes is the *concatenation* of two decreasing sequences - high buffers are used when the first decreasing sequence is being traversed, and low buffers are used for the second sequence of tags. A message switches from high buffers to low buffers whenever the node receiving the message has a larger address than the neighboring node which sent it. In a torus of any dimension and width, this only occurs when the wraparound links are traversed.

For example, consider the torus in figure 1.7. A message traveling within a dimension either moves from right to left or up to down, always moving to lower numbered nodes. The message is allowed to move to a *higher* numbered node at most *once* within each dimension, at which point it switches from a high class buffer to a low class buffer. Because the buffer tags form a decreasing sequence, it is guaranteed that deadlock cannot occur. Similar deadlock free routing schemes based on the same principles can be derived for the cube-connected cycles and shuffle exchange topology [DaSe87].

The torus routing chip was designed to efficiently implement communications in a two dimensional torus. Each chip contains three input links and three output links. Two of these links carry message traffic between distinct nodes of the torus. The third is used to cascade several chips, permitting construction of higher dimension tori.

Figure 1.8 shows a block diagram of the chip. The torus routing chip was implemented as a self-timed VLSI circuit. Five input controllers process incoming messages. Separate controllers process messages for different buffer classes. The link used to cascade chips requires only one buffer class, hence the five controllers. Similarly, five queues are provided, and multiplexers merge messages in the two buffer classes assigned to each link onto one physical set of wires. A five-by-five crossbar switch performs the actual switching function.

1.5. Outline of Text

The emergence of commercial multicomputer systems has sparked interest in the message passing paradigm for parallel computation. In this monograph we focus on

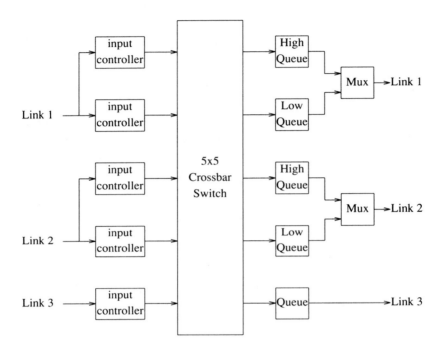

Figure 1.8
Data Paths in Torus Routing Chip.

the important issues in hardware, system software, and application program design for multicomputer networks. Our goal is to give the reader a better appreciation of the important issues that must be addressed and to provide the background knowledge necessary to anticipate future developments in multicomputer networks. Although we will discuss existing multicomputer networks, the primary focus will be the principles underlying the design of these systems.

1.5.1. Communication Systems

Repeated studies have shown that a system's performance is maximized when the components are balanced and there is no single system bottleneck [DeBu78]. Optimizing multicomputer performance requires a judicious combination of node computation speed and message transmission latency. For example, high speed processors connected by high latency communication links restrict the classes of algorithms that can be efficiently supported. Chapters two, three, and four discuss the design issues for multicomputer communication networks.

Chapter two presents analytic models of interconnection networks. Although hypercubes have been widely touted, many other topologies are not only possible, but are often preferable for certain algorithm classes. We analyze the effectiveness of several metrics for topology evaluation and present a new one based on asymptotic bound analysis. Using these metrics we evaluate several proposed network topologies.

Whether each node of a multicomputer network is implemented as a VLSI component or a printed circuit board, packaging constraints limit the number of connections to each node, and consequently, the communication bandwidth. As more links are added to each node, less bandwidth is available for each one. However, increasing the number of links usually reduces the average number of link crossings or hops required to reach a particular destination. In chapter three we examine the balance between link bandwidth and average hop count to determine the optimal number of links per node.

Because multicomputer networks are limited in extent to a few cabinets, rather than a large geographic area where transmission delays dominate, they require hardware, rather than software support for message transport, routing, buffer management, and flow control. In chapter four we examine design alternatives for each of these issues and estimate the circuitry required for one possible design.

1.5.2. Multicomputer Operating Systems

Chapter five examines operating system and load balancing issues in multicomputer networks. There are two primary approaches to parallel processing and task scheduling on a multicomputer network. In the first approach, all parallel tasks in a computation are known *a priori* and are statically mapped onto the network nodes before the computation begins. These tasks remain on their assigned nodes throughout the computation. In the second approach, a parallel computation is defined by a dynamically created task precedence graph. New tasks are initiated and existing tasks terminate as the computation unfolds, and tasks are assigned to network nodes dynamically. Although a single processor can schedule static tasks, dynamically created tasks must be assigned to network nodes by a distributed scheduling algorithm executing on the multicomputer network. We present approaches to the static scheduling problem, analyze the feasibility of dynamic task scheduling, and review the current state of the art.

1.5.3. Multicomputer Applications

The history of high speed computer design is replete with examples of computer systems whose realizable performance was but a small fraction of the theoretical maximum. Multicomputer networks are only viable if important applications execute efficiently. The application programs for multicomputer networks must be decomposed into a collection of parallel tasks that communicate using the message passing mechanisms provided by the machine.

We will explore the programming of multicomputer networks by examining case studies of two typical application areas: discrete event simulation and partial differential equations. Chapter six examines discrete event simulation of physical systems such as assembly lines and queueing networks. Although parallel simulation using multicomputer networks seems intuitively attractive, serious difficulties arise when one attempts to execute event driven simulation programs on a parallel machine. Most notably, deadlocks can occur. We will discuss several mechanisms that have been developed to permit parallel simulation.

Chapter seven discusses the solution of partial differential equations on a multicomputer network. We analyze the interaction of problem partitioning and architectural parameters and present a validated performance model that identifies the appropriate partitioning for a given multicomputer network.

1.5.4. Performance of Existing Machines

We conclude with a comparison of several commercial and research hypercubes. Chapter eight examines the hardware and software available on these machines and presents a comparative performance study using a set of processor and communication benchmarks. Based on this study, we suggest potential improvements in second generation multicomputer networks.

References

[Amda67]   G. Amdahl, "The Validity of the Single Processor Approach to Achieving Large Scale Computing Capabilities," *AFIPS Conference Proceedings* (1967), Vol. 30.

[ArBG85]   M. Arango, H. Badr and D. Gelernter, "Staged Circuit Switching," *IEEE Transactions on Computers* (February 1985), Vol. C-34, No. 2, pp. 174-180.

[ArKa81]   Arvind and V. Kathail, "A Multiple Processor that Supports Generalized Procedures," *Proceedings of the 8th Annual Symposium on Computer Architecture* (May 1981), pp. 291-302.

[BRKK68]   G. H. Barnes, R. M. Brown, M. Kato, D. J. Kuck, et al., "The ILLIAC IV Computer," *IEEE Transactions on Computers* (August 1968), Vol. C-17, No. 2, pp. 746-757.

[DaSe86]   W. J. Dally and C. L. Seitz, "The Torus Routing Chip," *Journal of Distributed Computing* (1986), Vol. 1, No. 3.

[DaSe87]   W. J. Dally and C. L. Seitz, "Deadlock-Free Message Routing in Multiprocessor Interconnection Networks," *IEEE Transactions on Computers* (May 1987), Vol. C-36, pp. 547-553.

[DeBu78]   P. J. Denning and J. P. Buzen, "The Operational Analysis of Queueing Network Models," *ACM Computing Surveys* (September 1978), Vol. 10, No. 3, pp. 225-261.

[Denn80]   J. B. Dennis, "Data Flow Supercomputers," *IEEE Computer* (November 1980), Vol. 13, No. 11, pp. 48-56.

[Fuji83]   R. M. Fujimoto, *VLSI Communication Components for Multicomputer Networks*. Ph.D. Dissertation, Electronics Research Laboratory Report No. UCB/CSD 83/136, University of California, Berkeley, California, 1983.

[GPKK82]   D. D. Gajski, D. A. Padua, D. J. Kuck and R. H. Kuhn, "A Second Opinion on Data Flow Machines and Languages," *IEEE Computer* (February 1982), Vol. 15, No. 2, pp. 58-69.

[GuHS86]   H. L. Gustafson, S. Hawkinson and K. Scott, "The Architecture of a Homogeneous Vector Supercomputer," *Proceedings of the 1986 International Conference on Parallel Processing* (August 1986), pp. 649-652.

[HMSC86]   J. P. Hayes, T. Mudge, Q. F. Stout, S. Colley, et al., "A Microprocessor-based Hypercube Supercomputer," *IEEE Micro* (October 1986), Vol. 6, No. 5, pp. 6-17.

[Hoar78]   C. A. R. Hoare, "Communicating Sequential Processes," *Communications of the ACM* (August 1978), Vol. 21, No. 8, pp. 666-677.

[Inmo84]   *Occam Programming Manual*. Prentice-Hall International, London, 1984.

[Inte86a]   *Intel iPSC System Overview, Order Number 310610-001*. Intel Scientific Computers, 1986.

[Jord78]   H. F. Jordan, "A Special Purpose Architecture for Finite Element Analysis," *Proceedings of the 1978 International Conference on Parallel Processing* (August 1978), pp. 263-266.

[KDLS86]   D. J. Kuck, E. S. Davidson, D. H. Lawrie and A. H. Sameh, "Parallel Supercomputing Today and the Cedar Approach," *Science* (February 1986), Vol. 231, pp. 967-231.

[Kogg81]   P. M. Kogge, *The Architecture of Pipelined Computers*. McGraw-Hill, New York, NY, 1981.

[Kung82]   H. T. Kung, "Why Systolic Architectures?," *IEEE Computer* (January 1982), Vol. 15, No. 1, pp. 37-46.

[KuWR82]   T. Kushner, A. Y. Wu and A. Rosenfeld, "Image Processing on ZMOB," *IEEE Transactions on Computers* (October 1982), Vol. C-31, No. 10, pp. 943-951.

[Lawr75]   D. H. Lawrie, "Access and Alignment of Data in an Array Processor," *IEEE Transactions on Computers* (December 1975), Vol. C-24, No. 12, pp. 1145-1155.

[LuMM85]   O. Lubeck, J. Moore and R. Mendez, "A Benchmark Comparison of Three Supercomputers: Fujitsu VP-200, Hitachi S-810/20, and Cray X-MP/2," *IEEE Computer* (December 1985), Vol. 18, No. 12, pp. 10-23.

[MeCo80]   C. Mead and L. Conway, *Introduction to VLSI Systems*. Addison-Wesley, Reading, Massachusetts, 1980.

[OrVo85]   J. Ortega and R. G. Voigt, "Solution of Partial Differential Equations on Vector and Parallel Computers," *SIAM Review* (June 1985), Vol. 27, No. 2, pp. 149-240.

[PBGH85]   G. F. Pfister, W. C. Brantley, D. A. George, S. L. Harvey, et al., "The IBM Research Parallel Processor Prototype (RP3): Introduction and Architecture," *Proceedings of the 1985 International Conference on Parallel Processing* (August 1985), pp. 764-771.

[Pott85]   J. L. Potter, *The Massively Parallel Processor*. MIT Press, Cambridge, Massachusetts, 1985.

[Ratt85]   J. Rattner, "Concurrent Processing: A New Direction in Scientific Computing," *Conference Proceedings of the 1985 National Computer Conference* (1985), Vol. 54, pp. 157-166.

[SeFu82]   C. H. Séquin and R. M. Fujimoto, "X-Tree and Y-Components," In: *Proceedings of the Advanced Course on VLSI Architecture*, P. Treleaven, ed. Prentice Hall, Englewood Cliffs, New Jersey, 1982.

[Seit85]   C. L. Seitz, "The Cosmic Cube," *Communications of the ACM* (January 1985), Vol. 28, No. 1, pp. 22-33.

[Snyd84]   L. Snyder, "Parallel Programming and the Poker Programming Environment," *IEEE Computer* (July 1984), Vol. 17, No. 7, pp. 27-36.

[Srin86]   V. P. Srini, "An Architectural Comparison of Dataflow Systems," *IEEE Computer* (March 1986), Vol. 19, No. 3, pp. 68-87.

[SuBa77]   H. Sullivan and T. R. Bashkow, "A Large Scale, Homogeneous, Fully Distributed Parallel Machine," *Proceedings of the Fourth Annual Symposium on Computer Architecture* (March 1977), Vol. 5, No. 7, pp. 105-117.

[Whit85]   C. Whitby-Strevens, "The Transputer," *Proceedings of the 12th International Symposium on Computer Architecture, Boston, Mass.* (June 1985), Vol. 13, No. 3, pp. 292-300.

[Witt80]   L. D. Wittie, "MICROS: A Distributed Operating System for MICRONET, A Reconfigurable Network Computer," *IEEE Transactions on Computers* (December 1980), Vol. C-29, No. 12, pp. 1133-1144.

2 Analytic Models of Interconnection Networks

> If one is working from the point of view of getting beauty into one's equations, and if one has a really sound insight, one is on a sure line of progress.
>
> Paul Dirac

The communication network plays a central role in determining the overall performance of a multicomputer system; all other components rest on its performance. If the network cannot provide adequate performance, nodes will frequently be forced to wait for data to arrive. To avoid this phenomenon, programmers must restructure their software, often in unnatural ways, to create ''larger grains'' of computation that require less frequent communications. Not only does this make the programmer's job more difficult, but this restructuring also reduces the amount of parallelism within the program. Tasks that might otherwise execute in parallel on several different nodes must now be combined to execute serially on a single node. Further, as technological improvements increase the computing power of individual processing elements, additional pressure is placed on the communication network to provide a comparable improvement in performance to avoid becoming a bottleneck.

In addition to performance considerations, the communication network must be resilient to failures. As the size of the network increases, the probability that some component in the system will fail increases proportionally. The effect of such failures must be isolated, or the system will be rendered inoperative. If care is not taken, users may find that their time is better spent executing their programs on a slower, more reliable, conventional uniprocessor rather than waiting for repair of the parallel computer.

In this chapter, we will focus attention on analytic models of multicomputer communication networks and examine the effect of certain design decisions on network performance and reliability. Chapters three and four will address network control and hardware implementation, and chapter eight presents experimental data on the communication capabilities of existing multicomputer networks, the hypercubes. Before beginning the discussion of analytic models, however, we must first define several important terms and concepts used to quantify the performance and reliability of networks.

2.1. Definitions

Because communication networks have been proposed for a plethora of different purposes, many metrics and models have been used to evaluate them. Of these, graphs are the most natural and widely used models.

A graph consists of a set of **vertices** or **nodes** $\{V_1, V_2, \cdots, V_N\}$ and a set of **arcs** or **links** connecting pairs of nodes. L_{ij} represents the link from node V_i to node V_j. Physically, the vertices correspond to computation processors with local memory and/or communication processors. The links represent the physical connectivity of the communication network. In some networks, links are bidirectional and operate in full duplex mode, i.e., each link can simultaneously transmit and receive data. In these situations, graphs with undirected arcs will be used.

A **path** through the network is a sequence of arcs from the **source node** where a message originates, up to and including the **destination node** that consumes the message. The **path length** or **distance** from one node to another is the *minimum* number of links in any path between the two nodes. Thus D_{AB}, the distance from node A to node B, refers to the minimum number of "hops" a message must traverse traveling from A to B. If no path exists between the two nodes, they are said to be **disconnected**, and the path length between them is undefined. A disconnected graph is one containing at least one pair of disconnected nodes.

The **out-degree** of a node is the number of outgoing arcs leaving the node. **In-degree** is similarly defined for incoming arcs. If all links are bidirectional, a node's in- and out-degrees must necessarily be equal, and the distinction will be dropped. Often we will assume that each node of the network has the same degree. This assumption is particularly appropriate when the network is constructed from a *single* network "building block" containing processor, memory, and communication circuitry within a single VLSI component. As later analysis will show, node degree is important. Limitations on the maximum number of physical connections to a node, e.g., the maximum number of pins on a VLSI chip, bound the maximum rate data can flow into or out of the node.

Given this basic graph terminology, it is possible to define a set of interconnection metrics:

- network connectivity [Tane81],
- network diameter [FiSo80],
- mean internode distance [Witt81],

• communication link visit ratios [ReSc83], and

• network expansion increments.

These metrics provide a framework to systematically compare various interconnection networks. In the following sections, we briefly review the definitions of these metrics and show how they can be applied to proposed interconnection networks. To do this, we introduce the basic notation shown in table 2.1.

2.1.1. Network Connectivity

Network nodes and communication links do fail and must be removed from service for repair. When components fail, the network should continue to function with reduced capacity, so communication paths that avoid inactive nodes and links are desirable. As noted earlier, this is particularly important for large networks because the probability of all network components operating correctly decreases as the size of the network increases.

Table 2.1

Notation for interconnection networks

Symbol	Definition
AC	arc connectivity
NC	node connectivity
K	number of network nodes
$lmax$	maximum internode distance
n	number of levels in an asymmetric interconnection network
CL	communication link
PE	processing element
$Net\text{-}type$	type of interconnection network (e.g., ring, mesh, etc.)
$Numlinks(K, Net\text{-}type)$	number of communication links in a network with K nodes
$Reach(l, Net\text{-}type)$	number of nodes reachable by crossing exactly l links in a symmetric interconnection network
$\Phi(l)$	probability of a message crossing l links

Network connectivity measures the resiliency of a network and its ability to continue operation despite disabled components. Informally, connectivity is the minimum number of nodes or links that must fail to partition the network into two or more disjoint subnetworks. More precisely, the **arc connectivity** $AC(i,j)$ between two nodes is the minimum number of links that must be removed from the network to disconnect nodes i and j. The arc connectivity of a network is

$$\min_{\substack{i,j \\ i \neq j}} AC(i,j).$$

For the ring network in figure 2.1, the arc connectivity is 2, because the failure of any two links will prevent some pair of nodes from communicating.

Similarly, **node connectivity** $NC(i,j)$ is the minimum number of nodes other than i or j that must be removed to disconnect i and j. The node connectivity of a network is

$$\min_{\substack{i,j \\ i \neq j}} NC(i,j)$$

The node connectivity for the ring network in figure 2.1 is also 2.

Larger node or link connectivity increases the resiliency of the network to failures, provided appropriate mechanisms exist to recover, e.g., new routing paths must be established. However, neither the node nor the arc connectivity of the network can exceed the smallest degree d of any node in the network: one can always remove the d

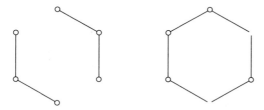

Two link failures   Two node failures

Figure 2.1
Device failures in a bidirectional ring.

links connected to that node, or the d nodes neighboring it. Also, the node connectivity must always be less than or equal to the arc connectivity [BoMu79]. This is because removing a node effectively removes *all* arcs connected to that node. Thus, a node failure is more "damaging" to network connectivity than an arc failure, and fewer node failures may be necessary to disconnect the graph.

In addition to being a measure of network reliability, connectivity is also a performance measure. Greater connectivity reduces the number of links that must be crossed to reach a destination node. Unfortunately, technological barriers such as pinout constraints limit the number of connections per node to a small constant, and other performance measures such as network diameter are necessary.

2.1.2. Network Diameter

The maximum internode distance, often referred to as the **diameter** of the interconnection network, places a lower bound on the delay required to propagate information throughout the network. It is simply the maximum number of communication links that must be traversed to transmit a message to any node along a shortest path. Formally, the network diameter is

$$\max_{\substack{A,B \\ A \neq B}} D_{AB}$$

where D_{AB} is the distance from node A to B. This notion is analogous to the diameter of a circle, which is the maximum length of any line segment between any two points on or within the circle. Networks that contain a relatively large number of nodes, but still maintain a small diameter, are often referred to as **dense** networks. Dense networks offer short internode distances but are more difficult to physically construct than other, less dense topologies, as the number of nodes becomes large.

2.1.3. Mean Internode Distance

The mean internode distance is the expected number of hops a "typical" message will need to reach its destination. This mean internode distance is a better indicator of average message delay than the maximum internode distance, but as we shall see, it too fails to completely capture the relative communication capacity of different interconnection networks.

Unlike the maximum internode distance, the average internode distance depends on the message routing distribution. This routing distribution specifies the probability that different network nodes exchange messages, and it ultimately depends on the communication requirements of the application and system programs as well as the mapping of these programs onto the network. Table 2.2 summarizes the notation needed to discuss message routing distributions.

In its most general form, the mean internode distance (number of Link Visits) is given by

$$LV = \sum_{l=1}^{lmax} l \cdot \Phi(l),$$

(2.1)

where $\Phi(l)$ is the probability of a message crossing l communication links, and $lmax$ is the maximum internode distance. Different choices for $\Phi(l)$ lead to different message

Table 2.2

Notation for message routing distributions

Symbol	Definition
$LV_{symmetric}^{uniform}$	mean message path length (Link Visits) for a symmetric interconnection network with uniform message routing
$LV_{asymmetric}^{uniform}$	mean message path length (Link Visits) for an asymmetric interconnection network with uniform message routing
$LV_{symmetric}^{local}$	mean message path length (Link Visits) for a symmetric interconnection network with sphere of locality message routing
$LV_{symmetric}^{decay}$	mean message path length (Link Visits) for a symmetric interconnection network with decreasing probability message routing
L	maximum internode distance within the locality when using the sphere of locality message routing distribution
ϕ	probability of sending a message to a node within a sphere of locality
$Decay(d, lmax)$	normalizing constant for decreasing probability message routing distribution
d	decay factor for decreasing probability message routing distribution

routing distributions and in turn, different mean internode distances. In the following, we consider three different message routing distributions for which it is possible to obtain closed forms for the mean internode distance. To do this, however, we must first distinguish between two types of networks: symmetric and asymmetric.

In a *symmetric* interconnection network there exists a homomorphism that maps any node of the network graph onto any other node. Intuitively, all nodes possess the same view of the network. A bidirectional ring network is a simple example of a symmetric interconnection network because each message can always reach two nodes by crossing any given number of communication links, and a simple node renumbering suffices to map any node onto any other.

An *asymmetric* interconnection network is any network that is *not* symmetric. A tree structured interconnection is a simple example.

2.1.3.1. Uniform Message Routing - Symmetric Interconnections

A message routing distribution is said to be *uniform* if the probability of node i sending a message to node j is the same for all i and j, $i \neq j$. Because we are interested in message transfers that require use of the interconnection network, we exclude the case of nodes sending messages to themselves.

Consider a symmetric interconnection network containing K nodes obeying the uniform message routing distribution. Define $Reach(l, Net-type)$ as the *number* of nodes reachable from an arbitrary node by crossing *exactly* l communication links. The probability of a message requiring l link traversals to reach its destination is

$$\Phi(l) = \frac{Reach(l, Net-type)}{K - 1},$$

and the mean internode message distance (average number of links traversed by a message) is

$$LV_{symmetric}^{uniform} = \frac{\sum_{l=1}^{lmax} l \cdot Reach(l, Net-type)}{K - 1}, \tag{2.2}$$

where $lmax$ is the network diameter.

The uniform message routing distribution is appealing because it includes no assumptions about the computation generating the messages. It also provides what is likely to be an upper bound on the mean internode message distance because most distributed computations should exhibit some measure of communication locality.

2.1.3.2. Sphere of Locality Message Routing - Symmetric Interconnections

Suppose the uniform message routing assumption were relaxed. We would expect any reasonable mapping of a distributed computation onto a multicomputer network to place tasks that communicate frequently close to one another in the network. One abstraction of this idea places each node at the center of a sphere of locality[1]. A node sends messages to the other nodes in its sphere of locality with some high probability ϕ, whereas messages are sent to nodes outside the sphere with low probability $1 - \phi$.

Iterative partial differential equations solvers, discussed in chapter seven, exemplify the sphere of locality communication model. Each parallel task exchanges data with its near neighbors during each iteration and periodically sends local convergence information to a global convergence checker.

If L is the maximum number of links a message can cross and remain in the sphere of locality centered at its source, i.e., L is the radius of the sphere, then the number of nodes contained in a sphere of locality is

$$LocSize\,(L, Net-type\,) \;=\; \sum_{l=1}^{L} Reach\,(l, Net-type\,)\,, \tag{2.3}$$

where $Reach\,(l, Net-type\,)$ is the number of nodes reachable by crossing exactly l links in a network of type $Net-type$. In a symmetric network containing K nodes, network symmetry implies that each node is contained in the localities of $LocSize\,(L, Net-type\,)$ other nodes and is outside the localities of $K - LocSize\,(L, Net-type\,) - 1$ nodes. Thus, the message traffic on the communication links is uniform even though the message routing distribution is not.

Given the values of ϕ and L, the message routing distribution is given by

$$\Phi(l) \;=\; \begin{cases} \dfrac{\phi\, Reach\,(l, Net-type\,)}{LocSize\,(L, Net-type\,)} & 1 \le l \le L \\[4mm] \dfrac{(1 - \phi)\, Reach\,(l, Net-type\,)}{K - LocSize\,(L, Net-type\,) - 1} & L < l \le lmax. \end{cases}$$

---

[1] Strictly speaking, the "sphere" is a polygon when distances are measured in discrete units.

The mean number of communication links traversed by a message under this message routing distribution is

$$LV_{symmetric}^{local} \; = \; \sum_{l=1}^{lmax} l \cdot \Phi(l) \tag{2.4}$$

$$= \; \frac{\phi \sum_{l=1}^{L} l \cdot Reach(l, Net-type)}{LocSize(L, Net-type)} \; + $$

$$\frac{(1 - \phi)\left[LV_{symmetric}^{uniform} \times (K - 1) - \sum_{l=1}^{L} l \cdot Reach(l, Net-type) \right]}{K - LocSize(L, Net-type) - 1} .$$

The first term is simply the product of the average number of links traversed when sending a message to a node in the locality and the probability of visiting the locality ϕ. The second term has a similar interpretation for nodes outside the locality and is obtained by substituting (2.2) in the summation.

2.1.3.3. Decreasing Probability Message Routing - Symmetric Interconnections

The previous definition of locality is useful if the probability of visiting the locality is high, and the size of the locality is small compared to the size of the network. There are, however, many cases when this is not an appropriate abstraction. An alternative, intuitively appealing notion of locality is that the probability of sending a message to a node decreases as the distance of the destination node from the source node increases.

Parallel functional programs create many small tasks during their execution lifetime. These tasks are *pure functions*, operating independently of all other tasks. After assignment to a processor, each child task produces a single function result that must be returned to its parent task. Keller and Lin [KeLi84] have suggested an elegant scheme, called **diffusion scheduling**, for assigning tasks to processors. Newly created tasks diffuse from areas of high processor utilization to areas of lower processor utilization

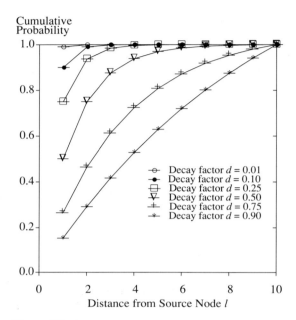

Figure 2.2
Cumulative probability of sending a message l links
20 node bidirectional ring.

with a bound on the maximum migration distance.[2] The decreasing probability message routing distribution is a natural abstraction of this diffusion process.

Many distribution functions exhibiting some rate of decay exist, but the function

$$\Phi(l) \;=\; Decay(d, lmax) \cdot d^l \qquad 0 < d < 1,$$

where $Decay(d, lmax)$ is a normalizing constant for the probability Φ, is particularly attractive. Figure 2.2 shows the cumulative distribution function (cdf) of Φ for different values of d. In the figure, $lmax$ is equal to 10 on a twenty node, bidirectional ring. As d approaches one, the cdf of Φ approximates a linearly increasing function of the distance from the source node, i.e., uniform routing. Conversely, as d approaches zero, the cdf of Φ approaches a nearest neighbor communication pattern. Choices of d between these two extremes lead to varying degrees of message routing locality.

---

[2] Chapter five discusses this algorithm in depth.

The normalizing constant $Decay(d, lmax)$ is chosen such that

$$Decay(d, lmax) \sum_{l=1}^{lmax} d^l = 1.$$

Simple algebra yields

$$Decay(d, lmax) = \frac{d-1}{d(d^{lmax}-1)},$$

and

$$\Phi(l) = \frac{(d-1)d^{l-1}}{d^{lmax}-1}.$$

Substituting this in (2.1), the formula for mean message path length, we have

$$LV_{symmetric}^{decay} = \sum_{l=1}^{lmax} l \cdot \Phi(l) \tag{2.5}$$

$$= \frac{(d-1)}{(d^{lmax}-1)} \sum_{l=1}^{lmax} l \cdot d^{l-1}$$

$$= \frac{(d \cdot lmax - lmax - 1)d^{lmax} + 1}{(d-1)(d^{lmax}-1)}.$$

Interestingly, $lmax$ is the only network dependent parameter in this formula.

2.1.3.4. Uniform Message Routing - Asymmetric Interconnections

In an asymmetric interconnection network, the number of nodes reachable by crossing L links from a given source node depends on the location of the source node. For example, the number of nodes reachable by crossing two links from the root of a binary tree is larger than the number reachable from a leaf node of the same tree.

Because each node or, at best, each group of similar nodes perceives a different set of internode distances, non-uniform message routing distributions require a separate analysis for each different set of nodes and the communication links connected to them. Hence, we restrict our attention to the conceptually simpler uniform message routing distribution for asymmetric interconnection networks.

Consider some interval during which each of the K network nodes sends a message to each of the other $K - 1$ nodes, and observe the total number of messages that cross each link l. Denote this number by $Msg(l, Net-type)$. During the interval, $K(K - 1)$ messages are sent, and the mean internode distance is

$$LV_{asymmetric}^{uniform} = \frac{\sum_{l=1}^{Numlinks(K, Net-type)} Msg(l, Net-type)}{K(K - 1)}, \tag{2.6}$$

where $Numlinks(K, Net-type)$ is the number of links in a network of type $Net-type$ containing K nodes.

Repeated studies [ReSc83, Witt81] have shown that asymmetric networks are ill-suited for general purpose multicomputer networks. Topological bottlenecks such as the root node in a binary tree limit the flow of messages unless the pattern of internode communication closely matches the network topology. Consequently, we exclude asymmetric networks from further analysis.

2.1.4. Visit Ratios

Each time a node sends a message to another node, the message must cross some communication links and pass through intermediate nodes before reaching its destination node. At the destination, it causes some computation to occur. Each of these link crossings and destination node computations constitutes a *visit* to that link or processing element. If all possible source-destination pairs and the probabilities that they exchange messages are considered, the number of visits to each communication link and node by an *average message* can be calculated. Now consider such an average message and an arbitrary node or link i. This average message will visit device i a certain number of times. This mean number of visits is called the *visit ratio* of device i and is denoted by V_i [DeBu78].

By analogy, imagine that each message deposits a "token" at a device every time it visits. After observing the system of nodes and links for some "reasonably long" interval, the visit ratios can be obtained by normalizing the token counts at each device, i.e., by dividing the number of tokens at that device by the total number of token-depositing messages that were created during the observation period. As we shall see, visit ratios can be used to locate those *bottleneck* devices in a network that most limit performance.

Under the uniform message routing distribution discussed earlier, it is obvious that the visit ratios for all network nodes must be the same. By definition, the probability of visiting each node is the same, and V_{PE}, the visit ratio for the nodes, is

$$V_{PE} \;\; = \;\; \frac{1}{K} \tag{2.7}$$

for a network containing K nodes.

Somewhat surprisingly, the node visit ratios are also given by (2.7) when the sphere of locality and decreasing probability message routing distributions are considered. This follows immediately from two features of the networks and the routing distributions:

- network symmetry and

- similar message routing behavior at all nodes.

That is, if all nodes behave similarly and the network is symmetric, each node is equally likely to be visited.

As we saw earlier, the mean message path length LV represents the average number of visits to *all* communication links by a message. Dividing this value by the number of communication links yields the communication link visit ratios:

$$V_{CL} \;\; = \;\; \frac{LV}{Numlinks\,(K,\,Net-type\,)}\,. \tag{2.8}$$

This quantity can be viewed as a measure of the message intensity supported by a single link. If V_{CL} is near one, then nearly all messages must cross *each* link at some point along a path to their destination.

Unfortunately this simple definition is accurate only if the interconnection network contains just one type of communication link. In a ring with chordal connections, one would expect the communication traffic on the two link types to be different, leading to different link visit ratios. To accurately analyze interconnection networks with multiple types of communication links, it is necessary to consider the visits to each link type separately. Such cases will be discussed as they arise.

2.1.5. Expansion Increments

Ideally, a network should be incrementally expandable, i.e., it should be possible to create larger and more powerful multicomputer networks by simply adding more nodes to the network. However, expandability may be restricted by limiting factors of the network. The node degree of the hypercube, for example, might increase as the network size increases. In addition, performance limiting bottlenecks may arise in some networks as the size increases. As a classical example, the nodes near the root of a tree quickly saturate for most message routing distributions as the number of nodes increases. Finally, the size of the network expansion increment may be restricted. Although arbitrary expansion increments are most desirable, many systems must be expanded in increments of the current network size. For example, the size of a hypercube can only be increased by doubling the number of nodes.

2.2. Single Stage Interconnection Networks

A plethora of interconnection network proposals have appeared in the research literature, and an enormous amount of research has centered on the design and analysis of these networks. Earlier, we classified networks as *symmetric* if there existed a homomorphism mapping any network node onto any other node, and *asymmetric* otherwise.

Networks are also frequently classified as **single stage** or **multistage**. A multistage network consists of several stages of switches [GKLS83]. Only the first and last stages of switches are connected to computation nodes. Switches in intermediate stages are connected only to other switches. Conversely, each switch in a single stage network is connected to one or more nodes. If *exactly* one switch is connected to each node, then the processor, local memory, and switch collectively form a building block. Historically, only single stage networks have been considered for use in multicomputer networks. Consequently, we concentrate the bulk of our analysis on single stage networks.

Among the proposed single stage interconnection network topologies are several that provide useful points of reference in the space of possible networks or have particularly attractive features:

- the single bus,
- complete connection,
- ring,
- chordal ring [ArLe80],
- spanning bus hypercube [Witt81],
- binary hypercube [Seit85],
- dual bus hypercube [Witt81],
- torus [SuBa77],
- lattice,
- cube-connected cycles [PrVu81],

- R-ary N-cube or butterfly [BuSl81],

- lens [FiSo81],

- X-tree or full ring binary tree [DePa78],

- B-ary Tree,

- snowflake [FiSo80], and

- dense snowflake [FiSo80].

Figure 2.3 illustrates the differences among the more interesting of these single stage networks. Because these networks will be discussed at length in the remainder of this chapter, we digress briefly to define those networks that may be unfamiliar.

The **chordal ring** introduces cross or *chordal* link connections between nodes on opposite sides of the simple ring, reducing the maximum number of links that must be traversed to reach a destination node. Arden and Lee [ArLe80] have shown that an optimal choice for chord placement can reduce the diameter of a K node ring from $O(K)$ to $O(K^{1/2})$.

The **spanning bus hypercube** [Witt81] is a D-dimensional lattice of width w in each dimension. Each node is connected to D buses, one in each of the orthogonal dimensions; w nodes share a bus in each dimension. Note that the **binary hypercube** used in the current generation of commercial multicomputer networks is a degenerate case of the spanning bus hypercube, arising when $w = 2$.

To reduce the number of connections to each node, the **dual bus hypercube** [Witt81] was proposed. It is obtained by pruning $D - 2$ bus connections from each network node. In particular, one dimension, the 0-th dimension, is distinguished, and all nodes are connected to a 0-th dimension bus. In each $(D - 1)$ hyperplane orthogonal to the 0-th dimension, all nodes have their second connection to buses spanning the same dimension. The second bus direction differs from hyperplane to hyperplane, but repeats if the width w of a dimension exceeds $D - 2$.

The **torus** is identical to the spanning bus hypercube except the bus connecting each group of w nodes is replaced with a ring of point-to-point connections. As a special case, the torus includes the two-dimensional **lattice** or square mesh. Other lattices include the hexagonal and octagonal meshes, obtained by connecting each node to its six or eight nearest neighbors, respectively.

Also proposed to limit the number of connections to each node, the **cube-connected cycles** [PrVu81] replaces each node of a D-dimensional cube, i.e., a binary hypercube, with a ring of D nodes. Each ring node connects to one of the D links incident on the vertex, fixing the node connectivity at three.

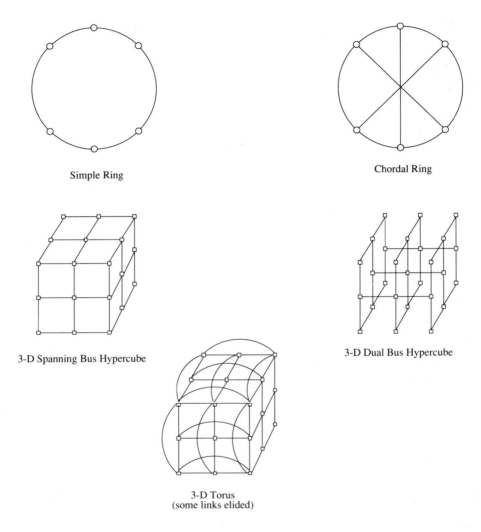

Simple Ring

Chordal Ring

3-D Spanning Bus Hypercube

3-D Dual Bus Hypercube

3-D Torus
(some links elided)

Figure 2.3
Single stage interconnection networks - part one.

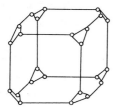

3-D Cube-connected Cycles

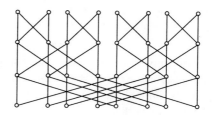

2-ary 3-cube

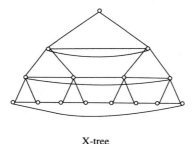

X-tree

Figure 2.3 (continued)
Single stage interconnection networks - part two.

The **lens**, a bus-connected network proposed by Finkel and Solomon, is created using a recursive construction algorithm described in [FiSo81]. Although the construction algorithm is too lengthy to describe here, an n level lens contains $n(b-1)^n$ nodes, each connected to b buses.

The **R-ary N-cube** is a generalization of the indirect binary n-cube or **butterfly network** originally proposed by Pease [Peas77], where N is the number of levels, and R^N is the number of nodes on each level. The network contains NR^N nodes, each connected to $2R$ other nodes. Unlike Pease's original proposal, the cube is closed, i.e., the top and bottom rows shown in figure 2.3 are the same. The R-ary N-cube or butterfly is equivalent to a multistage network [GKLS83] whose switches are replaced by processor/memory pairs.

An **X-tree** or **full ring binary tree** [DePa78] is a simple binary tree with all nodes at each level also connected in a ring, reducing the communication bottleneck near the tree root.

Finally, the **snowflake** and **dense snowflake** are two bus-connected, asymmetric networks also proposed by Finkel and Solomon [FiSo80]. As we shall see, their performance is limited, but we include them as representatives of the class of asymmetric, bus networks.

Each of these networks can be analyzed to determine its connectivity, network diameter, mean internode distance, communication link visit ratios, and expansion increments. These analyses are detailed, lengthy, and somewhat tedious; the interested reader can find details in [Reed83a]. Despite this, these analyses have intrinsic value for two reasons.

- To our knowledge, they represent the most extensive application of a uniform methodology to the proposed networks.

- Many of the techniques embodied in the analyses are generally applicable to other networks and will likely be helpful when analyzing networks that emerge in the future.

In the remainder of this chapter we will examine, by analytic models, the design of multicomputer networks at a *macroscopic* or system level, and evaluate the overall performance and reliability of several different designs. In chapters three and four, we will adopt a *microscopic* network view, examining the technological design issues and constraints faced when constructing a multicomputer network. Finally, in chapter eight, we will examine the performance of existing multicomputer networks. We begin, however, with an example of our analytic techniques, using the torus as a typical network.

2.3. Analyzing the Torus: An Example

The D-dimensional torus, a D-dimensional lattice of width w, connects each of its w^D nodes to a ring of size w in each of the D orthogonal dimensions (see figure 2.4). As the name implies, the interconnection network is topologically equivalent to a torus constructed in D-space.

Not only is the binary hypercube a special case of the spanning bus hypercube, it is also a special case of the torus, obtained when $w = 2$ and the degenerate, two node ring is replaced with a single link. We will return to the binary hypercube shortly.

Because each of the w^D nodes is connected to D rings, there are $2Dw^D$ total link connections to the Dw^D communication links.

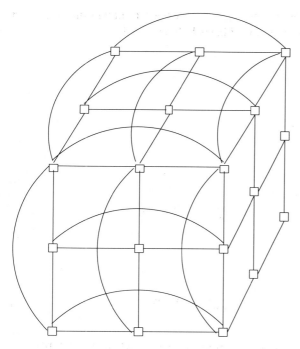

Figure 2.4
Three dimensional torus with $w = 3$ (some links elided for clarity).

Armstrong and Gray [ArGr81] have established node and arc connectivity results for the binary hypercube. Straightforward extension of these results leads to arc and node connectivities of $2D$ for a D-dimensional torus of width w.

Message routing is easy if source and destination addresses are viewed as D-digit, base w numbers. Each digit represents a ring of w nodes, and a message is routed to its destination by successively sending the message to the correct location on each of the D rings. Consequently, the network diameter is just $D \left\lfloor \dfrac{w}{2} \right\rfloor$, D times the maximum internode distance in any dimension using that dimension's ring. It initially appears that the mean internode distance under the uniform message routing assumption is also simply D times that for a simple bidirectional ring. However, this is incorrect. In the torus, some dimensions need no address resolution, i.e., the source and destination nodes share the same address on that ring. For these cases, this approach overestimates the mean path length. Instead, we must include the case of zero moves in each dimension and scale the sum of the moves in each dimension to obtain the true mean path length. Thus, the average distance moved in each dimension is

$$LV_{one\ dimension}^{uniform} \quad = \quad \frac{\displaystyle\sum_{k=0}^{w-1} \min\left\{ k, w-k \right\}}{w}$$

$$= \begin{cases} \dfrac{2\displaystyle\sum_{k=0}^{\left\lfloor \frac{w}{2} \right\rfloor} k \ - \ \dfrac{w}{2}}{w} \quad = \quad \dfrac{w}{4} \qquad w\ even \\[4em] \dfrac{2\displaystyle\sum_{k=0}^{\left\lfloor \frac{w}{2} \right\rfloor} k}{w} \quad = \quad \dfrac{w^2 - 1}{4w} \qquad w\ odd. \end{cases}$$

Because the dimensions are independent, the true mean path length is D times this distance scaled to exclude nodes routing messages to themselves:

$$LV_{torus}^{uniform} \quad = \quad D \left[\frac{w^D}{w^D - 1} \right] LV_{one\ dimension}^{uniform}$$

$$= \begin{cases} \dfrac{Dw^{D+1}}{4(w^D - 1)} \qquad w\ even \\[3em] \dfrac{Dw^{D-1}(w^2 - 1)}{4(w^D - 1)} \qquad w\ odd. \end{cases}$$

Network symmetry and the existence of only one type of communication link allow us to immediately obtain the link visit ratios by normalizing with the number of links:

$$V_{CL}^{uniform} = \frac{LV_{torus}^{uniform}}{Dw^D} = \begin{cases} \dfrac{w}{4(w^D - 1)} & w \ even \\[4mm] \dfrac{w^2 - 1}{4w(w^D - 1)} & w \ odd. \end{cases}$$

The derivation of mean path lengths and visit ratios for non-uniform message routing distributions, though conceptually straightforward, is computationally difficult. To simplify exposition, we consider only the case where w is odd. The motivation for this is simple; for w odd, we can, without loss of generality, assume the source node is at the center of a D-dimensional hyperspace. When w is even, only one node has maximum distance $\left\lfloor \dfrac{w}{2} \right\rfloor$ from the source node, making it more difficult to appeal to simplifying symmetry assumptions.

Let the source node be at the center of the hyperspace. Then it is at the center of a $(D - 1)$-dimensional hyperplane and has $\left\lfloor \dfrac{w}{2} \right\rfloor$ $(D - 1)$-dimensional hyperplanes "above" and "below" it. Suppose a message is sent to the hyperplane l links above or below the one containing the source node, and the message is permitted to cross a maximum of L links. Then only those nodes within $L - l$ links of the point of origin in the destination hyperplane can be reached. Figure 2.5 illustrates the 3-dimensional case. This view of message routing leads to the following recurrence,

$$Reach(L, D, w) = 2\sum_{l=1}^{L} Reach(L - l, D - 1, w) + Reach(L, D - 1, w)$$

where $Reach(L, D, w)$ is the number of nodes exactly L links from a source node in a D-dimensional torus of width w. The first term contains a factor of two because a message can, by symmetry, go "up" or "down" from the source node. The second term is the number of nodes reachable in the hyperplane where the source node lies. Although this formula is simple, it neglects the case where L is greater than $\left\lfloor \dfrac{w}{2} \right\rfloor$, the maximum distance in any dimension. A slight change in the sum is needed:

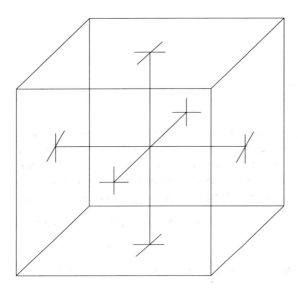

Figure 2.5
Sphere of locality routing in a 3-dimensional torus.

$$Reach(L, D, w) = 2 \sum_{l=1}^{\min\left\{L, \left\lfloor \frac{w}{2} \right\rfloor\right\}} Reach(L - l, D - 1, w)$$

$$+ \; Reach(L, D - 1, w).$$

Now only boundary conditions are needed to complete the description of the recurrence. First, if L is zero, only the current node can be reached, so $L = 0$ implies that $Reach(0, D, w) = 1$. For $D = 1$ and $0 < L \leq \left\lfloor \frac{w}{2} \right\rfloor$, $Reach(L, 1, w) = 2$ because moves are only along one ring. Finally, for $D = 1$ and $L > \left\lfloor \frac{w}{2} \right\rfloor$, $Reach(L, 1, w) = 0$ since $\left\lfloor \frac{w}{2} \right\rfloor$ is the maximum internode distance in any dimension.

With these boundary conditions, the recurrence becomes

$Reach(L, D, w) =$

$$
\begin{cases}
1 & L = 0 \\[2ex]
2 & D = 1 \ \text{ and } \ 0 < L \le \left\lfloor \dfrac{w}{2} \right\rfloor \\[2ex]
0 & D = 1 \ \text{ and } \ L > \left\lfloor \dfrac{w}{2} \right\rfloor \\[3ex]
2 \displaystyle\sum_{l=1}^{\min\left\{L, \left\lfloor \frac{w}{2} \right\rfloor\right\}} Reach(L - l, D - 1, w) & \text{otherwise} \\[1ex]
+ \ Reach(L, D - 1, w).
\end{cases}
$$

For any specified number of dimensions, a closed form for $Reach(L, D, w)$ can readily be calculated if $L \le \left\lfloor \dfrac{w}{2} \right\rfloor$. Including the case $L \ge \left\lfloor \dfrac{w}{2} \right\rfloor$ greatly complicates the formulas, and it is not obvious that any "locality" is of much practical interest when L is this large.

Given a closed form for $Reach(L, D, w)$, one can easily obtain the number of nodes in the sphere of locality, the mean internode distance, and the link visit ratios using equations (2.3), (2.4), and (2.8).

Likewise, given the network diameter $D \left\lfloor \dfrac{w}{2} \right\rfloor$, it is straightforward to obtain the mean message path length and visit ratios for the decaying probability message routing distribution.

Finally, the torus, with its lattice structure, has expansion increments of:

$w^D (w - 1)$ *increasing D*

$(w + 1)^D - w^D$ *increasing w.*

Because expanding the number of dimensions requires two additional link connections per node, it will generally be necessary to rewire the entire interconnection network if this method of expansion is chosen.

2.3.1. The Binary Hypercube: A Special Case

The binary hypercube, a special case of both the torus and the spanning bus hypercube, contains 2^D nodes each connected to a single node in each of the D orthogonal dimensions. Hence, there are $D\,2^D$ link connections and $D\,2^{D-1}$ communication links.

Message routing is a special case of torus routing, with D-digit binary node addresses. Crossing a single link resolves a bit difference between a source and destination address, and the network diameter is simply D. For uniform routing, bits in a message's source and destination node addresses differ with probability 0.5. The mean internode distance is the expected number of bit differences

$$LV_{hypercube}^{uniform} \;=\; \frac{D}{2}.$$

Similarly, the link visit ratio is

$$LV_{CL}^{uniform} \;=\; \frac{LV_{hypercube}^{uniform}}{D\,2^{D-1}} \;=\; \frac{1}{2^D}.$$

These formulas do not suffice to explain either the performance potential of the binary hypercube or the phenomenal interest currently shown in its topology. We will return to this topic in §2.5.1.

2.4. Analysis of Single Stage Interconnection Networks

The immense variety of application areas makes it difficult, if not impossible, to conclude with certainty that one network is best for all applications. Indeed, no generally accepted definition of *best* even exists. Some researchers have suggested that this pitfall be avoided by ranking networks using some weighted average of application specific evaluation criteria. This inevitably results in value judgements on the relevance of various criteria and the weights assigned to them. For example, is cost twice as important as network connectivity or only 1.5 times as important? Fortunately, no such ambiguity exists when ranking networks within each criterion. Hence, we have adopted a conservative approach, evaluating each network according to the criteria discussed earlier: expansion increments, connectivity, network diameter, mean internode distance, and communication link visit ratios.

2.4.1. Implications of Network Size

Several authors have speculated that inexpensive VLSI components will permit construction of massive multicomputer networks containing 10^5 or 10^6 nodes. Projecting trends in chip density shows that the technology will not reasonably support fabrication of chips with the requisite complexity for several more years. Meanwhile, economics dictate that any networks constructed most likely will contain no more than a thousand nodes. This limitation does more than preclude immediate construction of large systems; it creates a dilemma when extrapolating performance characteristics of large networks from small prototypes. Just as classical physics does not apply at atomic distances, postulating general principles from small networks is fraught with difficulties. Different interconnection networks may be appropriate for small or large multicomputer networks intended to solve the same problem. Whereas a single bus is likely optimal for a ten node system, it is infeasible for a ten thousand node system.

This range of network applicability compels us to examine networks in the three size classifications shown below: small, medium, and large. For small networks, constant factors can easily dominate, but the asymptotic behavior of a network becomes evident in the medium and large cases. Critical examination of results for small networks must precede any extrapolation to large ones lest apparently constant terms be confused with higher order terms.

2.4.2. Expansion Increment Comparison

Table 2.3 shows the number of nodes, links, and connections for the networks mentioned earlier. By comparison, table 2.4 shows the number of nodes and smallest expansion increment for these networks. Whereas small increments are preferred because they permit greater design flexibility, certain networks, most notably the snowflakes, R-ary N-cube, and lens expand extremely rapidly. Conversely, the bus hypercubes and torus have very small increments for limited dimensions (i.e., $D = 2, 3, 4$).

Classification	Number of Nodes
small	< 100
medium	100-1000
large	> 1000

Table 2.3
Network physical characteristics

Network	Number of Nodes	Number of Connections	Number of Links
Single Bus	K	K	1
Complete Connection	K	$K(K-1)$	$\dfrac{K(K-1)}{2}$
Ring	K	$2K$	K
Chordal Ring	K	$3K$	$\dfrac{3K}{2}$
Spanning Bus Hypercube	w^D	Dw^D	Dw^{D-1}
Dual Bus Hypercube	w^D	$2w^D$	$2w^{D-1}$
Torus	w^D	$2Dw^D$	Dw^D
Binary Hypercube	2^D	$D\,2^D$	$D\,2^{D-1}$
Cube-connected Cycles	$D\,2^D$	$3D\,2^D$	$3D\,2^{D-1}$
Lens	$n(b-1)^n$	$nb(b-1)^n$	$n(b-1)^n$
R-ary N-cube	NR^N	$2NR^{N+1}$	NR^{N+1}
Tree	$\dfrac{b^n-1}{b-1}$	$\dfrac{(b+1)(b^n-1)}{b-1}$	$\dfrac{b^n-b}{b-1}$
X-tree/Full Ring Tree	2^n-1	$5(2^n-1)$	$2^{n+1}-5$
Snowflake	b^n	$2b^n$	$\dfrac{b^n-1}{b-1}$
Dense Snowflake	b^n	$2b^n$	$2b^n-1$

b fanout (degree) per level
D dimension
K number of nodes
n number of levels
N number of levels
R fanout
w width

Table 2.4

Network expansion increments

Network	Number of Nodes	Increment	Factor of Increase
Single Bus	K	1	$\dfrac{K+1}{K}$
Complete Connection	K	1	$\dfrac{K+1}{K}$
Ring	K	1	$\dfrac{K+1}{K}$
Chordal Ring	K	2	$\dfrac{K+2}{K}$
Spanning Bus Hypercube	w^D	$(w+1)^D - w^D$	$\left[\dfrac{w+1}{w}\right]^D$
Dual Bus Hypercube	w^D	$(w+1)^D - w^D$	$\left[\dfrac{w+1}{w}\right]^D$
Torus	w^D	$(w+1)^D - w^D$	$\left[\dfrac{w+1}{w}\right]^D$
Binary Hypercube	2^D	2^D	2
Cube-connected Cycles	$D\,2^D$	$(D+2)2^D$	$2\left[\dfrac{D+1}{D}\right]$
Lens	$n(b-1)^n$	$\left[b(n+1)-2n-1\right](b-1)^n$	$\dfrac{(b-1)(n+1)}{n}$
R-ary N-cube	NR^N	$\left[N(R-1)+R\right]R^N$	$N\left[\dfrac{R+1}{R}\right]$
Tree	$\dfrac{b^n-1}{b-1}$	b^n	$\dfrac{b^{n+1}-1}{b^n-1}$
X-tree	2^n-1	2^n	$\dfrac{2^{n+1}-1}{2^n}$
Snowflake	b^n	$(b-1)b^n$	b
Dense Snowflake	b^n	$(b-1)b^n$	b

2.4.3. Network Connectivity Comparison

As table 2.5 illustrates, there is a wide variation in the arc and node connectivities of the proposed networks. It is important that alternate paths from each source to destination exist. Otherwise, the failure of a single node or link could partition the network into disjoint sections. The number of connections per node is currently technology limited. Varying the appropriate parameters for each network within the range of technology constraints shows that the torus, R-ary N-cube, lens, and hypercubes are clearly more resistant to node and link failures than the other networks.

2.4.4. Network Diameter Comparison

The network diameter is not a good general measure of a network's communication capacity because it is biased toward those networks constructed using buses; a single bus has the same maximum internode distance as the complete connection. Nevertheless, distributed algorithms requiring rapid dissemination of control or termination information are likely to execute more rapidly on networks with a small network diameter.

As table 2.6 shows, the diameter of most networks is $O(\log_p K)$ or $O(K^{1/p})$ where K is the number of nodes and p is a network dependent parameter. This is shown as a function of network size in figures 2.6 and 2.7.

The spanning bus hypercube networks emerge as clear winners because their diameter is a constant if the network is expanded by increasing the lattice width w while keeping the number of dimensions fixed.[3] Although wired-OR driver/receiver combinations can easily support ten nodes on a bus, there are limitations to the expansion of spanning bus hypercubes by increasing the lattice width. Bus contention rapidly becomes an important issue for significant numbers of nodes. This fact should be kept in mind when considering truly large systems.

2.4.5. Mean Internode Distance Comparison

Unlike the previous quantities, the mean internode distance requires specification of an item extrinsic to the network, namely the message routing distribution. Of the three distributions considered thus far — uniform, sphere of locality, and decay — only the uniform distribution requires no additional parameters, and we consider it in detail.

---

[3]Spanning bus hypercubes should not be confused with the binary hypercube. The former, as their name suggests, use buses connecting w nodes, the latter uses point-to-point connections.

Table 2.5

Arc and node connectivities

Network	Number of Nodes	Arc Connectivity	Node Connectivity
Single Bus	K	1	K
Complete Connection	K	$K - 1$	$K - 1$
Ring	K	2	2
Chordal Ring	K	3	3
Spanning Bus Hypercube	w^D	D	$D(w - 1)$
Dual Bus Hypercube	w^D	2	$2(w + 1)$
Torus	w^D	$2D$	$2D$
Binary Hypercube	2^D	D	D
Cube-connected Cycles	$D\,2^D$	3	3
Lens	$n(b - 1)^n$	b	b
R-ary N-cube	NR^N	$2R$	$2R$
Tree	$\dfrac{b^n - 1}{b - 1}$	1	1
X-tree	$2^n - 1$	2	2
Snowflake	b^n	1	1
Dense Snowflake	b^n	1	1

Table 2.6
Network diameters

Network	Number of Nodes	Network Diameter lmax	Order of lmax
Single Bus	K	1	1
Complete Connection	K	1	1
Ring	K	$\left\lfloor \dfrac{K}{2} \right\rfloor$	K
Chordal Ring	K	variable	$\sqrt{K}$
Spanning Bus Hypercube	w^D	D	$\log_w K$
Dual Bus Hypercube	w^D	$2(D-1)$	$\log_w K$
Torus	w^D	$D \left\lfloor \dfrac{w}{2} \right\rfloor$	$w \log_w K$
Binary Hypercube	2^D	D	D
Cube-connected Cycles	$D\,2^D$	$2D + \left\lfloor \dfrac{D}{2} \right\rfloor - 1$	$\log_2 K$
Lens	$n(b-1)^n$	$n + \left\lfloor \dfrac{n}{2} \right\rfloor$	$\log_{(b-1)} K$
R-ary N-cube	NR^N	$N + \left\lfloor \dfrac{N}{2} \right\rfloor$	$\log_R K$
Tree	$\dfrac{b^n - 1}{b - 1}$	$2(n-1)$	$\log_b K$
X-tree	$2^n - 1$	$2(n-2)$	$\log_2 K$
Snowflake	b^n	$2^n - 1$	$2^{\log_b K}$
Dense Snowflake	b^n	$2^n - 1$	$2^{\log_b K}$

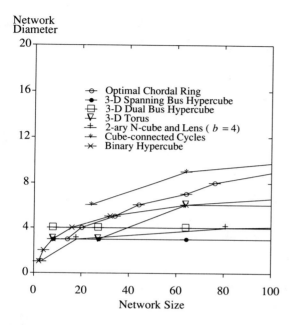

Figure 2.6
Network diameter for small networks.

Figure 2.8 shows the mean internode distance for the uniform message routing distribution as a function of network size. Those networks at the extremes of the spectrum are excluded: the single bus and complete connection with mean internode distances of one, and the ring with mean internode distance $O(K)$.

Because the sphere of locality and decay message routing distributions require extra parameters, and the mean internode distance is intimately related to the communication link visit ratios, we defer their analysis until discussion of the visit ratios.

For the uniform message routing distribution, the spanning bus hypercubes clearly have the smallest mean path length for all networks with greater than twenty nodes.[4] They are followed by the binary hypercube, R-ary N-cube, cube-connected cycles, and X-tree.

---

[4]Bus saturation becomes a crucial consideration for large spanning bus hypercubes, however.

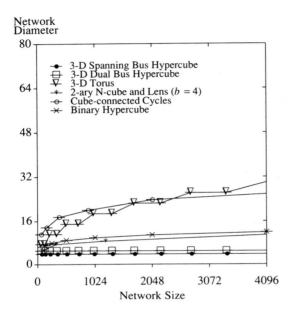

Figure 2.7
Network diameter for medium and large networks.

2.5. Communication Link Visit Ratios

In the formulation of message routing presented earlier, a message leaves a source node, crosses some communication links to reach its destination, and causes some computation to take place there. After normalization, the **visit ratio** V_i can be interpreted as the average number of visits made to device i by a message. Suppose we define S_i as the average amount of service required by a message during each visit to device i. Then the product $V_i S_i$ is the *total* amount of service required by an average message at device i, and the sum

$$\sum_i V_i S_i$$

is the total amount of service required by an average message at all devices.

If the average number of messages circulating in the network is steadily increased, the utilization of at least one device must approach unity. Which device will saturate

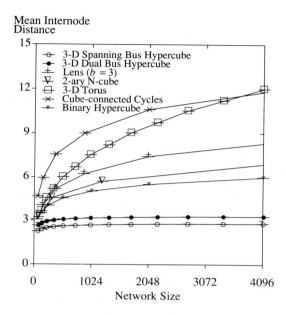

Mean Internode Distance vs Network Size

Legend:
- 3-D Spanning Bus Hypercube
- 3-D Dual Bus Hypercube
- Lens ($b = 3$)
- 2-ary N-cube
- 3-D Torus
- Cube-connected Cycles
- Binary Hypercube

Figure 2.8

Mean internode distance with uniform routing
medium and large networks.

first? Because $V_i S_i$ represents the average amount of service required at device i, the device with the maximum value of $V_i S_i$ will first limit the message circulation rate. If X_0 denotes the rate at which a network can route messages from source to destination, an absolute upper bound on X_0 is given by

$$X_0 \leq \frac{1}{V_b S_b},$$

where

$$V_b S_b = \max_i V_i S_i.$$

This technique, called asymptotic or **bottleneck analysis** in its most general form [DeBu78], applies to any closed queueing network in a steady state, i.e., any network where the message arrival rate at each device equals the message departure rate. No assumptions about service time or queueing distributions are necessary. This simplicity allows one to make minimal assumptions about network behavior and, consequently, leads to conclusions applicable to a wide range of intended network environments.

To simplify analysis, we assume that computations require the same mean time S_{PE} at all nodes and that all links require time S_{CL} to transmit an average message. We emphasize that this assumption is *not* required. The succeeding discussion can be applied in its entirety, albeit involving somewhat more arduous symbol manipulation, if each device has a distinct service time.

If there are T distinct link visit ratios, the bound on X_0, the network message completion rate, is

$$X_0 < \frac{1}{\max \{ V_{PE} S_{PE}, V_{CL}^1 S_{CL}, \cdots, V_{CL}^T S_{CL} \}}. \qquad (2.9)$$

Figure 2.9 illustrates the bounds on the message completion rate for the uniform message routing distribution, and figure 2.10 shows the effect of locality on the message completion rate. In both cases, unit node and link service times are assumed.

In the uniform routing case for medium to large networks, the binary hypercube has by far the largest message completion rate and is followed by the torus, R-ary N-cube, lens, spanning bus hypercube, and cube-connected cycles. Recall, however, that the binary hypercube is expanded by increasing the dimension D. Were the torus and bus hypercubes expanded by increasing their dimensionality rather than their width, they would exhibit a similar performance increase.

Although increased message routing locality obviously increases the message completion rate, the many different parameterizations of the locality distributions make it exceedingly difficult to draw conclusions without some specific application area in mind. In chapter five we will examine some simulation results for a model of distributed programs exhibiting high message routing locality.

2.5.1. Feasible Computation Quanta

In addition to providing bounds on the maximum rate of message transfer, the visit ratios can also be used to determine appropriate granules of computation, given the relative speeds of processors and communication links.

Bound on X_0

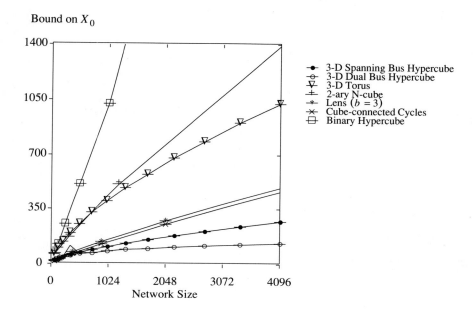

Figure 2.9

Upper bound on message completion rate
medium and large networks.

If K is the number of network nodes, the amount of service required at an average node by an average message[5] is

$$V_{PE} S_{PE} \;=\; \frac{S_{PE}}{K}.$$

A linear increase in the message completion rate could only be expected if the communication link VS products were no larger than this value. As prior figures have shown, the message completion rate is *not*, in general, such a linear function, implying

---

[5]A single message obtains service S_{PE} at one node, but this is statistically equivalent to obtaining $\frac{1}{K}$ of the total service at each node.

Bound on X_0

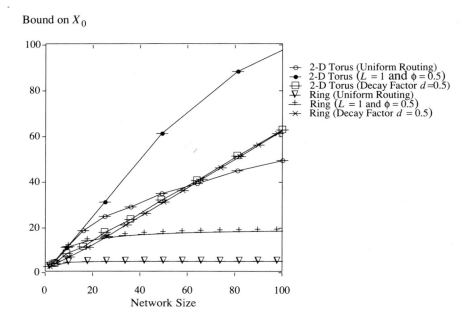

Figure 2.10
Upper bound on message completion rate
small networks with locality.

communication delays are limiting the message completion rate. Other than changing the message routing distribution, one can only adjust the ratio $\dfrac{S_{PE}}{S_{CL}}$ to insure that communication is not the performance limiting factor. Inspecting (2.9) shows that the minimum ratio of computation to communication where communication delays are not dominant occurs when

$$V_{PE} S_{PE} = \max \{ V_{CL}^1, ..., V_{CL}^T \} S_{CL}$$

or

$$\frac{S_{PE}}{S_{CL}} = \frac{\max \{ V_{CL}^1, \cdots, V_{CL}^T \}}{V_{PE}} \tag{2.10}$$

$$= K \cdot \max \{ V_{CL}^1, \cdots, V_{CL}^T \}.$$

In essence, the ratio of computation time to communication time for a message must be at least K times the maximum link visit ratio if the maximum computation rate is not to be limited by communication delays.

As an example, consider the simple ring with an odd number of nodes K. For the uniform message routing distribution, the communication link visit ratios are

$$V_{CL} S_{CL} = \frac{S_{CL} (K + 1)}{4K}.$$

In other words, each message visits roughly one fourth of the links, with service S_{CL} at each one. Applying (2.10) yields

$$\frac{S_{PE}}{S_{CL}} = \frac{(K + 1)}{4}.$$

This means that the ratio of computation time to communication time must increase at least linearly with the ring size if communication delays are not to dominate performance. Simply put, larger granules of computation are needed for larger rings if the greater average distance between nodes is to be offset.

As another example, consider the binary hypercube. The communication link visit ratios for uniform message routing are

$$V_{CL} = \frac{1}{2^D}$$

and the number of nodes is 2^D. Applying (2.10) yields

$$\frac{S_{PE}}{S_{CL}} = \frac{2^D}{2^D} = 1.$$

If the hypercube is expanded by increasing the dimension, the ratio of computation time to communication time remains constant, permitting development of application programs that are independent of the network size. *This is the performance motivation for binary hypercubes.*

Assuming communication delays are the performance limiting factor, one can also use a variation of this technique to determine the ratio of communication times for two different networks to have the same bound on the message completion rate. Consider again the ring and single bus networks, each with K nodes. Under the uniform message routing distribution, one obtains

$$V_{CL}^{ring} S_{CL}^{ring} = \frac{S_{CL}^{ring}(K + 1)}{4K}$$

and

$$V_{CL}^{bus} S_{CL}^{bus} = S_{CL}^{bus}.$$

Equating and rearranging terms yields

$$\frac{S_{CL}^{ring}}{S_{CL}^{bus}} = \frac{4K}{(K + 1)}.$$

Simply put, the mean message transmission time for the ring can be nearly four times larger than that for the bus, and the ring will still have the same bound on the message completion rate as the bus.

The lesson for designers of parallel algorithms is immediate and striking: the smallest feasible quantum of parallelism is dictated by the communication patterns of the algorithm *and* the network topology. At best, excessive parallelism leads to negligible performance gains. At worst, performance can decrease due to increased overhead.

2.5.2. Network Selection

Situations do arise where factors intrinsic to an intended application dictate the use of a specific ratio of computation to communication time for messages. When this occurs, the designer must realize that the range of optimality for a specific network does *not* span the entire spectrum of network sizes. This is clearly illustrated by the crossing of the bounds on message completion rate in figures 2.9 and 2.10. Thus, one might be justified in using one interconnection for ten nodes and a different one for one hundred nodes. One can analytically or numerically determine where the bounds for two networks cross by equating the *VS* products for the bottleneck devices of the networks and solving for K, the network size where they are equal.

Finally, the *VS* products can be used to derive performance bounds that are independent of network size. Consider the limit

$$\lim_{K \to \infty} \left(\frac{1}{\max_i V_i S_i} \right).$$

When the limit exists, it defines an absolute upper bound on the message completion rate of a network even if it contained an *infinite* number of nodes. Using the ring with uniform message routing as an example once more, we obtain

$$X_0 < \lim_{K \to \infty} \left(\frac{1}{\max \left\{ \dfrac{S_{PE}}{K}, \dfrac{S_{CL}(K+1)}{4K} \right\}} \right)$$

$$= \lim_{K \to \infty} \frac{4K}{S_{CL}(K+1)}$$

$$= \frac{4}{S_{CL}}.$$

No ring based system with uniform message routing can pass messages faster than this constant rate.

Needless to say, if performance improvement by incremental network expansion is important, those networks whose performance is bounded above by a constant, (independent of network size) should be avoided. Unfortunately, table 2.7 shows that several networks possess this property. These networks share one of two features; either the network diameter is linearly related to the number of nodes, or the networks are asymmetric, resulting in bottlenecks. We emphasize that these bounds apply *only* for the uniform message routing distribution. With enough locality in the message routing distribution, message passing rates greater than these bounds can be achieved.

Table 2.7
Finite bounds on throughput with uniform message routing

Network	X_0 Asymptote	Notes
Single Bus	$\dfrac{1}{S_{CL}}$	
Ring	$\dfrac{4}{S_{CL}}$	
Chordal Ring	$\dfrac{2(c + 1)}{S_{CL}}$	chord length c
Tree	$\dfrac{b^2}{2S_{CL}(b - 1)}$	branch factor b
X-tree	$\dfrac{64}{11S_{CL}}$	
Snowflake	$\dfrac{b}{S_{CL}(b - 1)}$	branch factor b
Dense Snowflake	$\dfrac{b}{S_{CL}}$	branch factor b

2.6. Nodes with Limited Communication Bandwidth

Heretofore we have assumed that all communication links connected to a node operate asynchronously and in parallel. Thus, a node could simultaneously transmit or receive on all links to which it is connected. This assumption accurately models the operation of the proposed X-tree communication processor [DePa78] and the JPL hyperswitch [Mada87]. However, it fails totally as a model of the MicroNet prototype [Witt80], where only one link connected to a transmitter and receiver node can be active at any given time.

In Goodman's view [GoSe81], it is more natural to view the communication bandwidth of a VLSI implementation of a communication controller as fixed. Thus, two networks, one with C connections per node and the other with $\hat{C}$, would be perceived as having effective message transmission times of CS_{CL} and $\hat{C}S_{CL}$

respectively, if the base time to transmit a single message across a single link were S_{CL}. One can view the communication controller as being multiplexed among the communication links attached to the node.

This simple technique permits us to determine the possible effects of limited communication bandwidth at the nodes. By scaling each of the communication link service times by the number of links connected to each node, a set of curves similar to those in figures 2.9 and 2.10 can be obtained. The results of such an analysis are the subject of chapter three.

2.7. A Comparison Based on Rankings

We have examined six characteristics of multicomputer networks and informally ranked networks within each characteristic. Whereas it is difficult to draw general conclusions concerning the relative merits of networks, general trends are apparent:

- The spanning bus hypercube ranks high in all categories except the maximum message passing rate defined by the communication link visit ratios.
- The R-ary N-cube and torus support by far the largest message passing rates when the network connectivity is constrained.
- If network connectivity can increase, the binary hypercube is the clear choice.
- The asymmetric networks are generally ill-suited to support communication patterns that do not closely match the network topology.

2.8. Network Performance at Finite Workloads

The asymptotic bounds on network message passing rates derived using bottleneck analysis provide a basis for ranking networks that is simple to apply and requires few assumptions. But because systems rarely if ever operate at their theoretical capacity, it is appropriate to ask if simple characterizations of message passing rates exist for networks operating under finite workloads. This question is important because different functions approach their asymptotes at different rates. Thus, even though the asymptotic message passing rate of network A is greater than that of network B, the message passing rate of B may really be larger for all workloads of interest.

Fortunately, characterizations of network message passing rates for finite workloads do exist. In general, they require assumptions stronger than the flow balance assumption for bottleneck analysis and may involve nontrivial amounts of computation [DeBu78]. We begin, however, with one simple technique for obtaining performance bounds that does not require sophisticated analysis.

2.8.1. Asymptotic Bound Analysis

If $V_i S_i$ is the total amount of service required by an average message at device i, the sum

$$R_0 = \sum_i V_i S_i$$

is the total amount of service required by an average message at all devices. We have already established that the network message passing rate X_0 is bounded above by

$$X_0 < \frac{1}{V_b S_b},$$

where

$$V_b S_b = \max_i V_i S_i.$$

Can anything be said about the message passing rate when only a few messages are circulating in the network? This question has been answered affirmatively [DeBu78].

Suppose only one message is present in the network. That message's completion rate must be simply $\frac{1}{R_0}$. Because the message passing rate can rise at most linearly with the number of messages in the network, $X_0(N)$, the network message passing rate when N messages are present is bounded above by

$$X_0(N) \leq \frac{N}{R_0}.$$

Combining this with (2.9) gives

$$X_0(N) \leq \min\left\{ \frac{N}{R_0}, \frac{1}{V_b S_b} \right\}. \tag{2.11}$$

As figure 2.11 illustrates, the two components of the bound in (2.11) must intersect, and they do so at

$$N^* = \frac{R_0}{V_b S_b} = \sum_i \frac{V_i S_i}{V_b S_b} \leq \textit{number of devices.}$$

Completion
Rate X_0

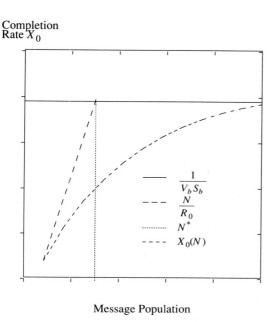

Message Population

Figure 2.11
Finite population asymptotic bound
on the message completion rate.

At the critical point N^* message queueing begins because at least two messages must be at the same device, one obtaining service and the other waiting for service.

The true message passing rate $X_0(N)$ is a monotonically increasing function bounded above by (2.11). For $1 \leq N \leq N^*$, the bound (2.11) provides a simple means of ranking the maximum message passing rates of networks. This ranking also captures something of the rate that networks approach their asymptotic message passing rate. This is illustrated for networks of 64 nodes under the uniform message routing distribution and unit device service times in figure 2.12.

2.8.2. Product Form Queueing Networks

Heretofore we have obtained only bounds on the network message passing rate. To efficiently evaluate the function $X_0(N)$, assumptions more restrictive than just steady state operation are needed.

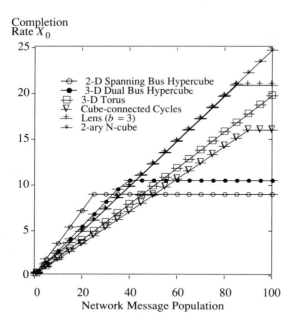

Figure 2.12
Asymptotic bound on the message completion rate
uniform message routing - 64 node networks.

The class of *product form queueing networks* [BCMP75] can be efficiently evaluated using several different algorithms [Buze73, ReLa80]. Although networks with a variety of queueing disciplines and service time distributions are product form, those whose devices have a first come first serve (FCFS) queueing discipline and a single negative exponential service time distribution suffice for our purposes.

The most intuitive of the solution algorithms for product form networks, mean value analysis [ReLa80], provides a basis for several optimizations and bounding techniques that take advantage of properties specific to interconnection networks. But before proceeding further with its description, we must define some notation unique to queueing network solution algorithms. This notation, summarized in table 2.8, will be used extensively throughout the remainder of this section.

Table 2.8

Queueing network notation

Symbol	Definition
M	number of network devices
N	network message population
$\bar{n}_i(N)$	device i mean queue length
O_i	number of occurrences of type i VS product
$R_i(N)$	single class device i response time
$R_0(N)$	system response time
S_i	device i mean service time
T	number of distinct VS products
V_i	device i visit ratio
$X_i(N)$	device i message completion rate
$X_0(N)$	system message completion rate

The mean value analysis (MVA) algorithm shown in figure 2.13 recursively computes $X_0(N)$ from $X_0(N-1)$ and requires $O(NM)$ operations, where M is the total number of nodes and communication links in the network. For networks with 10^4 to 10^6 devices, evaluation of $X_0(N)$ with a similar number of messages could require over 10^{12} operations, a prohibitive number. In our earlier analysis, we observed that all nodes had the same VS product and the communication link VS products could be grouped into a small number of types T. All devices with the same VS product should have the same performance characteristics, so finding these values for one device in each group of distinct VS products should suffice. A simple revision of the MVA algorithm takes advantage of these facts and requires only $O(NT)$ operations to evaluate $X_0(N)$. Because there are normally only three or four unique VS products for most networks, an appreciable savings is obtained.

Figure 2.14 shows the network message passing rate as a function of the number of messages circulating in each network obtained using the revised MVA algorithm; again, unit service times are assumed. As one can see, the message passing rate curves

$$\bar{n}_i(0) := 0.0 \qquad\qquad\qquad\qquad\qquad\qquad i = 1,...,M$$

for $N := 1$ to $N_{\max}$ do begin

$$R_i(N) := S_i [1.0 + \bar{n}_i(N-1)] \qquad\qquad\qquad i = 1,...,M$$

$$R_0(N) := \sum_{i=1}^{M} V_i \cdot R_i(N)$$

$$X_0(N) := \frac{N}{R_0(N)}$$

$$X_i(N) := V_i \cdot X_0(N) \qquad\qquad\qquad\qquad i = 1,...,M$$

$$\bar{n}_i(N) := R_i(N) \cdot X_i(N) \qquad\qquad\qquad\qquad i = 1,...,M$$

end

Figure 2.13

Single class mean value analysis algorithm.

cross in several places. These crossing points are important because they show where it would be advantageous to change from one network to another. They also show the range of network populations over which one network is preferred. Unfortunately, mean value analysis makes finding these points difficult because it is an *algorithm* and not a formula; the message completion rate for population N cannot be determined without calculating the message completion rates for all populations less than N. Thus, one must enumerate the message completion rates and search for crossing points.

If the requirement for an exact solution to the product form queueing network were relaxed, a formula approximating $X_0(N)$ might be found. The characteristics of such a formula are the subject of the next section.

2.8.3. Balanced Job Bound Analysis

Zahorjan *et al.* [ZSEG82] established the following bounds on the message completion rate of a closed, single class, load independent queueing network:

$$\frac{N}{R_0 + (N-1)V_b S_b} \leq X_0(N) \leq \min\left\{ \frac{1}{V_b S_b} \, , \, \frac{N}{R_0 + (N-1)V_a S_a} \right\}, \qquad (2.12)$$

Message
Completion Rate X_0

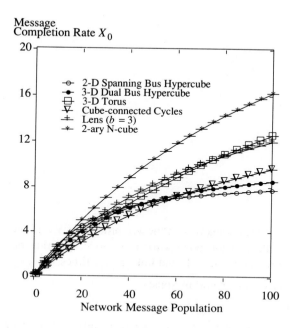

Figure 2.14
Network message completion rate with uniform message routing
64 node networks.

where

$$R_0 = \sum_{i=1}^{M} V_i S_i,$$

$$V_a S_a = \frac{R_0}{M},$$

$$V_b S_b = \max_{1 \le i \le M} V_i S_i,$$

and M is the number of nodes and links. In the particular case of interconnection
networks, this simplifies to

$$R_0 = \sum_{t=1}^{T} O_t \cdot V_t S_t,$$

$$V_a S_a = \frac{R_0}{\sum_{t=1}^{T} O_t},$$

and

$$V_b S_b = \max_{1 \le t \le T} V_t S_t,$$

where O_t is the number of devices (nodes or links) with the VS product $V_t S_t$. Figure 2.15 illustrates the accuracy of the balanced job bounds for a 64 node spanning bus hypercube with uniform message routing and unit node and link service times.

The balanced job bounds are attractive for several reasons:

• Only $O(T)$ operations are needed.

• Bounds for a single message population can be obtained independently of any other populations.

• Approximate intersection points of $X_0(N)$ for different networks can be obtained analytically.

This last point is of particular interest.

2.8.3.1. Approximate Intersection Points

Obtaining estimates of the point where network message passing rate curves intersect is easy with the balanced job bounds. Consider two networks with VS products denoted by $V_t S_t$ and $\hat{V}_t \hat{S}_t$. Equating the lower bounds obtained from (2.12)

$$\frac{N}{R_0 + (N-1)V_b S_b} = \frac{N}{\hat{R}_0 + (N-1)\hat{V}_b \hat{S}_b}$$

and solving for N gives

$$N_{low}^{cross} = \frac{\hat{R}_0 - R_0}{V_b S_b - \hat{V}_b \hat{S}_b} + 1.$$

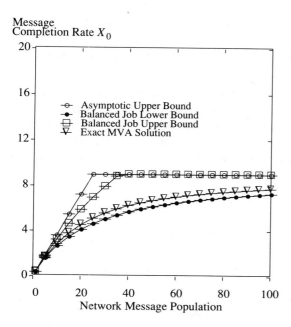

Figure 2.15
Completion rate for the 2-D spanning bus hypercube
uniform routing with 64 nodes.

A similar, though somewhat complicated, approach using the upper bounds gives
another approximate point of intersection, N_{high}^{cross}.

2.9. Summary

Selecting an interconnection network suitable for all applications is difficult, if not
impossible. However, a careful comparison of networks does show that there are
classes of networks with a range of performance, connectivity, and expansion
increments. Among these, networks such as the torus, R-ary N-cube, and the lens seem
most promising for truly large systems. For smaller systems within reach of current
technology, the binary hypercube is the network of choice. Until the number of nodes
exceeds a few thousand, the connectivity problems of the binary hypercube are easily
managed. This, coupled with its obvious performance advantage, makes the binary
hypercube extremely attractive.

When a network suitable for a specific application is needed, a systematic approach, based on a study of the most important applications, can expose the expected traffic patterns and computation requirements. Using these and the derived visit ratios, one can easily compare networks using asymptotic bounds or mean value analysis.

A systematic approach is imperative. New network topologies can be effectively compared to existing ones and networks suitable for specific applications can be selected via systematic application of the techniques presented in this chapter. Evaluating network topology is but the first step in a complete performance analysis. The design of communication hardware, the subject of chapter four, is equally important.

References

[ArGr81]   J. R. Armstrong and F. G. Gray, "Fault Diagnosis in a Boolean n-Cube of Microprocessors," *IEEE Transactions on Computers* (August 1981), Vol. C-30, No. 8, pp. 587-590.

[ArLe80]   B. W. Arden and H. Lee, "Analysis of a Chordal Ring Network," *Proceedings of the Workshop on Interconnection Networks for Parallel and Distributed Processing* (April 1980), pp. 93-100.

[BCMP75]   F. Baskett, K. M. Chandy, R.R. Muntz, F. G. Palacios, "Open, Closed, and Mixed Networks of Queues with Different Classes of Customers," *Journal of the ACM* (April 1975), Vol. 22, No. 2, pp. 248-260.

[BoMu79]   J. A. Bondy and U. S. R. Murty, *Graph Theory with Applications*. North Holland, Inc., New York, 1979.

[BuSl81]   F. W. Burton and M. R. Sleep, "Executing Functional Programs on a Virtual Tree of Processors," *Proceedings of the 1981 ACM Conference on Functional Programming Languages and Computer Architecture* (October 1981), pp. 187-194.

[Buze73]   J. P. Buzen, "Computational Algorithms for Closed Queueing Networks with Exponential Servers," *Communications of the ACM* (September 1973), Vol. 16, No. 9, pp. 527-531.

[DeBu78]   P. J. Denning and J. P. Buzen, "The Operational Analysis of Queueing Network Models," *ACM Computing Surveys* (September 1978), Vol. 10, No. 3, pp. 225-261.

[DePa78]   A. Despain and D. Patterson, "X-Tree: A Tree Structured Multiprocessor Computer Architecture," *Proceedings of the 5th Annual Symposium on Computer Architecture* (April 1978), Vol. 7, No. 6, pp. 144-151.

[FiSo80]   R. A. Finkel and M. H. Solomon, "Processor Interconnection Strategies," *IEEE Transactions on Computers* (May 1980), Vol. C-29, No. 5, pp. 360-371.

[FiSo81]   R. A. Finkel and M. H. Solomon, "The Lens Interconnection Strategy," *IEEE Transactions on Computers* (December 1981), Vol. C-30, No. 12, pp. 960-965.

[GKLS83]   D. Gajski, D. Kuck, D. Lawrie, A. Sameh, "Cedar - A Large Scale Multiprocessor," *Proceedings of the 1983 International Conference on Parallel Processing* (August 1985), pp. 524-529.

[GoSe81]   J. R. Goodman and C. H. Séquin, "Hypertree: A Multiprocessor Interconnection Topology," *IEEE Transactions on Computers* (December 1981), Vol. C-30, No. 12, pp. 923-933.

[KeLi84]   R. M. Keller and F. C. H. Lin, "Simulated Performance of a Reduction-based Multiprocessor,"," *IEEE Computer* (July 1984), Vol. 17, No. 7, pp. 70-82.

[Mada87]   H. Madan, "private communication," *Jet Propulsion Laboratory* (April 1987).

[Peas77]   M. C. Pease, "The Indirect Binary n-Cube Microprocessor Array," *IEEE Transactions on Computers* (May 1977), Vol. C-26, No. 5, pp. 548-573.

[PrVu81]   F. P. Preparata and J. Vuillemin, "The Cube Connected Cycles: A Versatile Network for Parallel Computation," *Communications of the ACM* (May 1981), Vol. 24, No. 5, pp. 300-309.

[Reed83a]   D. A. Reed, *Performance Based Design and Analysis of Multimicrocomputer Networks*. Ph.D. Dissertation, Computer Sciences Department, Purdue University, West Lafayette, 1983.

[ReLa80]   M. Reiser and S. S. Lavenberg, "Mean Value Analysis of Closed Multiclass Queueing Networks," *Journal of the ACM* (April 1980), Vol. 27, No. 2, pp. 313-323.

[ReSc83]   D. A. Reed and H. D. Schwetman, "Cost-Performance Bounds for Multimicrocomputer Networks," *IEEE Transactions on Computers* (January 1983), Vol. C-32, No. 1, pp. 83-95.

[Seit85]   C. L. Seitz, "The Cosmic Cube," *Communications of the ACM* (January 1985), Vol. 28, No. 1, pp. 22-33.

[SuBa77]   H. Sullivan and T. R. Bashkow, "A Large Scale, Homogeneous, Fully Distributed Parallel Machine," *Proceedings of the Fourth Annual Symposium on Computer Architecture* (March 1977), Vol. 5, No. 7, pp. 105-117.

[Tane81]   A. S. Tanenbaum, *Computer Networks*. Prentice-Hall, Englewood Cliffs, New Jersey, 1981.

[Witt80]   L. D. Wittie, "MICROS: A Distributed Operating System for MICRONET, A Reconfigurable Network Computer," *IEEE Transactions on Computers* (December 1980), Vol. C-29, No. 12, pp. 1133-1144.

[Witt81]   L. D. Wittie, "Communications Structures for Large Networks of Microcomputers," *IEEE Transactions on Computers* (April 1981), Vol. C-30, No. 4, pp. 264-273.

[ZSEG82]   J. Zahorjan, K. C. Sevcik, D. L. Eager and B. Galler, "Balanced Job Bound Analysis of Queueing Networks," *Communications of the ACM* (February 1982), Vol. 25, No. 2, pp. 134-141.

3 VLSI Constraints and the Optimal Number of Ports

The mightiest rivers lose their force when split up into several streams.

Ovid

The previous chapter highlighted the importance of selecting a suitable topology for the multicomputer network. This chapter and the next continue a top down examination of issues related to the design and implementation of the communication system. In particular, this chapter will examine the network design question when constraints imposed by a physical realization are included.

A general purpose VLSI **communication component** is envisioned that can be used as a building block for constructing large multicomputer networks. These components feature special purpose hardware to implement frequently used communication functions. The torus routing chip [DaSe86] discussed in chapter one is an example of a component that can be used to construct tori of arbitrary dimension and width. Another design is presented in chapter four that can be used to construct networks of arbitrary topology. This chapter will focus on VLSI constraints imposed on such a design, whereas chapter four will examine issues that must be considered in the design of any multicomputer communication system.

Whether each node of the multicomputer system is implemented as a VLSI chip or a printed circuit board, packaging constraints limit the number of connections that can be made to the node, placing an upper bound on the I/O bandwidth available for communication links. As more links are added to each node, less bandwidth is available for each one. However, increasing the number of links will usually reduce the average number of hops required to reach a particular destination. Therefore, a tradeoff exists between link bandwidth and average hop count as the number of links on each node is changed [Fuji83]. This, as well as other performance related issues such as the impact of virtual cut-through[1], are the focus of the present chapter.

---

[1] defined in §3.2.

First, a model is developed relating the number of links to the bandwidth of each one. This model will be used to evaluate the link bandwidth - hop count tradeoff. Two different network models are used in these studies: the **cluster node model** where a network node with an arbitrary number of links is implemented with several communication components; and the **topology class model** where two classes of network topologies, lattices and dense networks, are defined, and networks within each class are compared based on node degree. Queueing and simulation models are used extensively in these studies.

3.1. VLSI Constraints

A VLSI chip is subject to several technological constraints. In particular, the number of interconnections to the chip's periphery is limited and is increasing much more slowly than the exponential improvements in transistors per chip [Keye79]. Given N pins for p I/O ports, there are $\dfrac{N}{p}$ pins per port. Thus, bandwidth per port is proportional to $\dfrac{N}{p}$, assuming a constant bandwidth for each pin. Doubling the number of ports halves the bandwidth of each one, so bandwidth per port varies inversely with the number of ports. If B is the total I/O bandwidth provided by the chip, then the bandwidth of each link is simply $\dfrac{B}{p}$.

This model provides a useful but simplified view of the chip. It is deficient in two respects:

• pins for control lines are not considered, and

• data skew is not considered.

We will discuss each of these in turn.

The simplified model assumed that all pins of each link are used for transmitting data. In a real implementation, some of the external connections may be used for control lines. These control lines represent an overhead that increases with the number of links. Doubling the number of links doubles the number of control lines, implying a more than proportional decrease in link speed because fewer pins are available for transmitting data. Therefore, the linear model presented above is biased to favor a high node degree because it does not include this "per link" overhead as the number of ports is increased. It will be seen that analytic and simulation results using this biased model show that fewer ports are preferred, so a more precise model will only strengthen the conclusions that follow.

This model also neglects the effects of data skew. In a traditional implementation of a parallel communication link, the receiver must wait for all arriving bits to reach a stable value before clocking the data. Due to possible variations in propagation delay along the different wires of the link, a parallel link usually must operate at a slower clock rate than the corresponding serial link, an effect not included in the analysis presented above. However, these data skew problems can be alleviated by implementing the parallel link as a number of autonomous serial links, allowing the link to operate at the highest possible clock rate. This latter implementation leads to link speeds that are proportional to the number of pins per link, in accordance with the linear model presented above.

In effect, each chip has some total amount of I/O bandwidth that is equally divided among the existing communication links. This "constant bandwidth per chip" model will be used in all studies that follow. Although this model is predicated on the assumption that a limited number of pins constrains the design, it has also been argued that this model is adequate if one assumes power consumption is the limiting constraint [Fuji83].

In addition to its effect on link speed, the number of ports also affects the average hop count between two nodes in the network. For example, a ternary tree could be used rather than a binary tree if one more port were available on each node. As the number of links on each chip is increased, the average hop count between pairs of nodes is reduced. This tradeoff between link speed and hop count is explored in great depth in the sections that follow.

3.2. Virtual Cut-Through

The communication chip uses a **virtual cut-through** mechanism to transmit data packets through the network [KeKl79]. This means each node can immediately begin forwarding a packet once an output link has been selected assuming this output link is idle. In particular, forwarding can begin *before* the rest of the packet has been received. It will be seen that virtual cut-through can reduce message delays significantly and should be incorporated in any communication component design. One implementation of the cut-through mechanism is discussed in chapter four.

One consequence of using virtual cut-through is that error checking and retransmission must be left to an end-to-end protocol. If error checking and retransmissions were performed within the network on a hop-by-hop basis, packet forwarding could not begin until the entire packet had been received because the node might otherwise begin forwarding an erroneous packet. However, an end-to-end approach to error recovery is justified because error rates can be expected to be very low. Low error rates have already been observed in local computer networks [ShHu80]. Multicomputer networks cover an even smaller geographic area, so they are less susceptible to environmental noise and have even lower error rates.

3.3. Analytic Studies

In this section, the performance of networks constructed from p-port communication components is evaluated using analytic models. The performance metrics include:

- average "end-to-end" delay and

- maximum network bandwidth.

The delay from point A to point B in a network is defined as the elapsed time from the moment the packet header begins to leave A to the moment the entire packet arrives at B. As discussed in chapter two, the "hop count" or distance from A to B is the number of links in the minimum length path from A to B. Network bandwidth is the amount of traffic the network can carry over some fixed time interval. A more precise definition for bandwidth will be given later.

To evaluate the tradeoff between hop count and link bandwidth, two network models are developed. The first considers the implementation of a topology with nodes of degree b using p-port communication components ($p \leq b$). To achieve the necessary fanout, several components are interconnected to form a "cluster node" with b external branches. Each cluster node forms a single conceptual node of the desired topology. Delay and bandwidth are compared for various values of p. In general, a cluster node using components with a small number of ports will require more components than one using a larger number of ports. Thus, comparisons under this model neglect component count.

A second analysis compares networks using the same number of components. In this model, the hop count / link bandwidth tradeoff is evaluated within individual classes of network topologies. In particular, lattices and dense network topologies are studied.

A queueing model is used to evaluate the performance for each model. The assumptions used in these models are outlined in the next section. The effect of virtual cut-through is explored. Delay in a lightly loaded network and overall network bandwidth are compared for the different approaches.

3.3.1. Assumptions

As discussed earlier, it is assumed that the bandwidth of each communication link is a linear function of the number of links on each chip. Several additional assumptions are also used in the queueing model that follows:

- Message arrivals at different nodes are independent.
- Message arrival times follow a Poisson distribution.
- Message lengths follow an exponential distribution.
- Each node contains unlimited buffer space.
- Routing through each node is deterministic.
- Electrical propagation delays are negligible.
- Transmission error rates are negligible.

The first three assumptions are necessary to solve the queueing model. In particular, the first assumption, often referred to as the "independence assumption," states that "the exponential distribution [for message length] is used in generating a new length each time a message is received by a node ..." [Klei76]. This is clearly false because messages maintain their length as they pass through the network, but the effect of the assumption on the accuracy of message delay computations is negligible so long as the network does not contain long chains with no interfering traffic [KeKl79]. The assumption is reasonable for the analyses presented here.

Similarly, the Poisson arrival time and the exponentially distributed message length assumptions allow the use of M/M/1 queues that can be easily solved. Relaxing each of these assumptions results in G/M/1 and M/G/1 queues respectively that are difficult to solve for the large, complex networks studied here. Later, simulation studies relax these restrictions. Further, a second approximate queueing model using M/G/1 queues has also been developed [Klei76] and applied to the questions discussed here [Fuji83]. Although this second approximate model yields performance curves somewhat different from the first, the final conclusions drawn from the two models are identical.

The next assumption, unlimited buffer space, will be addressed in chapter four. It will be seen that components with a limited number of buffers can achieve the same performance as components with unlimited buffering capacity. The deterministic routing assumption is appropriate in a **virtual circuit** transport mechanism, also discussed in chapter four. A virtual circuit is a path through the network carrying messages from one processor to another. Packets traveling along the same virtual circuit follow the same path from source to destination ensuring that packets arrive in the same order in which they were sent. Because communication links are short, electrical propagation delays are negligible compared to the time to transmit a single packet. Finally, the assumption of low error rates is justified by the extremely low error rates measured in local communication networks [ShHu80], as discussed earlier.

In addition to the queueing model assumptions described above, we assume that the internal structure of each cluster node is a balanced tree topology, i.e., a tree with minimal average path length between the root and leaf nodes [Knut73]. This minimizes both the average hop count through the cluster node and the number of components required to implement a node with a fixed number of branches. Traffic distribution assumptions will be explained as the need arises.

3.3.2. Model I: Cluster Nodes

Consider the implementation of a network topology requiring b branches, i.e., communication links, for each node. Each node could be implemented with a single communication component requiring $b+1$ ports, assuming one port is connected to the computation processor for that node. Alternatively, each node could be implemented with a "cluster" of p-port communication components, where $3 \leq p \leq b+1$. For example, figure 3.1 shows a node with 4 branches ($b = 4$) implemented with 3-port communication components called "Y-components." This "cluster node" implementation implies a larger hop count between processors. However, it also uses links of higher bandwidth, because fewer ports are required on each VLSI chip.

Adding a p-port component to an already existing cluster node adds $p-2$ branches, assuming the cluster is implemented as a balanced tree. The one component cluster node has $p-1$ branches, so an n component cluster node has $(p-1) + (p-2)(n-1)$ branches. Thus, a b-branch cluster node uses

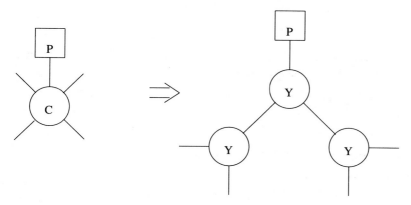

Figure 3.1
4-branch node built from Y-components.

$$n = \left\lceil \frac{b - (p - 1)}{p - 2} + 1 \right\rceil = \left\lceil \frac{b - 1}{p - 2} \right\rceil \tag{3.1}$$

components, where $\lceil x \rceil$ is defined as the smallest integer greater than or equal to x.

3.3.2.1. Queueing Model

The queueing model presented in [Klei76] is used to evaluate the performance of a b-branch "cluster node." The average delay T through the cluster node is

$$T = \sum_{i,j} \frac{\gamma_{ij}}{\gamma} Z_{ij} , \tag{3.2}$$

where γ_{ij} is the average number of messages per second entering branch i and leaving branch j ($\gamma_{ij} = 0$ if $i = j$), $\gamma = \sum_{i,j} \gamma_{ij}$ is the arrival rate for the entire cluster node, and Z_{ij} is the average delay for messages traveling from i to j. γ_{ij} and γ are determined by the traffic distribution. Let us now examine Z_{ij} in greater detail.

Consider the path taken by the virtual circuit from branch X to branch Y, as shown in figure 3.2. The average delay Z_{xy} along this path is equal to

$$Z_{xy} = \sum_{i=1}^{n_l} T_i ,$$

where T_i is the average delay at link i. Assume links are numbered sequentially from 1 to n_l, as shown in figure 3.2. With cut-through,

$$T_i = \frac{m_l}{C(1-\rho_i)} - (1-\rho_{i+1})(t_m - t_h) \tag{3.3}$$

as discussed below and in [KeKl79], where

m_l	= average message length
C	= capacity (bandwidth) of each link
ρ_i	= utilization of link i
t_h	= time to transmit a message header over the link
t_m	= time to transmit an entire message over the link

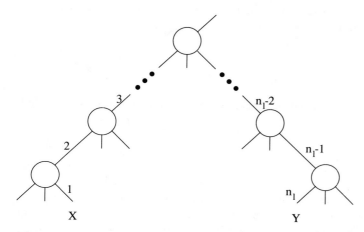

Figure 3.2
Virtual circuit from X to Y.

The message transmission time t_m includes the time to send both the data and header portions of the message. Assuming the total I/O bandwidth of each p-port component is B bits per second, C is equal to $\dfrac{B}{p}$. The first term of (3.3) is the solution of an M/M/1 queueing model and represents the amount of time required to obtain and transmit a message over the link. The second term reflects the effect of cut-through. $(1 - \rho_{i+1})$ is the probability that a cut-through occurs, and $t_m - t_h$ is the amount of time "saved" by beginning to forward the message as soon as the header has arrived. It is assumed that no "partial" cut-throughs occur. Forwarding begins either immediately after the header arrives or after the entire packet is received.

Thus the delay through the virtual circuit from X to Y is

$$Z_{xy} = \sum_{i=1}^{n_l} \left[\frac{p \, m_l}{B \, (1-\rho_i)} - (1-\rho_{i+1}) \, (t_m - t_h) \right] . \tag{3.4}$$

Equations (3.2) and (3.4) can be used to compute average message delay through the cluster node. γ_{ij}, γ, and ρ_i depend on the distribution of traffic through the node. Let us assume that there are two virtual circuits between every pair of branches in the cluster node, one in each direction, ignoring traffic to and from the processor attached to the cluster node. There are b branches, implying there are $b(b-1)$ virtual circuits. Assume that a traffic load of l messages per second exists on each of these virtual circuits, and each message consists of a single packet of data. In other words, $\gamma_{ij} = l$ and $\gamma = b \ (b-1) \ l$. Equation (3.2) becomes

$$T = \frac{1}{b \ (b-1)} \sum_{i,j} Z_{ij.} \tag{3.5}$$

The total traffic load on link k is equal to the number of virtual circuits using the link v_k times l, yielding

$$\rho_k = \frac{m_l \ l \ v_k \ p}{B} \quad \text{for } 1 \le k \le n_l.$$

Equation (3.4) for Z_{xy} measures the time from the instant the head of the packet enters until the time the *head* begins to leave the cluster node. To fulfill our definition of delay, we must also include the time that elapses while the remainder of the packet leaves the cluster. Setting ρ_{n_l+1} to 1 accomplishes this by, in effect, eliminating the "saved time" resulting from cut-through in the final node.

V_k can be easily computed for each link of a given cluster node, so the delay Z_{ij} for each virtual circuit can be found. Once Z_{ij} is known, (3.5) can be used to compute the average delay among all virtual circuits using the cluster node. Figure 3.3 shows the results of this computation for a 20-branch ($b = 20$) cluster node.

The various curves correspond to implementations that differ in two respects:

• the number of ports on each communication component and

• use of a cut-through mechanism.

The "without cut-through" curves are obtained by deleting the $(1 - \rho_{i+1}) \ (t_m - t_h)$ term in (3.3). Average delay is plotted in figure 3.3 as a function of the external load applied to each virtual circuit.

The computations assume that the average packet length m_l is 17 bytes, consisting of 16 data bytes and a one byte header. The total I/O bandwidth of each chip B is assumed to be 100 Mbits/chip-second and is equally divided among the existing links. This latter value was chosen arbitrarily but does not affect the relative ordering of the curves. These numerical values will be used in all subsequent computations unless indicated otherwise. Figure 3.3 shows that network performance deteriorates as p is increased for this particular cluster node.

For the purposes of these comparative studies, it suffices to evaluate network performance based on two metrics:

Delay (microseconds)

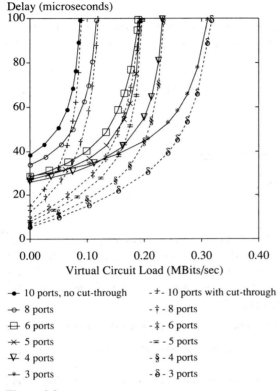

Figure 3.3
Queueing delay for 20-branch cluster node.

- T^*, the delay in a lightly loaded network, and

- L^*, the maximum traffic load the network can support.

T^* is the delay when ρ_i, the traffic load on each link, is zero. L^* is an asymptotic value for throughput in the cluster node, reflecting the point where links approach 100% utilization, leading (mathematically) to queues of infinite length. In the real network, a flow control mechanism would limit the actual queue size on each link. We will now examine delay and maximum throughput to determine the optimal number of ports for implementing cluster nodes of any size.

3.3.2.2. Delay

T^*, the delay through a lightly loaded cluster node, is obtained by setting the link utilization, ρ_i, equal to 0, except when $i=n_l+1$ in which case ρ_i is set to 1. Thus, from (3.3), the delay at each hop is

$$T_i^* \quad = \frac{p\ m_l}{B} \ - \ (t_m-t_h) \qquad\qquad \text{if } i\leq n_l$$

$$= \frac{p\ m_l}{B} \qquad\qquad\qquad\qquad \text{if } i=n_l+1$$

when cut-through is used, and the average delay through the cluster is

$$(LV-1)\left[\frac{p\ m_l}{B} \ - \ (t_m-t_h) \right] + \frac{p\ m_l}{B}\ , \tag{3.6}$$

where LV is the link visit ratio defined in chapter two, i.e., the average number of hops through the cluster node. A graph of T^* as the number of branches increases assuming a message is equally likely to enter (exit) any branch is shown in figure 3.4. As the figure shows, cluster nodes implemented using components with three ports yield the smallest delay when virtual cut-through is used.

Without cut-through, the delay of each hop through a lightly loaded b-branch cluster node implemented with p-port communication components is simply $\dfrac{p\ m_l}{B}$ and $T^* = \dfrac{LV\ m_l\ p}{B}$. T^* is also plotted in figure 3.4. The curves demonstrate that virtual cut-through can significantly reduce message delays and that clusters using components with three or four ports yield the least delay.

Assuming the cluster node is implemented by a balanced $(p-1)$-ary tree, at most $2\log_{p-1}b$ hops are required. The *worst case* delay through a cluster node without cut-through is

$$T^* \ = \ \frac{2\ m_l\ p\ \log_{p-1}b}{B} \ .$$

Differentiating with respect to p and setting the result equal to 0 reveals that minimum delay is achieved with approximately 4.6 ports per component, agreeing with the curves in figure 3.4.

Delay (microseconds)

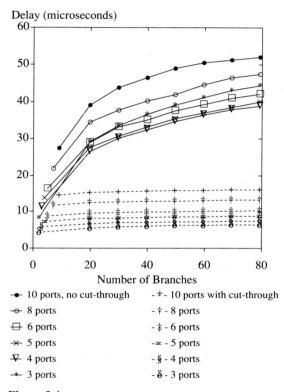

Figure 3.4
Delay through cluster node under light traffic loads.

3.3.2.3. Bandwidth

Consider the maximum throughput provided by the cluster node. This throughput is achieved when all links of the cluster node are equally utilized, i.e., the network is said to be "balanced." The bandwidth of a balanced network is equal to the sum of the bandwidths of all communication links divided by the average hop count through the network. Intuitively, each link adds some fixed amount of bandwidth to the network, and each virtual circuit uses bandwidth proportional to the number of hops. Thus, this figure is indicative of the number of active virtual circuits the network can support at one time, or alternatively, it is indicative of the total bandwidth allocated to a fixed set of virtual circuits. It will be seen later that this intuitive measure of bandwidth can also be derived from a queueing model for balanced networks.

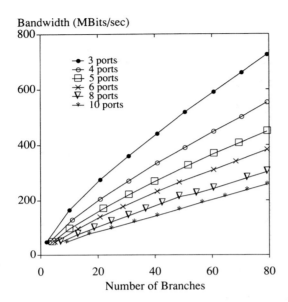

Figure 3.5
Maximum bandwidth of cluster node.

Using (3.1), a b-branch cluster node built from p-port communication components provides bandwidth:

$$BW_{max} = \frac{B\left\lceil \dfrac{b-1}{p-2}\right\rceil}{LV} \quad \text{for} \quad p \geq 3.$$

Figure 3.5 shows this measure of bandwidth for various values of p. Because a cluster node of n chips has a total link bandwidth that increases linearly with n, and the hop count increases only logarithmically in n, assuming a tree topology for the cluster node, one would expect the cluster node with the most chips to provide the most bandwidth. This corresponds to cluster nodes constructed with components using the minimum number of ports, or here, 3. The curves of figure 3.5 confirm this intuition. Virtual cut-through does not affect the bandwidth provided by a network.

Each cluster is implemented by a tree network, so it is possible that the balanced network assumption is inappropriate because bottlenecks can arise near the root node of the tree. An alternative model that considers this root bottleneck has also been studied;

however, the same result is obtained, namely, cluster nodes using components with a small number of ports yield greater bandwidth [Fuji83].

When constructing multicomputer systems with cluster nodes, congestion at the root can often be alleviated through the use of an appropriate routing algorithm. For example, figure 3.6 shows a grid topology implemented with Y-components. An appropriate routing algorithm for this topology is to route packets along one direction, say north/south, and then the other, east/west, using only one "90 degree turn." With this scheme, each packet travels through the root of a cluster node at most three times — at the source node, at the destination node, and at the node where the 90 degree turn

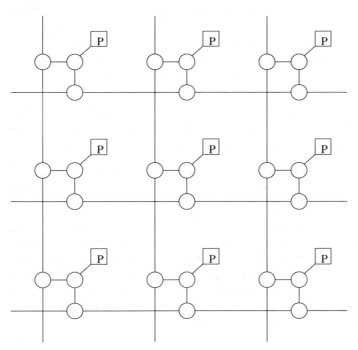

Figure 3.6
Grid topology built with Y-components.

is made. In general, this type of behavior can be exploited for any topology[2] by using a "global" shortest path routing algorithm through the network to increase use of the shorter paths that do not go through the root.

Thus, cluster nodes using communication components with a small number of ports, 3 or 4, yield the least delay, and cluster nodes using 3-port components yield the most bandwidth.

3.3.3. Model II: Fixed Sized Networks

The models in the previous section demonstrated that higher bandwidth and lower delays can be achieved by implementing b-branch cluster nodes with communication components using few ports. Such networks require more chips than networks constructed from components with a larger number of ports. In this section, we explore the tradeoff between hop count and link bandwidth for networks with the same number of switching components. Although many network topologies were discussed and compared in chapter two, simply comparing performance of networks is not sufficient for our purposes. Instead, classes of networks are first defined where distinct networks within each class differ according to node degree. Comparisons are then made *within* each class of networks.

Consider a large, unbounded symmetric network constructed from p-port communication components[3]. As before, assume that each port has a bandwidth proportional to $\frac{1}{p}$. Further, assume that there is one processor attached to each communication component in the network, using one of its p ports. Thus, in this model, p must be at least 4, because a 3-port component can only implement a ring topology.

The "sphere of locality" traffic distribution model discussed in chapter two is used for these studies. Suppose that each node must communicate with all nodes within R hops of it. Assume that there are M such nodes[4]. A small value for R, or equivalently M, indicates that traffic from each node is highly localized, whereas a larger value indicates more global communications. Consider one specific node in the network, say X, and number the M nodes to which it sends messages $1, 2, \cdots M$. The average distance, i.e., hop count, from X to these M nodes is

---

[2]except trees where there is only one path between any pair of processors.

[3]Recall symmetric networks were defined informally in §2.1.3 as networks which appear the same when viewed from any node.

[4]M is similar to *LocSize* defined in §2.1.3.2, but is not restricted to include all nodes in the outermost "shell."

$$LV^{local}_{symmetric} = \frac{1}{M}\sum_{i=1}^{M}d_i ,$$

where d_i is the number of links traversed in the shortest path from X to i. In the discussion that follows, $LV^{local}_{symmetric}$ will be abbreviated LV because symmetric networks using this traffic distribution will be used exclusively. Assume that traffic from X is uniformly distributed among the M nodes with which it communicates. As before, increasing p will reduce the average distance but at the cost of slower links.

The average distance LV is clearly dependent on the topology of the network. In general, more redundancy, i.e., distinct paths between pairs of nodes, implies a larger average distance assuming constant p. For the purposes of this discussion, different classes of network topologies will be characterized by the function $Reach(i)$ ($i=1, 2, \cdots, k$), defined in chapter two as the number of nodes whose minimum length path to node X is exactly i hops. One can envision a set of concentric shells with node X at the center. With this view, $Reach(i)$ is the number of nodes in the shell of radius i. Therefore, $M=\sum_{i=1}^{k}Reach(i)$ if the outermost shell is full.

The networks discussed here are symmetric and unbounded. Since one port leads to the computation processor, each node has $p-1$ ports for communication with other nodes, so $Reach(1)=p-1$. Two abstract cases will be discussed here:

$$
\left.
\begin{array}{ll}
lattices: & Reach(i)=Reach(i-1)+(p-1) \\
dense\ networks: & Reach(i)=(p-2)\times Reach(i-1)
\end{array}
\right\} \ i=2,...,k \ \text{and} \ p\geq 4
$$

The first represents regular two-dimensional lattices (see figure 3.7) and the second dense networks. The two-dimensional torus network discussed in chapter two is one example of a lattice network, whereas tree networks and cube-connected cycles are examples of dense networks. Lattices are attractive because they are easily mapped onto the two dimensional plane, facilitating physical implementation of the network. Dense network topologies are attractive because they feature small diameter and worst case internode distances that increase only logarithmically with the number of nodes.

3.3.3.1. Queueing Model

The cut-through queueing model discussed earlier can also be applied to the networks presented in this section. The symmetric nature of the traffic load and the network topology leads to links that are equally loaded, i.e., the network is balanced. As before, we will consider only traffic within the network itself. Delays on the links between the computation processors and communication components are ignored.

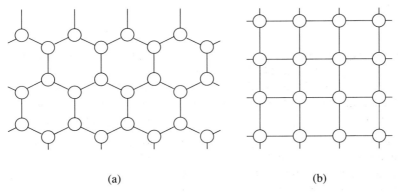

(a)   (b)

Figure 3.7
Regular two-dimensional lattices (port to processor not shown).
(a) $p=4$. (b) $p=5$.

A closed form solution for estimating network delay, including the effects of virtual cut-through, is known [KeKl79]. Using the same assumptions discussed earlier, it can be shown that the average delay to send a message through a balanced network is

$$T = \frac{m_l \, p \, LV}{B \, (1-\rho)} \; - \; (LV-1) \, (1-\rho) \, (t_m - t_h), \tag{3.7}$$

where:

LV	= average hop count
m_l	= average message length
B	= total I/O bandwidth of each communication component
p	= number of ports
ρ	= utilization of each link
t_h	= time to transmit a message header over the link
t_m	= time to transmit an entire message over the link

The first term of this equation is the delay when no cut-through is used. The second term is the improvement when cut-through is added. The effectiveness of cut-through in reducing delay increases with LV because there are more chances for cut-through to occur if the number of hops is large. As before, the model assumes that no "partial" cut-throughs occur, i.e., forwarding begins either immediately after the header arrives or after the entire packet is received. The cut-through mechanism has greater effect in lightly loaded networks (small ρ).

Table 3.1

Link Usage

p	Link Bandwidth (Mbits/sec)	Circuits per Link (Lattices)	Circuits per Link (Dense Networks)
4	25.00	65.00	57.33
5	20.00	42.50	32.50
6	16.67	30.00	24.00
7	14.29	23.33	18.00
8	12.50	18.57	13.43
9	11.11	15.00	11.50
10	10.00	12.67	10.11

Consider a network with N processors, each sending messages to the M processors closest to it. If LV is the average hop count to reach another processor, then there are $N \times M$ virtual circuits, each using LV links. Assume the load on each virtual circuit is l messages per second, or $l\ m_l$ bits per second. The network has $N \times (p-1)$ links, excluding those links connecting to the computation processors, so the average load on each link is

$$\frac{N\ M\ m_l\ l\ LV}{N(p-1)}$$

bits per second. Therefore,

$$\rho = \frac{M\ m_l\ l\ LV}{B}\ \frac{p}{p-1}\ . \tag{3.8}$$

LV can be computed numerically, given M and p, so we can use (3.7) and (3.8) to compute the average message delay.

Figure 3.8a shows delay in lattice topologies with and without a cut-through mechanism as a function of the load applied to each virtual circuit. Table 3.1 lists the number of virtual circuits using each link. M is fixed at 50 nodes. The optimal number of ports as a function of M will be studied in a later section. Under light traffic loads, networks with a smaller number of ports achieve lower delays, regardless of whether a cut-through mechanism is used. Figure 3.8a indicates, however, that the "knee" for curves with a large number of ports is further to the right than those with a small

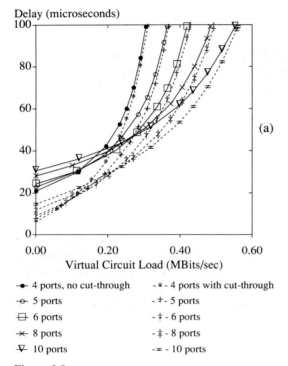

(a)

Figure 3.8a

Queueing delay for lattices, each node communicates with 50 others.

number of ports. This suggests that networks with a large number of ports can maintain reasonable delays for larger traffic loads than networks with a small number of ports. In other words, these curves show that components with a small number of ports yield networks with shorter delay but less overall bandwidth.

Figure 3.8b and table 3.1 present the same analysis for dense network topologies, also with M fixed at 50 nodes. Again, networks with a small number of ports yield better delay under light traffic loads but poorer overall bandwidth. The minimum number of ports achieves the least delay when a cut-through mechanism is used, as would be expected because cut-through diminishes the penalties of traversing additional hops. Networks without cut-through achieve minimal delay when 5 ports are used for this particular value of M.

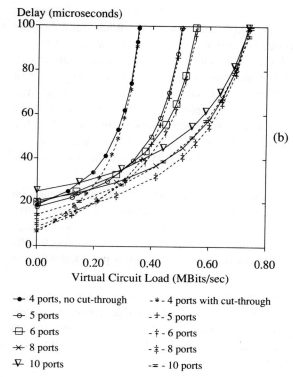

Figure 3.8b

Queueing delay for dense network, each node communicates with 50 others.

We will now analyze the optimal number of ports as a function of traffic locality M. T^*, the delay in a lightly loaded network, and l^*, the maximum virtual circuit traffic load supported by the network, will be evaluated and compared.

3.3.3.2. Delay

T^*, the delay in a lightly loaded network is again found by setting ρ equal to 0. Thus, from (3.7), one obtains:

$$T^* = \frac{m_l \, p \, LV}{B} - (LV-1)(t_m - t_h) \qquad \text{with cut-through}$$

$$T^* = \frac{m_l \, p \, LV}{B} \qquad\qquad\qquad \text{without cut-through}$$

These quantities are plotted in figure 3.9 as a function of M, the number of processors to which each processor sends messages, which determines LV. When cut-through is used, networks constructed with the smallest number of ports yield the least delay for both lattice and dense network topologies. The same is true for lattices without cut-through, indicating that the reduction in hop count caused by increasing the number of ports is not sufficient to adequately offset the lost bandwidth per port. The final case, dense networks without cut-through, is more complex. Figure 3.9b shows that the smallest number of ports ($p=4$) does not give minimum delay beyond $M=32$ nodes. Similarly, as M is increased further, larger values of p appear more attractive (see figure 3.10), although the optimal number never rises beyond 6. This case will be examined in more detail momentarily.

For both classes of networks, these results favor a communication component with relatively few ports, say from 4 to 6. A cut-through mechanism makes the optimal number closer to 4. Under the conditions stated above, dense networks will always yield lower delays than lattices because of lower hop count averages. Asymptotic values of T^* as a function of M when no cut-through mechanism is provided will now be derived.

Given these abstract topologies, we can treat M as a function of the continuous variable r, the distance of a node from the other nodes to which it is sending messages; previously, $Reach(i)$ was a function of the discrete variable i. As M grows toward infinity, $Reach(r)$ is asymptotically equivalent to $Reach(i)$. With this perspective, LV is an *integral* rather than a sum. Thus we have

$$LV = \frac{1}{M} \int_0^R r\, Reach(r)\, dr \qquad with \qquad M = \int_0^R Reach(r)\, dr$$

And the two cases discussed above reduce to:

$$\left. \begin{array}{l} lattices: \qquad Reach(r) = (p-1)r \\ dense\ networks: Reach(r) = (p-1)(p-2)^{r-1} \end{array} \right\} \ p \geq 4$$

Evaluation of the above integrals for the two cases results in the following equations for delay:

$$lattices: \qquad T^* = \frac{m_l\, LV\, p}{B} = \frac{m_l}{B} \left[\frac{8\,(p-1)M}{9} \right]^{\frac{1}{2}}$$

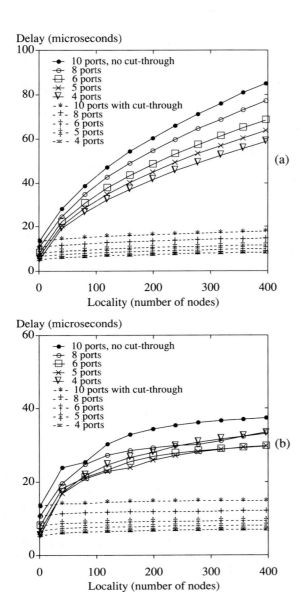

Figure 3.9

Delay under light traffic loads.

(a) lattices. (b) dense networks.

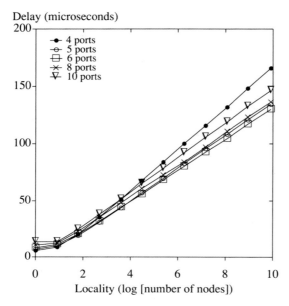

Figure 3.10
Delay under light traffic loads for dense networks (no cut-through).

$$dense\ networks: \quad T^* = \frac{m_l\ LV\ p}{B} = \frac{m_l}{B}\left[\frac{p\ R\ (p-2)^R}{(p-2)^R-1} - \frac{p}{\ln(p-2)}\right]$$

$$with \quad R = \frac{\ln[M\ (p-2)\ln(p-2)+p-1] - \ln(p-1)}{\ln(p-2)}$$

The equation for the first case again demonstrates that for any given M, a lower delay results if fewer ports are used. The equation for the second case, however, requires a more detailed analysis.

Minimizing T^* by taking the derivative with respect to p, and solving this equation numerically yields the curve in figure 3.11. This curve gives the optimal number of ports as a function of M, the number of nodes with which each node communicates.

The above derivations assume that traffic from a node is uniformly distributed among the nodes with which it communicates. In practice, one would map a specific problem onto the system so that there is more traffic with nearby nodes than with those further away. Traffic between neighboring nodes should then be weighted more heavily. If

Optimal Number of Ports

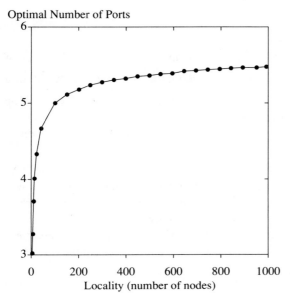

Figure 3.11
Optimal number of ports for dense networks (no cut-through).

one takes this into account, the case for the use of a few high-bandwidth links, rather than many slower links, becomes even stronger.

Based on these studies, it appears that a communication component with relatively few ports, say from 4 to 6, yields the least average delay. If cut-through is considered, the argument for a small number of ports becomes stronger.

3.3.3.3. Bandwidth

Let us consider increasing the load on all virtual circuits of the network. As before, network bandwidth is defined as the asymptotic traffic load supported by the network as it approaches saturation, i.e., as link utilization ρ approaches 1. From (3.8), the load per virtual circuit at saturation l^* is

$$l^* = \frac{B}{m_l \, M \, LV} \, \frac{p-1}{p}$$

messages per second. The total network bandwidth at saturation is

$$L^*m_l = \frac{BN}{LV} \frac{p-1}{p}$$

bits per second, because there are $M \times N$ virtual circuits, where N is the number of nodes in the network. Thus, neglecting the $\frac{(p-1)}{p}$ term, the maximum bandwidth of a network is asymptotically the sum of the link bandwidths divided by the average hop count, agreeing with the maximum bandwidth figure of merit derived intuitively for the cluster node model. This figure reflects the maximum number of active virtual circuits the network can support at one time.

When comparing networks with the same number of chips, the sum of the link bandwidths is constant, so the topology with the smallest average hop count will achieve the highest bandwidth. In this case, networks constructed with the largest number of links per node yield the most bandwidth. Bandwidths for dense and lattice networks are shown in figure 3.12 for various values of p, confirming this intuition[5]. The curves also demonstrate that network bandwidth diminishes rapidly as traffic becomes less localized.

3.3.4. Summary of Analytic Results

The analytic results for the optimal number of ports are summarized in table 3.2. When considering delay, the analytic models presented here indicate that better performance is achieved with communication components with a relatively small number of ports,

Table 3.2
Optimal number of ports

Model	Delay	Bandwidth
cluster nodes	3-4	3
fixed number of components	4-6	large

---

[5]This is also consistent with results derived in chapter two, e.g., the high completion rate for the hypercube depicted in figure 2.9.

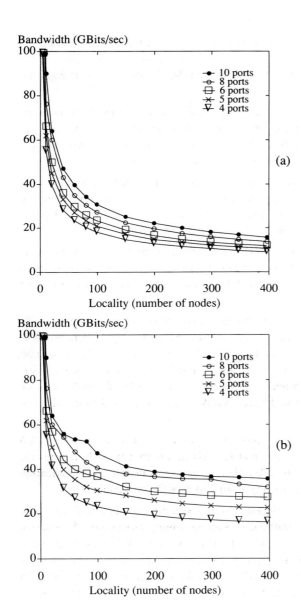

Figure 3.12
Maximum network bandwidth.
(a) lattices (b) dense networks.

say from 3 to 6. Virtual cut-through reduces the effect of larger hop counts, and pushes the optimal number of ports closer to 3. A cut-through mechanism can substantially reduce transmission delays in the network, so it is unreasonable to exclude it from any communication component design.

When considering bandwidth, the cluster node model favors components with the minimum number of ports, whereas the ''one communication component per processor'' model favors a large number of links. Despite the latter result, one can still argue that a small number of ports is preferred on the following grounds:

- The bandwidth result is only of practical interest if the traffic distribution is such that most of the links can be kept busy most of the time. If a few critical links are the bottleneck in the system, then it is better to maximize the bandwidth of these bottleneck links, implying few high bandwidth links are preferred.

- As demonstrated by the cluster node model, one can provide higher bandwidth by implementing the network with more communication chips. It is not as easy to overcome the delay limitations associated with components using many ports per node.

- The studies presented above measure the maximum bandwidth of the entire network. The bandwidth available to individual virtual circuits is bounded by the bandwidth of the links it uses and is greater if a small number of ports are used. The bandwidth between a pair of nodes can be improved by establishing several virtual circuits between them. However, this approach adds considerable complexity to the routing mechanism because the circuits should have no links in common for this technique to be effective.

Thus, one can make a good case for using few ports on each node even when bandwidth is used as the performance metric. When combined with the results concerning network delay, one concludes that a general purpose communication component with a small number of ports, say from 3 to 6, is the best choice.

The analysis presented above included several simplifying assumptions. The strongest assumption concerned the traffic distributions among processors. Simulation studies that explore a number of different traffic distributions will be discussed next. For the most part, these simulations support the conclusions derived analytically. When discrepancies do occur, the simulations indicate better performance for components with a small number of ports, strengthening the conclusion that a small number of ports should be used.

3.4. Simulation Studies

The analytic models presented above include some simplifying assumptions. In particular, traffic distributions implied equal link utilizations, message arrivals were assumed to follow a Poisson distribution, and message lengths were assumed to follow an exponential distribution. To evaluate the conclusions derived by the analytic models when these assumptions are relaxed, and to gain deeper insight into the tradeoffs between various network topologies and realizations of the communication components, a simulation program was developed. The results of these studies are discussed in this section. An instruction level simulator was used, and the respective speedups resulting from simulating several parallel application programs on various network structures are reported. Some of the issues evaluated by this study include the optimal number of ports and the effect of incorporating a mechanism in the communication hardware for efficiently handling multiple-destination messages.

3.4.1. Assumptions

The application programs that were executed on the simulator consist of a collection of statically defined tasks that execute concurrently and communicate through a message passing mechanism. Each task executes on a separate processor. Several assumptions are made in the simulation experiments reported here:

(1) Operating system overhead to send and receive messages is negligible.

(2) Processing elements are equivalent to a VAX™ 11/780 in computation speed.

(3) All packets contain a 1 byte header and 16 data bytes.

(4) Unlimited buffer space is available in each communication component.

(5) No errors occur in transmitting messages.

(6) All networks provide a virtual cut-through mechanism.

(7) Virtual circuits are statically defined and set up in advance.

(8) A shortest path routing algorithm is used to route messages.

Among these, the first four assumptions are perhaps the most significant and merit further discussion. The first assumption, negligible operating system overhead, allows separation of the penalty due to operating system overhead from that inherent in the communication switch. Studies that analyze the effect of operating systems overhead alone and assume negligible communication delays, will also be discussed. The second assumption concerning the speed of processing elements is appropriate for many 32 bit microprocessors. Packets consist of a single control byte followed by 16 data bytes. Fixed-size packets are used because of the difficulties associated with managing variable sized buffers, to be discussed in chapter four. This is in contrast to the analytic models that assumed message lengths follow an exponential distribution. The control byte is used to specify a virtual channel number, also discussed in chapter four. In the application programs discussed here, messages are short, typically consisting of a single floating point number, and fit within a single packet[6].

It is assumed that adequate buffer space is available in each component for holding packets waiting to be forwarded. It will be shown in chapter four that chip densities now allow each component to provide enough buffer space to achieve approximately the same performance as a component with an unlimited amount of buffering.

3.4.2. The Application Programs

Traffic distributions are generated by application programs executing parallel algorithms. For the purposes of this study, an application program is characterized by the communication pattern it generates. In particular, communications are characterized by the structure of interactions between the program and its surrounding environment and the pattern of interactions within the program among its constituent tasks.

External communications between the parallel program and its environment are assumed to fall into one of two categories:

- serial input, serial output (SISO), or
- parallel input, parallel output (PIPO).

These two communication patterns are shown in figure 3.13. In SISO, the input data arrive from (are sent to) a single source (destination). In PIPO, the data arrive (leave) in parallel from (to) several sources (destinations).

Several of the application programs implement signal processing functions using an SISO communication pattern. A single processor samples the input waveform and distributes the data values to other processors that collectively compute results. Another processor collects the output waveform. In other situations, a PIPO structure is more appropriate. For example, the application program could be one of several job steps, each of which is implemented as a separate parallel program. Because the input (output) of each job step comes from (goes to) another parallel program, one can expect data to arrive (leave) in parallel. Two other communication patterns are possible, i.e.,

---

[6]In contrast, messages in commercial multicomputers available today are usually much larger to offset inefficient communication mechanisms.

SERIAL INPUT
SERIAL OUTPUT (SISO)

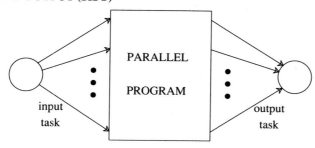

PARALLEL INPUT
PARALLEL OUTPUT (PIPO)

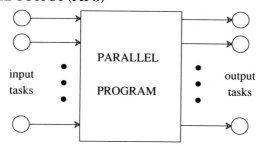

Figure 3.13
Communication patterns for application programs.

SIPO or PISO, but these are only combinations of the patterns presented above and are not fundamentally different.

The internal communication paths are either:

- global communications, or
- local communications.

As the name implies, global communications means that each task interacts with all, or nearly all, of the other tasks. Local communications mean each task interacts with a small subset of the other tasks. The programs that use local communications are pipelined. Thus, the communications are local in the sense that each stage of the pipeline sends messages only to the next stage and not to previous or subsequent stages. Although this communication structure does not contain loops among tasks in different stages of the pipeline, loops can exist among tasks within the same stage. Programs with loops among tasks in different stages are considered to belong to the class with global communications.

Six application programs demonstrating several different traffic patterns were executed on the simulator. Each uses one of the four combinations of the parameters described above. These are:

(1)   Barnwell, a signal processing program using Barnwell's algorithm (global SISO),

(2)   Block I/O, a signal processing program using block filters (local SISO),

(3)   Block State, a second program also using block filters (local SISO),

(4)   FFT, a program for computing Fast Fourier Transforms (local PIPO),

(5)   LU, a program for LU decomposition on a sparse matrix (global PIPO), and

(6)   Random, a program generating artificial traffic loads (global PIPO).

The communication patterns exhibited by these programs are summarized in table 3.3.

All of these programs frequently communicate small amounts of data. Typically, a task waits for data values to arrive from other task(s), performs some floating point operations, and then generates a result that is passed to another task(s). The number of processors ranges from 12 in the Barnwell program to 32 in the FFT. Each of these programs is discussed in greater detail below.

Table 3.3

Communication patterns used by test programs

	SISO	**PIPO**
global	Barnwell (12 tasks)	Random (12 tasks) LU (15 tasks)
local	Block I/O (23 tasks) Block State (20 tasks)	FFT (32 tasks)

3.4.2.1. Barnwell Filter Program (global SISO, 12 tasks)

The Barnwell filter, Block I/O, and Block State programs implement the digital filter defined by the equation:

$$Y_n = \sum_{i=1}^{N-1} b_i Y_{n-i} + \sum_{i=0}^{M-1} a_i X_{n-i} .$$

Vectors X and Y are the input and output waveforms, A and B characterize the filter being implemented, and N and M are the number of poles and zeros in the filter respectively. The programs presented here use $M = N = 7$.

An "input task" distributes sampled values of the input waveform to some number of "computation tasks." The real system would collect this data from a sensor at some sampling frequency. An "output task" collects the output waveform computed by the computation tasks. Thus, all three programs have an SISO communication pattern. When all of the input samples have been processed, execution terminates. It is assumed that the sampling frequency is large compared to the rate that data points can be processed. This ensures that the execution time is not limited by the input data rate.

The Barnwell program computes the filtering function using Barnwell's algorithm [BaGP78, BaHG79, HoBM80, BaHo82, Lu83]. Twelve tasks are used, as shown in figure 3.14. Each node in figure 3.14 represents a task and each arc a virtual circuit. An arc that fans out to several destinations represents a broadcast communication.

3.4.2.2. Block I/O Filter Program (local SISO, 23 tasks)

The Block State and Block I/O programs perform the filtering function described above by grouping the input samples into blocks and then processing each block as a single unit. The resulting communication patterns are local SISO. These algorithms have the advantage that the block size can be varied to change the performance of the system. A larger block size requires a larger number of processors but increases the rate at which input samples can be processed. Increasing block size does incur a latency penalty, however. The amount of time between reception of the first input sample and the generation of an output waveform increases. In practice, one would use the minimum block size that allows the input samples to be processed in real time; this minimizes the latency as well as the number of processors.

Here, the Block I/O and Block State programs use the minimum block size, minimizing latency. This minimum size is related to the number of poles in the filter. Given this block size, the computation is structured to use as many processors as required to exploit the parallelism inherent in the computation. The Block I/O program

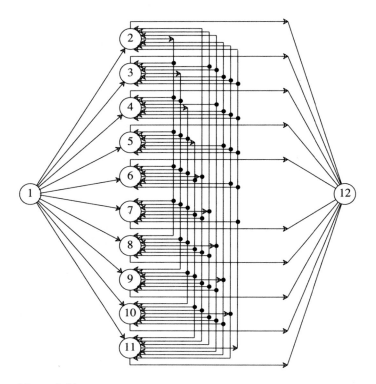

Figure 3.14
Communication paths for Barnwell program.

uses 23 tasks structured as a two-stage pipeline, as shown in figure 3.15. Communications within the second stage are global, so the program is actually somewhat intermediate between local and global SISO. Note that input samples must be broadcast to several other tasks. Details of the algorithms implemented by this program can be found in [Burr71, Burr72, MiGn78, Lu83].

3.4.2.3. Block State Filter Program (local SISO, 20 tasks)

The Block State program uses the same "blocking" techniques discussed in Block I/O. However, this program uses a somewhat different approach to perform the computation, and, as a result, includes information on the internal behavior of the filter as well as the input-output relationships. Thus, it allows the determination of some intermediate values that the Block I/O program does not compute. As before, the minimum block size is used, resulting in a computation that requires 20 tasks. The

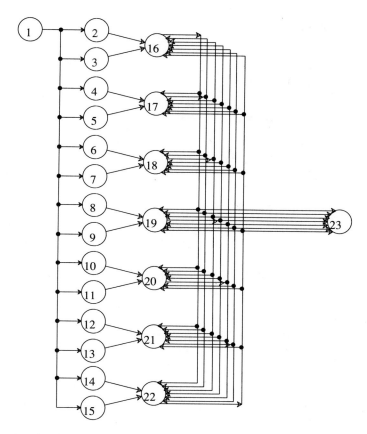

Figure 3.15
Communication paths for Block I/O program.

communication paths for this program are shown in figure 3.16. The computation uses a 4 stage pipeline and exhibits a local SISO communication pattern. Again, input samples are distributed via multiple-destination messages. Further details of the algorithms used in the Block State program can be found in [BaSh80b, BaSh80a, ZeLi81, Lu83].

3.4.2.4. FFT Program (local PIPO, 32 tasks)

This program performs a complex 16 point Fast Fourier Transforms on sets of input values. The FFT algorithm is used to compute the Fourier coefficients for an analog signal. The input consists of 400 sets of complex input values, $x_0 \cdots x_{15}$. The output

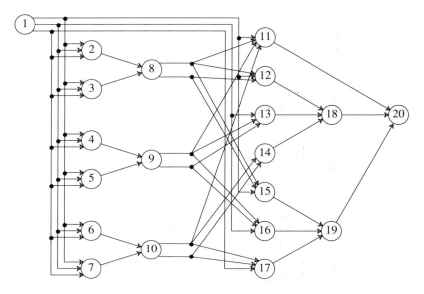

Figure 3.16
Communication Paths for Block State program.

consists of 400 sets of complex numbers $y_0 \cdots y_{15}$, such that

$$y_i = \sum_{k=0}^{15} x_k \exp((-2\pi/16)ik) \ .$$

Details of the algorithm used to perform this computation in time proportional to $N \log N$ (here, $N = 16$) are discussed in [Baas78] among others.

The communication paths used by this program are shown in figure 3.17. Because the same computation is performed on several sets of input data, it can be pipelined. The input data are assumed to reside in the processors comprising the first stage of the pipeline, so the resulting communication paths are local PIPO.

3.4.2.5. LU Decomposition (global PIPO, 15 tasks)

This program performs LU decomposition on a sparse matrix. LU decomposition is a well known technique for solving a set of linear equations. Suppose a set of equations is specified as

$AX = Y$

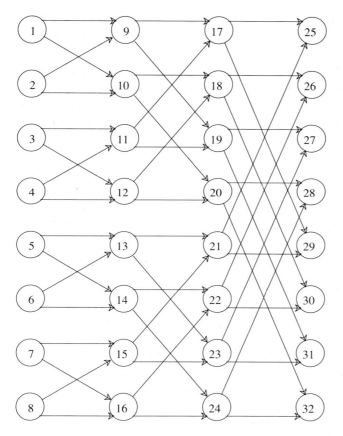

Figure 3.17
Communication paths for FFT program.

where A is a known n by n matrix, Y is a known column vector of length n, and X is an unknown column vector also of length n. The solution to this equation can be found by factoring the A matrix into two components, L and U, and then solving the equations

$$LB = Y \quad \text{and} \quad UX = B$$

in turn for B and then for X. L and U are upper and lower diagonal matrices respectively, i.e., all of the elements above (for L) or below (for U) the main diagonal are 0, so these two equations can be easily solved by forward and backward substitution respectively. If the equation $AX = Y$ is solved many times with different values for Y, then this method is more efficient than solving the original equation ($AX = Y$) repeatedly by, say, Gaussian elimination [DaBA74].

LU decomposition is one step in the inner loop of the circuit simulation program SPICE, so it must be executed repeatedly on each circuit simulation run [Nage75]. The parallel program used in these experiments performs the decomposition by using Doolittle's algorithm [ChLi75]. In this context, results computed by each processor remain in that processor and are used as input to the next step of the computation. Therefore, a PIPO communication pattern results.

Given a sparse matrix, the parallel program was generated by creating uniprocessor code for the computation, analyzing the data dependencies within this code, and then creating a parallel program from the data dependency graph [Yu84, WiHu80]. A global communication pattern resulted for the program in question. Input (output) values can be expected to arrive from (be sent to) another parallel program executing the previous (subsequent) step of the inner loop.

3.4.2.6. Artificial Traffic Loads (global PIPO, 12 tasks)

A program that created synthetic traffic loads using random number generators was also studied. In the discussion that follows, this program is called the "Random" program. In contrast to the other application programs, this program does not perform any useful computation. Its only function is to generate traffic for the communication network. The program consists of 12 tasks, each of which sends messages to all of the other tasks. Messages are uniformly distributed among other tasks, implying global communications. Because each processor originates its own messages, in contrast to a single processor generating all messages, the external I/O structure is PIPO. The mean time between messages is chosen from an exponential distribution. Loading on the network is increased by reducing the average time between messages.

3.4.2.7. Characterization of the Application Programs

To better understand the behavior of these application programs, their execution was simulated as a function of certain aggregate parameters of the communication network. Figure 3.18a shows the performance of these application programs using a fixed-delay, infinite-bandwidth switch. Speedup, defined as the execution time of the program on a uniprocessor divided by the execution time on the parallel system, is plotted as a function of communication delay. Here, delay is the end-to-end delay to send a message along a virtual circuit. It is assumed that this delay is the same along all circuits. Because the switch provides unlimited bandwidth, any number of processors can simultaneously send messages.

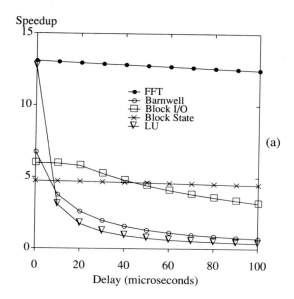

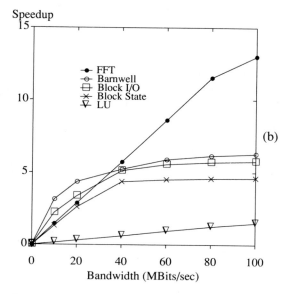

Figure 3.18
Speedup of application programs.
(a) vs. delay. (b) vs. bandwidth.

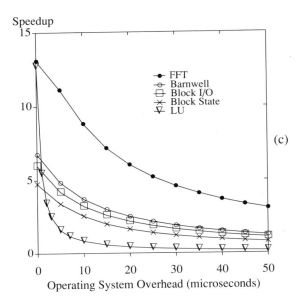

Figure 3.18c
Speedup of application programs vs. operating system overhead.

The two programs using global communications, Barnwell and LU, experience a severe degradation in performance as communication delays increase. This results from the relatively fine "granularity" of the computation and the pattern of data dependencies; communications are frequent, and delays have a significant impact on total execution time. On the other hand, the FFT and Block State programs exhibit little performance degradation as delays increase. These programs are pipelined, so delays only affect the amount of time required to fill and empty the pipe. Once the pipeline is filled, data arrive at each processor at a constant rate, independent of communication delay, so all of the processors remain busy. It is erroneous, however, to conclude that the interconnection switch does not affect the performance of these programs, because the curves in figure 3.18a assume unlimited network bandwidth.

The curves in figure 3.18b show the performance of the programs as a function of network bandwidth. Conceptually, the network can be viewed as an entity that provides a certain amount of bandwidth for transmitting messages. The optimistic assumption is made that all of the network's bandwidth can be allocated to a single virtual circuit on demand. In the simulator, this is accomplished by modeling the interconnection network as an "ideal bus." The communication network can be viewed as a bus of the indicated bandwidth. The full bandwidth of the bus is allocated to messages as they are generated. Conflicts to access the bus are queued in FIFO sequence, and propagation delays along the bus are assumed to be zero. The curves show that, although the performance of the pipelined programs is insensitive to communication delay, adequate network bandwidth is required to achieve good performance. The programs exhibiting global communication patterns behave similarly. The LU program in particular requires very high bandwidth before achieving good performance. Simulations at higher bandwidths indicate that a 500 Mbit/second network is required to achieve a speedup of 10.0. Speedup with an infinite bandwidth, zero delay switch is 12.7.

Finally, the curves in figure 3.18c show performance as a function of operating system overhead. Here, overhead is the time required to execute an operating system routine for sending or receiving a message. Transmission delays are assumed to be zero. Degradation is severe when delays in the operating system are only a few tens of microseconds. This result again is a consequence of the fine granularity of the computation. It demonstrates that hardware support for operating system primitives is required for full exploitation of the parallelism inherent in these programs. With a traditional software implementation, the time spent in the operating system will dominate the transmission time, negating the benefits of incorporating a high-performance communication network. In particular, because recovery from transmission errors is left to an end-to-end protocol, hardware support should be employed in the computation processor to keep these checks from degrading performance.

3.4.3. Issues Under Investigation

Three separate issues are studied in these simulation experiments:

- The optimal number of ports is explored and simulation results are compared with those predicted by the analytic models presented earlier.

- An alternative model where processor and communications are integrated onto the same chip is studied.

- Because many of the application programs send the same message to several different destinations, the benefit of incorporating a multicast mechanism for efficiently handling such messages is investigated.

To evaluate the optimal number of ports, the networks discussed in the analytic studies — cluster nodes and networks with a fixed number of components — were studied. In the first, each node of a topology requiring b branches per node is implemented with a cluster of p-port communication components. As p is reduced, the number of components required to construct the network is increased. Thus, the cluster node switch models do not keep the chip count constant. The second set of switch models compares networks with different values of p but with approximately the same number of components.

In addition to networks constructed from separate computation and communication components, networks with processor and communications on a single chip are studied. This is the building block for the "network computer" proposed by Wittie [Witt81]. In this model, the communication links between the computation and communication domains are eliminated. In communication component networks, these links sometimes become bottlenecks that bias the results. The simulations under this latter model eliminate this bias. Systems using the Wittie model do require more circuitry per chip than those using communication components, making direct comparisons unfair. Nevertheless, it is included as an alternative model for multicomputer networks.

Because the digital filtering algorithms (Barnwell, Block State, and Block I/O) transmit the same data to several destinations, a mechanism for distributing multiple-destination packets efficiently, i.e., a "multicast" mechanism, should improve performance. If a multicast mechanism is *not* used, one "single destination" packet must be generated at the source node for each destination. Each is routed separately using a shortest path routing algorithm. If one traces the paths followed by these packets through the network, one sees that packets follow each other up to a certain point, and then part and go their separate ways. The multicast mechanism combines the single destination packets that are "following each other" into a single "multicast packet." A new copy is not generated until one or more of the single destination packets incorporated into the multicast packet need to "go their separate ways." If several packets breaking off like this are all going in the same direction, only one new multicast packet is created. Multicast and broadcast mechanisms are described more fully in [DaMe78, BhJa83, McQu78]. Because virtual circuits are used, implementation of the multicast does not affect other parameters of the switching network. A longer header might be needed to provide a list of destination nodes. However in a virtual circuit mechanism, this information need only be sent when the multicast circuit is established.

3.4.4. Simulation Results on Cluster Node Networks

As discussed earlier, one can implement a node of a topology requiring b branches per node as a cluster of p-port communication components. The application programs described above were simulated using models for several different cluster node networks. The results of these simulation experiments are reported in this section.

For this study, four topologies are examined. All topologies use full duplex, bidirectional links. These topologies are:

- fully connected network,
- full-ring binary tree [DePa78],
- butterfly network, and
- ring network.

The topology within each cluster node is a balanced tree with the processor attached to the communication component at the root.

In all of the graphs that follow, speedup is shown as a function of B, the total I/O bandwidth of the communication chip. The only exception is the program that generates an artificial traffic load; there, the average message delay is plotted as a function of traffic load. We assume that the bandwidth B is equally divided among the existing communication links. Thus, a Y-component with bandwidth of 300 Mbit/second has three 100 Mbit/second communication links. For comparison, the speedup on a multicomputer system with a perfect switch, i.e., one that provides unlimited bandwidth and zero delay, is also shown. The perfect switch assumes that messages arrive instantaneously. This gives an upper bound on performance for any communication network.

3.4.4.1. Fully Connected Networks

The fully connected network is formed by placing a single link between every pair of nodes. Here, the number of nodes is equal to the number of tasks required by the parallel program and varies from application to application. This topology minimizes the number of hops between every pair of nodes at the expense of a larger number of branches on each node.

Figure 3.19 shows representative curves for the performance of application programs on fully connected networks constructed from cluster nodes using p port communication components. These curves indicate that performance improves as the number of ports is reduced, in agreement with the analytic results presented earlier. The curve labeled ''P+C'' corresponds to a single chip node.

The curves suggest that a significant performance improvement results from incorporating a multicast mechanism. If no multicast mechanism is provided, the processor must send a separate copy of the message to each destination. A queue rapidly develops in the processor sending the message leading to long delays and poor performance.

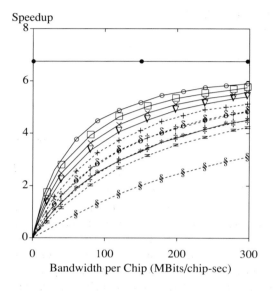

Speedup

Bandwidth per Chip (MBits/chip-sec)

-⊖- 3 ports with multicast   - +- 3 ports, no multicast
⊟ 4 ports   - ‡ - 4 ports
⋇ 5 ports   - ‡ - 5 ports
∇ 6 ports   -=- 6 ports
+ 12 ports   - § - 12 ports
•- ideal switch   - ∂ - 11 ports (P+C)

Figure 3.19
Speedup of Barnwell program on fully connected networks.

No multicast curve is shown when processor and communications form a single chip. A multicast mechanism has no effect for these networks because each processor has a direct link to every other processor. All "splitting" of the multicast packet is done at the source node.

3.4.4.2. Full-Ring Tree Networks

The second topology is the full-ring binary tree [DePa78]. This topology is constructed from a binary tree by adding links between siblings and cousins, as shown in figure 3.20. The average hop count grows logarithmically with the number of nodes, while the number of branches per node remains fixed at 5.

Representative performance curves for full-ring tree networks are shown in figure 3.21. Qualitatively, these curves agree with those presented for the fully connected networks. Again, components with a small number of high-bandwidth links achieve the best performance. Some curves in figure 3.21 show a linear increase in speedup as bandwidth per chip increases. The linear behavior arises when one virtual circuit remains the critical path for the program as chip bandwidth is varied. As bandwidth is increased, delay and execution time decrease in proportion. In the experiments, the pipelined programs often demonstrated this behavior, with the longest path from the first stage of the pipeline to the last forming the critical path. Many SISO programs behaved similarly. Here, the bottleneck is distribution of initial data samples to the computation processors. The problem is aggravated if multiple-destination messages are required to distribute the samples, particularly if the network does not include a multicast mechanism. The speed of the links near the input processor limits performance.

3.4.4.3. Butterfly Networks

The 32 node butterfly network shown in figure 3.22 was the third topology studied. Like the tree, the average hop count of the butterfly network grows logarithmically with the number of nodes. However, the butterfly network is less susceptible to bottlenecks for applications exhibiting global traffic patterns. Moreover, the butterfly is ideally suited for the FFT application program.

Performance curves for the butterfly network are shown in figure 3.23. Networks constructed with components using a small number of ports again achieve the best performance. The FFT program (figure 3.23a) performs unusually well at low chip bandwidths, demonstrating the reduction in bandwidth requirements with a good mapping between the application program and network topology.

The curves for the artificial traffic load program are shown in figure 3.23b. The curve with processor and communications on the same chip shows that the link between the processor and communication component is not a serious bottleneck. The provided bandwidth equals that of a network using communication components with the same number of ports. Delay and bandwidth both improve as the number of ports decreases, in agreement with the analytic models. Similar results exist for the other network topologies [Fuji83].

3.4.4.4. Ring Networks

The fourth topology, a bidirectional ring, minimizes the number of branches per node but maximizes the average hop count. Like the fully connected topology, the number of nodes is equal to the number of tasks in the application program.

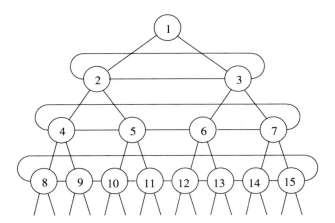

Figure 3.20
Full ring binary tree.

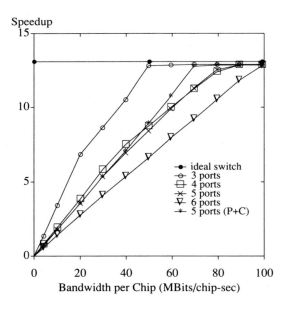

Figure 3.21
Speedup of FFT program on full ring tree.

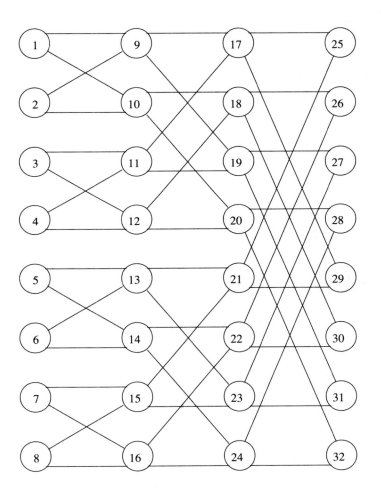

Figure 3.22
Butterfly topology.

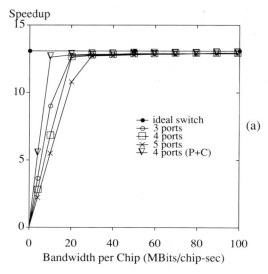

(a)

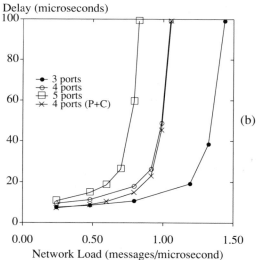

(b)

Figure 3.23

Speedup on butterfly network.

(a) FFT program. (b) Artificial traffic generator.

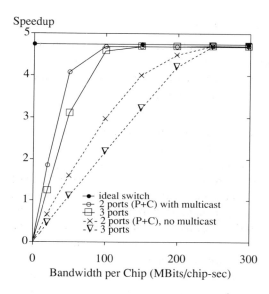

Figure 3.24
Speedup of Block State program on ring networks.

Results for the ring network agree qualitatively with those observed for the other topologies. The curves in figure 3.24 for the Block State program are typical. The network with communication circuitry on the processor chip yields better performance because it has higher bandwidth links (only 2 ports are needed) and smaller hop counts. Thus, networks constructed with components with a small number of ports again achieve the best performance.

3.4.4.5. Conclusions for Cluster Node Networks

The simulation results agree qualitatively with the analytic results presented earlier. Networks constructed from components using a small number of ports yield less delay than networks using components with many ports. Bandwidth can be increased by adding components to the communication domain. As network bandwidth increases, the rate at which processors can generate traffic limits performance. Also, the programs using multiple-destination communications show a significant performance improvement if the communication circuitry includes a multicast mechanism.

3.4.5. Simulation Results on Fixed Sized Networks

The studies presented above do not consider chip count because fewer components are required to implement each cluster node as the number of ports increases. In this section we consider networks using the same number of components. In addition to lattices, dense networks such as trees and De Bruijn networks are examined.

The analytic results indicated that networks constructed from components with a small number of ports yielded lower delay but less bandwidth than those using components with a large number of ports. Based on these results, one would expect networks using a large number of ports to yield better performance when the network is bandwidth limited. As the number of ports increases, the average hop count declines and additional paths are created in the network, tending to reduce traffic on congested links. If the reduction in congestion is significant, it will more than offset the disadvantage of using slower links and overall performance improves. Of course, if the network provides adequate bandwidth for the presented traffic load, then the queueing delays will be small, and networks using a larger number of ports will have poorer performance with the reduced link speed. Thus, networks with a large number of ports should perform better when the traffic load is heavy relative to total network bandwidth, but networks with a small number of ports should perform better otherwise.

In the studies that follow, the mapping of application program onto the network topology was optimized manually. Care was taken to ensure that these mappings did not bias the results. This issue is of less significance in the cluster node studies because comparisons are made within a single network topology, and identical mappings were used in all comparisons.

3.4.5.1. Lattice Topologies

The application programs were simulated on lattice networks such as those shown in figure 3.7. The FFT program (figure 3.25a) exhibited better performance with a large number of ports, as would be expected in bandwidth-limited networks. However, the remaining programs exhibit either little performance variation as the number of ports varies, or better performance with a small number of ports. For example, see the speedup curves for the Barnwell program in figure 3.25b. One reason is that the programs could not fully utilize the available network bandwidth. Increasing the number of ports, and thus the number of paths between pairs of nodes, did not eliminate all bottlenecks. In the SISO programs, for example, the bottleneck is around the input processor, and performance is determined largely by the speed of the communication links near this congested area. Because components with a small number of ports use faster links, they achieve better performance.

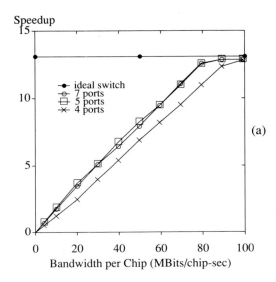

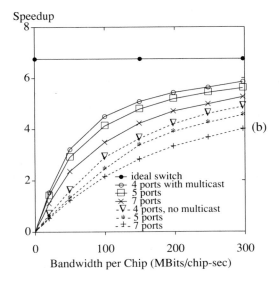

Figure 3.25

Speedup on lattice networks.

(a) FFT program. (b) Barnwell program.

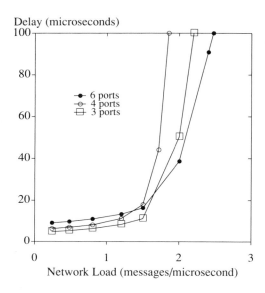

Figure 3.26
Average message delay for artificial traffic generator.
Lattice networks with processor and communications circuitry incorporated on the same chip.

Experiments were also conducted assuming communication circuitry is integrated onto the same chip as the processor. These results agreed qualitatively with those presented above. Performance curves for the artificial workload generator program are shown in figure 3.26. With the exception of the unexpectedly large bandwidth for the degree 3 network, the curves agree with the analytic results that predict less delay for lattices of low degree but more bandwidth for those with large degree. The anomalous behavior observed for degree 3 network may be a consequence of the limited size network that was simulated.

3.4.5.2. Tree Topologies

Tree topology networks are one example of a dense network whose diameter grows logarithmically with the number of nodes. Figure 3.27 shows a representative performance curve. Networks built from components with a small number of ports always yielded better performance than those using a larger number of ports. However, these results are a consequence of congestion around the root node rather than from the hop count/link bandwidth tradeoffs discussed earlier. In trees, a disproportionate

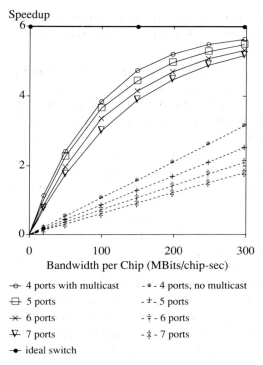

Figure 3.27
Speedup of Block I/O program on tree networks.

amount of traffic must flow through the root, leading to congestion in this portion of the network[7]. Increasing the number of links does not improve the amount of bandwidth allocated to this congested area. As a result, performance is determined largely by the speed of communication links near the root. Because components with a small number of ports have faster links, they yield higher performance.

3.4.5.3. De Bruijn Networks

The results for tree topologies were biased by the inherent bottleneck around the root. To provide a better test of the analytic results, a class of topologies is required that does not have this inherent bottleneck but also has an average hop count that grows

---

[7]This result is predicted by the analytic models of §2.5.2.

logarithmically with the number of nodes. For fair comparison, it must be possible to construct networks with approximately the same number of nodes as the node degree is varied.

One class of network topologies satisfying these requirements is the De Bruijn network [deBr46]. De Bruijn networks, defined only for even degree, are among the densest known infinite family of undirected graphs. Moreover, the De Bruijn networks are a set of graphs with diameter that is logarithmic in the number of nodes but does not contain the "root bottleneck" inherent in trees.

A De Bruijn graph is characterized by two parameters, a base b and an integer n. The graph consists of b^n nodes. The address of each node is defined by a string of digits, $x_0 x_1 \cdots x_{n-1}$, where $0 \le x_i < b$. The addresses of nodes directly connected to X are derived by shifting X's address left or right 1 digit and shifting in a new digit k, $0 \le k < b$. Thus, node X has links to nodes $yx_0 x_1 \cdots x_{n-2}$ and nodes $x_1 \cdots x_{n-1}y$, where $y = 0, 1, \cdots b-1$. Each node has at most $2 \times b$ links to other nodes. From this definition, it is clear that node X can reach any other node in at most n hops because an arbitrary address can be generated by shifting the X address n times. The topology does contain some degenerate cases. For example, with $b = 2$, nodes $00 \cdots 0$ and $11 \cdots 1$ have links to themselves, and nodes $0101 \cdots$ and $1010 \cdots$ have more than one link between them. However, these are the only special cases. The edges of the De Bruijn graph yield exactly the same interconnection as the permutation network sometimes called the single-stage shuffle-exchange [Ston71, Ston72]. A base 2, 8 node network is shown in figure 3.28.

For this study, three De Bruijn graphs were examined:

(1) $b = 2$, $n = 5$ (32 nodes),

(2) $b = 3$, $n = 3$ (27 nodes), and

(3) $b = 5$, $n = 2$ (25 nodes).

These graphs were selected because they have roughly the same number of nodes, and they provide enough processors to execute most of the application programs; the FFT is the only one requiring more than 25 processors. Communication components for these graphs require 5, 7, and 11 ports for each node, respectively, including one port for the node's computation processor, providing a wide range in values for p.

Representative performance curves for the De Bruijn networks described above are shown in figure 3.29. The results are qualitatively similar to those of the lattice topologies. The curves indicate that better performance is achieved when components with a small number of ports are used.

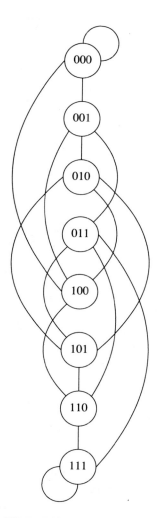

Figure 3.28
Base 2 De Bruijn network with 8 nodes.

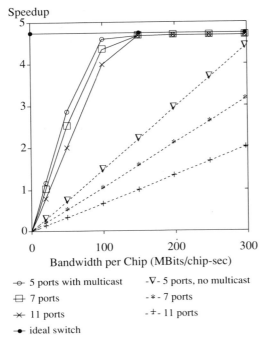

Speedup

Bandwidth per Chip (MBits/chip-sec)

-○- 5 ports with multicast   -▽- 5 ports, no multicast

⊟ 7 ports   -*- 7 ports

-✻- 11 ports   -+- 11 ports

-●- ideal switch

Figure 3.29
Speedup of Block State program on De Bruijn networks.

3.5. Summary

The results in this and the previous chapter highlight the importance of the communication system in deriving good performance from parallel application programs. Physical design constraints must be carefully considered during the design process. Whereas chapter two discussed the important problem of topology selection, this chapter addressed the network design problem given limited I/O bandwidth of a general purpose communication component.

The central result of this chapter is that from a performance standpoint, a small number of high bandwidth ports is generally preferable to many low bandwidth ports. Three to six ports are recommended. The implications of these results are threefold. When considerations such as characteristics of the expected workload dictate that a topology with high node degree is desired, one should consider a cluster node implementation of the network using switching chips with a small number of high bandwidth links rather than a direct, single chip per node implementation. A reasonable compromise must be found between decreasing the number of ports and increasing component count. Secondly, when one network among a family of topologies must be selected, e.g., a torus of some specific dimension and width, these analyses favor networks with low degree. Finally, a general purpose communication component applicable to a wide variety of network topologies and applications should be designed with three to six I/O ports.

Support for virtual cut-through can significantly reduce communication delays and should be included in any communication component design. Further, special mechanisms to efficiently handle broadcast and multicast messages should be considered if the algorithms used by the application program require it. These can also have an important effect on performance.

At present, many multicomputer designs require software intervention to forward messages, leading to very long delays for communications between processes on distant nodes. Future multicomputer designs will contain hardware support for this function. The next chapter will discuss design issues for a general purpose communication component that can be used to construct networks of arbitrary topology and present one design for such a component.

References

[Baas78]   S. Baase, *Computer Algorithms: Introduction to Design and Analysis*. Addison-Wesley, Reading, Massachusetts, 1978.

[BaGP78]   T. P. Barnwell III, S. Gaglio and R. M. Price, "A Multi-Microprocessor Architecture for Digital Signal Processing," *Proceedings of the 1978 International Conference on Parallel Processing* (August 1978), pp. 115-121.

[BaHG79]   T. P. Barnwell III, C. J. M. Hodges and S. Gaglio, "Efficient Implementations of One And Two Dimensional Digital Signal Processing Algorithms on a Multiprocessor Architecture," *1979 International Conference on ASSP, Washington, D. C.* (April 1979), pp. 698-701.

[BaHo82]   T. P. Barnwell III and C. J. M. Hodges, "Optimal Implementation of Signal Flow Graphs on Synchronous Multiprocessors," *Proceedings of the 1982 International Conference on Parallel Processing* (August 1982), pp. 90-95.

[BaSh80a]   C. Barnes and S. Shinnaka, "Finite Word Effects in Block-State Realizations of Fixed-Point Digital Filters," *IEEE Transactions on Circuits and Systems* (May 1980), Vol. CAS-27, pp. 345-349.

[BaSh80b]   C. Barnes and S. Shinnaka, "Block Shift Invariance and Block Implementation of Discrete-Time Filters," *IEEE Transactions on Circuits and Systems* (August 1980), Vol. CAS-27, pp. 667-672.

[BhJa83]   K. Bharath-Kumar and J. M. Jaffe, "Routing to Multiple Destinations in Computer Networks," *IEEE Transactions on Communications* (March 1983), Vol. COM-31, No. 3, pp. 343-351.

[Burr71]   C. Burrus, "Block Implementation of Digital Filters," *IEEE Transactions on Circuit Theory* (November 1971), Vol. CT-18, pp. 697-701.

[Burr72]   C. Burrus, "Block Realization of Digital Filters," *IEEE Transactions on Audio and Electroacoustics* (October 1972), Vol. AU-20, pp. 230-235.

[ChLi75]   L. Chua and P. Lin, *Computer-Aided Analysis of Electronic Circuits: Algorithms and Computational Techniques*. Prentice-Hall, Englewood Cliffs, New Jersey, 1975.

[DaBA74]   G. Dahlquist, A. Bjorck and N. Anderson, *Numerical Methods*. Prentice-Hall, Englewood Cliffs, New Jersey, 1974.

[DaMe78]   Y. K. Dalal and R. M. Metcalfe, "Reverse Path Forwarding of Broadcast Packets," *Communications of the ACM* (December 1978), Vol. 21, No. 12, pp. 1040-1048.

[DaSe86]   W. J. Dally and C. L. Seitz, "The Torus Routing Chip," *Journal of Distributed Computing* (1986), Vol. 1, No. 3.

[deBr46]   D. G. de Bruijn, "A Combinatorial Problem," *Koninklijke Nederlandsche Academie van Wetenschappen te Amsterdam, Proc. Section of Sciences* (1946), Vol. 49, No. 7, pp. 758-764.

[DePa78]   A. Despain and D. Patterson, "X-Tree: A Tree Structured Multiprocessor Computer Architecture," *Proceedings of the 5th Annual Symposium on Computer Architecture* (April 1978), Vol. 7, No. 6, pp. 144-151.

[Fuji83]   R. M. Fujimoto, *VLSI Communication Components for Multicomputer Networks*. Ph.D. Dissertation, Electronics Research Laboratory Report No. UCB/CSD 83/136, University of California, Berkeley, California, 1983.

[HoBM80]   C. J. M. Hodges, T. P. Barnwell III and D. McWhorter, "The Implementation of an all Digital Speech Synthesizer Using a Multimicroprocessor Architecture," *1980 International Conference on ASSP, Denver, Colorado* (April 1980), pp. 855-858.

[KeKl79]   P. Kermani and L. Kleinrock, "Virtual Cut Through: A New Computer Communication Switching Technique," *Computer Networks* (September 1979), Vol. 3, No. 4, pp. 267-286.

[Keye79]   R. Keyes, "The Evolution of Digital Electronics Towards VLSI," *IEEE Journal of Solid-State Circuits* (April 1979), Vol. SC-14, No. 4, pp. 193-201.

[Klei76]   L. Kleinrock, *Queueing Systems, Volume II: Computer Applications*. John Wiley & Sons, New York, New York, 1976.

[Knut73]   D. E. Knuth, *The Art of Computer Programming, Sorting and Searching (Vol. 3)*. Addison-Wesley, Reading, Massachusetts, 1973.

[Lu83]   H. Lu, *High Speed IIR Digital Filters*. Ph.D. Dissertation, University of California, Berkeley, California, 1983.

[McQu78]   J. M. McQuillan, "Enhanced Message Addressing Capabilities for Computer Networks," *Proceedings of the IEEE* (November 1978), Vol. 66, No. 11, pp. 1517-1527.

[MiGn78]   S. Mitra and R. Gnanasekaran, "Block Implementation of Recursive Digital Filters - New Structures and Properties," *IEEE Transactions on Circuits and Systems* (April 1978), Vol. CAS-25, pp. 200-207.

[Nage75]   L. W. Nagel, *SPICE2: A Computer Program to Simulate Semiconductor Circuits*. Ph.D. Dissertation, University of California, Berkeley, California, 1975.

[ShHu80]   J. Shoch and J. Hupp, "Measured Performance of an Ethernet Local Network," *Communications of the ACM* (December 1980), Vol. 23, No. 10, pp. 711-721.

[Ston71]   H. S. Stone, "Parallel Processing with the Perfect Shuffle," *IEEE Transactions on Computers* (February 1971), Vol. C-20, No. 2, pp. 153-161.

[Ston72]   H. S. Stone, "Dynamic Memories with Enhanced Data Access," *IEEE Transactions on Computers* (April 1972), Vol. C-21, No. 4, pp. 359-366.

[WiHu80]   O. Wing and J. W. Huang, "A Computational Model of Parallel Solution of Linear Equations," *IEEE Transactions on Computers* (July 1980), Vol. C-29, No. 7, pp. 632-638.

[Witt81]   L. D. Wittie, "Communications Structures for Large Networks of Microcomputers," *IEEE Transactions on Computers* (April 1981), Vol. C-30, No. 4, pp. 264-273.

[Yu84]   W. Yu, *LU Decomposition on a Multiprocessing System with Communication Delay*. Ph.D. Dissertation, University of California, Berkeley, California, 1984.

[ZeLi81]   J. Zeman and A. Lindgren, "Fast Digital Filters with Low Round-Off Noise," *IEEE Transactions on Circuit and Systems* (July 1981), Vol. CAS-28, pp. 716-723.

4 Communication Paradigms and Hardware Support

Always design a thing by considering it in its next larger context - a chair in a room, a room in a house, a house in an environment, an environment in a city plan.

Eliel Saarinen

Chapters two and three discussed the performance and reliability of interconnection networks at the *system level*. In this chapter, we will focus our attention on a finer level of detail and examine important issues and tradeoffs related to the design of hardware to support communication functions.

Communications functions have traditionally been implemented by software in loosely coupled communication networks such as the ARPANET, DECNET™, etc. Workloads for such systems are generated by processes that communicate infrequently to perform high level functions such as file transfers. The physical extent of these networks may cover extremely broad geographical areas, sometimes entire countries or continents. In contrast, multicomputer networks execute collections of *closely coupled* tasks that communicate frequently and are usually confined to a few cabinets in a single room. Therefore, although many of the same problems and issues that arise in loosely coupled networks also arise in multicomputer networks, the latter often require completely different solutions and implementations. In particular, rather than software implementation of communication protocols, hardware support is more appropriate.

Several key issues must be considered when designing a high performance communication network:

- **Transport Mechanism**. This defines the message forwarding facility that is used.

- **Routing Mechanism**. This implements the routing algorithm that determines the direction in which messages are forwarded.

- **Buffer Management**. Each message requiring the use of a busy communication link must be buffered until the desired link becomes available. Hence, circuitry is necessary to utilize the pool of message buffers efficiently.

- **Flow control**. Some mechanism must throttle the flow of incoming traffic when the pool of available buffers is exhausted.

In the sections that follow, we will discuss design alternatives for each of these issues. A sample design will be examined to illustrate the implementation of frequently used communication functions with special purpose hardware and to estimate the amount of necessary circuitry. Our discussion will be oriented toward design of a *general purpose* VLSI communication component that can be used as a building block for large multicomputer networks. Finally, we discuss simulation analyses of important communication component design parameters such as the number of buffers.

4.1. Transport Mechanisms

The transport mechanism provides a facility for moving data through the network. Several frequently used transport mechanisms and their distinguishing characteristics are shown in table 4.1. Briefly, these characteristics are:

- **Data Unit**: The indivisible unit of data transported through the network is either a variable-length message or a fixed-length packet.

- **Routing Overhead**: The overhead associated with message routing is incurred either on a hop-by-hop basis at each network node or only in the initial establishment of a circuit.

- **Bandwidth Allocation**: Bandwidth is allocated by the network either statically, e.g., when a circuit is established, or dynamically as messages are forwarded through the network.

- **Buffering Complexity**: The complexity of the buffering hardware varies with the sophistication of the chosen transport mechanism.

As shown in table 4.1, networks can be broadly classified as either **circuit-switched** or **store-and-forward**. The circuit-switched approach is best exemplified, at least conceptually, by the telephone system. When someone picks up a telephone and dials a phone number, a circuit is established between the caller and the party being called. Once this circuit is established, it remains intact until either party hangs up. Examples of circuit-switched networks are described in [Joel79, MaGN79]. The distinguishing characteristic of this approach is the fact that communicating parties are guaranteed a certain bandwidth and maximum latency when the call is established, an important consideration in applications with real time constraints. Because the communication network cannot know *a priori* when data will be transmitted, bandwidth must be allocated statically when the call is established. Otherwise, the bandwidth may not be available when it is needed. Circuits are allocated a certain amount of bandwidth regardless of its actual use. If communications are bursty, as is often the case in

Table 4.1

Transport Mechanisms

	Circuit Switch	Store-and-Forward		
		Datagrams	Packet Switch	Virtual Circuit
Data Unit	arbitrary	messages	packets	packets
Routing Overhead	set up only	per message	per packet (+reassembly)	set up
Bandwidth Allocation	static	dynamic	dynamic	dynamic
Buffering Complexity	low	high	moderate	moderate

computer networks, much of the network's bandwidth will be wasted. This is the primary disadvantage of the circuit-switched approach.

However, the circuit-switched approach also offers several advantages. Routing overhead is usually paid only when the circuit is set up, so subsequent messages can flow through the network with little delay. This reduces the average delay on circuits carrying more than one message. Also, buffering strategies are simpler than those required for store and forward networks because bandwidth allocation is performed statically. If circuit-switching is used, the network can be designed to ensure that the rate of traffic flow into each node of the network never exceeds the rate of flow out, alleviating buffer overflow problems. In fact, if each circuit is implemented as a physical electrical connection between the communicating parties, e.g., a series of relays, the network need not provide any buffering at all!

Store-and-forward networks avoid the wasted bandwidth problem just described by allocating bandwidth dynamically to messages as they flow through the network. Three types of store-and-forward networks are common:

- datagram networks,
- packet-switched networks, and
- virtual circuit networks.

Datagram networks are characterized by the unit of data sent through the network — variable length messages. Because each message can be relatively large, a substantial amount of circuitry in each network node must be devoted to message buffers. In addition variable size buffers must be used because messages vary in length. This increases the complexity of the buffer management circuitry significantly, because the buffer selected for a particular message must be at least as large as the message, or the buffer must be implemented as a chain of fixed sized buffers. The differences between variable sized and fixed sized buffers are not unlike those between segmentation and paging in virtual memory systems. Finally, routing overhead in the datagram approach is worse than that of circuit-switching because routing decisions must be made on a hop-by-hop basis for each message sent into the network.

The **packet-switched** transport mechanism eliminates many of the buffer management problems described above. Here, each message is divided into fixed-sized packets that are routed separately through the network. Because packets can be relatively small, buffering requirements in each component are reduced substantially. The use of fixed-sized packets also simplifies the buffer management circuitry. On the negative side, however, packets sent from one node to another are routed separately and may follow different paths to reach the destination. Therefore, they may arrive out of order. An end-to-end scheme is required to reassemble each message from its constituent packets, incurring some additional overhead not found in the other transport mechanisms. In addition to reassembly overhead, the other disadvantage of the packet-switched approach is that the routing overhead is greater than that of the datagram scheme, because this overhead now occurs on every *packet* rather than on every *message* sent into the network.

If we examine the transport mechanisms described thus far, we see that the circuit-switched approach suffers from static bandwidth allocation, whereas the packet switch approach suffers from reassembly and routing overhead. One might hope that a hybrid combining these two approaches would provide the best of both mechanisms without their respective disadvantages. This is the motivation behind the **virtual circuit** transport mechanism, which combines aspects of packet-switched and circuit-switched techniques. A virtual circuit is established between processors that wish to communicate. A virtual circuit is a fixed, unidirectional path through the network from one processor to another. All messages sent on this circuit travel along this path to reach their destination.

Consider the characteristics of the virtual circuit transport mechanism (see table 4.1). Like the packet-switched mechanism, the data unit is a fixed sized packet, so the buffering problems of the datagram mechanism are alleviated. Routing is similar to the circuit-switched approach because the routing algorithm need only be applied when the circuit is established, and not with subsequent packets. It will be seen, however, that some overhead is still required to route messages, so the routing overhead is intermediate between the circuit-switched and the datagram/packet-switched approaches. Because a store-and-forward mechanism is used, network bandwidth is allocated dynamically, although allocation is not as adaptive as it is in packet-switched networks because packets are constrained to follow a fixed path from source to destination. The fixed path restriction in the virtual circuit mechanism is necessary to reduce routing overhead and to avoid reassembly overhead. The virtual circuit mechanism can utilize multiple paths between two nodes by establishing several circuits between them. The disadvantages of this approach are that changing message routing on existing circuits is cumbersome, and recovery from node and link failures is more complex because broken circuits must be repaired or eliminated. Moreover, the virtual circuit mechanism requires more control circuitry than either the circuit-switched or packet-switched approach.

A communication network using virtual circuits was designed and partially implemented in the X-Tree project, a multicomputer system developed at the University of California in Berkeley [DePa78, Fuji83, Fuji80, Laur79, Grif79]. The remainder of this chapter will describe this design to highlight many of the important design issues and tradeoffs that arise during the development of an interconnection network for a multicomputer system. An overview of the design will first be presented, followed by discussions of the hardware required to support message routing, flow control, and buffer management.

4.2. A Virtual Circuit Based Communication System

We will now examine the design of a communication component using a virtual circuit transport mechanism. An overview of the transport mechanism will first be described, followed by a study of important issues faced during the design of this chip. This design was originally intended for use in the X-Tree project developed at Berkeley in the late 1970's and early 1980's. It is sufficiently general, however, to be applicable in a wide variety of multicomputer systems. The design features hardware implementation of frequently used store-and-forward communication functions.

4.2.1. Virtual Circuits

Sending a message is a three step process in a virtual circuit communication network. A virtual circuit, i.e., a path of time-multiplexed links to the destination processor, is first established by sending a message header containing routing information through the network. Once a circuit has been established, an arbitrary amount of data, consisting of one or more logical messages, can be sent along this circuit. Data can immediately follow the message header without an end-to-end handshake, so the sender need not wait for the circuit to be established before it begins to send data. Also, messages need not be transmitted continuously for the circuit to remain intact. Thus, this approach reduces routing overhead on all packets except the message header. When the circuit is no longer needed, it is torn down by sending a tagged message trailer.

The communication system provides only a data transport facility. With the exception of the header and trailer information, all data pass uninterpreted through intermediate nodes. The utility of a virtual cut-through mechanism was demonstrated in chapter three and will be used in the designs that follow. Error checking and retransmission are left to an end-to-end protocol.

4.2.2. Virtual Channels

The communication domain can be viewed as a simple, connected graph. Nodes and edges represent processors and links, respectively. A circuit from one processor to another corresponds to a path in this graph. Two distinct paths may use a common edge. For example, the two paths shown in figure 4.1 share the link from X to Y. Thus, this link must be multiplexed between the two paths, and provisions must be made to ensure that data from A are sent to B and not to D.

Each physical link is divided into some fixed number of unidirectional **virtual channels**. Each channel can carry data for one virtual circuit, i.e., one path. Thus, a circuit from one node to another consists of a sequence of channels on the links in the

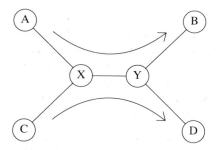

Figure 4.1
Two Paths Multiplexed through the Same Link.

path between the two nodes. The circuit from A to B in figure 4.1, for example, might use channel 3 to get to X, then 5 to get to Y, and finally 7 to get to B.

When node X sends data to node Y, the latter must determine the circuit associated with the data. Two commonly used techniques for providing this information are:

- Divide the link into a fixed number of *time slots* and statically assign each time slot to a channel, e.g., the first time slot might be assigned to channel 0, the second to channel 1, etc. The time slot on which the data arrive identifies the sending channel.

- Precede the data with a tag that identifies the channel on which it is being sent. In this scheme, the available bandwidth on the link is allocated to the various channels by some demand-driven scheduling algorithm.

In the first scheme, the link is effectively divided into several lower bandwidth links, with the sum of these bandwidths equal to that of the physical link. This approach is sometimes used in circuit-switched transport mechanisms. If a channel does not send any data, its allocated bandwidth is wasted. In addition, latency is increased because each channel must wait for its turn to send a unit of data. In the second scheme, the entire bandwidth of the link can be allocated to channels when they have data to send, so the inefficiencies associated with the previous approach are avoided. However, some bandwidth is required to carry the channel tag. Demand-driven time-multiplexing is superior if the degree of multiplexing on each link is high and communications is bursty. This is often the case in computer-to-computer communications, so the dynamic approach is more suitable for the networks described here.

4.2.3. Translation Tables

To route messages through each node of the network, channels entering a node (input channels) must be "linked" to channels leaving the node (output channels). Each node maintains a set of **translation tables** to perform this function. There is one translation table for each input port of each node. An entry of the translation table contains two fields: an output port and the number of a channel on that port. When data arrive on, say, input channel 3, entry 3 of the translation table for that port is read to yield the output port and the number of the channel on which the data are to be forwarded.

The translation tables logically link incoming and outgoing channels, and establish the virtual circuits through the node. Establishing these circuits involves allocating channels and updating translation tables along each path from source to destination. This task is performed by a **routing controller** residing in each communication node.

Initially, all translation tables specify that data are to be sent to the local routing controller. When a new circuit is established at a node, the routing controller analyzes the destination address in the header, determines the proper output port with the use of some routing algorithm, allocates a free output channel, and updates the translation table at the input port. Subsequent data are forwarded without intervention by the routing controller. Similarly, when the circuit is torn down, the channel is released, and the corresponding translation table entry is reset to point to the routing controller.

Thus, three types of packets are required: a "set-up packet" that establishes virtual circuits, a "trailer packet" that tears them down, and a "data packet" that carries data. In addition, it is useful to provide a "clear packet" that flows through a virtual circuit, removing any data packets it encounters along the way. Such a mechanism is useful in error recovery protocols to reset virtual circuits to a "known" state. Tag bit(s) in the packet header are used to distinguish the different types.

4.2.4. Switch Architecture

Any communication network must provide mechanisms for routing messages to their proper destination, managing the limited amount of buffer space, and controlling the rate at which packets flow from one node to another. Hardware implementation of these mechanisms is required to achieve high-performance.

A block diagram of the switching node we will be discussing is shown in figure 4.2. The distinguishing feature of this design is a single pool of buffers shared by all channels of the component. Because all packets traveling through a node must use this pool, it must provide sufficient bandwidth to avoid becoming a bottleneck. This is achieved by interleaving the memory 16 ways, assuming packets consist of 16 bytes. Byte i of each packet ($0 \leq i \leq 15$) is always stored in memory module i (MM_i). Each of the p ports can simultaneously load a packet into a buffer, provided no two simultaneously access the same memory module. In the worst case, p packets simultaneously arrive at a node. Because only one port can be granted access to MM_0, additional registers are required to temporarily buffer the arriving data bytes until they can be stored in MM_0. On the next clock cycle, when the second byte of each packet arrives, one of these newly arriving bytes will be loaded into MM_1, and one of the temporarily buffered bytes can now be written into MM_0. Similarly, three accesses to the buffer pool will occur on the third clock, and so on. Eventually, each port will be able to access a different memory module on each clock cycle.

If the links can transmit one data byte per clock cycle, then the communication circuitry must be able to transport p bytes from the input ports to the memory modules in each clock. A high-speed, time-multiplexed bus performs this function. Because this bus remains entirely within the chip, it can run several times faster than the I/O links that require off-chip communications [SeDP78]. Alternatively, multiple buses or a simple switching network can be used. A second high speed bus carries bytes from

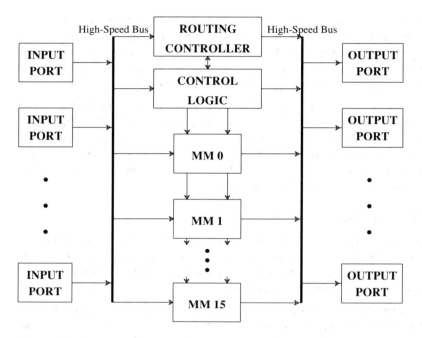

Figure 4.2
Block diagram of component design.

the memory modules to the output ports. Single-port memories can be used in the memory modules, provided the control logic only initiates one operation — forward a packet or receive a packet — per clock cycle. The designs that follow assume this is the case.

A block diagram of the control logic module is shown in figure 4.3. Consider the events that occur when a packet arrives at the node. First, the header containing the input channel number is received. The translation table is read to determine which output port and channel will be forwarding the packet. The output of the translation table is sent to both the buffer management and flow control modules. The buffer management module allocates an empty buffer to hold the newly arriving packet and records the location of this buffer as well as the output port/channel specified by the translation table. This information will be needed when it is time to forward the packet. The buffer module then sends the address of the buffer to MM_0, and the packet is stored, byte-by-byte, into successive memory modules on subsequent clock cycles. The flow control module notes that this output channel now has a packet waiting to be forwarded. When the output link specified by the translation table is free, the flow

High Speed Bus

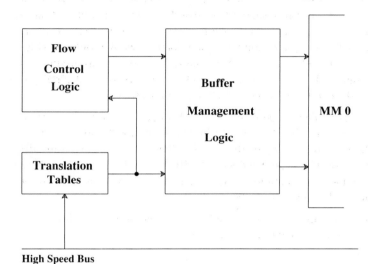

High Speed Bus

Figure 4.3
Control logic.

control logic signals the buffer management module to forward the next packet waiting on this output channel. The buffer management module finds the address of the buffer holding this packet and sends it to MM_0. The packet is read from the buffer byte-by-byte and forwarded over the output link. In both reading and writing a packet, the same memory address is pipelined from memory module to memory module on successive clock cycles. Because the pipelined structure of the memory modules allows the forwarding of a packet to begin before all of it arrives, a virtual cut-through capability is provided.

In the circuit diagrams that follow, the widths of data paths are based on a component with 4 I/O ports, 32 data buffers, and 128 channels per link. Thus, port numbers, buffer numbers, and channel numbers are 2, 5, and 7 bits in length respectively. The number of ports was discussed in chapter three. The number of buffers and channels will be discussed in §4.6.

4.3. Routing

All communication networks require some routing algorithm to build the paths between communicating nodes. A great deal of research has been done in the area of routing in loosely coupled computer networks, and much of this work is applicable here [Gerl81, Tane81]. In the context of the proposed communication domain, we will only consider distributed routing that does not rely on a centralized authority. For this discussion it is also appropriate to distinguish between regular networks with a predefined topology, such as arrays or trees, and irregular networks of arbitrary connectivity.

In regular networks, routing can be performed in each node by a state machine or microprogrammed engine using a fixed algorithm based on the local and destination addresses. In square lattices, for example, the routing controller could forward the message header in a direction that would reduce the difference between the x- or y-coordinates of the current and the destination nodes. Routing algorithms are known for many standard topologies such as the hypercube.

For irregular networks, routing must be based on suitable lookup tables. In a decentralized system each node i has entries of the form:

$$NN = R_i(DN),$$

implying that messages destined for node DN are forwarded by node i to neighbor node NN. This lookup table, commonly called a **routing table**, can be defined statically, or it can be maintained dynamically using information exchanged between neighboring nodes. The latter approach allows the network to automatically reconfigure itself should the topology change due to node failure or network expansion [Taji77].

If the network has many nodes, the routing table will be excessively large because a separate entry is required for each destination node. A common technique to reduce the size of this table uses hierarchical names and multiple routing tables per node [Kamo76]. An example of such a mechanism is seen in the telephone system where names (telephone numbers) consist of an area code and a seven digit number. When a call to a number with a different area code is made, the area code is first used to route the call to the correct area, and then the phone number is used to locate the final destination. Conceptually, routing could be performed as follows:

(1)   If the area code does not match that of the node doing the routing, then the area code is used to look up the next node via an ''area code'' routing table. The remaining seven digits in the phone number are ignored.

(2)   If the area code of the destination matches that of the router, then the seven digit number is used to locate the next node via a "neighborhood" routing table.

Thus, a two-level naming hierarchy is used along with a routing table for each level. Such a scheme reduces the table size by grouping distant nodes into a single entry in the "area code" routing table.

One can easily extend this principle to an arbitrary number of naming levels. To determine the number of levels to minimize the storage space required for routing tables, let there be l levels, with g_i entries in the level i table. The object is to minimize $g_1 + g_2 + \cdots + g_l$ subject to constant $N = g_1 \times g_2 \times \cdots \times g_l$, the maximum number of nodes in the network. It is easy to show that this sum is minimized for

$$g_1 = g_2 = \cdots = g_l = e \quad \text{and} \quad l = \ln N,$$

where e is approximately 2.718. Thus, to minimize the table size in each node, there should be many levels with few entries in each level [McQu74].

The reduction in table size resulting from a multi-level routing scheme can be substantial. A 16-bit destination address partitioned into eight 2-bit fields requires eight 4-entry routing tables, or a total of 32 entries. The single-level routing table would require 65,536 entries.

Let us consider what hardware is necessary to implement such a hierarchical table lookup scheme. This hardware is part of the routing controller that is responsible for establishing virtual circuits through the node. The routing controller also manages allocation of channels to new virtual circuits and performs higher level functions for fault tolerance and initialization. These functions could be implemented by the processor performing user computations or with a separate, dedicated microcoded engine.

We will discuss two hardware implementations of the hierarchical routing scheme. The first assumes that routing tables at all levels are the same size, some power of 2. The second design relaxes this assumption at the cost of added complexity.

An l-level hierarchical node address consists of a string of digits, $A_{l-1}A_{l-2} \cdots A_1 A_0$. Digit A_i is used to index the routing table at level i. A routing table entry contains either an output port number indicating the port to use or a "NULL" flag indicating that the table on the next level must be searched. Let RT_i denote the routing table at level i, with $0 \leq i < l$. The algorithm to determine the appropriate output port is as follows:

```
level := 0;          /* current level, 0, 1, ... l-1 */
while ((RT_level [A_level] = NULL) and (level < l))
          level := level + 1;
if (level < l )
          /* return output port */
          return (RT_level [A_level]);
else
          /* destination node reached */
          return (NULL);
```

If this routine returns NULL, then the destination address matches the local address, so the message has reached it's final destination. Otherwise, the number of the output port selected by the routing algorithm is returned.

The first implementation of this table lookup mechanism is shown in figure 4.4a. It is assumed that each table contains 2^k entries. The bus widths in figure 4.4a assume that there are 8 levels and 4 routing table entries in each level (i.e., $k=2$). The "address register" holds the destination address. The rightmost k bits of this register hold A_0, the next k bits hold A_1, etc. A single RAM holds all of the routing tables. The most significant bits of the address lines of this RAM specify a routing table, i.e., a level, and the remaining, least significant, bits specify an offset into this table. The k least significant bits of the address register (A_{level} above) are concatenated with the output of the level counter (*level*) to form this address. The shifter aligns the destination address bits by shifting out A_i and moving A_{i+1} into the rightmost position each clock cycle. Because each bit is shifted exactly k bits on each clock, the shifter can be implemented by an edge triggered register and a simple permutation of wires. Finally, the control logic that sequences through the various routing tables is not shown. Design of this finite state machine is straightforward, using the level counter and circuitry to detect NULL routing table entries, and generating signals to shift the address bits and increment the level counter.

A second implementation, shown in figure 4.4b, relaxes the "fixed routing table size" restriction of the previous design. The bus widths shown in this figure support up to 8 levels and a total of 256 routing table entries. The number of levels and sizes of the various routing tables is programmable at system initialization. The "address RAM" holds the base addresses of the various routing tables. Entry i contains the base address of the routing table at level i. The routing tables are again stored in a single RAM. The routing table offset, A_i, is generated by masking appropriate bits of the address register. This offset is added to the base address to generate an address for the routing table RAM. A barrel shifter is used to align data in the address register for the

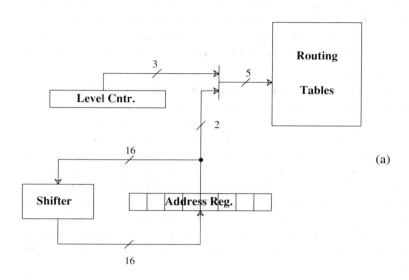

(a)

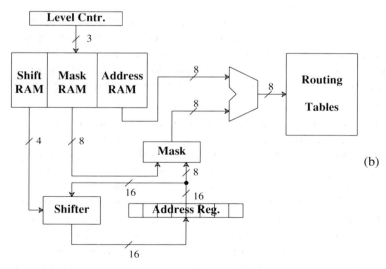

(b)

Figure 4.4
Hierarchical routing circuitry. (a) simple. (b) complex.

next iteration. The mask bits and the number of address bits to be shifted are stored in the "mask RAM" and "shift RAM" respectively. These RAMs are loaded by the routing controller at initialization. Together, their contents describe the format of the address register. The control logic for this second implementation is virtually the same as that of the previous design.

Finally, the designs presented here can be optimized in a straightforward manner to reduce the number of table lookups required to route messages. Assume that once a message enters a certain "area" it does not leave that area. For example once a message destined for node 5.4.3.2 enters area 5.4, it never leaves area 5.4. Subsequent nodes making routing decisions will all lie within area 5.4, so there is no need to keep reexamining these first two fields of the destination address. The nodes nodes in area 5.4 can instead begin by examining the third field. To implement this scheme, a new field must be added to the message header indicating the number of destination address fields that can be skipped. Each time the message moves one level closer to its destination, this field in the message header is incremented. This scheme avoids many unnecessary accesses to the routing table and improves the efficiency of the table lookup mechanism.

4.4. Buffer Management

Each message passed into the communication domain must be subdivided by the sender into some number of fixed-length packets. Packets form the indivisible unit of data transmitted through the communication network. Due to conflicts that arise when several packets simultaneously require the use of the same link, buffering is required in each node. The strategy for managing usage of these buffers can have a significant effect on performance.

A scheme is necessary to allocate a node's buffers among the virtual circuits using the node. One simple solution gives each channel on each link a separate buffer. This is inefficient, however, because much of the buffer space will be unused most of the time. By allowing several channels to share buffers, fluctuations in the need for buffer space can be averaged over a large number of communication paths, and fewer buffers are required to achieve the same performance. A mapping is then required to link each channel to the buffers holding packets for that channel so they can be found when it is time to forward them. Furthermore, when a new packet arrives, an empty buffer must be found. From this perspective, buffer management is similar to the management of a cache memory: a program (here, a channel) must fit blocks from main memory (packets) into cache blocks (buffers).

As in cache memory design, there are three common schemes for performing this mapping:

- direct mapping,
- set-associative mapping, and
- fully associative mapping.

In turn, these three schemes offer an increased degree of buffer sharing and improved memory utilization but at the cost of increased complexity in the control circuitry. They are distinguished by restrictions on the placement of each channel's packets. In the direct mapping scheme (minimal sharing), each channel has a set of dedicated buffers, i.e., its own FIFO queue. The set-associative scheme (moderate sharing) allows each channel to use a larger set of buffers, but the channel is no longer given sole access to them. This scheme might be implemented by letting all channels of a single port share a pool of buffers dedicated to this port. In the fully associative scheme (maximal sharing), each node has a centralized pool of buffers that all channels share.

Intuitively, one might think the fully associative scheme offers the most sharing, and is thus the method of choice, ignoring the cost of control circuitry. However, this is not the case because of a phenomenon known as **buffer hogging**. Buffer hogging occurs when one output port becomes congested and uses a disproportionately large portion of the buffer pool, impeding traffic on other ports. Under these circumstances, better performance is obtained if the degree of buffer sharing is limited, and each port is limited to some maximum number of buffers.

The buffer management hardware must perform two functions:

- locate a free buffer to hold a newly arriving packet, and
- locate the next packet waiting to be forwarded on a particular output channel.

Two implementations will be described for these functions. The first assumes that the number of packets waiting to use a given output channel can be larger than one. The second restricts this number to be at most one.

Because buffers are dynamically assigned to virtual channels on demand, a mechanism is required to keep track of the buffer assignment. In the presented solution, the buffers waiting to be forwarded on an output channel are "chained" into a linked list for that channel. Buffer chaining may also be used to implement variable length buffers in datagram networks. When a packet arrives, it is placed at the end of the linked list corresponding to the output channel on which the packet is to be forwarded. It is removed from the list after it has been successfully transmitted to the next node. The linked lists are managed as a FIFO queue to ensure that packets are forwarded in the same order in which they arrived. Linked list management is implemented in hardware so that packet forwarding can proceed as quickly as possible. A block diagram of one implementation is shown in figure 4.5a. In the discussion that follows, it is assumed that each p-port component has b buffers and c input (or output) channels per port, i.e., $c \times p$ channels per node.

A buffer consists of a 16 byte data portion that is physically distributed across the memory modules (see figure 4.2) and a single pointer word. The pointer word indicates the address of the next buffer in this buffer's linked list. The b-word "link" RAM in figure 4.5a holds these pointers. Each output channel has pointers to the buffers at the front and end of its linked list. The $c \times p$-word "front" and "rear" RAMs in figure 4.5a perform this function. Adding a new buffer to an output channel implies reading the rear RAM (to find the last buffer in the list) and writing the address of the new buffer into this address of the link RAM (to set the new link) as well as the rear RAM (to set the pointer to the new rear element). Deleting an entry implies reading the front RAM (to get the address of the buffer being deleted), reading the link RAM (to get the new front element), and writing this latter address into the front RAM.

Buffers not linked to any channel list are empty and are linked together in a separate "free list." A register, called the "free" register, points to the beginning of the free list. The arrival of a new packet implies removing an element, i.e., the address of a free buffer, from the free list and adding this address to an output channel's linked list. Sending a packet implies removing the front element from the channel list and adding it to the free list. Allowing simultaneous access to different memories, a buffer can be added to or deleted from a linked list in four and three clock cycles respectively, where each memory reference requires one clock cycle. The operations necessary to process an arriving/departing packet are shown in table 4.2.

The complexity of the design described above can be reduced significantly if any output channel can use at most *one* buffer at a time. The impact of this restriction on system performance will be discussed later. Most of the hardware for managing the linked lists can be eliminated, because the lists contain at most one element. This allows the three RAMs in figure 4.5a to be combined into one RAM, the "channel-to-buffer" RAM shown in figure 4.5b. This $c \times p$-word RAM maps output channels to buffer addresses. Word i holds the address of the buffer containing a packet for channel i. The list of free buffers is replaced by a b-bit latch, called the "free buffer latch." The free buffer latch is implemented as a bit-addressable latch, i.e., a memory device that is written as a RAM (one bit at a time), but read as a latch (all bits in parallel). Each bit indicates the status of a buffer: free (1) or in use (0).

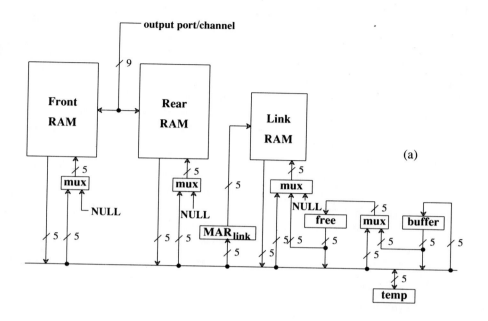

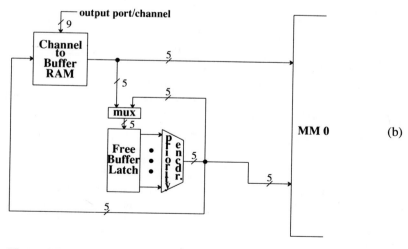

Figure 4.5
Buffer management circuitry. (a) >1 buffers/channel.
(b) 1 buffer/channel.

Table 4.2
Operations to send and receive packets

Packet arrives on channel "ich":

clock cycle	action	comments
1)	buffer ← free;	address of free buffer
	MAR_{link} ← free;	get ready to read new free list head
	if (free = NULL) abort;	no more free buffers
2)	free ← Link[MAR_{link}];	read new free list head
3)	Link[MAR_{link}] ← NULL;	mark pointer for new buffer
	temp ← Rear[ich];	locate end of linked list
	MAR_{link} ← Rear[ich];	get ready to add to end of list
4)	Rear[ich] ← buffer;	update pointer to end of list
	if (temp = NULL)	if channel list now empty
	Front[ich] ← buffer;	then update front pointer
	else	
	Link[MAR_{link}] ← buffer;	update previous last element

Packet forwarded on channel "och":

clock cycle	action	comments
1)	buffer ← Front[och];	get address of first buffer in list
	MAR_{link} ← Front[och];	
2)	if (buffer = NULL) abort;	abort if list empty
	temp ← Link[MAR_{link}];	address of new front element
3)	Front[och] ← temp;	update front pointer
	Link[MAR_{link}] ← free;	add buffer to free list
	free ← buffer;	new front of free list
	if (temp = NULL)	check if list now empty
	Rear[och] ← NULL;	

When a new packet arrives, the buffer management circuitry must perform two operations, assuming the flow control circuitry has first established that the packet can be accepted (discussed later):

- find and allocate a free buffer, and

- record the location of the buffer so that the packet can be found when it is time to forward it.

The address of a free buffer is determined by a priority encoder attached to the free buffer latch. The resulting address is sent to memory module MM_0. This address is also used to clear the corresponding bit in the free buffer latch, effectively allocating the buffer and completing the first operation. The second operation is accomplished by writing the address of the selected buffer into the channel-to-buffer RAM at the memory location corresponding to the output channel responsible for forwarding the packet. The latter is obtained from the translation table.

Sending a packet on output channel i also requires two operations:

- locate the buffer holding the packet for channel i, and
- release the buffer.

The first task is accomplished by reading address i of the channel-to-buffer RAM. The resulting address is used to set the corresponding bit in the free buffer latch, marking the buffer free to be used by other packets, thus accomplishing the second task.

Sending a packet requires two memory operations because the channel-to-buffer RAM read must be completed before the latch write can begin. These two steps are easily pipelined, however, allowing a "send packet" operation to be initiated every clock cycle. The operations for receiving a packet can be performed in a single clock cycle because both can be executed concurrently. This is in contrast to the four clock cycles required in the previous buffer management scheme that used linked lists.

4.5. Flow Control

Flow control is the mechanism that regulates the transmission of data packets along virtual circuits. The network must be able to "throttle" traffic on virtual circuits to prevent buffer overflow and to handle situations when a processor is sent more messages than it can immediately receive. In addition to providing a *mechanism* that allows components to throttle traffic, a *policy* is also required to determine which virtual circuits must be throttled, and when. Such a policy will be discussed next, followed by a discussion of different throttling mechanisms.

Because one of the purposes of flow control is to avoid buffer overflow, a natural policy is to begin throttling traffic when the pool of free, i.e., empty, buffers is depleted. If a node is inundated with data, packets will "back up" along the virtual circuits leading to it much like cars backing up on a congested freeway. This type of flow control, called "back pressure flow control," is analogous to water (packets) flowing through a pipe (buffers). If the pipe becomes blocked or constricted, water backs up to its source. Such a mechanism has been used successfully in TYMNET™, a loosely coupled, commercial communication network [Tyme81].

The flow control policy described above can lead to buffer hogging where one virtual circuit uses more than its share of the buffers in some node. If a virtual circuit becomes blocked, e.g., due to a congested output link, packets may continue to arrive on that virtual circuit and occupy most or all of the buffers in the node. Without some mechanism to restrict buffer sharing, buffer hogging will impede other traffic using the node and lead to deadlock situations. This situation can be avoided by controlling the maximum number of buffers each channel can use. The direct mapping scheme, and to a lesser extent the set-associative scheme, automatically provide some protection against buffer hogging, because they inherently restrict buffer sharing. All three schemes, however, need some mechanism to ensure that data are not lost if no free buffers are available.

In the design discussed here, buffer hogging is prevented by specifying that each output channel may not hold more than some "channel limit" of buffers at one time. Even with this restriction, however, another form of buffer hogging may still arise. A congested output link could use all of the node's buffers and block traffic on other links. To prevent this, each output port is restricted to using no more than some maximum number of buffers, determined by a higher level protocol. This maximum number, called the "port limit," can be changed dynamically to shift additional buffers to highly utilized ports, while still providing some space for traffic on lightly loaded ports. Studies indicate that by restricting the number of buffers an output port can use, "output port buffer hogging" is prevented, and a significant improvement in the bandwidth provided by the node is obtained [Irla78]. These studies also indicate that as a general rule, each port should not be allowed to use more than $\dfrac{b}{\sqrt{p}}$ buffers in a p-port node with b buffers.

Assuming a buffer allocation policy is used to control the rate of packet forwarding, let us now examine the throttling mechanism. Two mechanisms will be considered here: sender-controlled and receiver-controlled throttling. The receiver-controlled mechanism is the simpler mechanism and will be described first.

4.5.1. A Send / Acknowledge Protocol

A simple send/acknowledge protocol to transmit data over the link is the most straightforward example of receiver controlled flow control. Each node sends a packet and waits for the receiver to return a control signal indicating whether it accepted or rejected (and discarded) the packet. An "ack" signal denotes an accepted packet whereas a "nack" denotes a rejected packet. If a nack is returned, the packet must be retransmitted at a later time.

A receiver may choose to reject a packet because of buffer space limitations or transmissions errors. Here, it is assumed that only header information is checked for transmission errors, since the virtual cut-through mechanism prevents retransmission if errors in the data are detected. Errors in data bytes must be handled by an end-to-end protocol that detects and retransmits damaged packets.

It is also assumed that each link has a separate control line to carry the ack/nack signal. Alternatively, the control signal could be piggy-backed on a packet going in the opposite direction. However, this leads to a "looser coupling" between sender and receiver, forcing the sender to either deal with multiple unacknowledged packets pending over the link [PoZi78], adding a considerable amount of complexity to the circuitry in the port, or to stop using the link until the acknowledgement arrives, wasting bandwidth. Because the receiver can generate an acknowledgement after only the header is received, a direct connection to the sender offers the unusual feature that the sender will receive the acknowledgement before it has finished sending the packet! This allows a virtual circuit to "pipeline" a stream of packets through an otherwise idle node without incurring the delays associated with waiting for acknowledgements or the complexity of multiple unacknowledged packets.

To prevent buffer hogging, each output channel cannot use more than some channel limit of buffers, and each output port cannot use more than some port limit of buffers, as discussed earlier. Note that the port and channel limits only restrict the number of buffers the port and channel can use and do not represent an *a priori* allocation of buffer space.

A block diagram of the flow control circuitry for one port is shown in figure 4.6a. The circuitry performs two functions:

• select a channel waiting to use the link and initiate a request to the buffer manager to forward the next packet on this channel, and

• accept or reject arriving packets.

The flow control circuitry in this design does not process buffer numbers. The buffer manager records which buffers are assigned to which channels.

The first function is accomplished by the "channel FIFO" shown in figure 4.6a. This memory lists channels with packets waiting to be forwarded. When the link is ready to forward a packet, the first element of the channel FIFO is removed. The resulting channel number is sent to the buffer management circuitry indicating that the next packet on this output channel is to be sent over the link. If this packet is accepted by the neighboring node, the FIFO element is discarded. Otherwise, the channel number is reentered at the end of the FIFO.

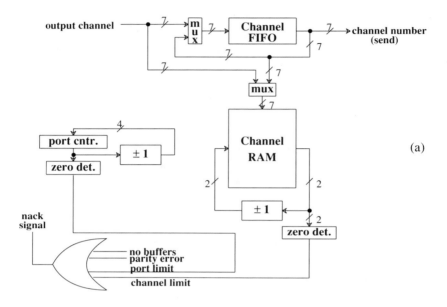

(a)

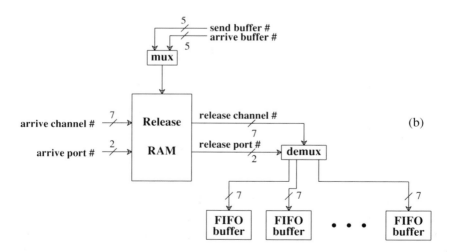

(b)

Figure 4.6

Flow control circuitry. (a) send/acknowledge.

(b) additional circuitry for remote buffer management.

The remaining circuitry in figure 4.6a performs the second function — determining if an arriving packet should be accepted or rejected. A packet may be rejected for any of four reasons:

- no buffers remain in the node to hold the packet,

- the parity check on the header indicates a transmission error,

- the output port is already using the maximum number allowed, or

- the output channel is already using the maximum number allowed.

The flow control hardware must detect each of these cases and generate a negative acknowledgement should any of them arise. If none of the conditions arise, the packet is accepted and a positive acknowledgement returned.

The first condition is detected by a control line from the buffer management module indicating when the free buffer pool has been exhausted. A NULL pointer in the free register in figure 4.5a, or a lack of '1' bits in the free buffer latch in figure 4.5b, indicates this condition. Similarly, a parity checker in the input port detects the second condition. A "port counter" is used to detect the third. This counter indicates the number of additional buffers that port can use before the port limit is reached. The counter is initially set to the port limit, decremented each time a packet is accepted, and incremented each time the port successfully forwards a packet. If the output of the counter is zero, the port cannot accommodate another packet. The zero-detection circuitry, implemented by a single NOR gate, identifies this situation.

To detect the final condition, a channel using its limit of buffers, circuitry similar to the port counter is required for each output channel. The c-word "channel RAM" indicates the number of buffers each channel can use before reaching its channel limit. Entry i is initially set to the channel limit for channel i, is decremented each time a packet is accepted by that output channel, and is incremented when the channel successfully forwards a packet. If a packet arrives and the corresponding channel RAM entry is zero, the packet must be rejected and a negative acknowledgement returned.

If each channel is restricted to use at most one buffer at a time, then the circuitry in figure 4.6a can be simplified. The channel RAM is now one bit wide, and indicates whether the channel has a packet waiting to be forwarded. The increment/decrement circuit attached to the channel RAM is no longer needed, because accepting a packet implies setting a bit in the RAM, and forwarding a packet implies resetting a bit. Similarly, the channel RAM's zero-detection circuitry is not required, because only a single bit is output from the RAM.

4.5.2. Remote Buffer Management

An alternative approach to flow control implements the buffer allocation policy for a node in its *neighboring* nodes; the flow of information is controlled from the sender rather than the receiver end of each link. For example, each output port could be statically assigned to manage some portion of the *neighboring* node's buffers. In this scheme, each output port maintains a table indicating the number of buffers in the neighboring node allocated to each output channel of the link connecting the two. A channel must wait if it is using "too many" of its neighbor's buffers or if there is insufficient free buffer space to hold a new packet. Control decisions are made by the sender, and receivers must accept all packets sent over the link. Whereas the send/acknowledge protocol described earlier is essentially a "request-to-send" protocol, the remote buffer management scheme is closer in spirit to a "clear-to-send" protocol, as will be seen momentarily.

Maintaining this remote status information requires some overhead. The fact that the receiver has freed a buffer must be reported to the transmitter. When a node forwards a packet, it must report back to the node from which it received the packet that the buffer is again available. This status information is equivalent to a clear-to-send message allowing the sender to forward another packet.

Finally, because packets cannot be retransmitted, transmission errors in packet headers result in lost packets. An end-to-end mechanism is required to retransmit these packets.

As in the send/acknowledge flow control scheme, channel buffer hogging is prevented by controlling the number of remote buffers used by each output channel. However, output port buffer hogging is much more difficult to prevent. This is because each node sending packets does not know which output port the receiving node will use to forward the packet. Thus, nodes have no direct control over the lengths of queues on output links of neighboring nodes, so nothing prevents a single output port from monopolizing the entire buffer pool. The receiving node must have more decision making power in the flow control mechanism to control the lengths of its own output port queues.

The flow control circuitry must perform four functions:

- select a channel waiting to use the link and initiate a request to the buffer manager to forward the next packet on this channel,

- generate release channel numbers to previous nodes indicating a buffer has been freed,

- process incoming release channel numbers indicating remote buffers are now available, and

- maintain information on buffer allocation in receiving nodes.

The physical circuitry for performing the first function is the same as that shown in figure 4.6a for the send/acknowledge scheme; however, the logical meaning of the information kept in the channel RAM is different. Instead of indicating the number of local buffers below the channel's limit in the local node, the RAM now indicates the number of *remote* buffers below the limit in the neighboring node. As long as entry i is not zero, channel i can send another packet, assuming the pool of remote buffers allocated to the port has not been exhausted. The port counter register indicates the number of buffers in the neighboring node used by this output port.

When a packet arrives, the number of the output channel responsible for forwarding the packet is added to the end of the channel FIFO. Because all packets are accepted, no further processing is required. To forward a packet, the next entry in the channel FIFO is removed. The corresponding channel number is used to address the channel RAM. If the corresponding entry of the channel RAM is not zero, and if the port counter is not zero, then the channel number is sent to the buffer module, and the next packet on this channel is sent over the link. The port counter and channel RAM entry are then decremented. If either of the counters is zero, the channel cannot forward the packet, so the channel number is reentered at the end of the channel FIFO.

Each time a packet is forwarded, a release channel number must be sent to the neighboring node that sent the packet. The circuitry in figure 4.6b performs this function. To generate release channel numbers, information must be kept with each packet that indicates the input port and channel on which it arrived. A b-word "release RAM" accomplishes this task. Element i indicates the input port and channel number where the packet in buffer i arrived. This information is placed in the release RAM when a packet arrives and read when it is forwarded. A small FIFO buffer in each output port holds the channel number portion of the word until it can be forwarded to the neighbor that sent the packet.

Finally, when a release channel number is received from a neighboring node, indicating that a certain channel is using one fewer buffer, the count of buffers the channel is allowed to use must be incremented. The appropriate entry of the channel RAM is read, incremented, and written back into the RAM, completing the processing of the release.

The simplifications resulting from constraining each output channel to use at most one remote buffer at a time are similar to those described in the send/acknowledge scheme. The channel RAM is again one bit wide. Forwarding a packet resets a bit in the RAM, effectively disabling the channel. Receiving a release channel number causes the bit to be set, reenabling the channel.

The send/acknowledge protocol leads to a simple implementation, whereas the remote buffer management approach prevents rejected packets and avoids retransmissions and waste of bandwidth. Both schemes require some overhead to provide the feedback signals necessary for flow control. The send/acknowledge scheme presented here uses dedicated pins, whereas the remote buffer management scheme uses piggy-backed control signals.

4.6. Evaluation of Design Parameters

Important parameters of the design described above include:

• the number of I/O ports,

• the number of virtual channels, and

• the number of buffers.

The first question was examined in detail in chapter three, where it was found that from 3 to 5 I/O ports should be used. The remaining two questions will be discussed next.

4.6.1. Number of Virtual Channels

Because each virtual channel requires a certain amount of overhead circuitry, the number of channels must be limited. In addition, it is desirable to limit the number of channels on each link to prevent "overbooking" the link's bandwidth, since this will lead to long queueing delays on the link. Conversely, providing too few channels per link will lead to a high failure rate in establishing virtual circuits, deadlock situations, and under-utilization of the link's bandwidth. Thus the number of virtual channels per link must be chosen to achieve good link utilization without requiring an excessive amount of circuitry.

One approach is to provide enough channels to accommodate a large number of low bandwidth circuits but also to provide a separate mechanism that prevents overbooking the link's bandwidth. New circuits cannot be established if the link's bandwidth is being fully utilized, regardless of the number of unallocated channels remaining.

With this approach, the bandwidth requirements of each circuit must be estimated. This could be accomplished statically when the circuit is established. For example, the operating system may be able to provide this information based on the type of traffic expected over the circuit. Alternatively, bandwidth requirements may be estimated dynamically by measuring traffic on the circuit. Of course, the latter scheme has the disadvantage that link bandwidth may still be overbooked because the amount of bandwidth required by the circuit is not known until after it has been established; a high bandwidth circuit may be established before it is known that the circuit's bandwidth requirements over-utilize the link.

Either scheme could be implemented with a "link bandwidth indicator" containing the anticipated bandwidth requirements of circuits using the link. When this bandwidth indicator exceeds some threshold, no more traffic is routed over that link. In the first scheme, using "hints" from the operating system, a field in the packet that establishes the virtual circuit could include the anticipated bandwidth requirements of that circuit. The link indicator is increased by the value of this field when the circuit is established and decreased when the circuit is torn down. The value of this field must be included in both the packet tearing down the circuit as well as the header unless the component records the bandwidth requirements of each channel. In the scheme using dynamic measurements, the bandwidth indicator could be incremented each time a packet is sent on that link. Periodically, the routing controller examines the indicator to determine if the link is overbooked and clears it. Finally, a third alternative is to measure the average queue length on each link and declare the link overbooked if this average exceeds a certain threshold.

If a separate mechanism is used to prevent overloading the link, each component should ideally provide an unlimited number of channels; this guarantees that it will never needlessly block circuits trying to use a link with excess capacity. However, this number can be reduced if the minimum bandwidth requirements of any virtual circuit can be established. The maximum number of channels the link will ever require can be calculated by dividing the total link bandwidth by this minimum channel bandwidth. Based in part on empirical simulation data from the fine grained computations discussed in the previous chapter, it has been argued that from 128 to 256 channels should be provided for an 80 Mbits/second link [Fuji83]. We note that the number of channels should increase with communication link bandwidth but may be reduced if processor computation speed increases. In the latter case, a given application program will generate messages at a faster rate, implying a higher traffic load on each virtual circuit.

4.6.2. Amount of Buffer Space

Buffers increase the total bandwidth provided by the network through pipelining and by "softening" the impact of statistical fluctuations in the traffic distribution. However, the law of diminishing returns applies when adding additional buffers to a switching node; a successively smaller improvement in performance is obtained with each additional buffer that is added. Intuitively, the node need not provide buffer space beyond that which is necessary to keep output links busy when there is traffic requiring use of the link.

In extreme cases, buffer deadlock will result. Buffer deadlock occurs when message traffic halts because two or more nodes have exhausted all available buffer space. A cycle is formed where each node in the cycle cannot forward a packet because no buffers are available to receive the packet, and no buffers can be freed because packets cannot be forwarded. An example of such a deadlock situation is shown in figure 4.7 where each node has a single buffer holding a packet waiting to be forwarded. The network will remain deadlocked until one or more packets are discarded, releasing buffer space.

Thus, sufficient buffer space must be provided to:

• reduce the probability of buffer deadlock, and

• ensure good performance.

Each of these issues will now be discussed in turn, as well as results from simulation studies that help determine the buffering requirements of each switching node.

4.6.2.1. Buffer Space: Deadlock Considerations

Buffer deadlock can be prevented if enough buffer space is provided in each node. A brute force solution is to provide each virtual channel with its own buffer. Because

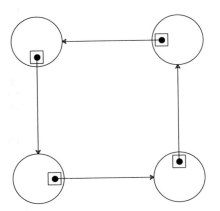

Figure 4.7
Example of buffer deadlock.

each circuit is allocated a buffer in each node it passes through, traffic on a circuit cannot be blocked by traffic on other circuits, and buffer deadlock cannot occur. Providing a separate buffer on each channel is wasteful, however, because each component must provide as many buffers as there are channels. It will be seen that similar performance can be achieved if many channels share a much smaller pool of buffers.

Several approaches have been proposed that avoid store-and-forward deadlock in networks of arbitrary topology [MeSc80a, MeSc80b, IsMa80, Gele81, ToUl81, SoAg83, Gopa85][1]. For example, assume each node has at least LV_{max} buffers, where LV_{max} is the maximum number of hops traversed by any virtual circuit. The node's buffer pool is partitioned into LV_{max} disjoint pools or levels, $1, 2, \cdots LV_{max}$. A register is associated with each circuit passing through the node indicating the number of hops remaining before the final destination is reached. A packet arriving on a circuit with i hops remaining can only be placed in a level i buffer.

Deadlock is avoided because all messages in the network can be delivered to their respective destinations, and all buffers holding messages can therefore be released. All level 1 buffers can be released because the messages they hold can immediately be forwarded to their final destinations. Because all level 1 buffers can be released, level 2 buffers can also be released by first emptying the level 1 buffers and forwarding the level 2 messages to these level 1 buffers, when the messages may leave the network. By applying this argument recursively, it is easy to see that all messages in the network can be forwarded to their respective destinations.

The central disadvantage of this scheme is that large networks require more buffers than smaller ones, so the switch must provide enough buffers to accommodate the largest possible network. This may require an excessively large amount of buffer space. In addition, if traffic is highly localized, many buffers are wasted because those reserved for higher hop counts are never used. Other schemes for avoiding deadlock have been proposed, but each has its respective disadvantages.

An alternative approach to the deadlock problem is to allow deadlock to occur but incorporate a mechanism that ensures that deadlocks are *broken* [BlBG84]. The deadlock breaking mechanism could be implemented as a side effect of an end-to-end protocol using timeout counters to retransmit lost messages. In such a scheme, each message sent over a virtual circuit must be acknowledged by the receiver. If an

---

[1]A deadlock free routing algorithm can be developed for certain topologies as was described in chapter one for the torus routing chip.

acknowledgement is not returned after a certain amount of time, the sender assumes that the message was lost and must be retransmitted. To avoid duplicate packets, the sender must first "clear" the virtual circuit by sending a special packet that flows through the circuit and destroys all packets it encounters. It then resends the lost message. If deadlock occurs, timeouts will result and circuits will be cleared. This releases buffer space and breaks the deadlock. Because such a timeout mechanism is already required to retransmit *lost* packets, the deadlock breaking mechanism incurs little additional cost. In this scheme, switching nodes are not required to ensure that buffer deadlock cannot occur, so they need not provide large amounts of buffer space. Finally, we note that some randomness should be introduced to avoid synchronously repeating the deadlock formation and breakup scenario.

A similar mechanism could be used to break deadlocks that arise when links use all of their virtual channels. Expiration of an end-to-end timeout during the establishment of a virtual circuit could trigger the release of a special packet that destroys the partially completed circuit, releasing channels and breaking the deadlock. This protocol also requires an end-to-end acknowledgement to mark the establishment of each virtual circuit.

Enough buffer space must be provided to ensure that deadlocks occur infrequently. Unfortunately, the likelihood of deadlock is dependent on the traffic distribution and is not yet fully understood. Some empirical evidence has been collected, however, that suggests that the probability of store-and-forward deadlock can be dramatically reduced with straightforward buffer allocation policies that reduce buffer hogging and require only a modest number of buffers [Fuji83]. This is the subject of the following discussion.

Simulation experiments similar to those discussed in chapter three were performed to evaluate the number of buffers each communication component should provide to avoid buffer deadlock. The six application programs discussed in chapter three were simulated for a hexagonal lattice network with 3 ports per node.

The first set of experiments assumed that each component provides b buffers, and there are no restrictions on buffer sharing; virtual circuits may use as many buffers as are available. A large number of buffers, over 100 for some of the programs, was required in each component to avoid buffer deadlock.

Buffer hogging was at the root of these deadlock problems. Consider the situation in figure 4.8. Virtual circuits 1 and 2 join at node A, sharing the link from A to B, and virtual circuit 3 uses the link from B to A. Suppose all three circuits carry a steady stream of packets, or equivalently, suppose a burst of packets simultaneously arrives on each circuit. The flow of packets entering node A on circuits 1 and 2 exceeds the flow

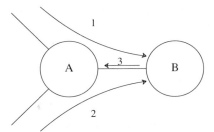

Figure 4.8
Example of congestion leading to deadlock.

leaving A toward node B because the latter is limited by the capacity of the link from A to B. A queue forms at node A. This queue will grow until the free buffer pool in node A is exhausted. When this happens, traffic on circuit 3 is blocked, and a queue of packets begins to grow in node B. Eventually, B's free buffer pool will also be exhausted, blocking traffic on circuits 1 and 2. The network is now deadlocked.

The scenario described above can be avoided if precautions are taken to avoid buffer hogging, e.g., by restricting the number of buffers each circuit can use. The simulation experiments were repeated assuming each circuit could not use more than one buffer in each node at one time. It was found that 12 buffers per node were sufficient to avoid buffer deadlock in the application programs that were tested.

The simulation experiments demonstrate the need for a flow control mechanism that prevents buffer hogging. These empirical studies also indicate that a few tens of buffers are sufficient to reduce the probability of buffer deadlock for the fine grained application programs that were tested. More research is required to understand the relationship between frequency of deadlock and the number of buffers per node, the buffer allocation policy, and characteristics of the traffic distribution. The results suggest, however, that proper design of the communication component can reduce the likelihood of deadlock significantly, allowing cruder, low overhead deadlock breaking mechanisms to be used rather than deadlock prevention techniques.

4.6.2.2. Buffer Space: Performance Considerations

Each switching node must provide sufficient buffer space to maintain a steady flow of traffic. Otherwise, communication bandwidth will be wasted. In the send/acknowledge flow control scheme, retransmissions are required to resend rejected packets, whereas in the remote buffer management scheme, links simply become idle. How many buffers are required to maintain this flow? Studies of multistage switching networks indicate that little performance improvement arises beyond three buffers per node [DiJu81b, DiJu81a]. However, as the studies of the previous section indicate, three buffers are not sufficient to avoid many deadlock scenarios in the single stage networks discussed here.

Simulation experiments were performed to answer the following questions:

• How many buffers should each component provide to achieve good performance?

• How many buffers should each virtual circuit be allowed to use at one time?

Buffering and flow control questions are of little consequence when the network is lightly loaded; buffering requirements are low and throttling mechanisms are not necessary. Therefore, we will only consider the case when links are congested. Such links often become bottlenecks that limit performance of the entire system.

The appropriate amount of buffer space depends on characteristics of the traffic distribution. Let us informally examine network behavior under heavy traffic loads. Consider the most heavily loaded link in the network, and assume it is saturated. Bottleneck analysis[2] tells us that this link will limit the overall performance of the system. Under these circumstances, traffic will back up on circuits "upstream," i.e., leading up to the bottleneck area, while circuits "downstream" will be starved waiting for messages to get past the bottleneck. The situation is not unlike that on a freeway near an accident where the road leading up to the accident is filled with delayed motorists, while the road just beyond the accident is almost empty. Intuitively, one would expect that only a modest amount of buffering is required by each output link or channel to keep the links busy and maintain a steady flow of traffic through the bottleneck. Just as the number of cars that can be "buffered" (say) a hundred feet in front of the accident is not very critical, the number of buffers in front of the bottleneck link also is not crucial, unless of course buffer hogging occurs and other output links are unnecessarily blocked.

Simulation experiments using the application programs described in chapter three were conducted. Figure 4.9 shows representative speedup curves for the FFT program on a degree three, hexagonal lattice network. Each switching component contains four ports including one to connect to the node's computation processor. A send/acknowledge protocol for flow control is assumed. If several packets are queued, waiting to use the same link, a round-robin algorithm selects the next packet to be sent over the link. This prevents a blocked virtual circuit from dominating use of the link by repeatedly sending negatively acknowledged packets.

---

[2]Bottleneck analysis was described in detail in §2.5.

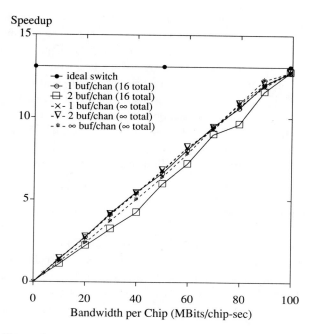

Figure 4.9

Limited buffer space, FFT program.

The curves in figure 4.9 are distinguished by the amount of buffer space provided in each switching node and the degree to which buffer usage is restricted. Four combinations of these two parameters result:

- unlimited buffer space and no restrictions on buffer usage,
- unlimited buffer space but with restrictions on buffer usage,
- limited buffer space and no restrictions on buffer usage, and
- limited buffer space but with restrictions on buffer usage.

As discussed earlier, the third class of networks, those with a limited amount of buffer space and no restrictions on buffer usage, resulted in deadlock situations for many of the application programs. All networks with limited amounts of buffer space provide 16 buffers per switching node. These networks also assume that each output port cannot use more than 8 buffers at one time, or $\frac{16}{\sqrt{4}}$ as suggested in [Irla78].

The curves indicate that networks with 16 buffers per component yield virtually the same performance as networks with an infinite amount of buffer space. Restricting virtual circuits to using at most one buffer at a time results in no significant degradation in performance. Networks using a send/acknowledge protocol for flow control yield virtually the same performance as networks with an infinite amount of buffer space and no restrictions on buffer usage. This indicates that the bandwidth wasted by negatively acknowledged packets does not have a significant effect on performance. This is due in part to the round-robin algorithm used for scheduling usage of the communication links. Blocked virtual circuits relinquish use of the link when a packet is rejected, allowing other traffic to use the link. Thus, the simulation results agree qualitatively with the intuitive arguments presented earlier.

4.7. Complexity of the Communication Circuitry

Using the results presented above, the complexity of the VLSI switch described here can be estimated. It is assumed that each component provides from 64 to 256 channels per link, 32 buffers, each large enough to accommodate 16 bytes of data, and 4 I/O ports. Transistor counts for different designs providing different levels of functionality are presented.

The switching chip consists of 6 modules:

- I/O ports,
- routing controller,
- translation tables,
- packet buffers,
- buffer management circuitry, and
- flow control circuitry.

Estimates of the amount of circuitry required for communication functions using each of the designs presented earlier are summarized in table 4.3. Circuitry for a communication processor that handles initialization and high level functions such as error recovery protocols is not included. We assume that the processor responsible for executing user computations performs those operations that are not critical from a performance standpoint.

The routing controller estimates assume a 256 entry hierarchical routing table is provided that supports up to 8 levels of lookup tables. The figures are based on the designs shown in figure 4.4a and 4.4b. The two buffer management hardware estimates

Table 4.3

Transistor counts for alternative designs

Module	Logic (transistors)	Memory (Kbits)		
	All Designs	64 Chan.	128 Chan.	256 Chan.
I/O Ports (4 ports)	8000	-	-	-
Routing controller				
simple	9000	0.6	1.1	2.1
complex	10000	1.4	1.9	2.9
Translation Table	-	2.2	5.0	11.0
Buffers (16 modules)	8000	4.0	4.0	4.0
Buffer Management				
$\leq$1 **buffer/vc**	2000	1.3	2.5	5.0
$\leq$4 **buffers/vc**	2000	2.7	5.2	10.2
Flow Control				
Send/Acknowledge				
$\leq$1 **buffer/vc**	11000	0.6	0.9	1.5
$\leq$4 **buffers/vc**	12000	0.9	1.4	2.5
Remote Buffer				
$\leq$1 **buffer/vc**	13000	1.0	1.3	2.0
$\leq$4 **buffers/vc**	14000	1.2	1.8	3.0
Totals				
Simplest	38000	8.7	13.5	23.6
Most Complex	42000	9.5	17.9	31.1

assume each virtual circuit can hold either one buffer at a time (figure 4.5b) or four buffers at one time (figure 4.5a). Four estimates of the flow control logic are shown. These represent the cross product of two parameters: send/acknowledge protocol versus remote buffer management; and virtual circuits limited to one, or up to four buffers at a time.

The figures in table 4.3 indicate that a minimal complexity switching chip with 4 I/O ports, 32 16-byte buffers, 64 channels per link, one buffer per virtual circuit, and a send/acknowledge flow control scheme, can be constructed with approximately 38,000 transistors for logic and 8.7 Kbits of RAM. Assuming single transistor dynamic RAM cells, less than 50,000 transistors are required. Except for the number of channels, this design is in accordance with the design recommendations derived throughout this chapter. A similar design using 256 channels per link and the more complex routing scheme requires 27,000 transistors of logic and 24.4 Kbits of RAM.

4.8. Summary

The designer of a switching component is faced with many important design decisions. Performance requirements dictate that special purpose hardware be used to implement frequently used communication functions. Key functions requiring hardware implementation include the basic message forwarding transport mechanism, routing, flow control, and buffer management.

Hierarchical techniques can be used to implement general lookup table mechanisms for message routing without excessively large memories. Memory size is minimized when many levels are used. Buffer management and flow control policies are required to avoid buffer hogging. Strategies that limit buffer usage by individual circuits appear to be effective in controlling this problem. Sufficient buffer space must be provided to obtain adequate performance and to reduce the frequency of deadlock. Simulations indicate that a relatively modest number of buffers suffices.

Complexity estimates of one possible design of a general purpose communication chip indicate that a moderately sophisticated design is well within the capabilities of technology available today. Such support will become prevalent in second and third generation multicomputer systems. Large communication delays for many first generation multicomputers require the application program to contain relatively coarse grains of computation and to map perfectly to the topology that is provided. Future machines can be expected that provide high performance communication systems, making them suitable for a much broader class of applications.

References

[BlBG84]   J. Blazewicz, D. P. Bovet and G. Gambosi, "Deadlock-Resistant Flow Control Procedures for Store-and-Forward Networks," *IEEE Transactions on Communications* (August 1984), Vol. COM-32, No. 8, pp. 884-887.

[DePa78]   A. Despain and D. Patterson, "X-Tree: A Tree Structured Multiprocessor Computer Architecture," *Proceedings of the 5th Annual Symposium on Computer Architecture* (April 1978), Vol. 7, No. 6, pp. 144-151.

[DiJu81a]   D. M. Dias and J. R. Jump, "Analysis and Simulation of Buffered Delta Networks," *IEEE Transactions on Computers* (April 1981), Vol. C-30, No. 4, pp. 273-282.

[DiJu81b]   D. Dias and J. Jump, "Packet Switching Interconnection Networks for Modular Systems," *IEEE Computer* (December 1981), Vol. 14, No. 12, pp. 43-53.

[Fuji80]   R. M. Fujimoto, *Routing Controller for X-Tree*. M.S. Thesis, Computer Sciences Division, University of California, Berkeley, 1980.

[Fuji83]   R. M. Fujimoto, *VLSI Communication Components for Multicomputer Networks*. Ph.D. Dissertation, Electronics Research Laboratory Report No. UCB/CSD 83/136, University of California, Berkeley, California, 1983.

[Gele81]   D. Gelernter, "A DAG-Based Algorithm for Prevention of Store-and-Forward Deadlock in Packet Networks," *IEEE Transactions on Computers* (October 1981), Vol. C-30, No. 10, pp. 709-715.

[Gerl81]   M. Gerla, "Routing and Flow Control," In: *Protocols and Techniques for Data Communication Networks*, F. F. Kuo, ed. Prentice-Hall, Inc., Englewood Cliffs, New Jersey, 1981, pp. 122-174.

[Gopa85]   I. S. Gopal, "Prevention of Store-and-Forward Deadlock in Computer Networks," *IEEE Transactions on Communications* (December 1985), Vol. COM-33, No. 12, pp. 1258-1264.

[Grif79]   M. Griffin, *X-Tree Communication Buses*. Master's Report, University of California, Berkeley, California, 1979.

[Irla78]   M. I. Irland, "Buffer Management in a Packet Switch," *IEEE Transactions on Communications* (March 1978), Vol. COM-26, No. 3, pp. 328-337.

[IsMa80]   S. S. Isloor and T. A. Marsland, "The Deadlock Problem: An Overview," *IEEE Computer* (September 1980), Vol. 13, No. 9, pp. 58-78.

[Joel79]   A. E. Joel, "Circuit Switching: Unique Architecture and Applications," *IEEE Computer* (June 1979), Vol. 12, No. 6, pp. 10-22.

[Kamo76]   F. Kamoun, *Design Considerations for Large Computer Communications Networks*. Ph.D. Dissertation, University of California, Los Angeles, California, 1976.

[Laur79]   M. J. Laurent, *Input-Output Ports for the X-Tree Nodes*. M.S. Thesis, Computer Sciences Division, University of California, Berkeley, 1979.

[MaGN79]   G. M. Masson, G. C. Gingher and S. Nakamura, "A Sampler of Circuit Switched Networks," *Computer* (June 1979), Vol. 12, No. 6, pp. 32-48.

[McQu74]   J. McQuillan, "Adaptive Routing Algorithms for Distributed Computer Networks", NTIS Report AD-781 467, U. S. Department of Commerce, May 1974.

[MeSc80a]   P. M. Merlin and P. J. Schweitzer, "Deadlock Avoidance - Store and Forward Deadlock,"
            IEEE Transactions on Communications (March 1980), Vol. COM-28, No. 3, pp. 345-354.

[MeSc80b]   P. M. Merlin and P. J. Schweitzer, "Deadlock Avoidance in Store and Forward Networks II -
            Other Deadlock Types," *IEEE Transactions on Communications* (March 1980), Vol. COM-28,
            No. 3, pp. 355-360.

[PoZi78]   L. Pouzin and H. Zimmerman, "A Tutorial on Protocols," *Proceedings of the IEEE* (November
            1978), Vol. 66, No. 11, pp. 1346-1370.

[SeDP78]   C. H. Séquin, A. Despain and D. Patterson, "Communications in X-Tree, A Modular
            Multiprocessor System," *Proceedings of the ACM National Conference* (December 1978), pp.
            194-203.

[SoAg83]   I. M. Soi and K. K. Aggarwal, "Some Aspects of Computer Deadlocks," *Computers and
            Electrical Engineering* (1983), Vol. 10, No. 2, pp. 99-107.

[Taji77]   W. Tajibnapis, "A Correctness Proof of a Topology Maintenance Protocol for a Distributed
            Computer Network," *Communications of the ACM* (July 1977), Vol. 20, No. 7, pp. 477-485.

[Tane81]   A. S. Tanenbaum, *Computer Networks.* Prentice-Hall, Englewood Cliffs, New Jersey, 1981.

[ToUl81]   S. Toueg and J. D. Ullman, "Deadlock-Free Packet Switching Networks," *SIAM Journal on
            Computing* (August 1981), Vol. 10, No. 3, pp. 594-611.

[Tyme81]   L. Tymes, "Routing and Flow Control in TYMNET," *IEEE Transactions on Communications*
            (April 1981), Vol. COM-29, No. 4, pp. 392-398.

5 Multicomputer Network Operating Systems

> Bad administration, to be sure, can destroy good policy; but good administration can never save bad policy.
>
> Adlai Stevenson

Like traditional, uniprocessor operating systems, multicomputer network operating systems define a *virtual machine* that not only extends the underlying hardware but also hides its idiosyncrasies. Typically, such virtual machines provide resource management, scheduling, and some measure of fault tolerance. In addition, a multicomputer network operating system should also provide support for scheduling parallel tasks, internode synchronization and communication, and recovery from node failures. These areas are united by their need for resource status information.

The types and amounts of status information that can readily be acquired by the nodes of a multicomputer network differ considerably from those for a uniprocessor. Most notably, the absence of global memory in a multicomputer network means that no single node can possess a complete or current description of the global network state. As van Tilborg has noted [vanT82], there are three basic reasons for limited information:

- memory constraints,
- communication delays, and
- network traffic constraints.

Augmenting processing capacity by incremental addition of nodes is one of a multicomputer network's primary advantages, and it should be possible to do so without structural modifications to the network operating system. If global state tables are required, each network node must allocate a larger fraction of its memory for network state information as nodes are added. This is unwieldy and intractable for networks containing thousands of nodes. Even without memory constraints, the overhead required to update state tables would quickly exceed both the processing capacity of individual nodes and the transmission capacity of the communication network.

Communication delays make it impossible to obtain *exact* information of the current network state. The analogy with observational astronomy is apt. Electromagnetic radiation received from a distant object reflects the object's state in the past; the current state cannot be observed. Distance and time are directly related by a proportionality constant, the speed of light. Similarly, status messages from distant network nodes must be transmitted via the communication network. The delays incurred include both transmission across communication links and queueing delays. Although transmission delays are linear in the number of links from origin to destination node, queueing delays are not. Thus, unlike observational astronomy, there is a *nonlinear* relationship between distance and time, and the time required to receive a single status message depends on unpredictable network traffic.

Continuing the physical analogy, electromagnetic radiation interacts with the interstellar medium and can, under certain circumstances, stimulate the birth of new stars. Similarly, status messages consume a portion of the communication network bandwidth, and this resource competition increases message latency. Acquiring a large volume of accurate status information involves two antithetical concepts, volume and accuracy. One can either acquire a small amount of accurate information or a large amount of inaccurate information; disseminating information perturbs the network state. This dilemma is analogous to the Heisenberg Uncertainty Principle - either position or momentum can be determined accurately, but not simultaneously.

These three areas, memory constraints, communication delays, and communication traffic, make it difficult for a multicomputer network to build and maintain an accurate self-model. Moreover, they highlight the primary difference between a uniprocessor operating system, where a consistent self-model is endemic, and a multicomputer operating system, suggesting that different techniques are appropriate for the latter.

A multicomputer operating system bears more similarity to a distributed operating system such as the V kernel [Cher84] or Accent [RaRo81] than to a uniprocessor operating system. There are, however, fundamental differences. A multicomputer network typically has a greater degree of node connectivity, fewer resources, e.g., secondary storage, at each node, and on average, a shorter lifetime of computational entities. Although these are purely *quantitative* differences, in the aggregate they create a set of *qualitatively* different problems. As an example, Cheriton claims transmission of a 1024 byte message across a 10M-bit Ethernet™ by the V kernel [Cher84] requires about 6 milliseconds. Although this is quite good for distributed applications, e.g., multiple processor programs such as Amaze [BeCh85], it is far too slow to support tightly coupled parallel computation. Why? Because the V kernel protocol is implemented in software, uses no DMA devices for message transmission, and supports a contention-based network (Ethernet)[1]. The appropriate technique for multicomputer networks is, as we saw in chapter four, implementation of simplified, point-to-point communication protocols in hardware, a qualitatively different approach. Two designs that use this approach are the torus routing chip [DaSe86] or the hyperswitch [Mada87].

The qualitative differences between distributed systems and multicomputer networks do not mean that techniques from the former are inapplicable, merely that they often cannot be co-opted without circumspection.

5.1. Overview

Earlier, we alluded to multicomputer operating system support for internode communication, task scheduling, and failure recovery. Chapters three and four considered the first; in this chapter we consider the latter two.

There are two primary approaches to parallel processing and task scheduling on a multicomputer network. In the first, all parallel tasks in a computation are known *a priori*, are statically mapped onto network nodes before the computation is initiated, and remain there throughout the entire computation. This paradigm corresponds naturally to two different software design styles:

- a universal task, and

- a network of communicating tasks.

As an example of the universal task design style, iterative parallel algorithms for solving the Poisson equation [OrVo85]

$$\nabla^2 u = \frac{\partial^2 u}{\partial x^2} + \frac{\partial^2 u}{\partial y^2} = f(x, y)$$

update a regular grid of points.[2] Figure 5.1 illustrates a function over a rectangular domain and an associated discretization grid. After solution, the grid points will collectively represent a discrete approximation of the function.

The value of each grid point is successively updated using values from neighboring points; the algorithm at each point is the same. Thus, it is natural to partition the grid

---

[1]It is ironic that the most successful commercial multicomputer network, the Intel iPSC [Ratt85, Inte86a], uses software protocols and point-to-point Ethernets, and its internode communication is only slightly faster than that of the V kernel.

[2]Chapter seven considers this problem in detail.

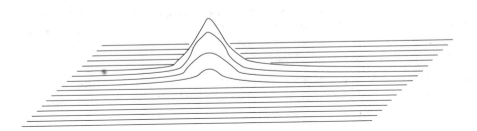

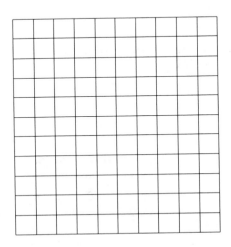

Figure 5.1
Uniform grid for solving partial differential equations.

into blocks and assign each block to an instantiation of the algorithm, a task. Although the tessellated tasks do communicate, the pattern is, by definition, regular. A static scheduling algorithm need only map the (fixed) tessellation of the single task onto the multicomputer network.

Alternatively, one can design a network of communicating tasks similar to that supported by CSP [Hoar78]. The topology of the network of communicating tasks can be arbitrary and irregular, unlike above, and both the amount and frequency of intertask data transfer may vary during the computation. Nevertheless, the number of tasks and their potential communication patterns are known, permitting a static mapping of tasks onto network nodes.

Regardless of the static computing paradigm, either a universal task or a task network, task scheduling is difficult. Indeed, optimal task scheduling that minimizes total execution time is known to be *NP*-complete even for a set of tasks that do *not* communicate [GaJo79].

In the second approach to parallel processing on a multicomputer network, a parallel computation is defined by a dynamically created task precedence graph. New tasks are initiated, existing tasks terminate as the computation unfolds, and the mapping of tasks onto network nodes is done dynamically. Precedence constraints among tasks arise because the initiation of new tasks depends on the completion of prior ones. This dynamic view of computation differs in several significant ways from the static view. In particular,

- the workload varies over time,

- multiple tasks may become eligible for execution given the results from a single task, but most importantly,

- tasks must be dynamically mapped onto network nodes using only partial knowledge of the global system state.

Returning to the partial differential equations example, the regular grid must be fine enough, i.e., contain enough grid points, to capture the behavior of f at its greatest variation. Where the variation is small, considerably less computation is required. Grid refinement techniques [OrVo85] adapt to the variation in f by repeatedly *refining* the grid in appropriate regions. This refinement, shown in figure 5.2, creates new tasks, each containing a new block of grid points, and disrupts the initially regular communication pattern. These new tasks must be dynamically mapped onto processors while simultaneously restricting the communication overhead to acceptable levels.

The static and dynamic views of multicomputer network computation are strikingly different. Not surprisingly, different scheduling techniques are appropriate for each. In

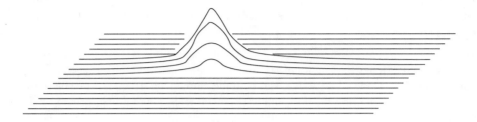

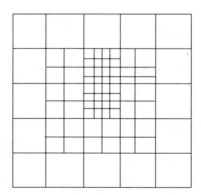

Figure 5.2
Non-uniform grid for solving partial differential equations.

the remainder of this chapter, we successively consider techniques for static scheduling and both the feasibility and potential algorithms for dynamic scheduling. We then consider the fault tolerance issues for multicomputer networks. We conclude with some thoughts on the future directions of multicomputer network operating systems.

5.2. Scheduling Static Tasks

Scheduling a group of tasks with known communication patterns requires only a mapping of the tasks onto network nodes before the computation begins. This mapping can be done *offline* on an ancillary scheduling processor, eliminating many of the information acquisition problems faced when scheduling using the multicomputer network. Even when the intertask communication pattern is known, however, the scheduling problem is still difficult. Usually the task communication pattern does not exactly match the network node connectivity. Portions of the network may already be in use by other computations, e.g., if the network is multiprogrammed, and multiple tasks may be mapped to a single node - causing a local scheduling problem.

The static scheduling problem is not unique to multicomputer networks. It also exists in many other guises, notably: data placement in distributed data base systems [FiHo80, MaRi76] file and resource placement in computer networks [MoLe77], and circuit routing in VLSI designs. Many approaches to its solution have been proposed, including graph theory [Ston77], integer programming [GyEd76], clustering techniques [Will83, Will84], partitioning algorithms [BeBo87], and, more recently, simulated annealing [FlOS86]. Graph theoretic techniques, although helpful for two or three processors, have limited applicability for large networks [Ston77]. Hence, we concentrate on integer programming, clustering techniques, and simulated annealing. Before examining these in detail, however, we formally define the scheduling problem. This formalization follows [CHLE80] and will provide both consistent notation and a means of comparing scheduling techniques. All notation defined below is summarized in table 5.1.

5.2.1. A Formal Model of Static Task Scheduling

Given a set T of m tasks, $\{T_1, T_2, \cdots T_m\}$, hereafter called a *task force*, and a set P of n nodes, $\{P_1, P_2, \cdots P_n\}$, we seek a task scheduling mechanism that assigns each of the m tasks to one of the n nodes. Obviously, if m is greater than n, at least two tasks will be assigned to the same node. Moreover, a task scheduler may opt to place multiple tasks on a single node even if m is less than n.

Table 5.1

Static scheduling notation

Quantity	Definition
$A_{i,j}$	average size of messages exchanged by tasks i and j
C_k	memory capacity of node k
D	matrix of message transmission delays
$d_{j,l}$	delay for message transmission from node j to node l
E_k	execution time limit for node k
$I_{i,j}$	interval between message exchanges by tasks i and j
L_i	average delay (latency) while awaiting messages at node i
M_i	maximum memory requirement of task i
m	number of tasks
N_i	number of tasks communicating with task i
n	number of network nodes
P_i	node (processor) i
S	binary matrix of scheduling decisions
$s_{i,j}$	binary one (true) if task i assigned to node j
Q	matrix of task execution times on potential host nodes
$q_{i,j}$	execution time of task i on node j
T_i	task i
$Td_{i,j}$	message transmission delay between nodes i and j
V	matrix of data transmission amounts between tasks
$v_{i,k}$	amount of data sent from task i to task k
ω	relative weight of computation and communication costs
$X_{i,j}$	count of messages exchanged by tasks i and j

Associated with T and P is a computation time matrix Q

$$Q = \{q_{i,j}\} \qquad i = 1,...,m \quad j = 1,...,n$$

where element $q_{i,j}$ is the execution time of task i on node j. If $q_{i,j} = \infty$, task i is ineligible for execution on node j. A task may have different execution times on different nodes, i.e., variations across a row of Q can occur, because

- the network contains different node types, e.g., special purpose nodes,

- other tasks are already executing on certain nodes, or

- external constraints on resource use have been imposed.

Because constructing the matrix Q requires *a priori* knowledge of task execution times, all or part of the matrix may be unknown.[3]

Task communication is represented by a volume matrix V

$$V = \{v_{i,k}\} \qquad i = 1,...,m \quad k = 1,...,m.$$

where $v_{i,k}$ is the total amount of data sent from task i to task k during their lifetimes. Similarly, the structure of the multicomputer interconnection network is approximated by a distance matrix

$$D = \{d_{j,l}\} \qquad j = 1,...,n \quad l = 1,...,n.$$

The value $d_{j,l}$ is the approximate transmission cost of a unit size message from node j to node l. Obtaining even approximate values for the matrix D requires knowledge of transmission link speeds and potential queueing delays at network nodes. Because the latter depend on the assignment of tasks to nodes, they are normally difficult, if not impossible, to obtain.

A static scheduling algorithm must select a binary matrix **S**, where

$$s_{i,j} = \begin{cases} 1 & \textit{if task } T_i \textit{ is assigned to node } P_j \\ \\ 0 & \textit{otherwise}, \end{cases}$$

---

[3]Pragmatically, this is the rule rather than the exception.

from the set of possible assignments. The complexity of this seemingly simple problem arises from the size of the search space, exponential in n and m.

5.2.2. Static Scheduling Via Integer Programming

The static scheduling problem described above can be cast as an integer programming problem by defining an objective function to be minimized subject to appropriate constraints. Chu [CHLE80] has suggested the following objective function:

minimize $R_0(\mathbf{S})$

where

$$R_0(\mathbf{S}) = \sum_{i=1}^{m}\sum_{j=1}^{n}\left[\omega q_{i,j}s_{i,j} + (1-\omega)\sum_{k=1}^{m}\sum_{l=1}^{n}v_{i,k}d_{j,l}s_{i,j}s_{k,l} \right] \qquad 0 < \omega < 1. \qquad (5.1)$$

The first term of (5.1), $q_{i,j}s_{i,j}$, is just the computation time for a task i on its assigned node j. In the second term, the product $v_{i,k}d_{j,l}$ is the communication delay to send data of total size $v_{i,k}$ from node j to node l. Thus, the second term of (5.1) sums the communication delays across all other tasks that must communicate with task i; recall that $s_{i,j} \neq 0$ if and only if task i has been scheduled on node j. Finally, ω weights the relative importance of computation and communication costs.

Minimizing (5.1) without constraints can lead to infeasible solutions, e.g., the memory of a node can be exceeded. Although the particular constraints imposed depend on the intended application, typical constraints include node memory capacity and execution delay on a single node. Limited node memory is reflected by

$$\sum_{i=1}^{m}M_i s_{i,k} \leq C_k \qquad k = 1,...,n \qquad (5.2)$$

where M_i is the maximum memory requirement of task i and C_k is the memory capacity of node k. This constraint simply says that the memory requirements of all tasks assigned to a node must not exceed its capacity. Similarly, the execution delay on each node can be constrained by

$$\sum_{i=1}^{m}q_{i,k}s_{i,k} \leq E_k \qquad k = 1,...,n \qquad (5.3)$$

where E_k is the limit on execution time for node k.

Combining (5.1), (5.2), and (5.3), the optimization problem becomes

mimimize $R_0(\mathbf{S})$

where

$$R_0(\mathbf{S}) = \sum_{i=1}^{m}\sum_{j=1}^{n}\left[\omega q_{i,j}s_{i,j} + (1-\omega)\sum_{k=1}^{m}\sum_{l=1}^{n}v_{i,k}d_{j,l}s_{i,j}s_{k,l} \right]$$

subject to

$$\sum_{i=1}^{m}M_i s_{i,k} \leq C_k \qquad k = 1,...,n$$

$$\sum_{i=1}^{m}q_{i,k}s_{i,k} \leq E_k \qquad k = 1,...,n.$$

This problem is a non-linear 0-1 integer (the matrix $\mathbf{S}$) programming problem solvable by standard techniques [Chva83]. Unfortunately, casting the scheduling problem in a form suitable for integer programming has several liabilities, notably computational expense. Scheduling even ten tasks via this method can take minutes of processing time on a high-speed computer. Although this overhead can be mitigated by precomputing solutions for important problem classes, it precludes use of integer programming in an environment where task forces have short lifetimes.

The absence of precedence relations is a far more critical shortcoming than computational expense. Typically, not all tasks in a task force execute concurrently; some await completion of other tasks while others await messages. In the former case, the tasks may be assigned to a single node without loss of concurrency. In the latter case, the frequency of communication is as important as the volume of data sent because waiting times increase with the number of message transmissions.

Finally, the crude model of communication afforded by the D and V matrices is a severe limitation. The communication delay in sending a message to another node is really a function of the task mapping, i.e., D is more properly a function of the mapping S. Moreover, values for D also depend on the frequency and size of messages sent, not just the total amount of data transmitted. Unfortunately, there is no accurate, non-empirical way to obtain values for D. Task forces already present in the network introduce additional variation in D, further exacerbating the difficulties.

In short, integer programming techniques have several important limitations. They are potentially valuable if the same computation is run repeatedly; communication delay estimates can then be acquired, allowing improved task mappings for successive executions. Otherwise, they are best suited to small task forces of long duration. As we shall see, approximation techniques based on task clustering and simulated annealing are more promising, both in reduced overhead and greater adaptability. However, these approximation techniques have limitations as well.

5.2.3. Static Scheduling Via Clustering

Casting the static scheduling problem as a mathematical optimization problem is artificial, omitting several important aspects of the problem to make solution tractable. Rather than tailor the problem definition to a mathematical technique, it is more natural to begin with problem characteristics and develop a mapping algorithm. Following this approach, Williams [Will83] has developed one set of task scheduling algorithms that not only cluster tasks and balance the workload across nodes, but also select an appropriate number of nodes and assign clusters to those nodes. These algorithms are iterative, rapidly giving near optimal task mappings.

As Williams [Will83] and others have noted, the operating continuum for scheduling algorithms is delimited by two extremes:

• message delays approaching zero

• extremely large message delays.

In the first case, the optimum assignment clusters and assigns tasks to balance the load over all available nodes. In the second, all tasks are assigned to the fastest node. Within this continuum, there are several conflicting optimization axes: load balancing, minimizing interprocessor communication, task clustering, and minimizing node loadings. Optimizing along any one of these axes leads to a non-optimal solution. Only when they are considered in concert can a satisfactory mapping be achieved. The first three axes are clear, but the latter is less intuitive. If tasks consist of compute-communicate cycles, several of these tasks should be assigned to each node. This reduces a node's idle periods when all its assigned tasks are awaiting messages. How many tasks should be assigned to each node depends on expected communication delays; large delays encourage use of fewer nodes, and smaller delays allow use of additional nodes. Simply put, using more nodes does *not* always imply reduced execution time.

As we noted earlier, the size and frequency of messages is more important than the volume of data transmitted. We let $X_{i,j}$ denote the number of messages *exchanged* by tasks i and j; see table 5.1 for a summary of notation. By assumption, $X_{i,j} = X_{j,i}$.

Similarly, $A_{i,j}$ denotes the average size of messages sent between tasks i and j. Clearly, the volume of traffic from task i to j is

$$v_{i,j} = X_{i,j} A_{i,j}.$$

We define $I_{i,j}$, the *average* processing interval between message transmission or receipt by task i on node j, as

$$I_{i,j} = \frac{execution\ time}{messages\ exchanged} = \frac{q_{i,j}}{\sum_{k=1}^{m} X_{i,k}}$$

Finally, define $Td_{i,j}$ as the transmission delay, excluding queueing, to send a unit of data from node i to node j. Then the delay incurred by a task while waiting for receipt of a message at node i is approximately

$$L_i = \min_{\substack{1 \le j \le n \\ i \le j}} Td_{j,i} \frac{\sum_{k'} A_{l,k}}{|k'|}$$

where

$$k' = \{k \mid 1 \le k, l \le m \text{ and } s_{k,i} = 1 \text{ and } s_{l,i} = 0 \text{ and } X_{k,l} \ne 0\}$$

and $|k'|$ is the number of elements in k'. Intuitively, k' is just the set of tasks not scheduled on node i that send messages to i. Informally, this delay to receive a message is approximated by the product of transmission delay and average message size for tasks not scheduled on i. Although this approximation can seriously underestimate the expected delay, only a trial execution of the program can provide accurate estimates.

Using these definitions, one can introduce the two constraints that any task mapping must satisfy: load balancing and minimum processing. The load balancing constraint for each node is

$$\sum_{i=1}^{m} q_{i,j} s_{i,j} \le Load \qquad 1 \le j \le n, \tag{5.4}$$

where *Load* is an adaptive bound on the amount of work to be assigned to each node. Similarly, each node should be assigned enough tasks to prevent excessive idle time while awaiting receipt of messages. This constraint is represented by

$$\sum_{i=1}^{m} I_{i,j} s_{i,j} > L_j \qquad 1 \leq j \leq n. \tag{5.5}$$

If $I_{i,j}$ is viewed as the "time slice" given to task j between message transmission or receipt, the constraint requires the sum of the time slices for all tasks assigned to a node to exceed the average message delay. Intuitively, each node needs sufficient work to prevent large idle times when awaiting messages, but not so much work that it is overloaded.

Given these two constraints, the load balancing heuristic operates in two stages, initialization and iterative assignment. Each is described below.

5.2.3.1. Initialization

Before iteratively assigning tasks to nodes, both the tasks and the nodes are ranked. This determines the selection order for task assignment and use of nodes. Tasks are ranked in decreasing order of the product of the total number of message transmissions or receipts *and* the number of logical neighbors.

$$\sum_{j=1}^{m} X_{i,j} N_j \qquad 1 \leq i \leq m$$

where N_j is the number of tasks communicating with task j. Similarly, nodes are ranked in decreasing order of speed (if applicable) and speed of their communication links (also if applicable). Thus, tasks requiring the most communication and nodes with the best performance are considered first. See [Will83] for further details.

5.2.3.2. Iterative Task Assignment

With the initialization described above, the heuristic repeatedly

- assigns enough tasks to one node to satisfy the minimum processing constraint (5.5),

- assigns additional tasks to the same node as long as the load balancing constraint (5.4) remains satisfied,

- selects a new node *nearest* the previous node, i.e., having minimal communication delay, and repeats the first two steps.

If all nodes have been filled, i.e., their load balancing constraints are met, the *Load* for each node is incremented, the current task assignment is discarded, and the iteration is repeated. Figure 5.3 summarizes this algorithm.

```
procedure Static;

   order tasks and processors;
   initialize Load;
   select initial_processor and initial_task;

   repeat
      current_processor := initial_processor;
      current_task := next_task (current_processor);

      repeat
            while (more_tasks_to_map and all_processors_not_full)) and
               (processing constraint for current_processor not satisfied)
               do begin
                  assign current_task to current_processor;
                  current_task := next_task (current_processor);
               end;

            while (more_tasks_to_map and all_processors_not_full)) and
               (load balance constraint for current_processor not satisfied)
               do begin
                  assign current_task to current_processor;
                  current_task := next_task (current_processor);
               end;

         if (current_task > 0) and (current_processor > 0) then
            begin
               mark current_processor full;
               current_processor := next_processor (current_processor);
            end;

         until (current_task = 0) or (current_processor = 0);

         if (all_processors_full) then
            increment Load;

   until (current_task = 0);

end; (* Static *)
```

Figure 5.3
Static task scheduling heuristic.

As an example, figure 5.4 shows a tree of tasks and the task assignment generated by the clustering heuristic for a 4×4 mesh of nodes. In the figure, the frequency of message exchange is shown on the arcs connecting tasks. By assumption, all tasks had the same computation requirement, and the ratio of node processing speed to link transmission rate was 10:1, i.e., the nodes are ten times as fast as the links.

As figure 5.4 shows, the heuristic places the four tasks with the most frequent communication on a single node. This is a consequence of the assumed (high) cost of communication. Moreover, the node selected for clustering was in the "center" of the mesh and had the greatest number of connections to other nodes. The remaining tasks were then clustered about the initial placement.

Although preferable to the mathematical programming approach, this heuristic shares many of the former's problems, notably the types and amounts of data required. For example, the expected time between message transmissions and the total execution time of tasks are rarely known *a priori*. In their absence, estimates must be used, limiting the effectiveness of the resulting schedule.

5.2.4. Static Scheduling Via Simulated Annealing

Simulated annealing has been widely touted as the method of choice for identifying the global minimum of a function with many local minima [KiGV83]. Although it cannot locate the global minimum of an arbitrary function exactly, it can approximate the minimum as closely as computational resources permit.

Simulated annealing is a mathematical analog of cooling. If a liquid is cooled rapidly, the crystals of the resulting solid will have many imperfections. These imperfections correspond to an energy state higher than the minimal energy state of a perfect crystal. If the liquid were cooled more slowly, fewer imperfections would develop, and the resulting crystal would be closer to the ideal, minimum energy state. In the limiting case, the cooling interval is infinite, the final temperature is absolute zero, the crystal is perfect, and all molecular motion ceases.

Just as natural annealing reduces an object's energy state during some interval, simulated annealing associates a "temperature" and a cooling interval with a function to be minimized. Longer cooling intervals typically yield smaller function values and require more exhaustive searches of the function domain. A naive minimization technique would select an initial point in the function domain and randomly vary the values of the function's independent variables, accepting all variations that reduce the function value. If the possible variations span the entire function domain and sufficient time is allocated to the search, this random search is guaranteed to converge to the global minimum, albeit at great computational expense.

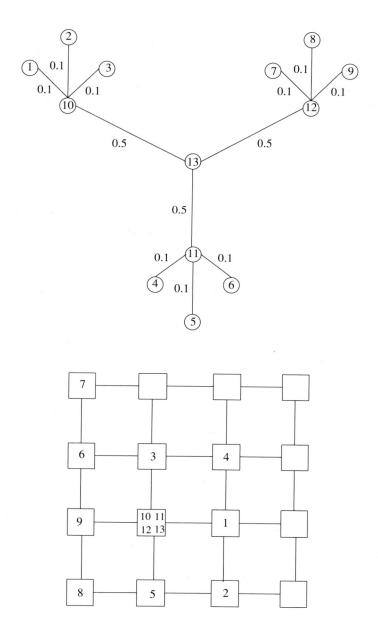

Figure 5.4
Static scheduling via clustering.

The efficiency of random search can be improved by accepting some changes in independent variables that *increase* the function value. This counterintuitive notion is the heart of the Metropolis Monte Carlo method [MRRT53]. Specifically, all random changes that reduce the function value are accepted, and any that increase the function value by ΔS are accepted with probability

$$e^{\frac{-\Delta S}{T}}$$

where T is the temperature. As the temperature decreases, the probability of selecting larger function values decreases.

Metropolis *et al.* showed that if the probability of moving from point i to point j in the function domain is the same as moving from point j to point i,[4] the **detailed balance criterion**, the probability density function for selecting points in the parameter space is the Boltzmann distribution. In statistical mechanics, this implies that the long-term mean of any quantity is equal to the thermodynamic average of the quantity at the chosen temperature. In the limiting case, a temperature of absolute zero constrains the thermodynamic range to a single minimum value. In layman's terms, the Metropolis Monte Carlo method is an exact mathematical analog of cooling. If the temperature is slowly reduced to zero while applying the Metropolis method, the method must converge to the global minimum of function.

5.2.4.1. A Sample Problem

Although it is possible to discuss simulated annealing in the abstract [KiGV83], it is more intuitive and instructive to consider its application to a specific load balancing problem. As an example, consider a metal plate with two bolt holes and a slot between the holes, shown in figure 5.5. Now consider the effect of a crack along the slot if the plate is subjected to forces orthogonal to the crack. In §5.1, we noted that iterative solution of partial differential equations often requires refinement of the iteration grid near regions of rapid function variation (see figure 5.2). A similar situation exists with the numerical solution of this stress problem via finite elements[5] [Adam82]. Near the crack in the plate, the mesh of finite elements must be very fine to capture the stress characteristics. If the plate were partitioned into regions of equal area, and each region were assigned to a processor, a small number of processors would receive most of the

---

[4]The probability of *choosing* moves is not related to the probability of *accepting* moves.

[5]Finite element methods tessellate the problem domain with small polygons, e.g., triangles, and iteratively calculate the stress interactions among these elements.

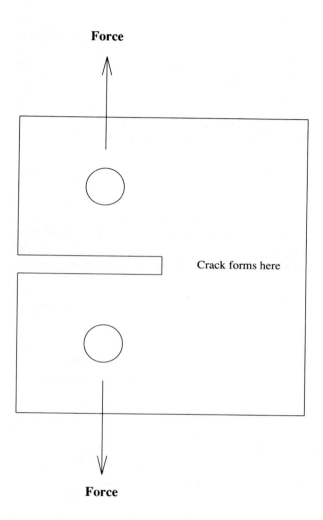

Figure 5.5
Metal plate with lateral forces.

computation, and the resulting load imbalance would be severe. The problem is simple, but deceptively difficult: partition the mesh into areas of equal computation cost and assign these areas to the nodes of a multicomputer network while minimizing internode communication costs.

5.2.4.2. Minimization Criterion

For the sample problem, Flower *et al.* [FlOS86] proposed the optimization criterion

$$S = S_{calc} + S_{comm} = \sum_{i=1}^{N} W_i^2 + \frac{t_{comm}}{t_{calc}} \sum_{p<q} C_{pq} \tag{5.6}$$

where N is the number of multicomputer nodes, W_i is the computation load on node i, C_{pq} is the communication overhead between finite elements p and q given their current node assignment,[6] t_{comm} is the mean time to exchange information between two finite elements, and t_{calc} is the mean number of floating point operations per finite element. Because the function

$$\sum_{i=1}^{N} W_i^2$$

is minimized when all W_i are equal, the first term of (5.6) reflects the goal of equally distributing the workload across all nodes. The second term of (5.6) represents the communication cost of the mesh partitioning.

The ratio t_{comm}/t_{calc} reflects the relative costs of internode communication and computation. If the ratio is large, the second (communication) term of (5.6) will dominate the cost of trial mesh partitions, and the simulated annealing will minimize the internode communication cost at the possible expense of computation load balance. Conversely, if internode communication is much faster than computation, the annealing will minimize the computation load imbalance even if the interpartition communication is large. Intuitively, the ratio t_{comm}/t_{calc} is a scale factor that determines the relative importance of computation balance and communication delays in execution time. Small ratios favor computation balance; large ratios favor minimal communication.

---

[6] If the finite elements p and q are assigned to the same multicomputer node, the communication overhead is zero.

5.2.4.3. Algorithm Implementation

Given the optimization function in (5.6), a single iteration of the simulated annealing algorithm consists of the following five steps for each finite element in the mesh:

- Temporarily move a finite element from its current multicomputer node to a different node, creating a new mesh partitioning.

- Calculate the change ΔS in the minimization criterion S.

- If $\Delta S < 0$, i.e., the change reduced the value of S, discard the old mesh partitioning and accept the new one.

- If $\Delta S > 0$, accept the new partitioning with probability $e^{-\frac{\Delta S}{T}}$.

- Discard the new partitioning if it is rejected.

The inputs to this algorithm include an initial mesh partitioning, an initial temperature T, and a schedule for varying the temperature over time.

Flower *et al.* [FlOS86] examined four possible initial mesh partitionings for the sample finite element problem: random, single node, list, and grid. With random partitioning, all elements of the mesh were distributed randomly across nodes. Similarly, single node partitioning placed all elements on a single node. List partitioning grouped elements canonically, e.g., by rows or columns, and assigned each group to a node. With grid partitioning, the elements were divided into bins of equal size, and each bin was assigned to a node (e.g., see figure 5.1). The choice of initial partitioning not only affects the annealing convergence rate, but also the final placement of elements. The more nearly the initial partitioning approximates the optimal partitioning, the greater the probability that a finite number of annealing steps will approach the true optimum.

The choice of initial temperature and the number of iterations between temperature changes is problem dependent and appropriate choices can only be determined empirically. The value of a particular placement can only be verified by annealing with multiple temperatures, iteration counts, and cooling schedules. This is a major limitation of simulated annealing.

5.2.4.4. Experiments

With $t_{comm}/t_{calc} = 1$ and an initial temperature $T = 1$, Flower *et al.* observed that all four of the initial mesh partitionings approached the minimum value of the minimization criterion S within ten annealing iterations. Because finite elements are computationally indistinguishable, assigning an equal number to each node is much simpler than balancing the communication load. Hence, the annealing balanced the computation load much more quickly than the communication load. Further analysis showed that many iterations were needed before the communication differences between initial placements disappeared. The small value of t_{comm}/t_{calc} masked these differences, emphasizing computation balance.

Table 5.2 shows the load balance achieved after 200 iterations with different combinations of temperature and computation/communication ratio. In the table, computation time is normalized to the minimum for the problem, i.e., $S_{calc}=1$ implies exact computation balance. Except for very large values of the ratio t_{comm}/t_{calc}, simulated annealing achieves near perfect computation balance. When this ratio is large, computation balance is less important given the (assumed) fast internode communication. Of the initial mesh partitionings, the grid is clearly superior to all others. This is not surprising; it most nearly reflects the logical contiguity of the finite elements.

5.2.4.5. General Observations

Experiments have shown that simulated annealing can quickly solve optimization problems of many variables [KiGV83], including static scheduling problems. Simulated annealing produces an assignment of tasks to nodes, given a minimization criterion and associated task parameters such as task computation times and amount of task communication. Simulated annealing's major limitations are the need for these task parameters and the empirical selection of both a temperature and an annealing schedule. The first limitation is shared with integer programming and task clustering. For data partitioning problems where the "tasks" are clusters of grid points or finite elements, the computation and communication costs can be estimated accurately. For arbitrary networks of communicating tasks, these costs are seldom known. The second limitation is philosophically troublesome but pragmatically unimportant. Experience and testing can identify appropriate temperatures and annealing schedules with only a modicum of overhead. Despite these limitations, simulated annealing is the static scheduling method of choice.

5.3. Scheduling Dynamic Tasks

Many multicomputer network algorithms create new tasks as they execute. Although it is possible for a *single* processor to assign dynamically created tasks to multicomputer network nodes, efficiency considerations make this impractical for large multicomputer networks. Thus, unlike static tasks, dynamically created tasks must be assigned to network nodes in real time by a distributed scheduling algorithm executing on the

Table 5.2

Simulated annealing experiments

Initial Placement	Temperature (T)	$\dfrac{t_{comm}}{t_{calc}}$	Normalized S_{calc}	S_{comm}
Single node	1.0	1.0	1.0040	617.0
	0.5	2.0	1.0002	592.0
	0.1	10.0	1.0180	488.0
	0.01	100.0	2.8262	358.0
Random	1.0	1.0	1.0004	663.0
	0.5	2.0	1.0002	592.3
	0.1	10.0	1.0016	600.0
	0.01	100.0	1.0004	556.0
List	1.0	1.0	1.0040	582.6
	0.5	2.0	1.0002	592.3
	0.1	10.0	1.0001	728.0
	0.01	100.0	1.0015	820.0
Grid	1.0	1.0	1.0004	578.2
	0.5	2.0	1.0020	423.4
	0.1	10.0	1.0089	422.0
	0.01	100.0	1.8000	326.0

multicomputer network. Not surprisingly, this scheduling problem is considerably more difficult than the already difficult static scheduling problem and published results are few [vanT81a, vanT81b, vanT84, BrFi81, Reed84, Bade86]. Its solution has, until recently, been further exacerbated by the paucity of multicomputer network test beds.

Algorithms for dynamic task scheduling can be classified as either placement or migration schemes. A **task placement algorithm** assigns tasks to nodes before the tasks begin execution, and all tasks execute where placed even if moving tasks might later reduce the load imbalance. In contrast, a **task migration algorithm** can move tasks after their initial placement. Although migration algorithms might seem superior, they must move the (potentially large) task execution state. Hence, the superiority of placement or migration depends intimately on the structure of the parallel computation.

Maintaining a consistent self-model is difficult in a multicomputer network, making even the feasibility of dynamic task scheduling suspect. Fortunately, a recent study has firmly established the efficacy of dynamic scheduling under worst case conditions [Reed84]. Although important, this study did not propose specific algorithms for solving the dynamic scheduling problem. Keller and Lin have, in turn, developed a gradient model of dynamic scheduling that transfers excess tasks to idle nodes via a *gradient plane* [Lin85]. An older algorithm, proposed by Bryant and Finkel [BrFi81] also distributes tasks to idle nodes. However, it obtains task behavior information by allowing them to begin execution before they are moved, a source of considerable overhead.[7]

Both Keller and Lin's and Bryant and Finkel's algorithms are fully distributed and stable. Stability, a notion pertinent only to task migration algorithms, means that a task does not continually migrate through the network without accomplishing any useful work. Its nearest analog in traditional operating systems is *thrashing*, where the majority of processor time is devoted to moving pages of virtual memory to and from secondary storage.

Van Tilborg and Wittie [vanT81a, vanT81b, vanT84] have also proposed and analyzed a distributed task scheduling algorithm. Unlike the other algorithms, which schedule individual tasks as they are created, the Van Tilborg algorithm schedules *task forces*, i.e., groups of interacting tasks. Because of this, the algorithm, although fully distributed, lies somewhere near the center of the spectrum between static and dynamic scheduling. Similarly, Baden's data partitioning algorithm [Bade86] periodically repartitions the task data allocation, e.g., after a grid refinement in a partial differential equations solver. These quasi-dynamic scheduling algorithms are applicable to only a subset of all problems. Before considering any of these scheduling algorithms, we return to the feasibility study, which shows *why* these algorithms are effective.

5.3.1. A Feasibility Study of Dynamic Scheduling

To investigate the feasibility of dynamic scheduling,[8] a model of dynamic task creation is needed. One such model is the dynamic task precedence graph. The tasks of such a graph are created and destroyed, subject to certain constraints, as the computation proceeds, and the dynamic scheduling algorithm maps this graph onto multicomputer

---

[7]This can be viewed as a degenerate migration algorithm that initially places all tasks at their creation point.

[8]This work originally appeared in the *Proceedings of the 1983 International Conference on Parallel Processing* [Reed83b]. A revised version appeared in *IEEE Transactions on Computers* [Reed84].

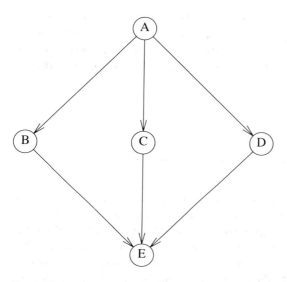

Figure 5.6
Precedence constraints for a simple graph.

network nodes. Clearly, the *structure* of the graph, i.e., the dynamic pattern of task creation and communication, determines both the potential network parallelism and the number of options available to a scheduling algorithm. For example, a broad, deep precedence graph affords much more parallelism and more task assignment choices than a very narrow graph. Examining the way these differences affect network performance requires a precise definition of a task precedence graph and a set of simulation experiments capable of quantifying the effects. These topics are the subject of this section.

5.3.1.1. Task Precedence Graphs

A precedence graph, illustrated in figure 5.6, represents a computation as a series of dependencies. Each node corresponds to a task and each arc represents a dependency. The results of all computations providing input to a task, its antecedents, must exist before the task is eligible for execution. In the figure, the evaluation of antecedent tasks B, C, and D must complete before the evaluation of task E can begin.

In each precedence graph, three types of tasks can be distinguished: fork tasks, join tasks, and regular tasks. A *fork* task has a single antecedent task and one or more consequent tasks; it represents the computation preparatory to initiation of parallel subtasks to solve a problem. A *join* task has one or more antecedent tasks and a single consequent task; it represents the combination of subproblem solutions to yield a solution to an entire problem. Finally, a *regular* task is any task that is not a fork or join task; it represents a simple computation. If we interpret the juxtaposition *AB* of tasks to mean ''*A* is an antecedent of *B* '', a task precedence graph can be formally defined by the following grammar.

<precedence graph> ::= *<regular task>* |

<fork task> <precedence graph>$^+$ <join task>

As illustrated in figure 5.7 and summarized in table 5.3, the characteristics of a precedence graph are determined by several parameters. Because the number of possible graph parameterizations is so large, we have somewhat arbitrarily selected a set of values, given in table 5.4, to be used as a reference point in this study. By systematically varying subsets of these parameters, we obtain different performance results. By comparing these results to those obtained using the reference parameters, we can estimate the effect of the variations.

5.3.1.2. Simulation Methodology

Given the computational expense of simulation, we limited our study to four interconnection networks that earlier analysis[9] had shown to have relatively good performance:

- 2-D spanning bus hypercube,

- 2-D torus,

- cube-connected cycles, and

- 2-ary N-cube.

To determine the performance degradation attributable to partially connected networks, we have also included the completely connected network.

For comparative purposes, we generated 25 task precedence graphs using the reference parameters shown in table 5.4. All service times were drawn from negative exponential distributions, the number of consequents of each fork task was uniformly distributed between B_{min} and B_{max}, and all graphs were constrained to have between

---

[9]See chapter two.

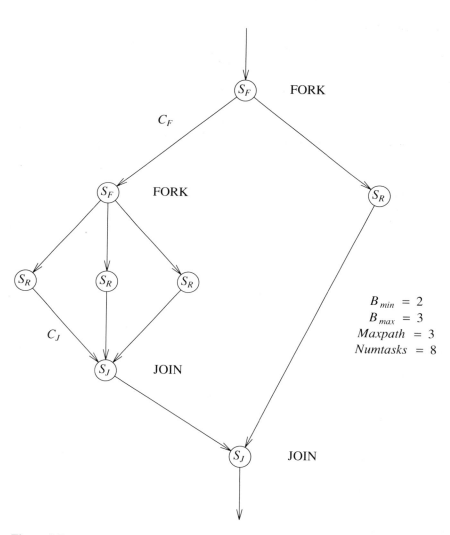

Figure 5.7
Illustration of precedence graph parameters.

Table 5.3
Precedence graph parameters

Quantity	Definition
B_{min}	minimum number of consequents of a fork task
B_{max}	maximum number of consequents of a fork task
C_F	mean data communication time to initiate a fork or regular task
C_J	mean data communication time to initiate a join task
$Maxpath$	maximum length path through the graph
$Numtasks$	number of tasks in the graph
S_F	mean fork task service time
S_R	mean regular task service time
S_J	mean join task service time

Table 5.4
Reference values for precedence graph parameters

Quantity	Value
B_{min}	1
B_{max}	4
C_F , C_J	1
$Maxpath$	60
$Maxtasks$	1024
S_F , S_R , S_J	10

Maxtasks/2 and *Maxtasks* tasks. Unless otherwise stated, we assumed that a task eligible for execution was scheduled on the idle node nearest its location. Finally, we scaled the mean data communication times by the number of link connections to each node to represent the fixed communication bandwidth of the nodes.

The average speedup S_p attained when evaluating a precedence graph on a network is the measure of performance. This speedup is

$$S_p = \frac{\sum_{i=1}^{Numtasks} S_i}{parallel\ execution\ time} \qquad where\ \ S_i\ \in\ \{S_F, S_R, S_J\}$$

and shows how many times faster the precedence graph executes on the multicomputer network than on a uniprocessor.

5.3.1.3. Simulation Experiments

Using the assumptions discussed above, we explored five different variations of precedence graph parameters and network characteristics and their effects on network performance:

● precedence graph structure,

● the event horizon of a distributed task scheduler,

● the maximum task branching factor,

● the mean computation time/communication time ratio, and

● the number of network nodes.

Each of these variations is discussed below; we conclude with some general observations.

Precedence Graph Structure

Figure 5.8 shows the average speedup when each of the 25 graphs derived from the reference graph parameters was simulated on the five networks with 64 nodes; table 5.5 shows the average speedup over the set of graphs using each network.

Two features of figure 5.8 are of particular interest. The first is that networks other than the complete connection exhibit the same performance trends from one precedence graph to another. This suggests that something inherent to the graphs is affecting the time required for their evaluation. To determine what this might be, we examined two precedence graphs, numbers nine and eleven in the figure, that

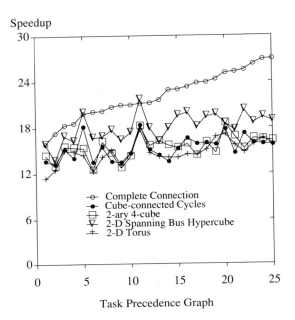

Figure 5.8
Average speedup for 64 node networks
using the precedence graph parameters.

Table 5.5
Average speedup
using precedence graph parameters

Network	Average parallelism	Fraction of complete connection
Complete Connection	22.17	1.00
Cube-connected Cycles	15.33	0.69
2-ary 4-cube	15.42	0.70
2-D Spanning Bus Hypercube	18.04	0.81
2-D Torus	14.75	0.67

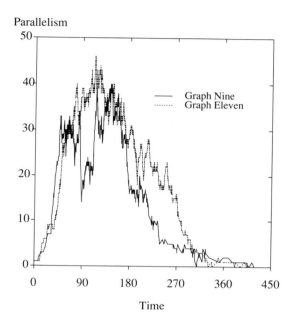

Parallelism

Figure 5.9

Time varying parallelism for two
precedence graphs on a 64 node torus.

represented two extremes of behavior. Figure 5.9 shows the time varying parallelism
when the two graphs were evaluated on a 2-D torus with 64 nodes. The simulation of
precedence graph nine exhibits a striking decrease in the number of parallel tasks near
simulated time 90. Because a similar simulation on the complete connection exhibits
no such decrease, we can only conclude that this variation is caused by a bottleneck in
the communication network during the collapse of a parallel subgraph, requiring the
communication of many results across communication links.

Figure 5.9 illustrates the constraints imposed by limited communication capacity. If
the underlying communication network cannot support the communication transients
created by parallel execution of task subgraphs, then either the level of parallelism must
be reduced or logically adjacent tasks must be scheduled with greater proximity.

The time required to evaluate a single precedence graph can vary considerably even
if no other computation is being performed in the network. As discussed earlier, a task
eligible for execution is scheduled on the nearest idle node. If more than one such node
is available, a single node is selected at random from among them. Different sequences

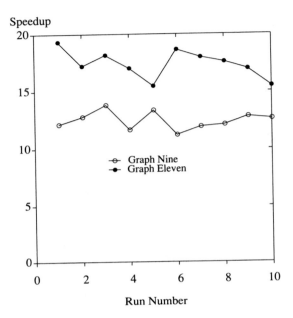

Figure 5.10

Variation in speedup due to scheduling decisions.

of choices can result in the placement of entire subgraphs in different parts of the network, causing increased communication delays.[10] This is illustrated in figure 5.10 for precedence graphs nine and eleven when they were evaluated ten times on the 2-D torus. The efficacy of this randomized scheduling is discussed in the next section.

Figure 5.8 also shows the performance differential between the spanning bus hypercube and the networks with dedicated links. Although this behavior may appear somewhat anomalous in light of the analytic results of chapter two, this is not the case. A detailed examination of the simulation results shows that tasks are scheduled for execution on nodes near their point of origin. In other words, the precedence graph evaluation exhibits considerable communication locality. For this communication pattern and the ratio of computation time to communication time for tasks, the utilization of the communication links is low. Because of this, the buses of the

---

[10]A scheduler that included task dependencies in its decision procedure should reduce this variation.

spanning bus hypercube permit more rapid distribution of tasks to other nodes than the dedicated links of the other networks. With a smaller ratio of task computation time to task communication time, this advantage disappears, showing the greater communication capacity of networks with dedicated communication links.

Event Horizon of a Distributed Scheduler

Heretofore we have assumed that a task scheduler always possesses complete knowledge of the global network state. In practice, only limited information is available and is often inaccurate by the time it is received from distant nodes.

To determine a scheduler's operation given partial knowledge, we postulated the existence of an *event horizon* for each network node. We assume the scheduler at each node has complete knowledge of network activity for all nodes within its event horizon but no knowledge of network activity at any other nodes. Finally, we assume that the scheduler must assign all eligible tasks to nodes within its event horizon. Figure 5.11 shows the average speedup as a function of the distance to the event horizon from a node when the precedence graph parameters of table 5.4 are used.[11] If the event horizon is too small, the probability that a scheduler can find an idle node is low, and the degree of parallelism is unnecessarily constrained. Conversely, if the event horizon is too large, the increased probability of finding idle nodes is offset by the increased cost of data migration and communication. Given sufficient state information, it is often better to reduce communication costs by scheduling some tasks sequentially.

Similar results arise when the ratio of computation times to communication times varies between 1:1 and 100:1. Based on this limited evidence, it appears that state knowledge of nodes within a *small* distance from each source node suffices.

Two final observations are appropriate. First, this dynamic scheduling strategy does *not* use the precedence graph structure to aid its decisions. Although optimal distributed scheduling is known to be *NP*-complete [GaJo79], it should be possible to design heuristics that take advantage of some graph specific information. Van Tilborg and Wittie [vanT81a, vanT81b] have obtained some promising preliminary results for hierarchical distributed schedulers that attempt to map subgraphs onto a small group of adjacent nodes. Unfortunately, the algorithm requires the subgraphs to be known *a priori*, and the tasks must represent a sufficiently large amount of computation to justify the nontrivial overhead required for scheduling. For scheduling dynamically created tasks of the size expected in mini-max game tree searches [Baud78] or distributed finite element problem solvers [SmLo82], Lin [Lin85] has proposed another heuristic.

---

[11]Note that in figure 5.11, the 2-D spanning bus hypercube has a network diameter of only two.

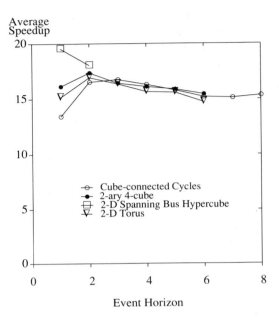

Figure 5.11
Average speedup for 64 node networks
with varying scheduler information.

Second, the acquisition of state information from nodes within an event horizon is decidedly more difficult for bus-connected networks than for those using dedicated communication links. This is primarily because so many more nodes are within a small number of bus crossings from a source node. Communicating state information to other nodes on the same bus could conceivably consume a significant portion of the available communication bandwidth.

Task Branching Factors

The average number of fork task consequents is a measure of the rapidity with which the computation is subdivided into independent tasks. If this division is done too slowly, the computation will not achieve sufficient parallelism to effectively use all of the network nodes. On the other hand, if tasks subdivide too quickly, they may not be able to diffuse through the network rapidly enough to find available nodes. If the average number of fork task consequents is greater than the number of link connections to each node, some tasks will be *forced* to wait for access to a communication link

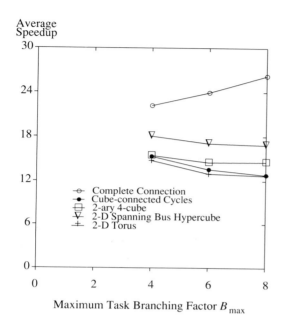

Figure 5.12

Average speedup for 64 node networks
with varying maximum branching factors.

before being scheduled on another node. Therefore, finding an acceptable task branching factor is an important consideration.

Figure 5.12 shows average speedup as a function of B_{max}, the maximum number of fork task consequents. Although the performance of the complete connection increases as B_{max} increases, no such gain is seen for partially connected networks. One should be somewhat chary about drawing general conclusions from such a paucity of data, but it is doubtful that branching factors much greater than the connectivity of a network are of great value.

Mean Ratio of Computation to Communication Time

Figure 5.13 shows the effect of increasing the ratio of computation time to communication time for tasks. As expected, the average speedup increases as each task represents more useful computation. Similarly, figure 5.14 illustrates network performance as a function of the number of nodes.

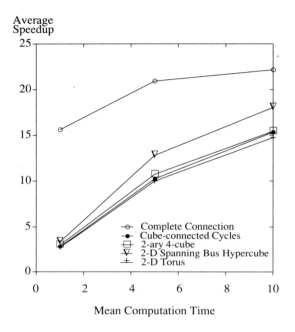

Figure 5.13

Average speedup for 64 node networks
with unit communication time.

5.3.1.4. General Observations

For small, dynamically created tasks and a limited number of nodes, the spanning bus hypercube appears to have better performance than the dedicated link networks. Why? Because it can diffuse work more rapidly. Clearly, the selection of a particular network must be made with knowledge of communication patterns and task sizes required by an algorithm. For larger problems and networks, the dedicated link networks are clearly superior.

Finally, and most importantly, dynamic task scheduling using only locally available information seems feasible for the class of algorithms represented by precedence graphs of the type we have discussed. Realizing the potential of dynamic scheduling algorithms is non-trivial. The remainder of this chapter examines proposed dynamic scheduling algorithms and evaluates their viability.

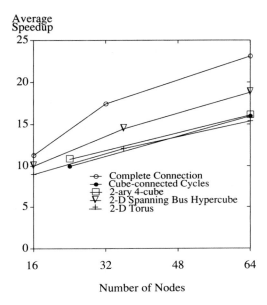

Figure 5.14
Average speedup for varying size networks.

5.3.2. Dynamic Scheduling Via Gradient Planes

Reed's study [Reed84], discussed in the previous section, established both the viability of distributed, dynamic scheduling, and the salient features of such schedulers:

- use of local status information,

- preference of nodes near the point of task creation, and

- stability, i.e., avoidance of processor thrashing.

However, this study did not propose specific algorithms. Following this lead, Lin and Keller [Lin85] recently proposed and analyzed a class of distributed scheduling algorithms, based on gradient planes, for the small tasks of parallel functional programs. During the lifetime of such a program, many hundreds or thousands of tasks are created. Each task is independent of all others, producing a result that is consumed by a single recipient task.

In the gradient plane algorithm, an idle node requests tasks from its immediate neighbors, those nodes directly connected to it. If a neighboring node has excess tasks awaiting execution, it transfers a task to the idle node. Otherwise, the request for tasks is modified and propagated to more distant nodes. Intuitively, an idle node creates a computation well into which extra tasks from other nodes flow.

5.3.2.1. Creating Gradient Planes

If tasks are to migrate from busy nodes to idle ones, a mechanism for creating and maintaining computation wells about idle nodes is needed; the gradient plane is one such mechanism. A *potential*, based on busyness, is associated with each node. Idle nodes, being least busy, have the lowest potential, and excess tasks flow along gradients to these nodes.

Defining the potential of each node does not suffice to create gradients known to all nodes. If the system is homogeneous, i.e., all nodes have equal computational power, one *can* form a gradient plane by defining the potential of each node as its distance to the nearest idle node. In this case, it is natural to view potential merely as proximity to idle nodes. Nodes with a low potential are near idle nodes and attract tasks from other nodes with high potentials.

Informally, proximity is determined by propagation of requests for work. If an idle node requests work from its neighbors, they transfer excess tasks if possible. Failing that, each neighboring node updates its proximity function to one, indicating it is adjacent to an idle node, and sends its updated proximity value to *its* neighbors. In this way, proximity information exchange between neighboring nodes establishes a system-wide gradient plane. If any node discovers that it has excess work and one of its neighbors has a smaller proximity function, it will transfer a task to that neighbor. By repeating this process, tasks move along gradients to idle nodes. This proximity function approach has several virtues:

- A node's proximity function is its network status.

- Based on the status of other nodes, the proximity function can be a request for work.

- As we shall see, a proximity function is a minimum distance routing pointer for load balancing.

- The load balancing is self-limiting. If all nodes are busy, gradients disappear and tasks are no longer transferred. This avoids unnecessary task movements when the system is busy.

5.3.2.2. The Gradient Plane Algorithm

Lin's implementation of gradient planes [Lin85] uses a two-tiered algorithm. First, each node determines its local state: *abundant*, *neutral*, or *idle*. *Abundant* nodes have excess, migratable tasks, *idle* nodes have too few tasks, and *neutral* nodes are neither abundant nor idle. These states are determined by evaluating a *pressure function* at each node. As an example, each node might evaluate the function

$$Pint\ (id) = sizeof\ (job\ queue)$$

$$+ \frac{ScaleFactor}{1 - memory\ utilization}.$$

The pressure of a node, its willingness to accept additional tasks, is a function of both the number of tasks already present and memory utilization. Using this pressure function, a node's state is finally determined by comparing the pressure to *watermarks*, as follows.

    if Pint [id] > high_watermark **then**
        state := ABUNDANT
    else if Pint [id] < low_watermark **then**
        state := IDLE
    else
        state := NEUTRAL;

After each node has determined its state, the second phase of the scheduling algorithm creates network gradients that allow tasks to be transferred. These gradients are based on proximities and can, in principle, be computed by each node as

$$proximity\ (i) = \begin{cases} distance\ to\ nearest\ idle\ node & if\ idle\ nodes\ exist \\ \infty & otherwise. \end{cases}$$

Figure 5.15 shows an example of proximities for a sixteen node mesh. This computation, as defined, requires each node to possess global knowledge of the network state, an unacceptable option. Fortunately, Lin has shown [Lin85] that the proximity function can be computed as follows:

$$proximity\ (i) = \begin{cases} 0 & node\ i\ idle \\ 1 + min\ \{proximity\ (j)\ if\ j\ is\ a\ neighbor\ of\ i\} & otherwise \end{cases}$$

using information solely from adjacent nodes. Although Lin presents a formal proof,

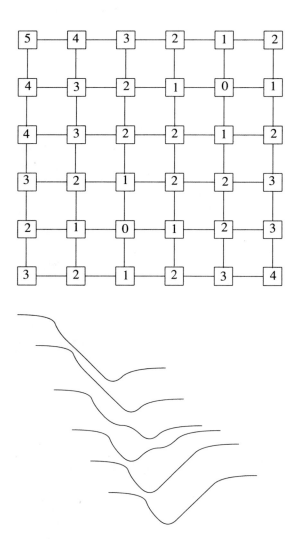

Figure 5.15
Two dimensional mesh and associated gradient plane.

the formula is intuitive: node proximity increases by unity each time another link leading away from an idle node is traversed.

Given a method for computing node proximities, the scheduling algorithm becomes clear; see figure 5.16 for a complete description. Idle nodes announce proximity zero to their neighbors; this is tantamount to a request for work. Neutral nodes, unable to satisfy requests for work, simply increment the minimum proximity received from their neighbors and propagate it. Finally, abundant nodes transfer tasks to the neighboring node with minimal proximity. In this way, tasks migrate toward idle nodes. Moreover, Lin has also shown that transferring tasks to nodes with minimal proximity provides a shortest path through the network to an idle node. Again, this is intuitive; proximities are distances.

As we noted earlier, this algorithm is self-limiting. If the workload at each node becomes large, i.e., the network is saturated, all nodes enter the *abundant* state, requests for work cease, and the induced gradient plane is flat. Only when one or more nodes service their backlog and return to the idle state will load balancing resume. Moreover, the algorithm is adaptive, asynchronous, and fully distributed. Different regions of a network can simultaneously adapt to workload variations in different ways.

5.3.2.3. Simulation Studies

However attractive or intuitive a distributed scheduling algorithm, the final test is its operation. Although no implementations yet exist, Lin has extensively simulated the gradient plane algorithm [Lin85] and compared its performance to an ideal, centralized scheduler. As in Reed's feasibility studies [Reed84], an artificial workload, consisting of randomly generated tasks, was used. Although this does not test the scheduling algorithm under ''real world'' conditions, it does allow stress testing at the limits of the operating region. Before presenting the results of this simulation study, we briefly digress to summarize both the assumptions and parameters.

The task arrivals in the artificial workload are determined by distributions in both time *and* space. In time, new tasks are assumed to be randomly created with a mean interarrival time drawn from a negative exponential distribution. In space, tasks may arrive either uniformly at all nodes or with a normal distribution centered at some node. The distribution in space is particularly important; systems with uniformly generated loads require much less load balancing than those with highly skewed distributions. Finally, task execution times are also drawn from a negative exponential distribution. To reduce simulation overhead to tractable levels, a set of values, given in table 5.6, was used as a reference point.

procedure Gradient (id);   /* id is the processor id   */

  repeat
    processor *id* determines its internal pressure *Pint* [*id*]
    using task backlog and/or memory usage;

    if Pint [id] > high_watermark **then**
        state := ABUNDANT
    else if Pint [id] < low_watermark **then**
        state := IDLE
    else
        state := NEUTRAL;

    case state **of**

        IDLE:
          ignore proximity information from neighbors;
          proximity [id] := 0;
          broadcast proximity [id] to all neighbors;

        NEUTRAL:
          proximity [id] := 1 + min_of_all_neighbors (proximity [j]);
          broadcast proximity [id] to all neighbors;

        ABUNDANT:
          if min_of_all_neighbors (proximity [j]) = *network diameter* **then**
              proximity [id] := *network diameter*
          else if min_of_all_neighbors (proximity [j]) < proximity [id] **then**
              transfer one task to neighboring node with minimal proximity;
    end;

  until network_idle;

end; (* Gradient *)

Figure 5.16
Gradient task scheduling heuristic.

Table 5.6

Reference values for gradient plane simulation

Quantity	Value
Simulation length	3000
Proximity update interval	1
Mean task execution time	50
Task creation distribution (space)	uniform
Network topology	4×4 mesh

The average waiting time W of tasks

$$W = \frac{\sum_{i=1}^{Numtasks} (W_i - S_i)}{Numtasks},$$

where W_i is the interval from task creation to completion, and S_i is the task execution time, is taken as the measure of performance. An ideal scheduling algorithm would, given enough computing capacity, reduce the average waiting time to zero. Unfortunately, this is impossible for two reasons. First, transient processing demands will exceed the computing capacity even if the mean parallelism is less than the number of network nodes. Second, even the best scheduling algorithm incurs communication delays moving tasks from their creation point to idle nodes. Unlike Reed's simulation study [Reed84], Lin omitted communication delays from his simulation. Although this permits comparison of the gradient plane model with an omniscient central scheduler, it unfortunately precludes comparison with Reed's feasibility study.

Figure 5.17 compares the gradient model, a centralized scheduler, and an execute-at-point-of-arrival paradigm where no dynamic load balancing is used for the reference parameters of table 5.6. The horizontal axis is the average processor utilization, i.e., the busy time divided by total time; it increases as the average time between task creations decreases. As can be seen, the gradient model schedules tasks almost as well as the ideal scheduler even at heavy loads. If communication delays were included, the communication bottleneck of the centralized scheduler would make the gradient algorithm preferable. It should be noted, however, that this observation is based on a 4×4 mesh network. Simulations of networks this small suffer from fringe effects; the

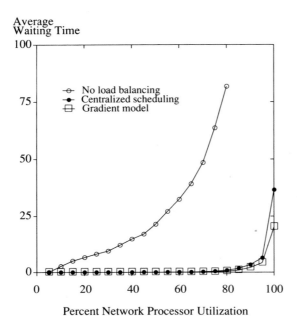

Figure 5.17
Comparison of gradient and centralized schedulers.

cross-mesh distance is only three communication links, and the delay to propagate state changes is very small. For larger networks, state changes propagate more slowly, and the efficiency of gradient scheduling is reduced.

Using variations of the base parameters of table 5.6, several aspects of the gradient plane model can easily be investigated. Among the most important aspects are the effect of the spatial arrival distribution of tasks, the proximity updating interval, and the importance of network topology.

The spatial distribution of task creations is perhaps more important than temporal distributions. A scheduler must disseminate tasks much more quickly if most tasks are created at only a few nodes than if tasks are created at all network nodes. Figure 5.18 compares the gradient model for three spatial distributions: uniform, where all nodes create tasks at an equal rate, normal, where the rate of task creation decays as a normal function of the distance from some distinguished node, and unitary, where all tasks are created by a single node. Node (2, 2) of the mesh was selected as the ''center'' of the normal and single node distributions. As can be seen, distinctions among the

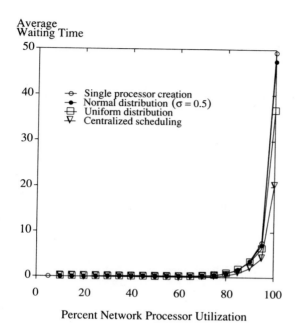

Average Waiting Time

Percent Network Processor Utilization

Figure 5.18
Effect of spatial task creation distribution.

distributions are small. However, we again caution that communication delays are omitted from this figure.

The frequency of proximity updates, i.e., the interval between exchange of proximity messages, determines the accuracy of each node's world view. One must balance the need for accurate information against the communication cost of its acquisition. Infrequent exchanges minimize communication overhead at the expense of accuracy, while frequent exchanges can delay transmission of task messages. In the simulations discussed above, nodes exchanged messages each time unit. Instantaneous proximity correspond to the omniscient, centralized scheme. At the other extreme, infinite delays for proximity exchanges correspond to no load balancing. Thus, as observed in figure 5.18, one expects implementations of the gradient model to lie between these two extremes. Figure 5.19 shows the influence of the proximity exchange interval. The mean task execution time is 50 time units. As can be seen, the proximity update interval must be a small fraction of the task execution time before the gradient scheduler approaches the centralized scheduler.

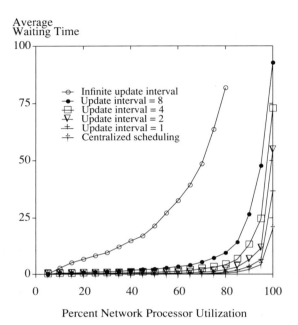

Figure 5.19
Effect of proximity update interval.

Finally, the underlying topology of the communication network can dramatically affect the delays needed to propagate node status information throughout the system. Wittie [Witt76] has argued that a good multicomputer network scheduler should be independent of network topology, adapting to the network on which it operates. Figure 5.20 compares the performance of the gradient scheduling algorithm for four different network topologies: a 2-D torus, a mesh, a ring, and a list, i.e., a ring with a broken connection. For the parameters of table 5.6, little distinction among the networks is seen at low workloads. Only at appreciable workloads does the topology delay the propagation of proximity messages significantly.

5.3.2.4. General Observations

Although the gradient model of dynamic scheduling holds promise, much further study is needed to assess its performance in an actual implementation. Among the issues that must be addressed are

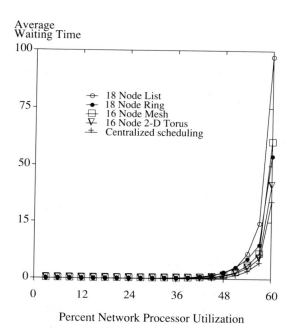

Figure 5.20

Effect of topology on gradient model.

• the presence of heterogeneous nodes,

• adaptive pressure functions,

• communication overhead for proximity messages, and

• locality.

Tamir, for example, has advocated replacing some computation nodes with I/O nodes [TaSe84]. Others have suggested distributing special purpose nodes such as FFT processors throughout the network. A realistic gradient algorithm must divert tasks to an idle node of the appropriate type. Similarly, node pressure functions should accommodate node heterogeneity and task priorities. Adaptive proximity updates are also desirable. When the network load is changing rapidly, updates should occur frequently. Conversely, a network in steady state should adapt infrequently. Finally, and perhaps most important, the gradient scheduling model should encourage locality of communication. Reed's feasibility study showed that identifying idle nodes and minimizing execution time were not always identical goals. If tasks are scheduled too far from their creation point, the communication cost may hide any gains via parallelism. Several obvious modifications to the gradient model, notably imposing maximum hop counts on tasks, can encourage locality.

At present, we know of no implementation of scheduling via gradient planes. However, the current availability of commercial message passing systems suggests that implementation and testing would be straightforward and instructive.

5.3.3. Dynamic Scheduling Via Waves

As defined, the gradient model of distributed scheduling does not readily accommodate a collection of cooperating tasks. Instead, each task is scheduled independently of its siblings, and any underlying structure of the parallel computation is ignored. To be fair, gradient scheduling was proposed for a class of functional programs [KeLi84] whose tasks communicate only on completion. Many computations, however, consist of a structured set of cooperating tasks.

Van Tilborg and Wittie [vanT84] have developed a distributed scheduling technique called *wave scheduling* that maps dynamically created groups of tasks onto available multicomputer network nodes. In its current implementation, wave scheduling does *not* permit dynamic creation of tasks, merely groups of tasks. Hence, these so called *task forces* cannot create new tasks after they have begun execution. Other than this restriction, wave scheduling makes no assumptions about task force arrivals, amount of intertask communication, or task resource requirements. Wave scheduling does, however, presume the existence of an underlying virtual machine that hides the topology of the communication network. As figure 5.21 shows, this virtual machine is a hierarchical arrangement of the network nodes. In the figure, the links delineate manager/subordinate relationships; they do *not* necessarily correspond to physical connections between nodes. The nodes at the lowest level of the hierarchy execute user tasks. Those at higher levels maintain the integrity of the communication network and allocate resources in a local region. To avoid overloads, each node can only exchange control information one level upward or downward. A manager node at each level maintains only summaries of the resource information known to its subnodes.

5.3.3.1. Management Hierarchies

The creation of a control hierarchy that does not correspond to the underlying network topology has both advantages and disadvantages. Among its advantages are the absence of topology dependent algorithms, allowing the control structures to be easily adapted to other networks. Moreover, scheduling need not depend on the operational status of all nodes. The potential performance degradation from eliding the topology is the most obvious disadvantage. In addition, algorithms for hierarchy creation are

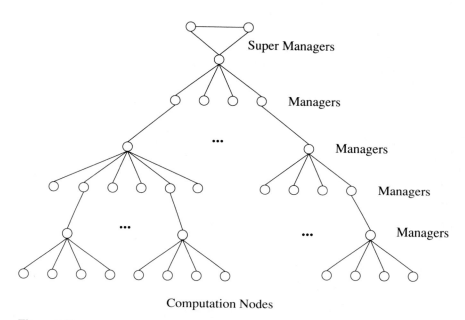

Figure 5.21
Wave scheduling control hierarchy.

needed. Van Tilborg and Wittie have extensively simulated algorithms for creating the hierarchy in an arbitrary network. The distributed algorithm they propose repeatedly forms clusters of nodes, clusters of clusters, etc., while attempting to minimize communication delays. These simulation studies [vanT80, vanT82] suggest that hierarchies with efficient communication paths *can* be created. Table 5.7 shows the result of several applications of the algorithm to a 27×27 mesh of nodes. In this example, the algorithm created two levels of manager nodes subject to constraints on the maximum number of communication links that could separate nodes. Although this algorithm succeeds in mapping the logical tree of the hierarchy onto the physical network, even the optimal mapping uses 90 of the 729 nodes, or about 12 percent, solely for management. For some applications, this penalty may be unacceptable.

5.3.3.2. Wave Scheduling Algorithm

Suppose a task force needing S nodes is created at an arbitrary node. All manager nodes attempt to schedule task forces that are no larger than some dynamically changing fraction of the computation nodes in their subtree. At an arbitrary time t, such

Table 5.7

Cluster results for Van Tilborg's
hierarchy creation algorithm on a 27×27 mesh

Definition	Optimal	Algorithm Values			
Requested number of children per manager	9	8	8	8	9
Requested maximum path length (level one)	2	3	3	6	3
Requested maximum path length (level two)	8	8	6	16	8
Average number of children per manager (level one)	7.89	6.59	6.62	7.55	7.22
Average number of children per manager (level two)	9.00	5.87	7.23	7.64	6.21
Average path length (level one)	1.49	1.73	1.72	1.85	1.74
Average path length (level two)	4.67	3.91	4.59	5.12	4.31
Number of computing processors (level zero)	639	619	622	634	628
Number of managing processors (level one)	81	94	94	84	87
Number of managing processors (level two)	9	16	13	11	14
Maximum number of paths sharing a link	3	7	7	7	7

a manager might schedule task forces containing no more than

$$S = K[1 - Util_i(t)]W_i$$

tasks, where $Util_i(t)$ is the fraction of busy computation nodes in subtree i, W_i is the number of nodes in the subtree, and K is the fraction of idle nodes in the subtree that can be safely scheduled. Recall that managers maintain only approximate status information using summaries received from the nodes in their subtrees.

If a task force is created at a manager with insufficient nodes to schedule the tasks, the task force is passed up the logical tree until a manager controlling enough nodes is found. Conversely, if a task force could be scheduled by a manager many levels below its point of entry in the hierarchy, it is passed down until it reaches a level that minimally satisfies its needs. The manager that finally schedules the task force becomes the *task force master*. These task force masters must reserve enough nodes for the task forces they control. Because the children of all managers are themselves managers, except for the lowest level, there is competition among task force masters for computation nodes. Hence, a task force master that needs S nodes gauges the activity of its subtree and reserves $R \geq S$ nodes to increase the likelihood of acquiring the needed S. A request for R nodes is divided among the submanagers of a task force manager and is propagated down the hierarchy as a wave of requests, hence the name *wave scheduling*. At each level, requests from parent managers take precedence over local task force arrivals, are further subdivided, and are passed downward. Effectively subdividing requests is not trivial, and no optimal algorithms are known. Ideally, a division should be proportional to the number of idle nodes in each subtree.

When a request reaches managers at the lowest level, just above the computation nodes, they reserve as many of the requested nodes as possible. These managers then tell their managers how many nodes were actually reserved. Managers at each level await responses from all requests issued to their children before advising their parent manager how many nodes were reserved. Finally, the requesting task force master learns how many nodes were secured. If enough nodes were obtained, the computation nodes are told where to obtain the code for their tasks and begin execution. If insufficient nodes were reserved, the scheduling pass fails, and the task force master issues a command releasing all reserved nodes. At a later time, the task force master will again try to schedule the task force. If, after several attempts, the master has been unable to obtain enough nodes, it will pass the task force upward to its parent, who controls more nodes.

5.3.3.3. Analysis of Wave Scheduling

Clearly, the effectiveness of wave scheduling rests on two premises: a control hierarchy with minimal communication delays and low reservation costs for computation nodes. As discussed earlier, Van Tilborg and Wittie believe their technique for constructing control hierarchies provides the former. The latter, however, is crucial. If the number R of nodes requested is too large, too much of the network's computation capacity will be reserved needlessly. If R is too small, many assignment passes will be needed, each reserving some number of nodes. In either case, the interval between reservation and release is wasted computing capacity. Van Tilborg and Wittie [vanT84] have developed a simple model of the expected node waste in wave scheduling. Using this model it is possible to determine appropriate values for R. The notation for this model is summarized in table 5.8.

Table 5.8
Wave scheduling notation

Quantity	Definition
c_h	mean wasted time when a single processor is reserved by a level h manager
F	expected number of failed scheduling passes
n_f	mean number of processors reserved by a failed scheduling pass
n_x	mean number of processors reserved by a successful scheduling pass
N	number of computation processors in a subtree
N_{opt}	size of subtree that minimizes wasted processor time
P	probability of reserving at least S processors in a subtree of size N
q	utilization of an individual processor
R	number of processors requested by a manager
S	number of tasks in a task force
T_s	expected waste of processor time scheduling a task force of size S

If T_s is the amount of node time wasted scheduling a task force, then

$$T_s = c_h(Fn_f + n_x),\tag{5.7}$$

where F is the mean number of failed scheduling passes, n_f is the mean number of nodes reserved on a failed pass, n_x is the mean number of excess nodes reserved on a successful pass, and c_h is the wasted time for a single node if it is reserved by a level h task force master. Computing F, n_f, and n_x requires further derivations.

For simplicity's sake, assume that the request size R is always equal to the number of nodes N in a subtree. This simplification introduces some inaccuracy [vanT84], but will provide a lower bound on the scheduling cost. A wave scheduling pass cannot reserve an arbitrary computation node with probability q, the utilization of the node. Then the probability of a successful pass, i.e., of reserving at least S nodes in a subtree of N computation nodes during one scheduling pass, is

$$P = \sum_{j=S}^{N} \binom{N}{j} (1-q)^j q^{N-j}.$$

The reservation process follows a geometric distribution with probability of success P, so the expected number of failed passes is simply

$$F = \frac{1-P}{P}.\tag{5.8}$$

If minimizing the number of failed passes were the only criterion of success, as many nodes as possible should be requested. This greatly increases the likelihood of reserving enough. However, unnecessary reservations are also expensive, making it important to know how many computation nodes are reserved during failed passes. This number is

$$n_f = \frac{1}{1-P} \sum_{j=0}^{S-1} j \; Prob \, (exactly \; j \; nodes \; reserved)\tag{5.9}$$

$$= \frac{1}{1-P} \sum_{j=0}^{S-1} j \binom{N}{j} (1-q)^j q^{N-j}$$

where the factor $\frac{1}{1-P}$ normalizes for the known failure of the scheduling pass.

Finally, the number of excess nodes reserved during a successful scheduling pass is

$$
n_x = \left[\frac{1}{P} \sum_{j=S}^{N} j \binom{N}{j} (1-q)^j q^{N-j} \right] - S. \tag{5.10}
$$

Substituting (5.8), (5.9), and (5.10) in (5.7) yields the desired expression for the expected waste of node capacity. Figure 5.22 shows (5.7) for one possible set of values for q and S. As the figure shows, a task force containing S tasks is optimally scheduled by a task force master with N_{opt} nodes. Unfortunately, the utilization q of nodes in (5.8), (5.9), and (5.10) is time varying and can never be known exactly. Consequently, N_{opt}, the value of N that minimizes (5.7), can never be determined exactly. Recall that N was assumed to be equal to R, the number of nodes requested during a scheduling pass. Van Tilborg and Wittie present heuristics for estimating N_{opt} [vanT84], and suggest the simple approximation

$$
N_{opt} = \frac{ScaleFactor \times S}{1-q}.
$$

The efficiency of wave scheduling remains an open question; no implementation exists. In one analytic study, Van Tilborg and Wittie [vanT81b] estimated that the efficiency of wave scheduling was 80 percent of an idealized, omniscient scheduler. It is clear, however, that the overhead of wave scheduling is significantly greater than that for the gradient model. Wave scheduling was designed for tasks with sizes typical of the processes on a uniprocessor. There, the costs of both the control hierarchy and multiple scheduling passes are mitigated by the large execution times of the tasks. The clustering of nodes in the control hierarchy also implicitly maps task forces onto neighboring nodes, allowing efficient intertask communication. The gradient model rapidly disseminates much smaller entities, perhaps as small as a few hundred instructions. There is, however, no means to cluster cooperating tasks.

Neither wave nor gradient scheduling is appropriate for all applications. A scheduling technique capable of clustering communicating tasks of any size is really needed. Only further research will resolve this dilemma.

5.4. Fault Tolerance

The computational demands of some algorithms are so large that they require weeks or months of processing even on highly parallel systems. As an example, the GF11, under development at IBM's Watson Research Center [BeDW85], is a 512 processor, eleven

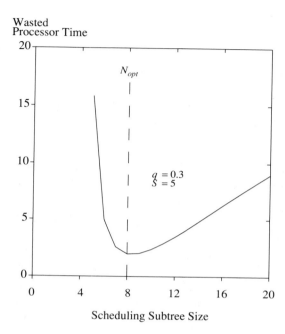

Wasted
Processor Time

Figure 5.22
Wasted processor time using wave scheduler.

gigaflop system designed for a Monte Carlo simulation of a quantum chromodynamics theory. To test this theory's prediction of a proton's mass, the simulation will run for one calendar year. During a one year interval, hardware failures will almost certainly occur. To insure that many months of computation are not lost, some form of fault tolerance is needed. Many methods of fault tolerance are possible, e.g., checkpointing or redundancy. The GF-11 achieves fault tolerance via both checkpointing *and* redundancy; a bank of 64 spare processors is included in the design.

Fault tolerance is important even for much shorter computations. As the number of components in a system rises, the likelihood that the entire system remains operational declines precipitously. Multicomputer networks, because they are based on the principles of modularity and incremental expansion to realize increased performance, are particularly susceptible to this problem. It is unreasonable to expect all of the (potentially) thousands of nodes and communication links in a multicomputer network to be simultaneously operational. As an example, if multicomputer network is configured as a hypercube containing 2^D nodes and $D\,2^{D-1}$ links, the mean time to failure is approximately

$$\min\left\{ \frac{T_p}{2^D}, \frac{T_l}{D\,2^{D-1}} \right\},$$

where T_p and T_l are the mean times to failure of nodes and links, respectively. Obviously, the mean time to failure declines linearly with the number of nodes. Equally clearly, a multicomputer network with some number of disabled nodes or links should *not* be considered disabled. Nevertheless, the presence *and* occurrence of failures force the multicomputer network to adapt to these failures. Moreover, failures can be either permanent, e.g., processor failure, or transient, e.g., transmission error, and failure recovery can occur in both hardware and software.

In the operating system, adapting to multicomputer hardware failures minimally involves adapting the message routing and task scheduling strategies, and checkpointing. Each of these techniques has been the subject of extensive research in other contexts. Little is known, however, about software fault tolerance for multicomputer networks [TaSe84, Lin85]. Rather than review research in other contexts, the following sections simply summarize the fault tolerance issues for multicomputer networks.

5.4.1. Recovery Methods

If one or more communication links are disabled, the topology of a multicomputer network is disrupted. A message routing algorithm must recognize failed links and route around them.[12] If a multicomputer network supports packet switching, then an adaptive routing algorithm [Sega77] can easily avoid disabled links and route packets along minimal delay paths. If packet switching is realized via virtual circuits, the circuit *setup* algorithm must avoid disabled links. In contrast to standard packet switching, virtual circuit and circuit switched mechanisms establish a path from a source to a destination node; after the path is established, no routing decisions need be made; all packets are routed along this path. If a link fails, the circuit will be broken. To recover from such a failure, the circuit must be reestablished by routing around the failing link, and the remnants of the broken circuit must be destroyed. All these problems have analogs in communication networks, and there is a substantial body of research literature on techniques and methods applicable to multicomputer networks [ChBN81, FrCh71, JuKe76, McRR80, MeSe79, Sega77, Sega81, Taji77].

---

[12]In contrast, all commercial multicomputer networks currently use fixed path routing.

However, there is one crucial difference between loosely coupled communication networks and tightly coupled multicomputer networks: the failure rate. Because a multicomputer network operates in a protected environment and is closely coupled, factors such as line noise that are important in long distance communication networks are much less significant. Thus, simpler and more efficient error recovery techniques, e.g., end-to-end error recovery versus link-by-link correction can be used. This is particularly important given the high speed of multicomputer network links.

Unlike an adaptive routing algorithm, a task scheduler must avoid both disabled nodes *and* links. The former is obvious; the latter is also important when scheduling a group of communicating tasks. Avoiding disabled links also avoids regions of the network with potentially large communication delays. The techniques for avoiding failed nodes and links depend on the design of the task scheduler.

In the gradient scheduling model [Lin85], discussed in §5.3.2, disabled nodes are avoided during calculation of the proximity function. Disabled nodes always appear *busy*, unable to accept new tasks. In the wave scheduling model [vanT84], disabled nodes and links are avoided during *creation* of the scheduler hierarchy. Because the scheduler creation algorithm [vanT80] is distributed and clusters nodes according to communication costs, disabled links and nodes do not participate in the hierarchy creation phase. Consequently, these links and nodes do not appear in the scheduler hierarchy and are never used during scheduling or computation.

If nodes fail during a computation, recovery techniques are necessary. The type of recovery technique depends on the underlying computation paradigm. In a functional computing paradigm, tasks are function evaluations and communication occurs only when a task is created or its result is returned to the creation point. Pictorially, a parallel computation is a tree of non-communicating function evaluations. Tasks that have failed can be restarted without disturbing the correctness of the computation. Hence, for the functional paradigm, *asynchronous* checkpointing and recovery suffice [Lin85]. Each time a new task is created, the creating node saves a copy of the creation environment. If the node executing the new task fails, the creating node need only reinstantiate the failing task; no global checkpoints are necessary. With a naive implementation, reinstantiation of the failing task would also implicitly reinstantiate all the task's children, i.e., the task subtree rooted at the failing task. Lin has developed distributed algorithms for *patching* the task subtree [Lin85]. This replaces only the failed task, eliminating a potentially enormous amount of redundant computation, the so called *rollback avalanche*.

If communicating tasks [Hoar78] are the computing paradigm, more complex recovery mechanisms are necessary. In contrast to the functional paradigm, message exchanges between tasks make it difficult to capture a consistent network state. Many proposed recovery techniques either assume a bus connection [BoBG83] or require a significant fraction of the system's computation and communication capacity [HoKR83]. Tamir recently presented a global checkpointing algorithm designed specifically for multicomputer networks [TaSe84]. In this algorithm, a *complete copy* of the entire multicomputer network state is periodically saved. Because this state is large and there are no direct connections between nodes and secondary storage, the state must be saved in secondary storage devices distributed throughout the network. Although this may seem prohibitively expensive for networks containing thousands of nodes, Tamir has argued that the overhead for this checkpointing can be reduced to negligible levels (1 to 3 percent). No implementation, however, exists.

5.4.2. Summary

As noted earlier, little is really known about fault tolerant multicomputer networks. Until recently, only experimental prototypes existed [Seit85]. With these machines the primary goal has, justifiably, been increased performance. The availability of commercial multicomputer networks [Ratt85] should encourage implementation and testing of failure detection and recovery techniques in all areas: routing, scheduling, and checkpointing.

5.5. Future Directions in Operating Systems

Although a few experimental multicomputer network operating systems have been designed and partially implemented [Witt80, SoFi79], there exists no fully integrated operating system providing distributed task scheduling, message routing and management, and fault tolerance. Commercial systems [Ratt85] merely provide cross-compilers, software for downloading programs, and rudimentary error detection facilities. Other than basic communication support, all software resides on a companion development system, not the multicomputer network. This suffices for a set of static tasks; it is woefully inadequate, however, for dynamically created tasks.

The feasibility of dynamic task creation has been established [Reed84]; scheduling algorithms for both the functional [Lin85] and communicating task paradigms [vanT84] are known; rudimentary fault tolerance algorithms have been developed [Lin85, TaSe84]; the research literature is rich with algorithms for message routing and management in both long distance networks [ChBN81, McRR80] and multicomputer networks [FuSe82]. Simply put, the components of a true multicomputer network operating system exist. Only their integration into a functional but unobtrusive operating system is lacking. Although unobtrusiveness is not a feature normally associated with operating systems, it is crucial in a multicomputer network whose raison d'etre is performance. The facilities of a single multicomputer network node are not large. It is unreasonable to consume much more than ten percent of a node's capacity managing its meager resources. Thus, there is a delicate balance between functionality and excessive intrusion.

In summary, commercial hardware is currently available, and the components of a multicomputer network operating system exist. The time for development and experimentation is now.

References

[Adam82]   L. M. Adams, *Iterative Algorithms for Large Sparse Linear Systems on Parallel Computers.* Ph.D. Dissertation, Department of Applied Mathematics and Computer Science, University of Virginia, 1982.

[Bade86]   S. B. Baden, "Dynamic Load Balancing of a Vortex Calculation Running on Multiprocessors", Lawrence Berkeley Laboratory, University of California, Berkeley, CA, December 1986.

[Baud78]   G. M. Baudet, *The Design and Analysis of Algorithms for Asynchronous Multiprocessors.* Ph.D. Dissertation, Department of Computer Science, Carnegie-Mellon University, 1978.

[BeBo87]   M. J. Berger and S. H. Bokhari, "A Partitioning Strategy for Nonuniform Problems on Multiprocessors," *IEEE Transactions on Computers* (May 1987), Vol. C-36, No. 5, pp. 570-580.

[BeCh85]   E. J. Berglund and D. R. Cheriton, "Amaze: A Multiplayer Computer Game," *IEEE Software* (May 1985), Vol. 2, No. 3, pp. 30-39.

[BeDW85]   J. Beetem, M. Denneau and D. Weingarten, "The GF11 Supercomputer," *Proceedings of the Twelfth International Symposium on Computer Architecture* (June 1985), pp. 108-115.

[BoBG83]   A. Borg, J. Baumbach and S. Glazer, "A Message System Supporting Fault Tolerance," *Proceedings of the Ninth Symposium on Operating Systems Principles* (October 1983), pp. 90-99.

[BrFi81]   R. M. Bryant and R. A. Finkel, "A Stable Distributed Scheduling Algorithm," *Proceedings of the Second International Conference on Distributed Computing Systems* (April 1981).

[ChBN81]   W. Chou, A. W. Bragg and A. A. Nilsson, "The Need for Adaptive Routing in the Chaotic and Unbalanced Traffic Environment," *IEEE Transactions on Communications* (April 1981), Vol. COM-29, No. 4, pp. 481-490.

[Cher84]   D. R. Cheriton, "The V Kernel: A Software Base for Distributed Systems," *IEEE Software* (April 1984), Vol. 1, No. 2, pp. 19-42.

[CHLE80]   W. W. Chu, L. J. Holloway, M. Lan and K. Efe, "Task Allocation in Distributed Processing," *IEEE Computer* (November 1980), Vol. 13, No. 11, pp. 57-69.

[Chva83]   V. Chvátal, *Linear Programming.* W. H. Freeman and Company, New York, 1983.

[DaSe86]   W. J. Dally and C. L. Seitz, "The Torus Routing Chip," *Journal of Distributed Computing* (1986), Vol. 1, No. 3.

[FiHo80]   M. L. Fisher and D. S. Hochbaum, "Database Location in Computer Networks," *Journal of the ACM* (October 1980), Vol. 27, No. 4, pp. 718-735.

[FlOS86]   J. W. Flower, S. W. Otto and M. C. Salama, "A Preprocessor for Irregular Finite Element Problems," *CalTech Concurrent Computation Project Memorandum 292* (July 1986).

[FrCh71]   H. Frank and W. Chou, "Routing in Computer Networks," *Networks* (1971), Vol. 1, No. 2, pp. 99-112.

[FuSe82]   R. M. Fujimoto and C. H. Séquin, "The Impact of VLSI on Communications in Closely Coupled Multiprocessor Networks," *Proceedings of IEEE COMPSAC 1982* (November 1982).

[GaJo79]   M. R. Garey and D. S. Johnson, *Computers and Intractability, A Guide to the Theory of NP-Completeness*. W. H. Freeman and Company, San Francisco, 1979.

[GyEd76]   V. B. Gylys and J. A. Edwards, "Optimal Partitioning of Workload for Distributed Systems," *Proceedings of the Fall IEEE COMPCON* (September 1976), pp. 353-357.

[Hoar78]   C. A. R. Hoare, "Communicating Sequential Processes," *Communications of the ACM* (August 1978), Vol. 21, No. 8, pp. 666-677.

[HoKR83]   S. H. Hosseini, J. G. Kuhl and S. M. Reddy, "An Integrated Approach to Error Recovery in Distributed Computing Systems," *Proceedings of the 13th Fault-Tolerant Computing Symposium* (June 1983), pp. 56-63.

[Inte86a]   *Intel iPSC System Overview, Order Number 310610-001*. Intel Scientific Computers, 1986.

[JuKe76]   R. R. Jueneman and G. S. Kerr, "Explicit Path Routing in Communications Networks," *Proceedings of the International Conference on Computer Communications* (August 1976), pp. 340-342.

[KeLi84]   R. M. Keller and F. C. H. Lin, "Simulated Performance of a Reduction-based Multiprocessor,"," *IEEE Computer* (July 1984), Vol. 17, No. 7, pp. 70-82.

[KiGV83]   S. Kirkpatrick, C. D. Gelatt, Jr. and M. P. Vecchi, "Optimization by Simulated Annealing," *Science* (May 1983), Vol. 220, No. 4598, pp. 671-680.

[Lin85]   F. C. H. Lin, *Load Balancing and Fault Tolerance in Applicative Systems*. Ph.D. Dissertation, Department of Computer Science, University of Utah, 1985.

[Mada87]   H. Madan, "private communication," *Jet Propulsion Laboratory* (April 1987).

[MaRi76]   S. Mahmoud and J. S. Riordon, "Optimal Allocation of Resources in Distributed Information Networks," *ACM Transactions on Database Systems* (March 1976), Vol. 1, No. 1, pp. 66-78.

[McRR80]   J. M. McQuillan, I. Richer and E. C. Rosen, "The New Routing Algorithm for the Arpanet," *IEEE Transactions on Communications* (May 1980), Vol. COM-28, No. 5, pp. 711-719.

[MeSe79]   P. M. Merlin and A. Segall, "A Failsafe Distributed Routing Protocol," *IEEE Transactions on Communications* (September 1979), Vol. COM-27, No. 9, pp. 1280-1288.

[MoLe77]   H. L. Morgan and K. D. Levin, "Optimal Program and Data Locations in Computer Networks," *Communications of the ACM* (May 1977), Vol. 20, No. 5, pp. 315-321.

[MRRT53]   N. Metropolis, N. Rosenbluth, A. Rosenbluth and E. Teller, "Equation of State Calculations by Fast Computing Machines," *Journal of Chemical Physics* (June 1953), Vol. 21, No. 6, p. 1087.

[OrVo85]   J. Ortega and R. G. Voigt, "Solution of Partial Differential Equations on Vector and Parallel Computers," *SIAM Review* (June 1985), Vol. 27, No. 2, pp. 149-240.

[RaRo81]   R. Rashid and G. Robertson, ''Accent: A Communication-Oriented Network Operating System Kernel,'' *Proceedings of the Eighth Symposium on Operating System Principles* (December 1981), Vol. 15, No. 5, pp. 64-75.

[Ratt85]   J. Rattner, ''Concurrent Processing: A New Direction in Scientific Computing,'' *Conference Proceedings of the 1985 National Computer Conference* (1985), Vol. 54, pp. 157-166.

[Reed83b]   D. A. Reed, ''A Simulation Study of Multimicrocomputer Networks,'' *1983 International Conference on Parallel Processing* (August 1983), pp. 161-163.

[Reed84]   D. A. Reed, ''The Performance of Multimicrocomputer Networks Supporting Dynamic Workloads,'' *IEEE Transactions on Computers* (November 1984), Vol. C-33, No. 11, pp. 1045-1048.

[Sega77]   A. Segall, ''The Modeling of Adaptive Routing in Data-Communication Networks,'' *IEEE Transactions on Communications* (January 1977), Vol. COM-25, No. 1, pp. 85-95.

[Sega81]   A. Segall, ''Advances in Verifiable Fail-Safe Routing Procedures,'' *IEEE Transactions on Communications* (April 1981), Vol. COM-29, No. 4, pp. 491-497.

[Seit85]   C. L. Seitz, ''The Cosmic Cube,'' *Communications of the ACM* (January 1985), Vol. 28, No. 1, pp. 22-33.

[SmLo82]   C. U. Smith and D. D. Loendorf, ''Performance Analysis of Software for MIMD Computer,'' *Proceedings of the 1982 ACM Symposium on Measurement and Modeling of Computer Systems* (August 1980), Vol. 11, No. 4, pp. 151-162.

[SoFi79]   M. H. Solomon and R. A. Finkel, ''The Roscoe Distributed Operating System,'' *Proceedings of the Seventh Symposium on Operating Systems Principles* (December 1979), pp. 108-114.

[Ston77]   H. S. Stone, ''Multiprocessor Scheduling with the Aid of Network Flow Algorithms,'' *IEEE Transactions on Software Engineering* (January 1977), Vol. SE-3, No. 1, pp. 85-93.

[Taji77]   W. Tajibnapis, ''A Correctness Proof of a Topology Maintenance Protocol for a Distributed Computer Network,'' *Communications of the ACM* (July 1977), Vol. 20, No. 7, pp. 477-485.

[TaSe84]   Y. Tamir and C. H. Séquin, ''Error Recovery in Multicomputers Using Global Checkpoints,'' *Proceedings of the 1984 International Conference on Parallel Processing* (August 1984), pp. 32-41.

[vanT80]   A. M. van Tilborg and L. D. Wittie, ''High-Level Operating System Formation in Network Computers,'' *Proceedings of the 1980 International Conference on Parallel Processing* (August 1980), pp. 131-132.

[vanT81a]   A. M. van Tilborg and L. D. Wittie, ''Wave Scheduling: Distributed Allocation of Task Forces in Network Computers,'' *Proceedings of the Second International Conference on Distributed Computer Systems* (1981).

[vanT81b]   A. M. van Tilborg and L. D. Wittie, ''Distributed Task Force Scheduling in Multimicrocomputer Networks,'' *Proceedings of the National Computer Conference* (1981), Vol. 46, pp. 283-289.

[vanT82]   A. M. van Tilborg, *Network Computer Operating Systems and Task Force Scheduling.* Ph.D. Dissertation, Department of Computer Science, State University of New York at Buffalo, 1982.

[vanT84]   A. M. van Tilborg and L. D. Wittie, ''Wave Scheduling - Decentralized Scheduling of Task Forces in Multicomputers,'' *IEEE Transactions on Computers* (September 1984), Vol. C-33, No. 9, pp. 835-844.

[Will83]   E. A. Williams, *Design, Analysis, and Implementation of Distributed Systems From a Performance Perspective*. Ph.D. Dissertation, Computer Science Department, University of Texas, Austin, 1983.

[Will84]   E. A. Williams, "The Effect of Queueing Disciplines on Response Times in Distributed Systems," *Proceedings of the 1984 International Conference on Parallel Processing* (August 1984), pp. 330-332.

[Witt76]   L. D. Wittie, "Efficient Message Routing in Mega-micro-computer Networks," *Proceedings of the Third Annual Symposium on Computer Architecture* (January 1976), Vol. 4, No. 4, pp. 136-140.

[Witt80]   L. D. Wittie, "MICROS: A Distributed Operating System for MICRONET, A Reconfigurable Network Computer," *IEEE Transactions on Computers* (December 1980), Vol. C-29, No. 12, pp. 1133-1144.

6

Applications: Distributed Simulation

There's no limit to how complicated things can get, on account of one thing always leading to another.

E. B. White

The previous chapters focused on the design and implementation of hardware and system software for multicomputer networks. While the design of a highly parallel computer is certainly an important problem in its own right, it is nevertheless only half of the story. Algorithms must be developed to effectively utilize the parallelism available in the hardware. Therefore, we will shift our attention to applications for multicomputer networks. In particular, this chapter will examine discrete event simulation, whereas chapter seven examines the solution of partial differential equations on a multicomputer.

Computer simulation of discrete systems has long been a task with computational requirements that far exceed the computing capabilities of the fastest available machines. For example, it is not unusual for simulations of large communication networks to require hours or even days of CPU time. Many of the simulations discussed in chapters three and five required hours of CPU time to complete. Many large systems cannot be simulated with sufficient detail. The need for high performance, coupled with the parallelism inherent in many of the systems being modeled, has made the execution of simulation programs on a parallel processor an area of considerable interest.

6.1. Simulation of Discrete Systems

A simulation program is a model of a real world system. We shall refer to this real world system as the **physical system**. We will only consider **discrete** models whose state transitions occur at discrete points in time. In continuous simulation models transitions occur "all of the time," and the system is described by a set of differential equations. Simulation of assembly lines and queueing networks are examples of discrete simulators, whereas weather modeling and circuit level simulation of electronic components typically use continuous simulation models.

The relationship between the physical system and the simulation program is summarized in table 6.1. Informally, the physical system can be conceptualized as a state machine. The current state of the physical system is described by a **system state**, and its behavior over time is described by a sequence of **state transitions**. In the simulation model, the state of the system is modeled by a collection of **program** or **state variables**, and state transitions are modeled by **events**. Each event causes some code in the simulation program to be executed. This code modifies the state variables to reflect the new state of the physical system after the transition occurs. The set of values assigned to the state variables after an event has been processed is called a **state vector**. Each state vector corresponds to a state in the physical system. Time in the physical system, referred to here as **physical time**, is replaced in the simulation program by the notion of **simulated time**. Each event has a timestamp associated with it indicating the physical time when the corresponding state transition occurs.

6.1.1. The Causality Principle

One important aspect of simulation models must be explained before we begin discussing execution on a parallel processor. With the exception of time travel in science fiction novels, physical systems always obey the **causality principle**. This simply states that the future cannot affect the past. Causality imposes a partial ordering on state transitions in the physical system. If a state transition has some effect on another state transition, then the former must always occur before the latter, i.e., the cause must always precede the effect. State transitions that have no direct or indirect cause/effect relationship on one another have no such sequencing constraints and need not occur in any specific time sequence in the physical system. Therefore, causality imposes a *partial* ordering on all state transitions.

Table 6.1
Physical systems and simulation models

Physical System	Simulation Program
system state	state vector
state transitions	events
physical time	simulated time
causality	event synchronization
physical process	logical process
process interaction	timestamped message

This partial ordering of state transitions in the physical system imposes a partial ordering on events in the simulation model. In particular, the order that the simulator processes events must be consistent with this partial ordering if the simulation model is to faithfully reproduce the behavior of the physical system. For example, if state transition A in the physical system occurs at time 3 and has some influence on transition B occurring at time 5, then the simulation program must process the event modeling transition A before it processes the event modeling transition B. If it were to simulate transition B *first*, the simulator would not accurately model the physical system because the computation for transition B would not include the effects of transition A. When events are not processed by the simulator in a correct sequence, we say that a causality constraint has been violated, and the simulator is erroneous.

In a uniprocessor implementation of a simulation program, causality is easily ensured by ordering events in increasing simulated time sequence and always following the rule that the "oldest" event, i.e., the one with the smallest timestamp, is processed next. This is easily implemented by a time sorted list of events. The simulation program repeatedly removes the next (oldest) event from the event list and calls a procedure to model that event. This procedure updates the state variables to reflect the new state of the system and schedules any new events as needed. This scenario is repeated until the event list is empty or an "end of simulation" event is processed.

It is much more difficult to avoid violation of the causality constraint when the simulation program is executed on a parallel processor because many events are executed concurrently. Ensuring that causality constraints are not violated is at the root of the distributed simulation problem.

6.1.2. What is Distributed Simulation?

Distributed simulation is the execution of discrete simulation programs on a parallel processor. This requires partitioning the program into distinct computational units. Fortunately, this is straightforward if an appropriate methodology is used.

The *physical* system can be visualized as some number of independent, concurrently executing entities, i.e., **physical processes**, that interact in some fashion. A natural methodology for developing a distributed simulation program is to create a simulation model that is topologically identical to the physical system. Each physical process is modeled by a separate simulation program called a **logical process**. Interactions *between* physical processes are modeled by timestamped messages exchanged between the corresponding logical processes. The timestamp denotes the point in simulated time when the event occurs in the receiving process. State transitions that only affect the internal behavior of a physical process can be modeled by the process sending a message to itself, allowing all events to be modeled as messages.

For example, consider the simulation of airline traffic throughout the world. To simplify this example, we will focus our attention on two airports, ORD in Chicago and SFO in San Francisco, each of which forms a single physical process. For the purposes of this example, we will coalesce all other airports into a third physical process called ''EOE'' (EveryOne Else). Using the paradigm discussed above, three logical processes are created, one each for ORD, SFO, and EOE (see figure 6.1). Each process might contain queues of airplanes waiting to take off, land, enter or leave gates, etc. An airplane flying from one city to another is modeled by a message sent between the corresponding logical processes that carries a timestamp indicating the time of the airplane's arrival at the destination airport.

A few basic rules must be obeyed by each logical process. A logical process can receive and read the contents of messages, generate and send new messages, and update its internal state variables. There are no variables shared between distinct logical processes. Each process maintains a local clock variable containing the current value of simulated time, i.e., the timestamp of the last message processed by the logical process. The timestamp on each message generated by a process must be at least as large as the local clock of the process sending the message. Otherwise, processes could create events ''in the past,'' a clear violation of the causality constraint. We will assume for now that the sequence of timestamps on messages sent over each link must be nondecreasing. Further, all computation in the logical process must be initiated by a locally generated event or a message from another process. In other words, processes cannot spontaneously begin new computations. A more complete list of constraints will be presented later.

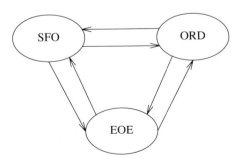

Figure 6.1
Simulator for Airline System.

6.1.3. Why is Distributed Simulation Hard?

The paradigm described above is a straightforward partitioning of the global model for the system into a collection of smaller models. This simple mapping demonstrates that *spatial* aspects of the physical system correspond naturally to a parallel simulation program. Unfortunately, *temporal* aspects do not map so easily.

In uniprocessor simulation programs, time in the physical system is modeled by a single *global* variable holding the current value of simulated time. Causality is preserved through strict adherence to the rule that events are processed in nondecreasing timestamp order. This paradigm imposes a strict serialization on the execution of the program that must be relaxed if parallel execution is to be exploited. In particular, two events that have no direct or indirect effect on each other can be executed in any order, regardless of their respective timestamps, without violating causality constraints. Such events can be processed concurrently.

Two problems related to *simulated* time must be addressed by any distributed simulation program:

- How can the single global clock variable of uniprocessor simulation programs be replaced by a distributed clock?

- How does one ensure that the partial ordering of events imposed by causality in the physical system are not violated by the distributed simulator.

Two approaches have been developed to address the first question. In the first, a *global* clock process is used to ensure that all logical processes advance together in lock step. This method is sometimes referred to as **time driven** simulation. The global clock process repeatedly waits until all activity has ceased in the current time step and then broadcasts a message allowing processes to advance to the next time step. It is easy to see that this approach guarantees causality constraints are not violated, however, its usefulness is limited to situations where the number of events per unit of simulated time is high. Otherwise, most processes will lie idle waiting for the global clock to advance to the time of their next event.

The second approach, often referred to as the **event driven** method, provides each logical process with its own local clock. Each logical process is responsible for advancing its own clock as it simulates events in the physical system. In general, the clocks in different processes are advanced *at completely different rates*. This approach eliminates the problems associated with time driven simulation and is the subject of the remainder of this discussion.

Of course, the fundamental problem which arises in the event driven approach is guaranteeing that causality constraints are not violated. Each logical process can receive timestamped messages from several other processes. Clearly, we must ensure that messages arriving from these processes are processed in increasing timestamp order, lest we allow the future to influence the past. This implies the following "local" causality constraint must not be violated:

> **Definition 6.1:** The **Local Causality Constraint** is satisfied by a logical process if and only if messages received by that process are processed in nondecreasing timestamp order.

Local causality only requires a nondecreasing timestamp order *within* each logical process. It does not constrain different processes to *collectively* process messages in nondecreasing timestamp order; we allow any logical process to "get ahead" of any other as long as the sequencing constraints within each process are not violated.

Adherence to local causality in each process is sufficient to ensure global causality if we assume that all interactions between processes are through timestamped messages. This is because a violation in a causality constraint can only occur when an event A with timestamp T_A has a direct effect on an event B with timestamp T_B, with $T_A < T_B$, but the simulator erroneously processes B *before* it processes A. In the simulation program, event A can affect event B in one of two ways:

- Processing event A causes the creation of event B.

- Event A modifies state variables used by B.

The first situation clearly cannot lead to a situation where B is processed before A, so no violation of causality can occur here. The second situation implies that events A and B are both processed by the *same* logical process, because state variables are local to each process and cannot be accessed directly by other logical processes. Because adherence to local causality ensures that events are processed within each process in increasing timestamp order, it is again not possible for the events to be processed out of order. Therefore, adherence to local causality is sufficient to ensure no causality constraints are violated globally. Therefore we have:

> **Theorem 6.1:** If each logical process does not violate the local causality constraint and if all interactions between pairs of logical processes are through timestamped messages, then the simulation processes events in an order consistent with the partial ordering imposed by causality constraints in the physical system.

The key assumption is that *all* interactions between logical processes are through timestamped messages. In particular, logical processes cannot share global variables. If the two processes did share global state variables, access to them must be properly sequenced in nondecreasing timestamp order.

Thus, the causality problem reduces to ensuring that each logical process obeys the local causality constraint. This must be achieved despite the fact that processes are advancing in simulated time at different rates. Whenever a process has a message waiting to be processed, it must decide whether to process this message now or wait for a new message to appear with a smaller timestamp. If the process does decide to wait, a deadlock situation can result. Ensuring that local causality constraints are not violated within each process and addressing deadlock problems are at the core of the distributed simulation problem. Several approaches have been developed that solve these problems, as will be discussed momentarily.

Before discussing distributed simulation strategies, it is instructive to discuss an example which uses a naive approach to ensure that local causality is never violated. It will be seen that this scheme quickly leads to deadlock.

6.1.4. An Example

Let us again consider the air traffic example depicted in figure 6.1. The three logical processes are labeled ORD, SFO, and EOE. Each process contains a program modeling the airport(s) at that site. Interactions between airports are through airplane arrival events. Assume that an airport schedules a departure event by sending a message to itself when it has determined the time that the airplane will leave. When this event is processed, an arrival event message is sent to the process modeling the destination airport with timestamp denoting the time that the plane will reach its destination. This arrival event causes a new departure event to be scheduled. The simulator for an airport might schedule other internal events such as gate or runway allocation. However, we will ignore these in the present example.

Let us consider a simple strategy to ensure causality constraints are not violated. Each logical process contains the following:

- A local event queue is associated with each input port containing messages from a neighboring process.

- Another event queue contains locally scheduled departure events.

- State variables indicate the current state of the airport.

- Procedures describe the behavior of the airport. One procedure processes airplane arrivals and a second processes locally scheduled departure events.

- Another procedure is responsible for ensuring that events are properly sequenced by the simulator. This procedure determines which event is to be processed next, updates the current simulated time of the process to equal the timestamp on this event, and then calls the procedure responsible for processing that event.

This last procedure is of primary interest here. Consider a naive scheme to ensure local causality is not violated. Assume that the timestamps on messages sent from one process to another (or itself) form a nondecreasing sequence of values. Therefore, when a message arrives at process ORD from SFO with timestamp T_{SFO}, it is guaranteed that subsequent messages from SFO will have timestamps greater than T_{SFO}.

To ensure causality constraints are not violated, messages must be processed *within* each process in nondecreasing timestamp order. Consider the ORD logical process. Assume the next message in each of the queues from SFO, EOE and itself have timestamps T_{SFO}, T_{EOE}, and T_{ORD} respectively. Among these three events, the one with the smallest timestamp should be processed next. Further, because events are generated in nondecreasing order, local causality is guaranteed.

For example, consider each process in figure 6.2a. Each process is receiving a message from its neighboring processes, one with timestamp 10 and another with timestamp 20. Locally scheduled messages are not shown to simplify the presentation. Assuming the next locally scheduled event has timestamp greater than 10, it is clear that each airport simulator should process the timestamp 10 message next.

This scheme works perfectly until we reach a point where one of the event queues is empty. Figure 6.2b shows the state of the system after the timestamp 10 messages have been processed. This message has led to the generation of a timestamp 25 message that has been returned to the sender of the timestamp 10 message. Consider the ORD

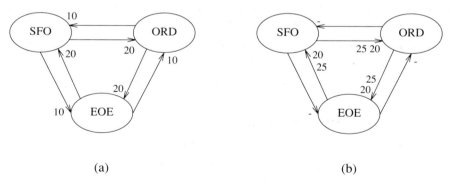

(a)   (b)

Figure 6.2
State of Simulator. (a) Before deadlock. (b) Deadlocked.

process; the other processes face an identical situation. The timestamp of the last message received from EOE had a timestamp of 10. The only messages that are ready to be processed came from SFO and have timestamps of 20 and 25. ORD cannot process either of these messages lest it later receive a message from EOE with timestamp less than 20. Therefore, ORD decides to *wait* for the next message from EOE. Assuming each process follows the same protocol of waiting until it is sure local causality is guaranteed, the situation in figure 6.2b is a deadlocked one. ORD is waiting for EOE, EOE is waiting for SFO, and SFO is waiting for ORD.

The scenario described above illustrates a deadlock situation where processes are blocked on one another while waiting to *receive* new messages from neighboring nodes. A similar kind of deadlock can also result from blocking induced by a flow control mechanism. Because the message queues in each process are necessarily finite, a "fast" sender may be forced to block while waiting for a receiver to absorb the messages it generates. In situations where communications are completely synchronous, i.e., the sender and receiver must concurrently be executing send and receive primitives to communicate, there is effectively no buffering between the communicating parties. This creates a second type of blocking that can also contribute to deadlock.

6.1.5. Overview of Distributed Simulation Strategies

Although the protocol presented above is prone to deadlock, it serves as a good starting point in discussing distributed simulation strategies. The three strategies we will describe follow the paradigm discussed above but provide mechanisms to address the deadlock problem while maintaining local causality. These approaches attack this problem in three different ways:

- Strategy 1 *avoids* deadlock by generating "NULL" messages to distribute information concerning the simulated time of neighboring processes.

- Strategy 2 allows deadlock to occur but provides a mechanism to *detect and recover from* deadlock situations.

- Strategy 3 avoids deadlock by allowing processes to process events on *any* nonempty queue, regardless of the number of other input queues that are empty. This can lead to violation of local causality, so an additional *rollback* mechanism is provided to undo erroneous computations and return to some point before the causality constraint was violated, giving the process another chance to perform the computation correctly.

In the discussions that follow, we make a number of assumptions concerning the parallel computer and the behavior of logical processes:

- Messages sent from one process to another arrive in the same order they were sent.

- Messages are transmitted through the network without error, and no messages are lost.

- Sufficient memory is available on each processor to hold the simulation program, message queues, local variables, etc.

- The timestamps on messages transmitted from one process to another form a nondecreasing sequence. This is strengthened in the deadlock avoidance approach to require that the sequence be strictly increasing.

- All computation occurs as the result of processing a received message. No computation can "spontaneously" begin.

- The timestamp of each message must be at least as large as the timestamp of the message that initiated the computation generating the message.

These restrictions are required in strategies 1 and 2. Several of these assumptions will be relaxed for strategy 3. The discussion of strategy 1 and 2 also assumes a synchronous communication model where the process sending a message must block until the receiver executes the corresponding receive primitive. However, it is straightforward to extend these approaches to use asynchronous communication primitives.

6.2. The Deadlock Avoidance Approach

The first approach, developed by Chandy and Misra [ChMi79], uses a deadlock avoidance technique. Each logical process must partition its set of unprocessed messages into two categories: those that can be processed immediately without fear of violating the local causality constraint and those that cannot. A key observation is that this task is easily accomplished if the process can determine a lower bound on the timestamp of any message it could receive in the future. All messages with timestamps less than or equal to this lower bound can be processed immediately, whereas those with timestamps larger than the bound cannot.

Consider a **link** from logical process i (LP_i) to logical process j (LP_j), indicating that LP_i can send messages to LP_j. Let us associate a variable with this link whose value indicates a lower bound on the timestamp of any future message that can be sent over that link. We refer to this value as the *LINKCLOCK* value for that link. Suppose each process knows the respective *LINKCLOCK* values of all *incoming* links. The minimum of these values is a lower bound on the timestamp of any message the process will receive in the future. Messages on input ports that have timestamps smaller than this lower bound can be processed immediately. Messages with timestamps larger than this lower bound cannot because they may later be "preempted" by some other message carrying a smaller timestamp.

How are these *LINKCLOCK* values computed? We assume each process is responsible for computing *LINKCLOCK* values on all *outgoing* links. Recall that the timestamps on messages sent from one process to another form a nondecreasing sequence of values. Therefore, the timestamp of the last message sent over the link is one lower bound on the timestamp of future messages. However, this may not be a very tight bound, particularly if messages are sent infrequently over the link. The last message sent may be rather "old" and contain outdated information. A second lower bound for *LINKCLOCK* on an outgoing link is the timestamp of the next message that will be processed by the sender. An incoming message with timestamp T cannot cause a new message to be created with timestamp less than T. A lower bound for this quantity is simply the minimum of the *LINKCLOCK* values on *incoming* links. The larger of these two bounds can be used as the *LINKCLOCK* value on the outgoing link.

For example, consider the process in figure 6.3a. The two input links have *LINKCLOCK* values of 6 and 7. The last messages sent on its two output links carried timestamps of 3 and 10, respectively. Therefore, the *LINKCLOCK* values on these output links are 6 (max [3, min (6, 7)]) and 10 (max [10, min (6, 7)]), respectively.

Although this derivation of *LINKCLOCK* values ensures that local causality is not violated, it unfortunately is not sufficient to avoid deadlock. For example, consider the *LINKCLOCK* values depicted in figure 6.3b. This set of values could be generated by

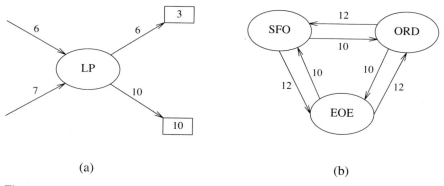

(a)   (b)

Figure 6.3
(a) Computation of LINKCLOCK values. (b) Example of Deadlock.

the following scenario: each process simultaneously receives a message with timestamp 10 which causes a ''reply'' message with timestamp 12 to be returned. Each process has only a single timestamp 12 message waiting to be processed on the link with LINKCLOCK value 12. The simulation strategy described above instructs each process to wait. Consider the ORD process, for example. Only one message is available to be processed, the timestamp 12 message from EOE. However, this timestamp is larger than the LINKCLOCK value on the incoming link from SFO, however. The message cannot be processed yet because ORD has no guarantee from SFO that the latter will not send it a message with, say, timestamp 11. Similarly, SFO must wait for EOE to advance the LINKCLOCK value on the link from EOE to SFO, and EOE similarly waits for ORD. Therefore, the system is deadlocked.

To circumvent this problem using deadlock avoidance, it is necessary to introduce an additional notion called **lookahead**. Lookahead states that a message with timestamp T cannot cause a new message to be generated with timestamp less than T *plus* L, where L is strictly greater than 0. L is the degree of lookahead. The basis for this assumption is that the physical process cannot instantaneously react to an input stimulus. In the airport example, suppose the minimum time for an airplane to land, move to a gate, unload and load passengers, taxi to the runway and depart for the nearest airport is ten time units. The lookahead L is then ten.

Lookahead allows a tighter bound to be derived for *LINKCLOCK*, the lower bound on the timestamp of future messages sent on that link. In particular, each process can compute the *LINKCLOCK* values on outgoing links using the minimum of the incoming *LINKCLOCK* values *plus* the lookahead value, rather than simply the minimum.

This added constraint allows deadlock situations to be avoided. In our example, assuming a lookahead of 1 time unit is used, the *LINKCLOCK* values in figure 6.3b can be increased from 10 to 11 (min $[10, 12] + 1$), and then later to 12. The incoming messages with timestamp 12 can now be safely processed.

Using positive lookahead to derive *LINKCLOCK*, the simulation cannot deadlock. Deadlock is avoided because the process(es) with the smallest *LINKCLOCK* value on an outgoing link can advance this value to the minimum of its incoming *LINKCLOCK* values plus the lookahead value. Because some process is always able to advance its *LINKCLOCK* value, the computation will always be able to advance and deadlock situations cannot appear. A formal proof of this statement is presented in [ChMi79], where it is shown that it is sufficient that nonzero lookahead is present on some link in any loop of links among processes.

The scheme outlined above is the distributed simulation strategy based on deadlock avoidance developed by Chandy and Misra. The details of this strategy will be discussed momentarily. One final detail remains, namely, how does a process determine the *LINKCLOCK* values on incoming links since they are computed by the neighboring processes? If the *LINKCLOCK* value is determined by a message modeling an interaction between the corresponding physical processes, then this value is simply the timestamp of the received message. Otherwise, a special "NULL" message is sent that carries the new *LINKCLOCK* value. Unlike other messages, NULL messages do not correspond to any interaction between physical processes.

Let us first define the notation which will be used:

- T_{ki} is the clock value of the link from LP_k to LP_i. It holds the timestamp of the last message transmitted over the link, including NULL messages. If no messages have been transmitted, it is assumed to be 0. T_{ki} indicates the extent to which LP_i and LP_k have simulated interactions between the corresponding physical processes.

- T_i is the clock value of LP_i, defined as

$$T_i = \min_{j,k} (T_{ij}, T_{ki}).$$

T_i reflects the extent to which LP_i has simulated physical process i.

- $L_{ij}(t)$ is defined as the **lookahead function** for communications from LP_i to LP_j at time t. This defines the extent to which LP_i can determine the timestamp of the next message it will send to LP_j, assuming it has received all incoming messages with timestamps of t or less.

- $LINKCLOCK_{ij}$, is defined as

$$LINKCLOCK_{ij} = \min_k T_{ki} + L_{ij}(\min_k T_{ki}).$$

Logical process i can determine all messages sent to process j up to time $LINKCLOCK_{ij}$. This differs from T_{ij} because the latter is affected only when a message is sent from LP_i to LP_j. $LINKCLOCK_{ij}$ can change whenever a new message is received.

Simulation using the deadlock avoidance scheme consists of three distinct phases that are executed repeatedly until termination of the simulation program:

(1) **Selection Phase.** Select input and output links on which messages will be transmitted. Let $NEXT_i$ be the set of processes with which LP_i is to communicate on this iteration of the algorithm.

(2)   **Computation phase.** For each *output* port in $NEXT_i$, determine the next message to be sent on that link. The next message will either be a message modeling an interaction in the physical system or a NULL message.

(3)   **I/O phase.** Perform the I/O operations for each link in $NEXT_i$.

Each of these operations will now be discussed in turn.

6.2.1. The Selection Phase

The set of processes with which LP_i exchanges messages is

$$NEXT_i = \{k \mid T_{ki} = T_i\} \cup \{j \mid (T_{ij} = T_i) \text{ and } (T_{ij} < LINKCLOCK_{ij})\} .$$

$NEXT_i$ identifies the input and output links of LP_i whose clock values equal the clock value of LP_i. The simulation strategy continually seeks to advance the process's clock T_i. Because T_i is by definition the minimum of the clock values of input (T_{ki}) and output (T_{ij}) links, I/O operations are required on those links that keep T_i at its current value. The constraint $T_{ij} < LINKCLOCK_{ij}$ is necessary because the message stream of the link to LP_j is only known with complete certainty up to time $LINKCLOCK_{ij}$.

6.2.2. The Computation Phase

If $NEXT_i$ contains only *input* links, then LP_i does not perform any computation during this phase. The computation phase determines what message is to be sent on each *output* link in $NEXT_i$. The selection phase dictates that if j is in $NEXT_i$, then $T_{ij} < LINKCLOCK_{ij}$. All messages with timestamp $LINKCLOCK_{ij}$ or less can be computed without any additional input. Two cases exist:

• If physical process i (PP_i) sends a message to physical process j (PP_j) in the time interval (T_{ij}, $LINKCLOCK_{ij}$], then send the corresponding message from LP_i to LP_j.

• If no messages are sent from PP_i to PP_j in this interval, send a NULL message to LP_j with timestamp $LINKCLOCK_{ij}$ indicating this fact.

6.2.3. The I/O Phase

I/O operations are now performed simultaneously on all links in $NEXT_i$. The clock value for each link is updated to the timestamp of the message sent or received on that link. The clock value of the process is updated to equal the minimum clock of any I/O link for the process. Following this step, we return to the selection phase of the algorithm. It has been shown that the deadlock avoidance scheme described above correctly sequences events and is free from deadlock [ChMi79].

6.2.4. Initialization and Termination

Initially, the input and output link clocks of each process are set to 0. The process clock is also set to 0. The distributed simulator then begins the selection phase described above. Processes with no input ports, i.e., source processes, immediately begin generating messages. If the simulator contains no source processes, then the logical processes composing the simulator will exchange NULL messages until some process's clock has advanced to a point when it can generate a non-NULL simulation message.

Termination can be handled by specifying the length of (simulated) time which the simulator should run. Assume the simulator is to run until each process reaches time Z. If a process generates a message with timestamp greater than Z, the message is replaced with a NULL message with timestamp Z. Logical processes continue executing the selection, computation, and I/O phases until all link and process clocks equal Z.

6.3. The Deadlock Detection and Recovery Approach

The second distributed simulation strategy allows the simulator to deadlock rather than generate NULL message to advance local clocks. Separate mechanisms are required to detect and break the deadlock. In this light, the simulation strategy becomes a sequence of parallel job steps:

(1) Simulate until deadlock.

(2) Detect the deadlock.

(3) Break the deadlock and return to step 1.

This approach, also developed by Chandy and Misra [ChMi81], is discussed next.

Each of the three job steps involves a parallel computation. The transition from one phase to the next is managed by a central controller process. The controller is not a bottleneck because it does not perform any significant computation. It only signals the transition from one job step to the next.

6.3.1. The Simulation Phase

As before, T_{ij} denotes the timestamp of the last message sent from LP_i to LP_j. T_i, the clock value in logical process LP_i, is defined as $\min_{j,k} (T_{ij}, T_{ki})$ and is a lower bound on the timestamp of the next message that will be sent or received by LP_i. Unlike the deadlock avoidance approach, no notion of lookahead is necessary.

A logical process waits for a message to arrive using the following rules:

• LP_i waits on all *input* links which have a link clock value T_{ki} equal to T_i.

• LP_i waits on all output links on which it has a message to send.

After sending/receiving a message, the process executes until the next communication is required.

The system described above can deadlock just as the airport simulation program described earlier. A controller process detects deadlock using a distributed computation. A signaling scheme developed by Dijkstra and Scholten can be used for this purpose [DiSc80]. The Dijkstra and Scholten algorithm (DSA) assumes processes never have to wait to send a message. Later, we will present another algorithm developed by Chandy and Misra (CMA) that allows processes to be blocked when sending messages [ChMi82].

6.3.2. The Dijkstra Scholten Algorithm (DSA)

The distributed simulation is characterized as a "diffusing computation." The simulation program is a collection of logical processes and a single controller. Initially, the computation is deadlocked and all *LPs* are idle because no process is able to execute any code for fear of violating the local causality constraint. The controller selects one or more processes and instructs them to advance their local clocks and resume execution, as will be discussed later. The processes that have been started will send messages that start other processes, and so on. The computation "diffuses" across the entire system in a manner similar to the diffusion of perfume molecules across a room. However, as time progresses, processes will begin to block again, and eventually the computation grinds to a halt. At this time, the controller must again nudge some process(es) ahead to resume the computation. To implement this scheme, we will define a signaling protocol to be superimposed on the message sending system so that the controller can detect the end of the diffusing computation.

One can view the dynamic behavior of the diffusing computation as the growth and shrinkage of a tree, where the controller is the root and logical processes form the other nodes of the tree. Processes contained in the tree are said to be *engaged*, and the remaining processes are said to be *disengaged*. When the computation is deadlocked, all processes are disengaged. A process becomes engaged and is added to the tree when it receives a message from another engaged process or the controller. Thus, the tree grows as the controller sends messages to processes to restart the computation and as engaged processes send messages to other disengaged processes. When a process becomes engaged, it is added to the tree as a descendant of the process that engaged it, i.e., the process which sent it a message.

For an engaged process to become disengaged and removed from the tree it must:

- be in an idle state where it cannot perform any new computation or generate any new messages unless some additional messages arrive, and

- be a leaf node of the tree.

When these conditions become true, the leaf process signals its parent process to indicate that the leaf has removed itself from the tree and has become disengaged. The signaling protocol must ensure that each process can determine when it creates a new descendant, i.e., when it sends a message to a previously disengaged process, as well as when a descendant becomes disengaged. With this information, each engaged process can determine if it is a leaf node, as required in the second condition above. The tree will continually grow and shrink as processes are added to and removed from the tree. As the computation approaches deadlock, more and more processes become disengaged, and the tree shrinks to fewer and fewer nodes. The network is deadlocked when all of the processes have been removed from the tree and only the root, i.e., the controller, remains. Once the controller detects that it has become a leaf, it concludes the system is deadlocked.

To implement this scheme, a signaling convention must be adopted to control the growth and shrinkage of the tree. The goal of the signaling convention is to allow a process to determine when it has become a leaf node of the tree. Therefore, a process must determine when it has spawned a new descendant, i.e., when it has engaged a previously disengaged process, and when descendants that it earlier engaged become disengaged. A simple signaling protocol that achieves this consists of the following rules:

- When an *engaged* process receives a message, it immediately returns a signal to the process that sent the message. In this case, the message did *not* spawn a new descendant, and the signal informs the sender of this fact.

- When a disengaged process receives a message, it becomes engaged and does *not* return a signal to the process that engaged it until it becomes disengaged again. This corresponds to the creation of a new descendant.

- Each process maintains a count of the number of messages it has sent that have yet to be signaled. Each unsignaled message denotes either (a) a descendant in the tree remains, or (b) the message or the returned signal has been delayed in the communication network, or (c) a "slow" receiver that has not yet responded to its messages. When this count is zero, the process must be a leaf process because signals have been returned from all processes that this process engaged. If the process now has no work to do, it becomes disengaged and returns a signal to its parent.

More formally, the signaling scheme operates as follows:

- Each process maintains two variables, C and D, which always assume nonnegative values. C denotes the number of messages received from neighboring processes that have yet to be signaled, and D denotes the number of messages sent to other processes for which a signal has yet to be returned.

- A process is in the disengaged state whenever $C = 0$ and $D = 0$.

- Sending a message to another process causes D in the sending process to be incremented by 1 and C in the receiving process to be incremented by 1.

- Sending a signal to another process causes C in the sender to be decremented by 1 and D in the receiver to be decremented by 1.

- Each process is constrained so that the following condition is always true: $C > 0$ OR $D = 0$.

This last condition ensures that the process is either engaged and has yet to return a signal for the message that engaged it, and possibly some others as well ($C > 0$), or if C is 0 then D is also 0, meaning the process is disengaged. It can be shown that as long as each process adheres to these rules, the controller will detect deadlock a finite amount of time after the computation has ceased [DiSc80].

6.3.3. The Chandy Misra Algorithm (CMA)

Chandy and Misra have extended DSA to operate in a synchronous message passing environment such as Hoare's Communicating Sequential Processes (CSP). The essential difference between CSP and the communication mechanism assumed in DSA is that processes in CSP may have to wait when *sending* a message as well as when receiving. In DSA, processes only block when receiving. The principal consequence that a blocking send primitive has on the algorithm is that processes in CSP can no longer determine if they are idle based on local information alone. Recall that this information is essential in DSA because it is a necessary condition for a process to become disengaged. A process blocked on a send may or may not be able to send more messages, depending on the state of the receiver. Thus, in CMA we need information in each process regarding the state of its neighbors.

CMA uses two signaling schemes: A-signals are similar to the signals used in DSA to manage the tree of engaged processes, and B-signals are used to inform processes of the state of their neighbors (blocked or running). It is assumed that signals can be processed even if the logical process is waiting to send or receive a message.

In DSA, a process must determine if it is blocked, i.e., unable to perform any more computation or generate any new messages unless additional messages arrive. Here, a process cannot determine this with absolute certainty because remote information is required. Instead, each process LP_j computes a boolean value called *thinkblocked(j)* based on locally available information. *Thinkblocked(j)* is true if LP_j thinks it is blocked, and false otherwise. To compute *thinkblocked*, process j maintains local boolean variables $r_j(i)$ and $s_j(i)$ for each neighbor i. $r_j(i)$ is true if process j thinks that neighboring process i is waiting to receive a message from it. Similarly, $s_j(i)$ is true if process j thinks that process i is waiting to send a message to it. Note that $r_j(i)$ and $s_j(i)$ may be inaccurate because the status of the neighbor may have changed since the neighbor last sent a message. *Thinkblocked (j)* is true if each of the following three conditions is true:

- LP_j is not executing,

- for each process i to which j is waiting to send a message, $r_j(i)$ is FALSE, and

- for each process k from which j is waiting to receive a message, $s_j(k)$ is FALSE.

Because *thinkblocked* is based on information that may be out of date, it may not reflect the true status of the process. Chandy and Misra show, however, that the algorithm operates correctly despite this inconsistency.

Three types of communications can occur among processes:

- *Messages* are used to model interactions among physical processes.

- *A-Signals*, or activity signals, are used to construct the engagement tree discussed in DSA.

- *B-Signals*, or blocking signals, are used to inform neighbors of changes in the status of processes. For example, a B-Signal is sent whenever a process becomes blocked attempting to send or receive a message.

The rules governing the signaling scheme are as follows:

- *Condition for sending B-signals.* Process i sends a B-signal to neighboring processes whenever its waiting status changes. Formally, LP_i sends a B-signal to LP_j if and only if $r_j(i)$ or $s_j(i)$ is inconsistent with LP_i's true waiting status. LP_i can deduce remote values of r and s from the B-signals it has already sent.

- *Condition for sending A-signals for nontree arcs.* An incoming nontree arc corresponds to a communication that did not engage the process. Recall in DSA, these arcs were removed by returning a signal as soon as the message was received by the already engaged process. In CMA, each process eliminates all nontree arcs when that process thinks it is blocked. LP_j sends an A-signal to LP_i where the arc from LP_i to LP_j is a nontree arc if *thinkblocked(j)* is true. This deletes the nontree arc.

• *Condition for sending A-signals for tree arcs.* Process j deletes its incoming tree arc by sending an A-signal when: (1) *thinkblocked(j)* is true, (2) process j has no other incoming or outgoing arcs, and (3) LP_j has ensured that for each neighbor k, $r_k(j)$ and $s_k(j)$ accurately reflect the true waiting status of LP_j. LP_j ensures this latter condition by sending appropriate B-signals.

Initially, processes must ensure that $r_j(i)$ and $s_j(i)$ reflect the true waiting status of LP_i and LP_j for each i and j. The controller is initially engaged, and all other processes are disengaged. Chandy and Misra prove that the signaling scheme outlined above always detects deadlock a finite amount of time after it occurs and never indicates a deadlock situation when none has occurred [ChMi81].

6.3.4. Deadlock Recovery

Once deadlock has been detected, the controller initiates a distributed computation to break the deadlock. The purpose of this computation is to determine how far the clock on each link can be advanced.

A simple means of breaking the deadlock can be seen if we consider the operation of a *sequential* event driven simulation program. Events to be processed are placed in a list that is sorted in increasing timestamp order. The operation of the simulator consists of repeatedly removing the "oldest" event from the queue and executing some procedure assigned to processing the event. This scenario can also be used to break deadlocks in a distributed simulator. Because the message with minimum timestamp certainly can be safely processed, the deadlock can always be broken by processing this message next.

More precisely, for any link from LP_i to LP_j, let U_{ij} be the timestamp of the next message sent over this link, assuming no further messages will be received by LP_i. Let U_{kr} be the minimum of all U_{ij}. This is the oldest message in the simulator. It can be processed next to break the deadlock. One need only compute U_{kr} in a distributed manner, signal LP_k and LP_r to resume computation, and transmit the message with this timestamp.

This approach described above is overly conservative because it may be possible to start several logical processes to break the deadlock. For example, consider the simulator depicted in figure 6.4. If the oldest message is on the link from LP_3 to LP_5, and the second oldest is from LP_2 to LP_4, we can immediately begin processing both of these messages because the communication paths used by this simulator make it impossible for the oldest message to affect the second oldest.

In general, a process can transmit a message if the timestamp of that message is smaller than the timestamp of messages generated by processes "upstream." A process

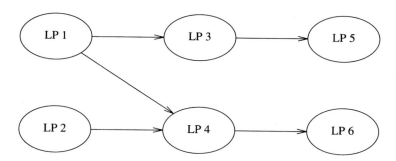

Figure 6.4
Deadlock Breaking Example.

"upstream" from LP_i is defined as any process with a path of links leading to LP_i; for example, in figure 6.4, LP_1, LP_2, and LP_4 are upstream from LP_6. The smallest timestamp of any message LP_6 can receive is the minimum of $U_{1,4}$, $U_{2,4}$, and $U_{4,6}$.

Before defining the deadlock breaking computation formally, let us observe one more fact. Suppose, as in figure 6.4, LP_4 is waiting to send a message with timestamp T^* to LP_6. Because successive messages contain nondecreasing timestamps, T^* is a lower bound of any message sent over that link, independent of the timestamps of messages sent on the links from LP_2 to LP_4 or LP_1 to LP_4.

The distributed computation for breaking deadlock requires the computation of the quantity W_{ij}, the lower bound of any timestamp of future messages transmitted from LP_i to LP_j. In general, W_{ij} is a tighter lower bound than U_{ij} discussed earlier. This new bound is defined as:

$$
W_{ij} = \begin{cases} f \text{ if } LP_i \text{ is waiting to output a message with timestamp } f \text{ to } LP_j \\ \max (T_{ij}, \min [U_{ij}, \min_{r} \{W_{ri}\}]) \text{ otherwise.} \end{cases}
$$

The first case follows from the discussion in the previous paragraph. In the second case, T_{ij} is the timestamp of the last message sent over the link and serves as one lower bound on W_{ij}. The second term is another lower bound representing the minimum timestamp of messages we already know will be generated without any additional information (U_{ij}) and messages that can arrive in the future and cause a new message to be sent to LP_j (W_{ri}).

W_{ij} may be computed iteratively in a distributed manner. The computation for LP_i is:

(1)   Set $W_{ij}^{(1)} = U_{ij}$ and send it to LP_j, set $k = 2$.

(2) $W_{ij}^{(k)} = \begin{cases} f \text{ if } LP_i \text{ is waiting to output a message with time stamp f to } LP_j \\ \max (T_{ij}, \min[U_{ij}, \min_r \{W_{ri}^{(k-1)}\}]) \text{ otherwise.} \end{cases}$

$W_{ri}^{(k-1)}$ was computed by LP_r on the previous iteration and was sent to LP_i at the end of that iteration.

(3)   Send the value $W_{ij}^{(k)}$ to neighbor LP_j.

(4)   Let N be the number of logical processes in the network. If $k = N$, go to the next step, else $k = k + 1$ and go to step 2,

(5) $W_{ij} = W_{ij}^{(N)}$

No future messages sent from LP_i to LP_j will carry a timestamp smaller than W_{ij}. The clock value of every link T_{ri} can be updated to W_{ri}. If the set of links on which LP_i now waits is different from that before the update, the process is said to be resumable and can continue execution. Each process signals the controller to indicate if it is resumable. These signals indicate which processes have become engaged.

6.3.5. Simulation Using Deadlock Detection

We can now describe the entire simulation algorithm using deadlock detection and recovery. Each logical process executes the following:

Initialization:
>   Initialize the clock on each link to 0.
>   Define this *LP* to be resumable if it is waiting to send along some link.

LOOP:
>   Send a message to the controller indicating if it is resumable.
>   Simulate, using the waiting rules defined earlier to send and receive messages.
>   Compute *U* and *W* values when the controller indicates deadlock has occurred.
>   **END-LOOP**

The controller performs the following actions:

LOOP:
>   Receive signals from processes indicating if they are resumable.
>   Receive signals denoting deadlock.
>   Send signals to all processes to initiate *W* computations.
>   **END-LOOP**

6.4. The Time Warp Mechanism

The approaches presented thus far are "conservative" because processes cautiously advance their clocks only when they are sure this will not violate the local causality constraint. The Time Warp scheme takes a more liberal viewpoint and allows processes to progress as rapidly as possible, sometimes risking an erroneous simulation. When an error does occur, it is erased by *rolling back* the computation to a point in simulated time before the error. The computation then proceeds forward until the next error is detected.

The rollback scenario is complicated by the fact that the computation that was rolled back may have sent messages to other processes which in turn may have triggered the generation of other erroneous messages. Thus, the rollback may not be confined to a single process. This approach to distributed simulation was first proposed by Jefferson and Sowizral [JeSo83, Jeff83, Jeff85].

6.4.1. Assumptions

Many of the assumptions required in the previously discussed methods can be relaxed in Time Warp. In particular, we need not assume that messages are delivered in the same order they were sent. The sequence of timestamps on messages transmitted from one process to another need not be nondecreasing, however, processes cannot generate messages with timestamps less than its local clock. The communication paradigm is now assumed to be asynchronous, i.e., the sender need not block and wait for the receiver. Queues hold messages waiting to be delivered to destination processes. We still assume, however, that communications are reliable, that sufficient memory resources are available, and that all computation is initiated by received messages.

Previously, we have implicitly assumed that no logical process could be created once the simulation began. Dynamic creation of processes is difficult to implement in the previously described strategies because each process must know which other processes can send it a message that could violate local causality constraints. In contrast, dynamic creation of processes is not incompatible with the Time Warp approach; this is beyond the scope of the present discussion, however.

6.4.2. Logical Processes

Each logical process contains state for several distinct purposes:

- *state variables* that model the state of the physical process;
- a *single input queue* containing a time sorted list of messages yet to be processed;

- a *local clock variable* indicating the current value in simulated time of the process;
- an *output queue* containing messages waiting to be transmitted;
- a list of *previous state vectors* and associated clock times, necessary for rollback;
- a list of *previous messages* sent by the process.

Each logical process removes messages from its input queue and processes them one by one. This activity proceeds regardless of the local clock in other processes. As each message is processed, the process's local clock is set to the timestamp of that message. If the input queue is empty, the local clock is set to "infinity."

Each message contains the identity of the sending and receiving processes, the timestamps in simulated time when the message was sent and received, and an arbitrary data field defined by the application program. The send time of any message can never exceed the receive time.

6.4.3. Error Detection and Roll Back

Each process must determine when it has processed incoming messages (events) out of order. A process can detect a violation of local causality by checking that the timestamp on the next message to be processed is at least as large as the last message that was processed. If an error has occurred, a rollback is necessary.

Let M be the message causing the rollback and M_T be the timestamp on this message. When M arrives, the computation must be rolled back to a point in simulated time earlier than M_T. The current state of the logical process must be replaced with that before M_T. Consider the types of state that exist in the process and how they are updated:

- *State Variables:* The most recent state vector with timestamp less than or equal to M_T is retrieved from the list of previous state vectors and is used to restore the system state. Assume the system state is restored to that at simulated time T.

- *Input Queue:* This is restored to its value at simulated time T as part of the state vector restoration, and M is inserted into its proper position.

- *Local Clock Variable*: This is reset to the timestamp of the first message in the input queue after the restoration to time T. This may *not* be M_T if state vectors are saved less frequently than after each message has been processed.

- *Output Queue:* The queue is reset in accordance with the rules describing anti-messages (discussed below).

- *Previous State Vectors:* State vectors with timestamps less than T are kept; others are discarded.

• *Previous messages sent by the process:* Those messages with timestamps larger than T must be "unsent" using anti-messages, discussed below. Unsent messages are discarded, whereas earlier messages remain in the history list.

6.4.4. Anti-Messages

Messages sent by the process during a computation that has been rolled back must somehow be "unsent." **Anti-messages** are defined for this purpose. An anti-message is identical in format and content to a message sent by a process, except in a single boolean flag field that distinguishes it from the corresponding normal message. We will refer to the original message as the "positive" copy of the message, and the anti-message as the "negative" copy. When a rollback occurs to simulated time T, an anti-message is sent for each message sent by the process with timestamp larger than T. Messages that must be unsent reside in the list of previously sent messages. When positive and negative versions of a message meet, the two annihilate each other in much the same way as an atom of anti-matter annihilates an atom of matter.

When the anti-message is generated, one of four possible scenarios will ensue:

• The anti-message and corresponding message meet in the output queue of the process being rolled back. In this case, they annihilate each other, and all is well.

• The two meet in the input queue of the process receiving the message. They again annihilate each other, and all is well.

• The positive message has already been received and processed by the receiving process. This is detected by noting that the matching message is stored in the input history queue for that process. In this case, the anti-message must undo any work triggered by the original message. This is accomplished by rolling back the computation in the receiving process to a time preceding the timestamp of the anti-message. This rollback may in turn generate new anti-messages, allowing all effects of the erroneous message to be rolled back across the entire system.

• One other case exists. The corresponding message may not have arrived at the receiving process yet. This situation may arise if the communications system does not guarantee that messages will arrive in the same order they were sent. This situation is detected by the receiving process when it cannot find any record of the positive message. The process then enqueues the anti-message and waits for the corresponding positive message to arrive, at which time the two will annihilate each other.

Therefore, to "unsend" a message, it suffices to send the corresponding anti-message. Jefferson has shown that a computation always progresses, despite rollback, and will eventually terminate if the simulation program terminates [Jeff83].

6.4.5. Global Virtual Time

The discussion so far has assumed that processes retain state information from the beginning of the computation. Maintaining all previous state vectors requires an unbounded amount of memory, and is not feasible for long simulations. Furthermore, one might expect that as the local clocks advance in simulated time, the likelihood of rolling back to a point in time near the beginning of the simulation becomes increasingly remote. **Global virtual time**, defined below, provides a mechanism for determining when it is safe to "forget" old state information. Reclaiming memory resources used by old state vectors that are no longer required is called **fossil collection**.

Suppose the simulator has reached a point where all local clocks exceed a value of T, and all messages bearing a timestamp less than T have been processed. Then it is clear that no message or anti-message can be created with timestamp less than T. Because rollback can only be triggered by a message or anti-message, it follows that no rollback message with timestamp less than T can be created. Therefore, each process need only remember one state vectors with timestamp less than T. One state vector is needed in case a rollback message occurs with, say, timestamp T.

Global virtual time (GVT) is a lower bound on the timestamp of any message causing a rollback. The value of GVT never decreases during the simulation. It is defined as the minimum of (a) all virtual clocks at that time in the simulation and (b) the send timestamp of all messages that have been sent but have not yet been processed by the receiver. The send time rather than the receive time of messages is used because of the flow control mechanism used in Time Warp (described later). It can be shown that GVT never decreases in value as the simulation progresses. A process need only remember the most recent state vector with timestamp less than GVT. Earlier state vectors can be forgotten and their memory resources reclaimed.

At a particular point in the simulation, GVT can be computed by determining the minimum of (a) all local clocks, (b) the send times of all messages "in transit," i.e., all messages which have been sent, but not yet acknowledged, and (c) the send times of all messages in input queues which have not yet been processed. Each process can easily compute these quantities locally, so we only need to find the minimum value across the entire system. Due to communication delays, computation of GVT is necessarily imprecise. However, a value of GVT no smaller than the true value when the GVT computation begins and no larger than the true value when the computation completes can be derived in the time required for a broadcast communication. Further details of a protocol for this computation are discussed in [Sama85].

6.4.6. Flow Control

When messages arrive at a process at a higher rate than they can be processed, the incoming flow of traffic must be throttled. Otherwise, the input queue will eventually overflow. The approach usually taken is to block the process generating the messages until the receiver can reduce the size of its input queue.

Jefferson proposes an alternative approach in Time Warp. Rather than blocking the sender, receivers can return messages to the originating process forcing the sender to rollback to a time before the message was sent. Because this rollback uses the send time of the message rather than the receive time, the GVT calculation described earlier must be based on the message send time. This provides a rather simple means of implementing flow control, although the expense of additional rollbacks which may ensue has yet to be evaluated.

6.4.7. I/O and Runtime Errors

I/O presents an interesting problem in the Time Warp scheme. A process cannot simply send data to an output device, say a terminal display, because the computation which generated that output may later have to be rolled back. This problem is solved by treating an output request as a message, and the output device as a separate process. The output process buffers output requests and only performs a physical output operation when the timestamp on the request exceeds the GVT value. This guarantees that output operations never need to be rolled back.

Similarly, runtime errors can occur, e.g., by receiving an inconsistent sequence of events. However, the error may later be erased by a rollback. In Time Warp, an error causes the process to mark its state as an error state. However, the user cannot be notified that an error has occurred until GVT exceeds the timestamp on this error state. Whenever an attempt is made to fossil collect an error state, the process is terminated and the error reported to the user.

6.4.8. Termination Detection

GVT also provides a convenient means for detecting when the computation has completed. The simulation has terminated when all logically processes are idle, and there are no messages in transit to specific destinations. Earlier we said that an idle process sets its local clock to infinity. Hence, the computation is complete when GVT also reaches infinity.

6.5. Summary

We have described three proposed strategies for distributed simulation. Each strategy has its respective advantages and drawbacks. Other strategies have been reported in the literature [Brya77, PeWM79, PeWM80, Reyn82].

The deadlock avoidance approach is completely distributed and does not require any global resources. It is relatively intuitive and straightforward to implement. The central disadvantage of this approach is that a large fraction of the message traffic generated by the simulator may be NULL messages. In addition to placing an extra burden on the communications system, a significant amount of processor time may be spent processing these NULL messages. Hence, this approach to distributed simulation is not appropriate for modeling all physical systems.

The deadlock detection approach avoids NULL messages at the cost of added complexity to detect and break the deadlock. Although a centralized controller is required, it does not perform any substantial computations and should not present any significant problem. Like deadlock avoidance, the memory requirements of deadlock detection and recovery are bounded and are not significantly greater than that required by an equivalent single processor simulation program.

Finally, the Time Warp scheme offers a more flexible and robust approach than the other, more conservative approaches. Fewer constraints are placed on the application program. In particular, dynamic creation of logical processes is permitted. Time Warp also has a great intuitive appeal because it does not unnecessarily block a process to avoid violating causality constraints. The central drawbacks of this approach are the overhead to perform the state saving and rollback tasks and the potentially large amounts of memory required to implement it.

Although several schemes exist for distributed simulation, and certainly one could devise several others, we must hasten to point out that relatively few implementations exist and little empirical data have been collected which demonstrates conclusively that these approaches achieve good speedups. Hence, the effectiveness of these approaches across a wide variety of application areas is currently an open question. Comprehensive comparisons of the usefulness of alternative approaches have yet to be performed. Not surprisingly, speedup is heavily dependent on characteristics of the system being modeled.

References

[Brya77]   R. E. Bryant, *Simulation of Packet Communication Architecture Computer Systems*. M.S. Dissertation, Massachusetts Institute of Technology, Cambridge, Massachusetts, 1977.

[ChMi79]   K. M. Chandy and J. Misra, "Distributed Simulation: A Case Study in Design and Verification of Distributed Programs," *IEEE Transactions on Software Engineering* (September 1979), Vol. SE-5, No. 5, pp. 440-452.

[ChMi81]   K. M. Chandy and J. Misra, "Asynchronous Distributed Simulation via a Sequence of Parallel Computations," *Communications of the ACM* (April 1981), Vol. 24, No. 4, pp. 198-206.

[ChMi82]   K. M. Chandy and J. Misra, "Termination Detection of Diffusing Computations in Communicating Sequential Processes," *ACM Transactions on Programming Languages and Systems* (January 1982), Vol. 4, No. 1, pp. 37-43.

[DiSc80]   E. W. Dijkstra and C. S. Scholten, "Termination Detection for Diffusing Computations," *Information Processing Letters* (August 1980), Vol. 11, No. 1, pp. 1-4.

[Jeff83]   D. R. Jefferson, "Virtual Time," *Proceedings of the 1983 International Conference on Parallel Processing* (August 1983), pp. 384-394.

[Jeff85]   D. R. Jefferson, "Virtual Time," *ACM Transactions on Programming Languages and Systems* (July 1985), Vol. 7, No. 3, pp. 404-425.

[JeSo83]   D. R. Jefferson and H. Sowizral, "Fast Concurrent Simulation Using the Time Warp Part I: Local Control", Technical Report, Rand Corporation, Santa Monica California, June 1983.

[PeWM79]   J. K. Peacock, J. W. Wong and E. G. Manning, "Distributed Simulation Using a Network of Processors," *Computer Networks* (February 1979), Vol. 3, No. 1, pp. 44-56.

[PeWM80]   J. K. Peacock, J. W. Wong and E. G. Manning, "Synchronization of Distributed Simulation Using Broadcast Algorithms," *Computer Networks* (February 1980), Vol. 4, No. 1, pp. 3-10.

[Reyn82]   P. F. Reynolds, "A Shared Resource Algorithm for Distributed Simulation," *Proceedings of the 9th Annual Symposium on Computer Architecture, Austin, Texas* (April 1982), Vol. 10, No. 3, pp. 259-266.

[Sama85]   B. Samadi, *Distributed Simulation: Performance and Analysis*. Ph.D. Dissertation, University of California, Los Angeles, California, 1985.

7 Applications: Partial Differential Equations

Numbers are limits, and perfection doesn't have limits.

Richard Bach

Many physical phenomena can best be modeled by elliptic, parabolic, or hyperbolic partial differential equations. In two variables, these equations take the form

$$a\frac{\partial^2 u}{\partial x^2} + b\frac{\partial^2 u}{\partial x \partial y} + c\frac{\partial^2 u}{\partial y^2} = f,$$

where a, b, c are functions of x and y, and f is a function of $x, y, u, \partial x$, and ∂y [OrVo85].

For an **elliptic** partial differential equation, the coefficients must satisfy:

$$b^2 - 4ac < 0.$$

Problems of this type arise naturally in the study of various time-independent physical problems such as the steady-state distribution of heat in a plane region, the potential energy of a point in a plane acted on by gravitational forces in a plane, and two-dimensional steady-state problems involving incompressible fluids.

Parabolic partial differential equations must satisfy:

$$b^2 - 4ac = 0.$$

This equation can describe the heat flow along a rod, assuming uniform temperature within each cross-sectional element. In addition, the parabolic partial differential equation is also important in gas diffusion study.

Finally, a **hyperbolic** partial differential equation satisfies:

$$b^2 - 4ac > 0.$$

The one-dimensional wave equation is an example of this type. Suppose an elastic string of length l is stretched between two supports at some horizontal level. If the string is set in motion so that it vibrates in the vertical plane, then the vertical displacement $u(x,t)$ of a point x at time t satisfies the above equation if damping effects are neglected. Other physical problems involving the hyperbolic partial differential equation occur in the study of vibrating beams with one or both ends clamped, and in the transmission of electricity in a long transmission line when there is some current leakage to the ground.

The example applications just described are among the simplest. Partial differential equations can also describe the air flow over wing surfaces, atmospheric circulation, galactic evolution, and material stress. Unfortunately, closed form solutions rarely if ever exist, and numerical solution of these partial differential equations is at best extremely expensive and often intractable. Of the three types, elliptic partial differential equations [OrVo85] are the simplest, and they present many of the same problems in algorithm design and task scheduling as the others. Hence, we consider only the solution of elliptic partial differential equations in this chapter.

Given an elliptic partial equation on some planar region, the classical central difference technique, discussed in the next section, covers the region with a rectangular grid and replaces the derivatives at each grid point with central differences. The resulting system of linear equations can then be solved in parallel. Within this framework there remain several alternatives, and an optimal choice depend on the problem. Finally, if multiple multicomputer nodes are to cooperate, each solving the linear equations corresponding to a portion of the grid, the selection of grid partitions and their assignment to nodes are crucial to good performance.

Historically, only rectangular partitions of the discretization grid have been assigned to nodes, primarily because the resulting data structures are regular. However, triangles, squares, and hexagons also tessellate the plane. Partitions like hexagons have a higher area to perimeter ratio than squares and potentially less interpartition communication. Hence, the interaction of partition, discretization stencil, and multicomputer architecture must be investigated to determine the optimal combination.

In this chapter, we present a formal method for analyzing the performance of a stencil and grid partition when the partitions are mapped onto the the nodes of a multicomputer network. In section §7.2, we compute the total number of points in a partition and the number of points that must be transmitted between partitions, given the discretization stencil and the partition shape.[1] In sections §7.3 and §7.4, these results are used to determine those pairs of stencil and partition that maximize the ratio of computation to communication. In section §7.5, we derive a performance model of the solution of Laplace's equation on a multicomputer network. The section concludes with an experimental validation of the performance model. We begin, however, by describing solution techniques for partial differential equations.

7.1. Solution Techniques

Elliptic partial differential equations, particularly the Laplace and Poisson equations, have long been used to test new solution algorithms and parallel architectures. Consequently, our study is based on the following problem formulation.

The Problem: Consider the Laplace equation

$$\frac{\partial^2 u}{\partial x^2} + \frac{\partial^2 u}{\partial y^2} = 0, \tag{7.1}$$

an elliptic partial differential equation with Dirichlet boundary conditions, on some square region R. If R is discretized to contain $N = n^2$ points, we wish to iteratively solve the resulting linear system on a multicomputer network containing p processors (nodes), where $p \leq N$.

Although the Laplace equation can be solved directly using a fast Poisson solver [Swar77], many problems that arise during its iterative solution are shared with more complex problems, whence its status as a test problem.

Because few differential equations have closed form solutions, determining the numerical solution at points in the function domain must suffice. The number of points necessary depends on the rate of function change. Where there are large variations, many points will be needed to accurately capture the function behavior. A uniform grid with point spacing sufficiently close to capture the most rapid function variation will result in unnecessary computation. By using a non-uniform grid, computation can be concentrated on those areas where it is needed (see figure 5.2). To simplify analysis, we concentrate on uniform grids. However, the techniques presented are applicable to each of the sub-grids in a non-uniform grid.

---

[1]A portion of this work appeared in *IEEE Transactions on Computers* [ReAP87].

Each grid point represents a linear equation obtained by applying a **discretization stencil**, a discrete approximation to the partial derivatives. The calculus defines the derivative of $u(x)$ as

$$\lim_{h \to 0} \frac{u(x+h) - u(x)}{h}.$$

Two applications of this definition yield the discrete approximation of the partial derivative with respect to x:

$$\frac{\Delta^2 u}{\Delta x^2} = \frac{u(x+h, y) - 2u(x, y) + u(x-h, y)}{h^2}. \tag{7.2}$$

Substituting (7.2) and an equivalent approximation for the partial derivative with respect to y in (7.1) give

$$\frac{u(x+h, y) - 4u(x, y) + u(x-h, y) + u(x, y-h)}{h^2} = 0.$$

With rearrangement of terms, we obtain

$$u_{i,j} = \frac{1}{4}\left[u_{i-1,j} + u_{i+1,j} + u_{i,j-1} + u_{i,j+1} \right], \tag{7.3}$$

where $u_{i,j} \equiv u(x_0 + ih, y_0 + jh)$, (x_0, y_0) is the lower right corner of the square domain, and h is the horizontal and vertical spacing between grid points. Applying this centered **5-point stencil** (see figure 7.1b) at each of the n^2 grid points in the domain converts the partial differential equation in (7.1) to a system of n^2 linear equations.

Although the system of equations can be solved directly, e.g., via Gaussian elimination, the linear system is extremely sparse; each grid point depends on only its four nearest neighbors. Direct solution techniques require $O(n^6)$ time and $O(n^4)$ storage for a system of n^2 linear equations. However, iterative techniques require no extra storage, and with appropriate restrictions, converge quickly [Youn71].

The classical **Jacobi iterative method** rewrites (7.3) as

$$u_{i,j}^{i+1} = \frac{1}{4}\left[u_{i-1,j}^{i} + u_{i+1,j}^{i} + u_{i,j-1}^{i} + u_{i,j+1}^{i} \right], \tag{7.4}$$

where the superscript i is the iteration number. Given initial approximations for $u_{i,j}^{0}$, at each iteration the Jacobi method computes the average of each point's four neighboring

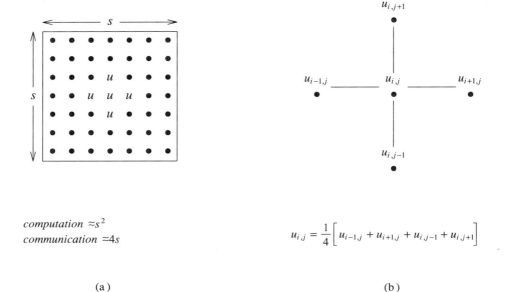

computation $\approx s^2$

communication $\approx 4s$

$$u_{i,j} = \frac{1}{4}\left[u_{i-1,j} + u_{i+1,j} + u_{i,j-1} + u_{i,j+1} \right]$$

(a)   (b)

Figure 7.1
Square partitions with 5-point stencil.

points *from the previous iteration.* The iteration continues until the difference between successive iteration values lies below some threshold ε.

Because the value of each point can be computed independently, the Jacobi technique is completely parallel; however, it converges slowly. Variations on the Jacobi method, e.g., Gauss-Seidel and SOR, increase the convergence rate at the expense of parallelism. In (7.4), each grid point is updated using only values from the previous iteration. If some values from the current iteration were used, one would expect the convergence rate to increase. The **Gauss-Seidel method** updates the grid beginning with the lower right corner

$$u_{i,j}^{i+1} = \frac{1}{4}\left[u_{i-1,j}^{i+1} + u_{i+1,j}^{i} + u_{i,j-1}^{i} + u_{i,j+1}^{i+1} \right]. \tag{7.5}$$

Intuitively, (7.5) is a sequential algorithm, and grid points must be updated from ''left to right'' and ''bottom to top.'' However, if alternate grid points are colored ''red'' and ''black,'' all ''red'' points depend only on the neighboring ''black'' points. By alternately updating all red then all black points, the parallelism is but a factor of two less than the fully parallel Jacobi method.

The convergence rate can be further increased by introducing a *relaxation* factor

$$u_{i,j}^{i+1} = \omega u_{i,j}^i + \frac{\omega}{4}\left[u_{i-1,j}^{i+1} + u_{i+1,j}^i + u_{i,j-1}^i + u_{i,j+1}^{i+1} \right],$$

where ω weights the new iterate and the old. This **successive over-relaxation** (SOR) technique converges more quickly than either the Jacobi or Gauss-Seidel methods.

The solution of the large, sparse linear systems arising from discretization of partial differential equations has been the subject of extensive research, and a detailed discussion of these methods is beyond the scope of this book; for surveys see [Adam82, HoJe81, OrVo85]. More sophisticated methods than Jacobi or SOR have been proposed and other discretization stencils used (e.g., see figure 7.8), but the parallelization of these methods shares many problems with the Jacobi or SOR methods. Hence, we concentrate on the simplest solution method, Jacobi iteration. Most techniques described in the remainder of this chapter can be applied in their entirety to other iterative solution methods.

7.2. Grid Partitions

Given a grid of points, how should the associated linear system be mapped onto the nodes of a multicomputer network? Suppose the grid were divided with each grid partition placed in a different node and that each node used the Jacobi iterative solution technique.[2] In this scenario, each node repeatedly updates its partition of grid points and sends values associated with its partition boundary to logically adjacent partitions. What partition structure would maximize the ratio of computation to communication? Maximizing this ratio minimizes the fraction of idle processor time and, in turn, the parallel execution time. One immediately observes that

- computation is a function of a partition's area,
- communication is a function of a partition's perimeter, and

---

[2]The iterates generated by this parallel Jacobi method are the same as those generated by the sequential Jacobi method in (7.4). We emphasize that the following analysis can be applied to other point iterative solvers, e.g., multicolor SOR and conjugate gradient, as well.

• the partition's perimeter that must be sent to other partitions is a function of the stencil.

As an example, figure 7.1 illustrates square partitions with a 5-point stencil. Each partition communicates with four neighboring partitions, and the amount of data transferred is directly proportional to the perimeter of the partition.[3]

7.2.1. Related Work

Although the efficiency of a sequential, iterative technique depends only on the discretization stencil and iterative algorithm, e.g., Jacobi, the efficiency of a parallel, iterative technique depends on the partitioning of the discretization grid, its associated stencil, *and* the underlying multicomputer architecture. Fox and Otto [FoOt84] confirmed that the efficiency of partial differential equation solution on a multicomputer network depends not on the amount of internode communication but the ratio of communication to computation. In their study, they considered the solution of Laplace's equation over a square region using a 5-point discretization stencil. Their partitioning placed squares of grid points on each node of a hypercube, using only nearest neighbor communication.

Vrsalovic *et al.* [VGSS85] considered the solution of Poisson's equation over a square region using a 5-point discretization stencil. Unlike Fox and Otto, they tested triangular, square, and hexagonal partitions. Their study used the ratio of processing time to data access time as one performance metric on a general class of multiprocessor systems. Their hypothetical multiprocessor systems were assumed to have both local memory attached to each processor and global memories accessible via an interconnection network. Of the three partitions, hexagonal decomposition produced the largest speedup.

In an experimental study, Saltz *et al.* [SaNN87] considered solution of the heat equation using successive over-relaxation (SOR) on an Intel iPSC [Ratt85, Inte86a], using rectangular strips and squares as grid partitions. They observed that the Intel iPSC's high startup costs for message transmission often favored decreasing the number of messages sent, even if that meant sending more bytes of data. Hence, partitions of rectangular strips were often more efficient that square partitions.

Superficially, these results by Fox and Otto, Vrsalovic *et al.*, and Saltz *et al.* seem mutually contradictory - each favoring different partition shapes. However, these

---

[3]Although convergence checking for an iterative scheme also involves communication, the amount and cost of this communication is independent of stencil type and partition shape and will not be considered.

studies considered only a small portion of the possible parameter space of stencils, partitionings, and multicomputer architectures; and the underlying assumptions differ. Hence, we begin by formalizing the relation of computation and communication, noting that they are functions of a partition's area and perimeter, respectively. Given this formalization, we then consider architectural ramifications.

7.2.2. Five Point Stencil

Figure 7.1b shows the 5-point stencil and the the unknowns in Laplace's equation that arise from the centered difference approximation to the partial derivatives, i.e., equation (7.3). With an iterative solution of these equations, e.g., via the Jacobi method, the new value computed at each grid point depends on the previous values from its north, south, east, and west grid point neighbors.

Now consider the influence of partition shape on internode communication. To ease comparison, assume each partition contains n^2/p grid points, i.e., each multicomputer nodes's computation is proportional to n^2/p.

7.2.2.1. Rectangular Partitions

Suppose the grid of n^2 points were partitioned into p/r horizontal strips, and each strip were again partitioned into r rectangles (see figure 7.2a). Assuming all rectangles are of equal size, each contains n^2/p grid points with sides n/r and nr/p. As illustrated in figure 7.2b, the perimeter contains

$$2\left[\frac{n}{r} + \frac{nr}{p}\right] - 4$$

grid points and all are involved in data transfer. However, the four corner points in each rectangle involve two data transfers. Therefore, the amount of data transferred from each interior rectangle is

$$2\left[\frac{n}{r} + \frac{nr}{p}\right].$$

To find an optimal value for r, the number of horizontal rectangles, we need only maximize the ratio of computation to communication

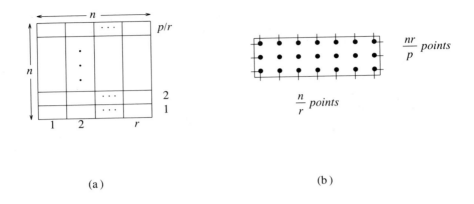

(a)   (b)

Figure 7.2
Rectangular partitions with 5-point stencil.

$$F(r) = \max_{\substack{r>1 \\ r \le p}} \frac{\dfrac{n^2}{p}}{2\left[\dfrac{n}{r} + \dfrac{nr}{p}\right]} = \max_{\substack{r>1 \\ r \le p}} \frac{nr}{2(p+r^2)}$$

in a single node. Differentiating and setting the derivative equal to zero, we obtain $p=r^2$ or $r=\sqrt{p}$ as the optimal value of r. Therefore, *squares are the optimal rectangular partitioning for the 5-point stencil* with a communicating perimeter of $4n/\sqrt{p}$. With the 5-point stencil, this result has a simple geometric interpretation: of all rectangular partitions, the square maximizes the ratio of area to perimeter.

Finally, as an interesting special case, note that if $r = 1$, the grid of n^2 points is partitioned into p strips each containing n^2/p points. In this case, there is no communication to the east or west and $2n - 4$ values ($n - 2$ north and $n - 2$ south) are communicated from each partition.[4]

7.2.2.2. Triangular Partitions

To partition an $n \times n$ grid into p triangles, we assume $n = 2\sqrt{p}\,l$ and divide the grid into $p/2$ squares with sides $s = 2\sqrt{2}l$. Each of these $p/2$ squares will contain $8l^2$ grid points.

---

[4]The four corner points of the partition are fixed boundary values that need not be transmitted.

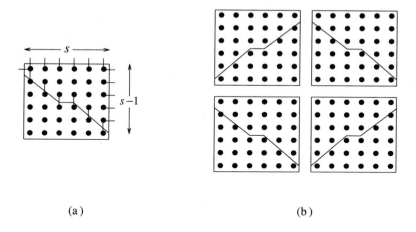

(a)   (b)

Figure 7.3
Triangular partitions with 5-point stencil.

Each of the squares is then divided into the two "approximate" triangles shown in figure 7.3a. Each of the p triangles contains $4l^2$ grid points and has height s and base $s-1$.

Now consider the communicating perimeter of the upper triangle in figure 7.3a, assuming a 5-point stencil. By observation, s values are sent north, $s-1$ values east, s values south, and 1 value to the west, for a total of $3s$. Note that $s-2$ of the values transmitted south are used twice by the receiving triangle. The other triangles are reflections of this case. Because $n = 2\sqrt{p}\,l$ and $s = 2\sqrt{2}l$, the total number of values sent from each triangle is

$$\frac{3\sqrt{2}n}{\sqrt{p}}.$$

7.2.2.3. Hexagonal Partitions

Suppose the $n \times n$ grid were divided into p hexagonal partitions. We again assume that $n = 2\sqrt{p}\,l$, implying each partition has $n^2/p = 4l^2$ grid points. Figure 7.4 shows how this partitioning can be accomplished. Each hexagon has $l+1$ grid points at the north and south edges and l grid points on each of the four remaining sides. The number of grid points in the upper or lower half of each hexagon is

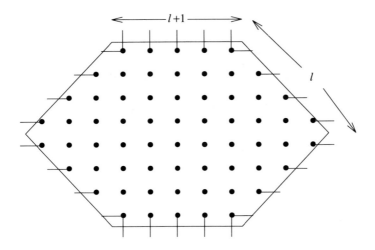

Figure 7.4
Hexagonal partitions with 5-point stencil.

$$\sum_{i=1}^{l}\left[(l+1)+2(i-1)\right]=2l^2,$$

for a total of $4l^2$ in each hexagon.

As figure 7.4 shows, $l+1$ values must be sent north, $l+1$ values south, l northeast, l southeast, l southwest, and l northwest, a total of $6l+2$. Because $l=\dfrac{n}{2\sqrt{p}}$, each hexagon must communicate $\dfrac{3n}{\sqrt{p}}+2$ values.

7.2.3. Nine Point Stencil

The 9-point stencil, shown in figure 7.5, is a higher order finite difference approximation to the partial derivatives than the 5-point stencil discussed earlier. When using this stencil, the iteration value computed at each grid point is a function of its north, northeast, east, southeast, south, southwest, west, and northwest grid point neighbor values. In this section we examine the amount of internode communication for the same partitions discussed earlier and observe the change in a partition's communicating perimeter as the stencil changes.

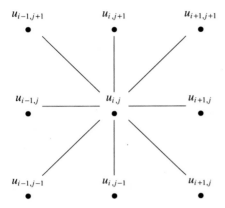

$$u_{i,j} = \frac{1}{5}\left[u_{i-1,j} + u_{i+1,j} + u_{i,j-1} + u_{i,j+1} \right] +$$

$$\frac{1}{20}\left[u_{i-1,j+1} + u_{i+1,j+1} + u_{i-1,j-1} + u_{i+1,j-1} \right]$$

Figure 7.5
9-point star stencil.

7.2.3.1. Rectangular Partitions

Figures 7.2 and 7.5 show that the communicating perimeter of rectangular partitions for the 9-point stencil is nearly the same as the communicating perimeter for the 5-point stencil. Only the four corner points of a partition are each involved in an additional communication. As before, squares are the optimal rectangular partitioning with a communicating perimeter of

$$\frac{4n}{\sqrt{p}} + 4.$$

Because there is no communication to the left or right, rectangular strips ($r = 1$) have the same communicating perimeter for both the 5 and 9-point stencils.

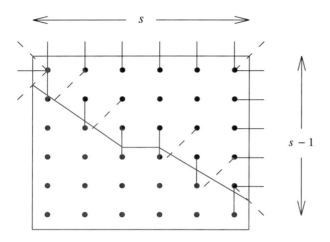

Figure 7.6
Triangular partitions with 9-point star stencil.

7.2.3.2. Triangular Partitions

The dashed lines between grid points in figure 7.6 denote the additional communications required for triangular partitions when using the 9-point stencil rather than the 5-point stencil. The solid lines between grid points are the communicating perimeter for the 5-point stencil ($3s$). The 9-point stencil requires the following additional communications: 1 to the northeast, 1 to the southeast, 1 to the northwest, 1 to the southwest, and $s-2$ to the south. This yields a total communicating perimeter[5] for an interior triangular partition with the 9-point stencil of $4s + 2$ or $\dfrac{4\sqrt{2}n}{\sqrt{p}}+2$.

7.2.3.3. Hexagonal Partitions

The dashed lines in figure 7.7 illustrate the the additional communications required with hexagonal partitions when using the 9-point stencil rather than the 5-point stencil. The solid lines of figure 7.7 correspond to the communicating perimeter of the 5-point stencil, shown to be $6l + 2$ in §7.2.2.3. The 9-point stencil requires l communications

---

[5]"Perimeter" is perhaps a misnomer here, for the perimeter of points along the diagonal in figure 7.6 is "two deep" for the 9-point stencil.

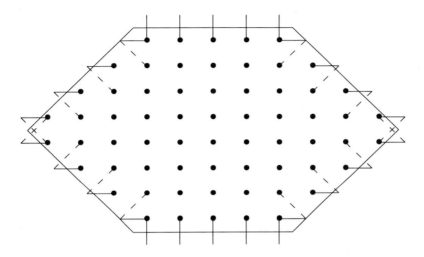

Figure 7.7
Hexagonal partitions with 9-point star stencil.

to the northeast, southeast, southwest, and northwest in addition to those for the 5-point stencil. For interior hexagonal partitions, this gives a total communicating perimeter of

$$10l + 2 = \frac{5n}{\sqrt{p}} + 2$$

where

$$l = \frac{n}{2\sqrt{p}}.$$

Note that the communicating "perimeter" is depth 2 along four of the six edges.

7.2.4. Other Stencils

Many stencils other than the 5-point and 9-point stencils just analyzed are frequently used when solving partial differential equations. Figure 7.8 illustrates some of the most common. We omit the analysis of the communication required for their associated partitions, however, the results of this analysis are summarized in table 7.2. The interested reader can verify these results by applying the methods discussed earlier to compute the additional grid points involved in data transfer for each of these stencils.

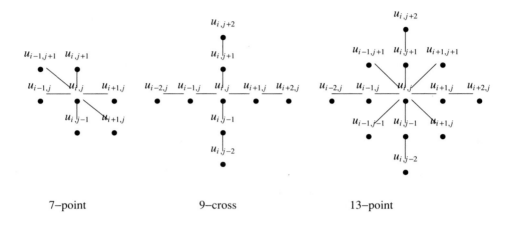

Figure 7.8
Frequently used discretization stencils.

7.3. Computation/Communication Ratios

Using the notation of table 7.1, table 7.2 shows the relative amounts of computation and communication for selected pairs of stencil and partition. For simplicity, the effects of boundaries on communication have been elided.[6] Table 7.2 also includes one quantity not discussed earlier, parallel communication, the amount of data transfer if partition sides can communicate in parallel. This parallel communication will later allow us to determine if the optimum pair of stencil and partition changes when communication to neighboring partitions occurs in parallel.

The entries of most interest in table 7.2 are the ratio of computation to communication (R) and the ratio of computation to parallel communication (PR). Table 7.3 illustrates the relative magnitude of these quantities for a square grid containing 256×256 points and a multicomputer network with 64 nodes.

An inspection of table 7.3 shows that hexagonal partitions yield the highest ratio of computation to serial communication, except for the 9-point star stencil, where squares are preferable. However, if one assumes the inter-partition communication occurs in parallel, i.e., all edges of a partition can be transmitted in parallel, then hexagons yield

---

[6]Recall that n^2 is the number of grid points, and p is the number of multicomputer nodes.

Table 7.1

Complexity notation

Quantity	Definition
Comp	$\dfrac{n^2}{p}$, the computational complexity of a stencil/partition pair
Comm	communication complexity of a stencil/partition pair
Pcomm	parallel communication complexity of a stencil/pair
R	the ratio $\dfrac{Comp}{Comm}$
PR	the ratio $\dfrac{Comp}{Pcomm}$

the highest ratio in all cases. With parallel communication, the improvement obtained with hexagons is even greater. For example,

$$\frac{R_{hexagon}}{R_{square}} = 1.33$$

for the 5-point stencil, but

$$\frac{PR_{hexagon}}{PR_{square}} = 2$$

The patterns in table 7.3 suggest there is some formal relation between partitions and stencils, with certain combinations preferred. In the next section we develop techniques for selecting optimal partition/stencil combinations.

7.4. Optimal Pairs of Stencil and Partition

A partition can be categorized *with respect to a given stencil* by the number of partition perimeters that must be communicated. Thus, a partition is a *k-partition with respect to stencil S* if k perimeters are communicated when stencil S is used. For example, the square is a 1-partition with respect to the 5-point, 7-point, and 9-point star stencils but is a 2-partition with respect to the 9-point cross and 13-point stencils. The hexagon is a

Table 7.2
Summary of stencil/partition analysis

Partition	Stencil				
	5-point	**7-point**	**9-point star**	**9-point cross**	**13-point**
Strips					
Comm:	$2n$	$2n$	$2n$	$4n$	$4n$
Pcomm:	n	n	n	$2n$	$2n$
R:	$\dfrac{n}{2p}$	$\dfrac{n}{2p}$	$\dfrac{n}{2p}$	$\dfrac{n}{4p}$	$\dfrac{n}{4p}$
PR:	$\dfrac{n}{p}$	$\dfrac{n}{p}$	$\dfrac{n}{p}$	$\dfrac{n}{2p}$	$\dfrac{n}{2p}$
Triangle					
Comm:	$\dfrac{3\sqrt{2}n}{\sqrt{p}}$	$\dfrac{3\sqrt{2}n}{\sqrt{p}}+2$	$\dfrac{4\sqrt{2}n}{\sqrt{p}}+2$	$\dfrac{6\sqrt{2}n}{\sqrt{p}}$	$\dfrac{6\sqrt{2}n}{\sqrt{p}}+2$
Pcomm:	$\dfrac{\sqrt{2}n}{\sqrt{p}}$	$\dfrac{2\sqrt{2}n}{\sqrt{p}}-2$	$\dfrac{2\sqrt{2}n}{\sqrt{p}}-2$	$\dfrac{2\sqrt{2}n}{\sqrt{p}}-1$	$\dfrac{2\sqrt{2}n}{\sqrt{p}}-1$
R:	$\dfrac{n}{3\sqrt{2p}}$	$\approx\dfrac{n}{3\sqrt{2p}}$	$\approx\dfrac{n}{4\sqrt{2p}}$	$\dfrac{n}{6\sqrt{2p}}$	$\approx\dfrac{n}{6\sqrt{2p}}$
PR:	$\dfrac{n}{\sqrt{2p}}$	$\approx\dfrac{n}{2\sqrt{2p}}$	$\dfrac{n}{2\sqrt{2p}}$	$\dfrac{n}{2\sqrt{2p}}$	$\approx\dfrac{n}{2\sqrt{2p}}$
Square					
Comm:	$\dfrac{4n}{\sqrt{p}}$	$\dfrac{4n}{\sqrt{p}}+2$	$\dfrac{4n}{\sqrt{p}}+4$	$\dfrac{8n}{\sqrt{p}}$	$\dfrac{8n}{\sqrt{p}}+4$
Pcomm:	$\dfrac{n}{\sqrt{p}}$	$\dfrac{n}{\sqrt{p}}$	$\dfrac{n}{\sqrt{p}}$	$\dfrac{2n}{\sqrt{p}}$	$\dfrac{2n}{\sqrt{p}}$
R:	$\dfrac{n}{4\sqrt{p}}$	$\approx\dfrac{n}{4\sqrt{p}}$	$\approx\dfrac{n}{4\sqrt{p}}$	$\dfrac{n}{8\sqrt{p}}$	$\approx\dfrac{n}{8\sqrt{p}}$
PR:	$\dfrac{n}{\sqrt{p}}$	$\dfrac{n}{\sqrt{p}}$	$\dfrac{n}{\sqrt{p}}$	$\dfrac{n}{2\sqrt{p}}$	$\dfrac{n}{2\sqrt{p}}$
Hexagon					
Comm:	$\dfrac{3n}{\sqrt{p}}+2$	$\dfrac{4n}{\sqrt{p}}+2$	$\dfrac{5n}{\sqrt{p}}+2$	$\dfrac{6n}{\sqrt{p}}+4$	$\dfrac{6n}{\sqrt{p}}+8$
Pcomm:	$\dfrac{n}{2\sqrt{p}}+1$	$\dfrac{n}{\sqrt{p}}$	$\dfrac{n}{\sqrt{p}}$	$\dfrac{n}{\sqrt{p}}+2$	$\dfrac{n}{\sqrt{p}}+2$
R:	$\approx\dfrac{n}{3\sqrt{p}}$	$\approx\dfrac{n}{4\sqrt{p}}$	$\approx\dfrac{n}{5\sqrt{p}}$	$\approx\dfrac{n}{6\sqrt{p}}$	$\approx\dfrac{n}{6\sqrt{p}}$
PR:	$\approx\dfrac{2n}{\sqrt{p}}$	$\dfrac{n}{\sqrt{p}}$	$\dfrac{n}{\sqrt{p}}$	$\approx\dfrac{n}{\sqrt{p}}$	$\approx\dfrac{n}{\sqrt{p}}$

Table 7.3

Ratio of computation to communication ($n = 256$ and $p = 64$)

Partition Type	Stencil				
	5-point	**7-point**	**9-point star**	**9-point cross**	**13-point**
Rectangle					
R:	2	2	2	1	1
PR:	4	4	4	2	2
Triangle					
R:	7.5	7.5	5.65	3.75	3.75
PR:	22.5	11.3	11.3	11.3	11.3
Square					
R:	8	8	8	4	4
PR:	32	32	32	16	16
Hexagon					
R:	10.66	8	6.4	5.3	5.3
PR:	64	32	32	32	32

1-partition for the 5-point and a 2-partition with respect to the 9-point cross and 13-point stencils.

Moreover, the value of k can be fractional. The hexagon, for example, is a $1\frac{2}{6}$ partition for the 7-point stencil and a $1\frac{4}{6}$ partition with the 9-point star stencil. Why? Because only some sides of the hexagon are involved in multiple data transfers. This categorization of partitions with respect to stencils permits the ranking of pairs of stencil and partition. Hence, one can determine those stencils where l-partition hexagons are preferable to k-partition squares.

When communication from a partition to each of its neighboring partitions is serial, the communicating perimeter for square k-partitions is nearly $4kn/\sqrt{p}$, and the corresponding ratio of computation to serial communication is

$$\frac{n}{4k\sqrt{p}}.$$

The communicating perimeter for hexagonal l-partitions is approximately $3ln/\sqrt{p}$, and the corresponding ratio of computation to serial communication is

$$\frac{n}{3l\sqrt{p}}.$$

Clearly, an l-partition hexagon yields a higher ratio when

$$\frac{n}{3l\sqrt{p}} > \frac{n}{4k\sqrt{p}}$$

or when

$$k > \frac{3}{4}l. \tag{7.6}$$

If one adopts parallel rather than serial communication, the communicating perimeter for square k-partitions is, except for a small constant, $kn/\sqrt{p}$, and the ratio of computation to parallel communication is

$$\frac{n}{k\sqrt{p}}.$$

Similarly, the communicating perimeter for hexagonal l-partitions is

$$\frac{ln}{2\sqrt{p}}$$

and the corresponding ratio of computation to parallel communication is

$$\frac{2n}{3l\sqrt{p}}.$$

With parallel communication, l-hexagons are preferable to k-squares when

$$\frac{2n}{l\sqrt{p}} > \frac{n}{k\sqrt{p}}$$

or

$$k > \frac{l}{2}. \tag{7.7}$$

Table 7.4

Comparison of Square and Hexagonal Partitions

Stencil	Square k-value (serial, parallel)	Hexagon l-value (serial, parallel)	Optimal partition serial/parallel
5-point	(1,1)	(1,1)	hexagon/hexagon
7-point	(1,1)	$(1\frac{2}{6},2)$	equal/equal
9-point star	(1,1)	$(1\frac{4}{6},2)$	square/equal
9-point cross	(2,2)	(2,2)	hexagon/hexagon
13-point	(2,2)	(2,2)	hexagon/hexagon

Using inequalities (7.6) and (7.7), table 7.4 shows optimal pairs of stencil and partition, based on the maximum ratio of computation to communication. In table 7.4, square partitions are preferable to hexagons in only one of the 10 cases.[7] Based solely on table 7.4, hexagonal partitions are superior to square partitions because they minimize the interpartition data transfer.[8] Similarly, triangles are clearly inferior.

7.5. Performance Models

The foregoing analysis did not include architectural considerations, save for the inclusion of results for both serial and parallel communication. However, the stencil and grid partition cannot be divorced from the topology of the multicomputer interconnection network, e.g., square or hexagonal grid. Optimal performance can be achieved only via judicious selection of a trio: stencil, partitioning, and multicomputer architecture.

---

[7]Note that the k and l-values for parallel communication in table 7.4 were obtained by rounding the fractional values for serial communication up to the next largest integer, i.e., a parallel communication of $1\frac{2}{6}$ perimeters requires two transmissions.

[8]The underlying parallel architecture also influences the choice of partition shape.

Deriving expressions for parallel execution times and speedups for a trio of stencil, partition, and architecture requires a model of execution. Our parallel execution time model is a variation of one developed earlier [RePa85] and is similar to the one used by Vrsalovic *et al.* [VGSS85]. In this model, the parallel iteration time for evaluating one partition of grid points is

$$t_{cycle}^{p-processor} = t_{comp} + t_a + t_w$$

where t_{comp} is the iteration computation time, t_a is the data access/transfer time, and t_w is the waiting/synchronization time.

The computation time t_{comp} depends on the partition size and stencil and is independent of the architecture except for the time, T_{fp}, to execute a floating point operation. Formally, t_{comp} is

$$t_{comp} = \frac{E(S)n^2}{p} T_{fp}$$

where $E(S)$ is the number of floating point operations required to update the value of a grid point, given a stencil S, n^2/p is the number of grid points in a partition, and T_{fp} is the time for a single floating point operation.

The *speedup* obtained using parallel iterations is simply

$$S_p = \frac{t_{cycle}^{uniprocessor}}{t_{cycle}^{p-processor}},$$

where the single processor iteration time is

$$t_{cycle}^{uniprocessor} = E(S)n^2 T_{fp}.$$

Specific values for the speedup depend not only on the trio of stencil, partition, and network chosen, but also on technology constants such as floating point operation time and packet transmission time. The other components of the execution time model, t_a and t_w, depend on the particular combination of partitioning, stencil, and multicomputer architecture and are analyzed below.

Clearly, the performance of a pair of stencil and partition depends heavily on the performance of the multicomputer interconnection network. Although a plethora of multicomputer interconnection networks have been proposed [ReSc83, Witt81], figure 7.9 shows those networks (meshes) that are directly relevant to iterative solution of

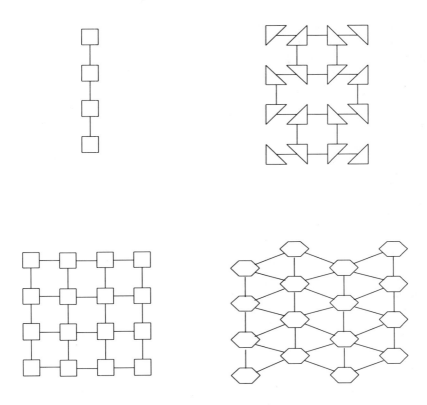

Figure 7.9
Selected interconnection networks.

elliptic partial differential equations.[9] Each interconnection network has an associated "natural" partition, for example, square partitions on a square mesh.

Consider an interior node in a mesh with an associated grid partition. During each iteration (cycle), two groups of data must cross each communications link, one in each direction from neighboring nodes. There are several possible interleavings of computation and remote data access. These range from a separate request for each communicating "perimeter" grid point to a request for an entire "side" of the

---

[9]The hypercube topology used in commercial multicomputer networks includes all but the hexagonal mesh as special cases.

communicating "perimeter" of the partition. These requests can, in turn, be either overlapped or non-overlapped with computation. Similarly, the hardware support for internode communication must be specified. As chapters three and four showed, a variety of designs exist, each with differing performance. The simplest design allows only one link connected to each node to be active at any time, increasing the data transfer time. With additional hardware, each node link can be simultaneously active.

Each combination of data access patterns and hardware design alternatives leads to an implementation with different performance characteristics. Rather than cursorily examine a wide variety of alternatives, we assume

- communication links are half-duplex, i.e., data can flow along links in only one direction at a time, and

- nodes request and wait for all perimeter values before starting computation.

Currently, these assumptions correspond to all commercial hypercube implementations [Ratt85, GuHS86, HMSC86].

Whether the communication is serial or parallel, some node P_i in the interior of the network will need data from another node P_j that is some number of links l_{ij} away (see table 7.5 for notation). The amount of data to be transmitted, $d_{ij}(S, P)$, depends on both the stencil S and the grid partitioning P. Ignoring synchronization and queueing delays, the time to transmit data from node P_i to P_j, crossing l_{ij} links, is

$$t_{send}(i,j) = t_{startup} + \left\lceil \frac{d_{ij}(S, P)}{Ps} \right\rceil l_{ij} t_{comm} + (l_{ij} - 1)t_{forward}, \qquad (7.8)$$

where $t_{startup}$ is the fixed overhead for sending data, t_{comm} is the packet transmission time, and $t_{forward}$ is the message forwarding overhead incurred at intermediate nodes. The ceiling function reflects the redundant communication due to the fixed packet size Ps.

In general, data destined for other nodes *will* encounter queueing delays, both at their origin and at intermediate nodes. The latter is expected, but the former is counter-intuitive. As an example of this phenomenon, consider the mapping of hexagonal partitions onto either a square or hexagonal mesh. On a square mesh, data from the six sides of the hexagons must exit via only four connecting links. Even with all links simultaneously active, some data will be delayed.

With hexagonal partitions on a hexagonal mesh, each partition edge is directly connected to its six neighboring partitions. However, each pair of neighbors must

Table 7.5

Execution time model notation

Quantity	Definition
$d_{ij}(S,P)$	amount of data sent from i to j
l_{ij}	number of links between i and j
P	partition
P_i	processor i
Ps	packet size
S	discretization stencil
S_p	speedup
T_{fp}	time for a single floating point operation
$t_a^{parallel}$	parallel access time
t_a^{serial}	serial access time
t_{comm}	time to send a packet across one communication link
t_{cycle}	time for one iteration
$t_{forward}$	time (possibly zero) to interrupt an intermediate processor and forward a message
$t_{send}(i,j)$	data transmission time from processor i to j
$t_{startup}$	overhead for preparing a communication
t_w^{serial}	serial waiting time

exchange data. Thus, two transmission delays are needed on each of the six links before exchanges are complete. If all links can simultaneously be active, two transmission delays will suffice to exchange boundary values. Conversely, twelve delays will be needed if only one link per node can be active at any time.

There are two general approaches to managing the interpartition communication problem. The first relegates management of message passing and the associated queueing of messages for available links to system software residing in each node. With this approach, each partition simply passes the data to be delivered to other partitions to the system software. No consideration is given to the pattern of communication in time. As an example, each partition might successively send boundary values on each of its links, then await receipt of boundary values from neighboring partitions. Although this approach is easily programmed, it hides the performance issues and can increase contention for communication links.

The second approach requires programming the exchange of partition boundaries in a series of *phases*, each phase corresponding to a particular pattern of communication. In the example of hexagonal partitions on a hexagonal mesh, discussed above, the communication pattern of neighboring partitions would be alternating sends and receives. Sender and receiver would cooperate, each expecting the action of the other. This *crystalline* communication mode [FoOt84] leads to regular communication patterns with minimal delays. Application of this approach is the subject of the next section.

7.5.1. Message Passing Analysis

Because the range of partition and network possibilities is so large, we present only the analysis of the 5-point stencil with square and hexagonal partitions on square and hexagonal interconnection networks. The triangular partitions were omitted because, as a cursory examination of figure 7.3 shows, they require data transmission to four adjacent partitions. Because square partitions also transmit to only four adjacent partitions and have a higher ratio of computation to communication, they are always preferable to triangles. The analysis for 9-point stencils is similar to that presented below; only the case analysis is more complex.

When partitions are mapped onto an interconnection network, the processors may permit communication on only one link or on all. In the following we consider only the serial case; similar analysis applies to simultaneous communication on all links.

We begin with the simplest case: square partitions on a square interconnection network. Each partition must exchange $n/\sqrt{p}$ values with each of its four neighbors. Because only one link per processor can be active, we expect the data exchange to require four phases, i.e., time proportional to $4n/\sqrt{p}$. However, this would require *all* processors to simultaneously send and receive. At any given instant, only half the processors can send; the other half must receive. Hence, eight phases are needed, and the total time for data exchange is

$$t_a^{serial} + t_w^{serial} = 4t_{startup} + 8\left\lceil \frac{n}{Ps\sqrt{p}} \right\rceil t_{comm}.$$

Four startup costs are needed to initiate message transmissions to neighboring processors. Because square partitions map directly onto the square mesh, no intermediate node forwarding costs arise. Because the square mesh can be directly embedded in the hexagonal mesh, the data exchange delay for square partitions on a hexagonal mesh is identical to that for the square mesh.[10]

Like square partitions on a square mesh, hexagonal partitions map directly onto a hexagonal mesh. Recalling that the north and south sides of a hexagon contain $\frac{n}{2\sqrt{p}} + 1$ points, and the other four sides contain $\frac{n}{2\sqrt{p}}$ points each, the data exchange delay is

$$t_a^{serial} + t_w^{serial} = 6t_{startup} + 4\left\lceil\frac{\frac{n}{2\sqrt{p}} + 1}{Ps}\right\rceil t_{comm} + 8\left\lceil\frac{\frac{n}{2\sqrt{p}}}{Ps}\right\rceil t_{comm}.$$

The first ceiling term corresponds to the north and south exchange and requires four phases. Similarly, the second term represents the exchange of data along the four diagonal connections and requires eight phases.

Finally, hexagonal partitions can also be mapped onto a square mesh. Unlike the other mappings, this one requires data exchange between non-adjacent nodes. In this case, we assume that rows of hexagons are mapped onto corresponding rows of the square mesh. With this mapping, north and south connections and half the diagonal connections are realized directly. The remaining diagonal connections require traversal of two links to ''turn the corner'' in the square mesh. Hence, the total communication delay due to data exchange is

$$t_a^{serial} + t_w^{serial} =$$

$$6t_{startup} + 4\left\lceil\frac{\frac{n}{2\sqrt{p}} + 1}{Ps}\right\rceil t_{comm} + 4\left\lceil\frac{\frac{n}{2\sqrt{p}}}{Ps}\right\rceil t_{comm} + 8\left\lceil\frac{\frac{n}{2\sqrt{p}}}{Ps}\right\rceil t_{comm} + 4t_{forward}.$$

The first ceiling term corresponds to the north and south connections and the second to the directly connected diagonals, each with four phases. The third term represents

---

[10]This is only true for the 5-point stencil. With the 9-point and other stencils, the distinction between square and hexagonal meshes is important.

Table 7.6
Message passing data exchange

Partition	Mesh	Stencil	Communication Count	Phase-Data Transmission Products	Order of Expected Delay
Square	Square	5-point	4	$\dfrac{8n}{\sqrt{p}}$	$\dfrac{8n}{\sqrt{p}}$
Square	Square	9-point	8	$\dfrac{8n}{\sqrt{p}} + 16$	$\dfrac{8n}{\sqrt{p}}$
Square	Hexagon	5-point	4	$\dfrac{8n}{\sqrt{p}}$	$\dfrac{8n}{\sqrt{p}}$
Square	Hexagon	9-point	8	$\dfrac{8n}{\sqrt{p}} + 12$	$\dfrac{8n}{\sqrt{p}}$
Hexagon	Square	5-point	6	$4\left[\dfrac{n}{2\sqrt{p}}+1\right] + \dfrac{4n}{2\sqrt{p}} + \dfrac{8n}{2\sqrt{p}}$	$\dfrac{8n}{\sqrt{p}}$
Hexagon	Square	9-point	6	$4\left[\dfrac{n}{2\sqrt{p}}+1\right] + \dfrac{4n}{\sqrt{p}} + \dfrac{8n}{\sqrt{p}}$	$\dfrac{14n}{\sqrt{p}}$
Hexagon	Hexagon	5-point	6	$4\left[\dfrac{n}{2\sqrt{p}}+1\right] + \dfrac{8n}{2\sqrt{p}}$	$\dfrac{6n}{\sqrt{p}}$
Hexagon	Hexagon	9-point	6	$4\left[\dfrac{n}{2\sqrt{p}}+1\right] + \dfrac{8n}{\sqrt{p}}$	$\dfrac{10n}{\sqrt{p}}$

indirectly connected diagonals, requiring eight phases. Half these phases require forwarding through intermediate nodes, hence the four forwarding costs.

Similar analysis can be applied to other meshes and stencils. Table 7.6 shows the number of other partitions with which each partition must communicate, i.e., the number of required communications, and transmission delays are shown as a sum of terms. Each term is a product of the amount of data exchanged between logically adjacent partitions and the number of phases necessary to accomplish the exchange. In the table, the potential effects of packet size on transmission delay are ignored, as are the times for startup and forwarding. Table 7.6 suggests that hexagonal partitions are preferable for 5-point stencils, and square partitions are more appropriate for 9-point stencils, confirming our earlier, mesh independent analysis. As we shall see, however, both the number of message startups *and* amount of data must be considered when estimating the performance of a trio of stencil, partition, and mesh.

7.5.2. Performance Prediction

Equation (7.8), the delay to send data, includes parameters for startup, forwarding cost, packet size, and packet transmission time. Because our primary interest is the effect of transmission time, we have ignored the effects of startup and forwarding, i.e., we have assumed those parameters are zero. When evaluating the relative performance of a trio of stencil, partition, and mesh, we have used values for packet size and packet transmission time similar to those for commercial multicomputer networks.

Figure 7.10 shows the speedup, obtained using (7.8), for square and hexagonal partitions on both square and hexagonal meshes, using a 5-point stencil. In the figure, 1K byte packets are used. We see that *square* partitions yield significantly larger speedup than hexagonal partitions, regardless of the underlying mesh. This is counter-intuitive and seems to contradict table 7.6. Careful inspection of (7.8), however, shows that packet size is crucial. The term

$$\left\lceil \frac{d_{ij}(S,P)}{Ps} \right\rceil l_{ij} t_{comm}$$

in (7.8) reflects the discretization overhead caused by packets. If Ps, the packet size, is large, the number of partitions that must receive data from each partition is much more important than the total amount of data to be sent. For example, sending 4 bytes to 6 partitions is much more expensive than sending 6 bytes to 4 partitions if the packet size is 1024 bytes. The former requires 6 packet transmissions, the latter only 4 transmissions. Square partitions, because they require communication with only four neighboring partitions, are preferable to hexagonal partitions with six neighboring partitions, *even though more data must be transmitted with square partitions.*

With a 4 byte floating point representation, a 1024×1024 grid, 1024 byte packets, and square partitions (the assumptions of figure 7.10), using more than 16 partitions will not decrease the communication delay because, beyond this point, the total number of packet transmissions does not change. Instead, the ratio of useful computation to communication begins to degrade.

As the packet size decreases, we would expect the differential in amount of transmitted data to become more important. For small enough packets, the total amount of data accurately reflects the delay. Figure 7.11 shows just this result. For smaller 16 byte packets, hexagonal partitions are preferable to square partitions.

Figures 7.10 and 7.11 show the effects of varying the number of nodes. For a small number of nodes, the iteration is *compute bound.* As the number of nodes (and

Speedup

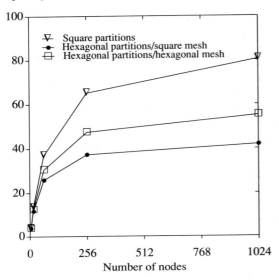

Parameter	Value
Packet size	1024
Startup	0.0
Forwarding	0.0
Packet transmission	$6\times10^{-3}\ sec$
Floating point operation	$1\times10^{-6}\ sec$

Figure 7.10
Speedup for 5-point stencil
1024 X 1024 grid with 1024 byte packets.

Speedup

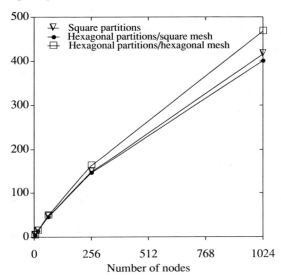

Parameter	Value
Packet size	16
Startup	0.0
Forwarding	0.0
Packet transmission	9.375×10^{-5} *sec*
Floating point operation	1×10^{-6} *sec*

Figure 7.11
Speedup with 5-point stencil
1024 X 1024 grid with 16 byte packets.

partitions) increases, the distinction between differing partition shapes becomes apparent. With 1024 nodes, only one grid point resides in each partition, and the effects of packet size on performance are striking.

Figures 7.12 and 7.13 illustrate phenomena similar to those in figures 7.10 and 7.11. For the large packet sizes in figure 7.12, hexagonal partitions are preferable to square partitions because the hexagons communicate with only six other hexagons, rather than eight other squares. However, the square partitions require less interpartition data transfer. Only when the packet size becomes small, figure 7.13, does the potential advantage of square partitions become apparent.

Stencil, partition, mesh, and hardware parameters interact in non-intuitive ways. For 5-point stencils, square partitions, with their smaller number of communicating neighbors, are appropriate for large packet sizes. Likewise, hexagonal partitions, with smaller interpartition data transfer, are appropriate for small packet sizes. The reverse is true for 9-point stencils: hexagonal partitions are appropriate for large packet sizes, even though they are $1\frac{4}{6}$ partitions for the 9-point stencil, and square partitions are best for small packet sizes. The interaction of parameters cannot be ignored when considering the performance of an algorithm on a particular architecture.

7.5.3. Experimental Validation

Recognizing the interdependence of algorithm and architecture parameters, Saltz *et al.* [SaNN87] benchmarked a 64 node Intel iPSC hypercube, using successive over-relaxation (SOR) to solve the heat equation. These experiments, discussed below, included measurement of efficiency as a function of grid size, investigation of partition shape, and comparison of convergence checking schemes.

Repeated studies have shown that a system's performance is maximized when the components are balanced [DeBu78]. For message passing systems, neither computation nor communication costs must dominate. Unfortunately, commercial multicomputer networks, including the Intel iPSC, are communication bound. The time to initiate a message transfer, i.e., $t_{startup}$ in (7.8), is approximately 2 milliseconds on the Intel iPSC,[11] regardless of the message length. Following this startup penalty, the per byte transfer time is 3 microseconds.[12]

---

[11]Saltz *et al.* [SaNN87] conducted their experiments on an earlier version of the Intel iPSC system software whose delay was nearly 6 milliseconds.

[12]See chapter eight for an evaluation of the Intel iPSC communication hardware.

Speedup

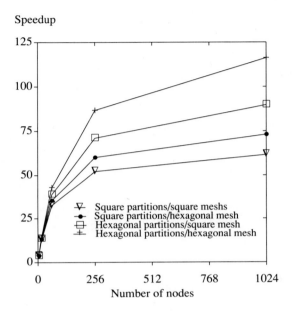

Parameter	Value
Packet size	1024
Startup	0.0
Forwarding	0.0
Packet transmission	$6\times10^{-3}\ sec$
Floating point operation	$1\times10^{-6}\ sec$

Figure 7.12
Speedup with 9-point stencil
1024 X 1024 grid with 1024 byte packets.

Speedup

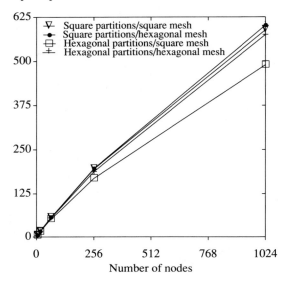

Parameter	Value
Packet size	16
Startup	0.0
Forwarding	0.0
Packet transmission	9.375×10^{-5} sec
Floating point operation	1×10^{-6} sec

Figure 7.13
Speedup with 9-point stencil
1024 X 1024 grid with 16 byte packets.

Unlike many parallel algorithms, the tasks of iterative linear systems solvers can be scaled to increase the ratio of computation to communication. Because the computation time of each task is proportional to the area of the associated grid partition, and the communication cost is proportional to the perimeter, one can increase the partition size to offset the effects of poorly matched computation and communication hardware.

In their first experiment, Saltz *et al.* examined the *efficiency* of the Intel iPSC as a function of the grid partition size, using square partitions and convergence checking after each iteration. Efficiency is defined as the speedup obtained on an N node system divided by the N; an efficiency of one reflects linear speedup. They observed that efficiency declines most rapidly with small grid sizes because there are fewer points to distribute among the nodes. For example, a 64 by 64 point grid partitioned among 32 nodes, a 5-dimensional hypercube, places only 4 points on each node. The computation time needed to update 4 grid points is dwarfed by the millisecond startup penalty for message transmission; processors are idle the majority of the time. In contrast, the partitioning of a 256 by 256 mesh places 64 grid points on each node, greatly increasing the ratio of computation to communication. This phenomenon mirrors the behavior predicted in figure 7.10 where the rate of increase in speedup, given a fixed size grid, decreases as the number of nodes increases.

Saltz *et al.* also examined the influence of partition shape on performance. Earlier, we showed that square partitions were the optimal rectangular partition, maximizing the area to perimeter ratio and minimizing the internode communication. Similarly, hexagonal partitions were superior to square partitions. However, as figures 7.10 and 7.11 show, packet size or equivalently, transmission startup time, determines the relative importance of the number of messages and quantity of data. Large startup penalties favor a small number of large messages; small startup penalties favor a larger number of smaller messages. Figure 7.14 illustrates the relation of message size to number of messages using square partitions and horizontal strips on the Intel iPSC. For small grids, partition boundaries can be transmitted in a single message, and horizontal strips minimize the number of message transmissions. For larger grids, the partition boundaries are sufficiently large that the reduced internode communication of squares offsets the message startup penalties for the additional messages.

The high cost of internode communication on the Intel iPSC also manifests itself in convergence checking. In a multicomputer implementation of an iterative algorithm, each node computes its local convergence using some norm,[13] producing a local

Communication delay (milliseconds/iteration)

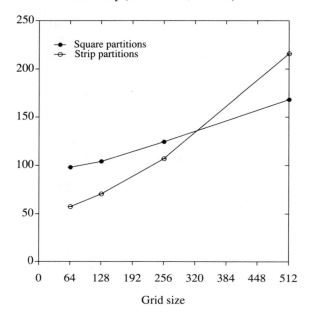

Figure 7.14
Communication time for square and strip partitions.

convergence flag. The iteration has converged only if the global "and" of all local convergence flags is true. Unlike the exchange of partition boundaries, convergence checking requires global interaction of all nodes. A naive implementation requires all nodes to broadcast their convergence flag after each iteration. After receiving flags from all other nodes, each recipient node would compute the global "and" of all flags, determining global convergence. Unfortunately, dissemination of global information is expensive on the Intel iPSC.

To reduce the cost of convergence checking, Saltz *et al.* investigated several alternate convergence strategies, including tree cascades, asynchronous checking, and scheduled convergence [SaNN87]. The simplest of these, tree cascade, forms a logical

---

[13]If $X_{i,j}$ denotes the vector of grid values in processor j after iteration i, the norm $//X_{i,j} - X_{i-1,j}//_\infty$ is the maximal absolute difference between components of $X_{i,j}$ and $X_{i-1,j}$. If the value of the norm is less than some ε, the node has locally converged.

tree connecting the nodes. Each node accepts convergence flags from its descendants, computes their logical ''and,'' and sends the result to its parent. The root of the tree determines the global convergence and broadcasts this value to all nodes. This strategy reduces internode communication and can determine convergence in $\log(N)$ time for N nodes. Asynchronous checking, the second scheme, overlaps convergence checking with iteration. This masks communication delays and permits the iteration to continue during convergence checking. Drawing on statistical techniques, scheduled convergence predicts the next iteration when convergence should again be checked based on the rate of decrease in the error norm. Experiments on the Intel iPSC show that asynchronous checking and scheduled convergence are greatly superior to both the naive broadcast *and* tree cascade.

The experiments by Saltz *et al.* confirm the predictions of §7.5.2. This validation of our analytic techniques suggests that they can effectively be used to determine the appropriate combination of partition shape and size given the architectural parameters of the underlying parallel machine.

7.6. Summary

The trio of iteration stencil, grid partition shape, and underlying multicomputer architecture must be considered together when designing parallel algorithms for solution of elliptic partial differential equations. Isolated evaluation of one or even two components of the trio is likely to yield non-optimal algorithms.

We have seen, for example, that an abstract analysis of iteration stencil and partition shape suggests that hexagonal partitions are best for 5-point stencils, whereas square partitions are best for 9-point stencils. Further analysis shows that this is only true in a message passing implementation if small packets are supported. For large packets, the reverse is true, i.e., square partitions are best for 5-point stencils and hexagonal partitions are best for 9-point stencils. Likewise, the type of interconnection network is crucial. Mapping grid partitions onto a network that does not directly support the interpartition communication pattern markedly degrades performance.

In summary, stencil, partition shape, and multicomputer architecture must be considered in concert when designing an iterative solution algorithm. They interact in non-intuitive ways and ignoring one or more of the three almost certainly leads to sub-optimal performance.

References

[Adam82]   L. M. Adams, *Iterative Algorithms for Large Sparse Linear Systems on Parallel Computers*. Ph.D. Dissertation, Department of Applied Mathematics and Computer Science, University of Virginia, 1982.

[DeBu78]   P. J. Denning and J. P. Buzen, "The Operational Analysis of Queueing Network Models," *ACM Computing Surveys* (September 1978), Vol. 10, No. 3, pp. 225-261.

[FoOt84]   G. C. Fox and S. W. Otto, "Algorithms for Concurrent Processors," *Physics Today* (May 1984), Vol. 37, pp. 50-59.

[GuHS86]   H. L. Gustafson, S. Hawkinson and K. Scott, "The Architecture of a Homogeneous Vector Supercomputer," *Proceedings of the 1986 International Conference on Parallel Processing* (August 1986), pp. 649-652.

[HMSC86]   J. P. Hayes, T. Mudge, Q. F. Stout, S. Colley, et al., "A Microprocessor-based Hypercube Supercomputer," *IEEE Micro* (October 1986), Vol. 6, No. 5, pp. 6-17.

[HoJe81]   R. W. Hockney and C. R. Jesshope, *Parallel Computing*. Adam Hilger, Limited, Bristol, 1981.

[Inte86a]   *Intel iPSC System Overview, Order Number 310610-001*. Intel Scientific Computers, 1986.

[OrVo85]   J. Ortega and R. G. Voigt, "Solution of Partial Differential Equations on Vector and Parallel Computers," *SIAM Review* (June 1985), Vol. 27, No. 2, pp. 149-240.

[Ratt85]   J. Rattner, "Concurrent Processing: A New Direction in Scientific Computing," *Conference Proceedings of the 1985 National Computer Conference* (1985), Vol. 54, pp. 157-166.

[ReAP87]   D. A. Reed, L. M. Adams and M. L. Patrick, "Stencils and Problem Partitionings: Their Influence on the Performance of Multiple Processor Systems," *IEEE Transactions on Computers* (July 1987), Vol. C-36, No. 7, pp. 845-858.

[RePa85]   D. A. Reed and M. L. Patrick, "Parallel, Iterative Solution of Sparse Linear Systems: Models and Architectures," *Parallel Computing* (1985.), Vol. 2, pp. 45-67.

[ReSc83]   D. A. Reed and H. D. Schwetman, "Cost-Performance Bounds for Multimicrocomputer Networks," *IEEE Transactions on Computers* (January 1983), Vol. C-32, No. 1, pp. 83-95.

[SaNN87]   J. H. Saltz, V. K. Naik and D. M. Nicol, "Reduction of the Effects of the Communication Delays in Scientific Algorithms on Message Passing MIMD Architectures," *SIAM Journal of Scientific and Statistical Computing*. (January 1987), Vol. 8, No. 1, pp. 118-134.

[Swar77]   P. Swarztrauber, "The Methods of Cyclic Reduction, Fourier Analysis and the FACR Algorithm for the Discrete Solution of Poisson's Equation on a Rectangle," *SIAM Review* (1977), Vol. 19, pp. 490-501.

[VGSS85]   D. Vrsalovic, E. F. Gehringer, Z. Z. Segall and D. P. Siewiorek, "The Influence of Parallel Decomposition Strategies on the Performance of," *Proceedings of the 12th Annual International Symposium on Computer Architecture* (June 1985), Vol. 13, No. 3, pp. 396-405.

[Witt81]   L. D. Wittie, "Communications Structures for Large Networks of Microcomputers," *IEEE Transactions on Computers* (April 1981), Vol. C-30, No. 4, pp. 264-273.

[Youn71]   D. Young, *Iterative Solution of Large Linear Systems*. Academic Press, New York, NY, 1971.

8   Commercial Hypercubes: A Performance Analysis

For a successful technology, reality must take precedence over public relations, for nature cannot be fooled.

Richard Feynman

The development of multicomputer systems clearly depends on the recent appearance of powerful single-chip processors and inexpensive memory. However, the recent explosion of interest in multicomputers can be traced to the CalTech Cosmic Cube [Seit85], a group of Intel 8086/8087 chips with associated memory connected as a D-dimensional cube[1]. Following the success of the Cosmic Cube, four companies quickly began delivery of multicomputer networks configured as hypercubes. Using existing chips, Intel developed the iPSC™ [Ratt85], a hypercube of 32, 64, or 128 Intel 80286/80287 processor pairs configured as 5, 6, or 7 dimensional cubes. Processor interconnection in the Intel iPSC is via point-to-point Ethernets. As configuration options, Intel also provides memory expansion and vector processor boards. Ametek countered with the System/14™, also based on the Intel 80286/80287 chip set.

Both the Intel iPSC and Ametek System/14 designs use an existing microprocessor coupled with additional logic to manage communication. If communication is considered initially, it can be integrated with the processor. As an example, the Inmos Transputer [Whit85] is a single chip, 32-bit processor containing 2K bytes of memory, a 32-bit external memory interface, and four, full duplex communication ports. By connecting Transputers, large multicomputer networks can be constructed using minimal ancillary support hardware. The Floating Point Systems T Series™ hypercube [GuHS86] typifies this approach. Following the Transputer lead, Ncube [HMSC86] developed a new VLSI chip containing hardware instructions for message passing and now markets the Ncube/ten™, a hypercube whose nodes each contain only seven chips, a processor and six memory chips.

---

[1]The design and development history of multicomputer networks is rich and varied and predates the Cosmic Cube. From a historical perspective, notable multicomputer research projects include the Finite Element Machine [Jord78], MICRONET [Witt80], the Stony Brook Network [ArBG85], X-Tree [SeFu82, Fuji83], and Zmob [KuWR82].

The appearance of any new computer system raises many questions about its performance, both in absolute terms and in comparison to other machines of its class. Multicomputer networks are no exception. Repeated studies have shown that a system's performance is maximized when the components are balanced and there is no single system bottleneck [DeBu78]. Optimizing multicomputer performance requires a judicious combination of node computation speed, message transmission latency, and operating system software. For example, high speed processors connected by high latency communication links restrict the classes of algorithms that can be efficiently supported.

Analytic models, such as those described in chapter two, capture the average, equilibrium behavior of multicomputer networks and can be used to examine the interaction between computation and communication. However, dynamic behavior and the idiosyncrasies of system software can only be captured by observation and measurement. For example, some commercial hypercubes such as the Ametek System/14 [Amet86] support only synchronous communication between directly connected nodes; others such as the Intel iPSC [Ratt85] provide asynchronous transmission with routing. The effects of these differences are difficult to model, but they can be easily measured.

As figure 8.1 illustrates, there are three levels in the hierarchy of performance analyses. At the lowest level, there is the performance of the hardware design. Determining this performance provides both a design validation and directives for

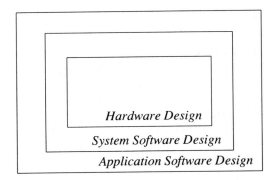

Figure 8.1
Performance analysis hierarchy.

system software design. Only by understanding the strengths and weaknesses of the hardware can system software designers develop an implementation and user interface that maximizes the fraction of the raw hardware performance available to the end user. As an example, consider a hypothetical multicomputer operating system that provides dynamic task migration to balance workloads and adaptive routing of data to avoid congested portions of the network. To meet these goals, it must be possible to rapidly transmit small status messages. It is fruitless to design such a system if the underlying hardware provides only high-latency message transmission. Finally, given some characterization of the balance between processing power and communication speed resulting from the system software, users can develop application algorithms that are best suited to the machine [SaNN87].

In this chapter, we discuss the hardware and software organizations of several commercial and one research multicomputer, each configured in a hypercube topology. Based on these descriptions, we examine their performance using a series of computation and communication benchmarks that highlight the interaction between hardware and software. Using the results of this performance analysis, we compare and contrast the strengths and weaknesses of each system. We conclude with an outline of desirable features for second generation multicomputer networks.

8.1. Hypercube Architectures

We begin with an examination of four commercial multicomputer networks, the Intel iPSC [Ratt85], Ametek System/14 [Amet86], Ncube/ten [HMSC86] and the FPS T Series [GuHS86], and one research machine, the Mark-III prototype [PTLP85] developed by the NASA Jet Propulsion Laboratory and the California Institute of Technology.

8.1.1. Intel iPSC

The Intel iPSC is a direct outgrowth of a licensing agreement between Intel and the California Institute of Technology (CalTech). Although this license provided access to both the hardware and software design of the Cosmic Cube [Seit85], Intel redesigned much of the hardware to improve its performance. In contrast, the software interface seen by users changed only cosmetically.

8.1.1.1. Hardware Organization

As originally announced, the iPSC product family contained three members: the iPSC/d5, iPSC/d6, and iPSC/d7, respectively five, six, and seven dimensional binary hypercubes.[2] Each group of 32 nodes is a single cabinet, and the nodes are connected via the cabinet backplane. Larger configurations of 64 and 128 nodes are formed by connecting multiple cabinets via cables.

Each system also contains an Intel System 310 **cube manager** that runs a variant of XENIX™. This cube manager supports program development, applications execution, and hypercube diagnostics.

As figure 8.2 shows, each iPSC hypercube node [Inte86a] contains an 8 MHz (Intel) 80286 microprocessor, a 6 MHz 80287 floating point co-processor, 512K bytes of dynamic RAM, and 64K bytes of PROM. All nodes are individually clocked. The 80286 in the iPSC operates in ''protected mode'' [Inte87], providing an address space of 16 megabytes. The programmable read-only memory (PROM) on each node occupies the highest portion of the 80286 address space and contains a node confidence test that is executed when the hardware is powered on, a loader that is used to load the node operating system from the cube manager, and a debug monitor that is used for diagnostics after initialization. The 512K byte dynamic memory occupies the lowest portion of the address space and contains the node operating system as well as user programs and data. This memory is dual ported and shared by both the 80286 and the communication hardware.

Communication, both internode and node-to-manager, is provided via eight 82586 Ethernet transceiver chips on each node board. All Ethernet transceivers are controlled via Intel 8254 and 8255A programmable peripheral interface chips, shown as the input-output control in figure 8.2. Up to seven of these transceivers connect the nodes in a binary hypercube, whence the maximum configuration of seven dimensions. The eighth transceiver connects the node to a global Ethernet, shared by all nodes and the cube manager.

Finally, each node contains a MULTIBUS II iLBX connector to the processor bus. On the system backplane, the iLBX of each even numbered node is connected to the adjacent odd numbered node. By replacing the hypercube node boards in the odd numbered positions, hypercube variations containing additional memory or vector processors can be configured. Naturally, replacing alternate node boards reduces the dimensionality of the hypercube. Given the fixed number of Ethernet transceivers on each node board, variations are configurable only in 16, 32, and 64 node sizes. Currently, Intel offers two extensions of the basic iPSC, the expanded memory iPSC/MX and vector processor iPSC/VX.

---

[2]Later variations on these designs will be discussed shortly.

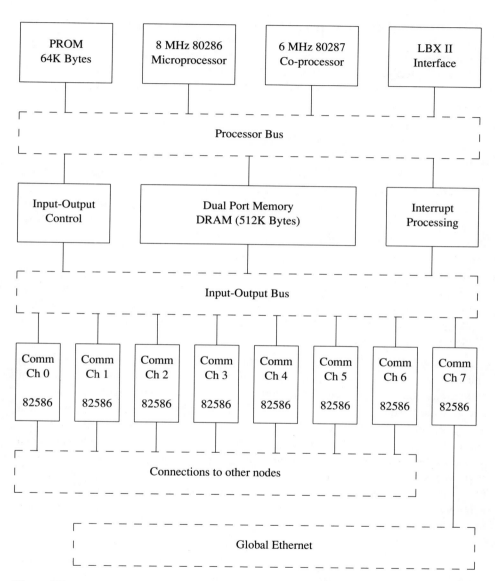

Figure 8.2
Intel iPSC node organization.

The expanded memory option replaces all odd numbered node boards with 4 megabyte memory boards. This memory resides between the PROM and 512K byte node memory in the 80286 address space. Because the node operating system and its associated buffers occupy approximately 200K bytes of the 512K byte node memory, this expansion is crucial for large memory applications. For example, Intel's parallel implementation of Common Lisp [Stee84] can only execute in expanded memory iPSC/MX configurations.

The vector processor iPSC/VX configuration also has additional memory on the vector boards. Each vector board contains one megabyte of dynamic RAM for user data, 16K bytes of static RAM, and 32K bytes of microcode (vector program memory) that control the vector pipeline. The dynamic RAM has a 250 nanosecond cycle time for 64-bit operands. The 100 nanosecond static RAM is partitioned into 4K bytes of user-accessible scratchpad memory and 12K bytes for intermediate results and table lookup. Data can be allocated to this memory via Fortran COMMON blocks.

Because the vector board is attached via the iLBX connector, all memory on the board is shared with the 80286, just as with the expanded memory option. Although the 80286 can access the vector memory, the vector processor cannot access the 512K bytes of memory on the node itself. Hence, the entire memory is not, properly speaking, dual ported; operands must initially be placed in the vector memory, or the 80286 must move the operands there.

As figure 8.3 shows, the vector processor is organized as an arithmetic unit, data unit, and control unit. The vector unit is synchronously clocked with a cycle time of 100 nanoseconds. The arithmetic unit contains twelve registers, used to store intermediate results and stage data for the two functional units. The adder and multiplier conform to the IEEE floating point standard,[3] and also support 32-bit logical and integer operations. The three stage adder, with 100 nanosecond stage delay, can produce either a single 32-bit or 64-bit result in 300 nanoseconds. With pipelining, a result is produced each 100 nanoseconds. In contrast, the multiplier can produce a 32-bit result in 300 nanoseconds and, after pipeline startup, a 32-bit result each 100 nanoseconds. For 64-bit operands, the multiplier delays increase by 200 nanoseconds for both scaler and vector operands.

The vector control unit, with its 50 nanosecond, 32K byte writable control store (WCS), coordinates operation of the data and arithmetic units. The WCS contains both a run time monitor and a library of vector, scalar, and logical operations.

---

[3]Excluding gradual underflow.

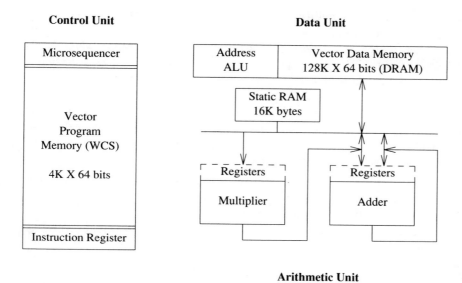

Figure 8.3
Intel iPSC vector processor.

Software support for vector processing includes a vectorizing preprocessor, a library of vector mathematical functions, and microcode development tools. The performance of the iPSC vector processor and its associated vector libraries will be discussed in §8.2.3.

8.1.1.2. Software Organization

The application programmer's model of the iPSC is one of a hypercube whose nodes are all connected to the cube manager. Application programs consist of a set of processes that interact via message passing. These programs usually contain a single **parent** or **master** process that executes on the cube manager; all other processes execute in the individual nodes. Typically, the master process is responsible for loading the node memories with the user processes, sending initialization parameters to these processes, and printing the results received from the hypercube processes.[4]

---

[4]Although the master process on the cube manager can participate in the computation, the contention overhead for access to the global Ethernet generally makes this alternative undesirable.

Figure 8.4 shows the system software organization of both the cube manager and the iPSC proper. As noted earlier, the cube manager interacts with hypercube nodes via the global Ethernet. On the cube manager this communication is realized via a XENIX Ethernet driver for the CNA960 hardware controller. All user processes executing on the cube manager interact with their hypercube siblings via this software and firmware. In addition to the standard XENIX command set, the cube manager also provides commands for controlling access to the nodes (see table 8.1). Finally, the master process executing on the cube manager interacts with node processes via calls to the manager application library. This library provides message transmission primitives analogous to those for internode communication on the hypercube.

At the lowest level, the node system software includes standard operating system support for memory management, process creation, and interrupt processing. The message passing routines, both for internode and node to cube manager communication, use these facilities to allocate message buffers and initiate message transfers. The application interface is analogous to the manager application library; it provides the user visible communication library and ancillary support. Finally, the process loader responds to manager commands that load and kill user processes.

Table 8.1

Intel iPSC cube manager commands

Command	Function
GETCUBE	Acquire exclusive access to the hypercube. No other users can load processes into the nodes until a corresponding RELCUBE command is issued.
CUBELOG	Maintain a time stamped log of events and errors in a specified file.
LOAD	Load node operating system software or user processes into the nodes.
LOADKILL	Kill the specified node processes.
LOADSTART	Begin execution of processes loaded via an earlier LOAD command.
LOADWAIT	Wait for the specified processes to complete.
RELCUBE	Release exclusive access to the hypercube.

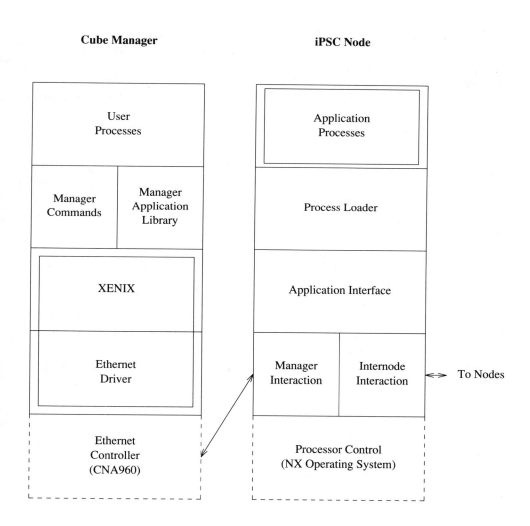

Figure 8.4
Intel iPSC software organization.

The node system software, collectively known as the Node Executive (NX), is designed to maximize the message throughput of the communication hardware. Experiments have shown that message buffer copying is a major source of overhead on the iPSC. To mitigate the effects of this overhead, the application interface provides both synchronous and asynchronous versions of message send and receive routines (see table 8.2). A complete description of these routines can be found in [Inte86b], however, a cursory description is sufficient to understand the interaction of the communication library and the node communication hardware.

For two node processes or a node process and a cube manager process to communicate, they must first open a **channel**. Because the two processes are physically separated, they may open or close the channel at different times. Any messages sent on a channel that has been closed by the destination process are buffered until the process opens the channel or the process terminates.

After opening a channel, a process can send messages either synchronously (**sendw**) or asynchronously (**send**). In both versions, the sender specifies the buffer containing the message, its length, the destination node, and the identifier of the process on the destination node. If the send is synchronous, the send invocation does not return until the message has been transmitted. This does not mean the message has reached its destination, merely that the message has been sent to an adjacent node and the buffer can be reclaimed. In contrast, an asynchronous send returns immediately, allowing the node to continue its computation. However, the **status** routine must be used to determine when the message buffer can be safely reclaimed. By forcing the application program to verify that buffers are free, the node executive NX avoids expensive copies of messages to system buffer space.[5]

Analogously, there are two versions of receive routines, **recv** and **recvw. Recvw** forces the receiver to wait until a message is actually received. In contrast, **recv** merely provides a user buffer to the system for message receipt. Again, the **status** routine must be used to verify receipt of a message. If no messages are outstanding for the specified channel when the **recv** is executed, no copying from system buffers need be done when a message arrives. If messages have arrived on this channel before the **recv,** they are buffered and copied on execution of the **recv.** Thus, asynchronous receives are only of value if they predate message arrival. If so, asynchronous receipt significantly reduces delays by eliminating buffer copy overhead.

---

[5]Normal implementation of an asynchronous send copies the message buffer from the process' address space to the operating system's address space before initiating the transmission.

Table 8.2

Intel iPSC node communication library

Procedure	Invocation	Function
COPEN	channel = copen (process_id);	Creates a communication channel for a node process.
CCLOSE	cclose (channel);	Closes a communication channel.
SEND	send (channel, type, buffer, buffer_length, node, process_id);	Initiates a message transmission to another process, perhaps on another node. The message buffer, passed as a parameter, must not be modified until the STATUS routine indicates the send is complete (i.e., non-blocking send).
SENDW	sendw (channel, type, buffer, buffer_length, node, process_id);	Initiates a message transmission to another process, perhaps on another node. The sending process is blocked until the message has been transmitted. This does not imply that the message has reached its destination, merely that the message buffer can be reclaimed.
RECV	recv (channel, type, buffer, length, &count, &node, &process_id);	Initiates receipt of a message from another process by providing a message buffer. Completion does not imply that a message has been received, merely that the system has accepted the buffer for eventual message receipt.
RECVW	recv (channel, type, buffer, length, &count, &node, &process_id);	Initiates receipt of a message from another process. The receiving process is blocked until the message has been received.

Table 8.2
Intel iPSC node communication library (continued)

Procedure	Invocation	Function
STATUS	result = status (channel);	Returns the state of the specified message buffer indicating whether the previous send or receive has completed.
PROBE	result = probe (channel, type);	Returns the availability of messages of a specified type on the channel.

Below the application interface, the communication routines interact with the node communication hardware in several ways. When an application process executes a **send** or **sendw,** several events occur; see [Inte86a] for complete details. First, the 80286 partitions the message into packets of maximum length 1024 bytes. Figure 8.5 shows the packet format used. Using the 82586 Ethernet transceiver chips imposes a sizable overhead in hardware header information. This is reflected in the bytes prepended to the software header of figure 8.5. Messages are packetized to reduce buffer requirements and to permit pipelining of transfers through the network.

After packetization, the 80286 determines the next node in the path to the destination node. The iPSC uses fixed path routing that successively resolves bit differences between the source and destination addresses, beginning with the low-order bit. Hence, the 80286 need only identify the bit position where the the current node address and the destination node address differ. This bit position, obtained via the exclusive OR of the two addresses, is the communication link to use.

Finally, the 80286 directs the Ethernet transceiver (the 82586) to initiate a message transfer. The transceiver reads the packets from the dual ported dynamic RAM via direct memory access and begins transfer to the adjacent node. When the transmission completes, the transceiver interrupts the 80286 to inform it that the message has been transmitted; this information is used by the **status** routine.

At intermediate nodes, the message packets are buffered and forwarded. When packets arrive at the destination node, they are reassembled to form the complete message and placed in either system buffers or an application program's buffer, depending on posting of an appropriate receive.

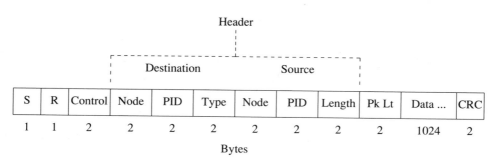

Figure 8.5
Intel iPSC packet format.

8.1.2. Ametek System/14

Like the Intel iPSC, the Ametek System/14 [Amet86] is based on research at the California Institute of Technology and the Jet Propulsion Laboratory (JPL). The collaborative effort between CalTech and JPL spawned two hypercube computing paradigms. The first, based on the Cosmic Cube [Seit85] and incorporated in the iPSC, provides asynchronous message transmission and message routing. The CalTech and JPL physics communities observed that many scientific computations are grid or lattice based. These computations require only nearest neighbor communication among processes that execute identical code. Consequently, there is little or no asynchrony and no need for message routing. By omitting asynchronous message transmission and routing, message transmission latencies can be reduced, albeit with corresponding loss of functionality. These **crystalline** operating systems (CrOS) formed the basis of the Ametek System/14 software.

8.1.2.1. Hardware Organization

The Ametek System/14 [Amet86] product family contains five members ranging from 16 to 256 nodes: the 14/16, 14/32, 14/64, 14/128, and 14/256. Each group of 16 nodes is a module. The 14/16, 14/32, and 14/64 contain 1, 2, or 4 modules stacked vertically in a single cabinet. Larger systems consist of multiple cabinets connected via cables.

The **host** for the System/14 is either a VAX-11™ or a MicroVAX II™, connected to the System/14 via direct memory access (DMA) ports. Like the iPSC cube manager, this host supports program development, applications execution, and cube diagnostics.

As figure 8.6 shows, each System/14 node contains an 8 MHz (Intel) 80286 microprocessor, an 8 MHz 80287 floating point co-processor, an 80186 communications co-processor, and 1 megabyte of dynamic RAM. The System/14

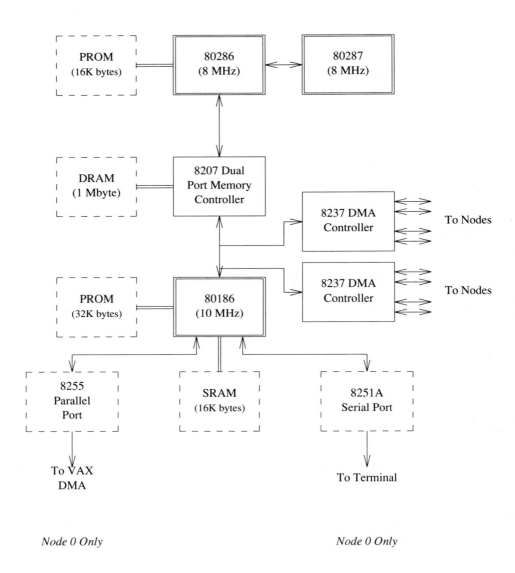

Figure 8.6
Ametek System/14 node organization.

nodes are individually clocked, but unlike the iPSC, the 80286 operates in "real mode" providing an address space of 1 megabyte. The two programmable read-only memories (PROMs) on each node store software monitors. At power-on, these monitors initialize the node, perform a consistency check, and determine the number of nodes in the system. The 1 megabyte dynamic RAM is dual ported and shared by both the 80286 and 80186. The 80186's 16K static RAM is mapped to the lowest portion of the address space, so it cannot access the lowest portion of the dynamic RAM.

Unlike the Ethernet transceivers used for internode communication on the Intel iPSC, the Ametek System/14 contains a dedicated 80186 communications co-processor. By offloading communication to a separate processor, the 80286 is potentially free to overlap computation with communication. This co-processor manages two DMA controllers, each with up to four connections to other nodes, whence the maximum configuration of eight dimensions. Each 16 node module is augmented with an additional parallel port interface (PPI) that connects with the host via a standard DMA connection[6] and to node 0 of the 16 node module. Interaction between the host and hypercube nodes is via the PPI; messages are first sent from the host to node 0 via the PPI and then sent via the hypercube links to the appropriate node. Because each group of 16 nodes contains a PPI, there can be separate paths from the host to distinct sub-cubes if the host contains the requisite DMA connections. This functionality permits **cube sharing**; discussed below. Finally, each group of 16 nodes also contains an RS-232 serial connection to the host. This connection is used for diagnostics and for interaction with the PROM monitors.

8.1.2.2. Software Organization

The programming model or *Weltanschauung* for the System/14 is similar to that for the Intel iPSC: a hypercube whose nodes are all connected to the host. Like the iPSC cube manager, the System/14 host executes a **parent** process that interacts with **child** processes executing on individual nodes. Although the host is connected to the hypercube via DMA channels, the communication overhead for node to host interaction is too high for the host process to participate as an equal partner in any computation.

The primary difference between the iPSC and System/14 programming models is the absence of asynchrony in the System/14. All System/14 internode communication is synchronous and unbuffered; there is no implicit message forwarding. Consequently, the system software organization for the System/14 is considerably simpler than that for the Intel iPSC; compare figures 8.4 and 8.7.

---

[6]A DRE-11/CC for a VAX-11 or a DRV-11/WA for a MicroVAX II.

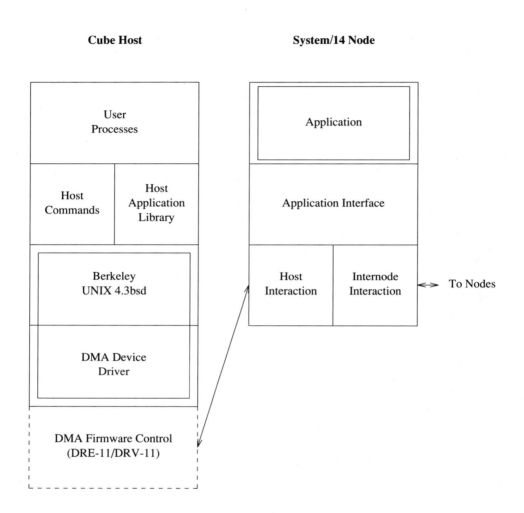

Figure 8.7
Ametek System/14 software organization.

Table 8.3

Ametek System/14 host commands

Command	Function
RTOT	Reset all hypercube nodes prior to loading user code.
RSPLIT	Split the hypercube into two systems of equal size. Each of the resulting sub-cubes can be used independently.
RSUB	Reset a sub-cube obtained via RSPLIT.

The hypercube host interacts with the nodes via a DMA interface. This communication is realized via a Unix™ device driver for the DRE-11 (VAX-11) or DRV-11 (MicroVAX II). Host interaction with the nodes takes two forms, hypercube control and process execution. The host commands, shown in table 8.3, enable the user to reset the hypercube and to partition it into disjoint subcubes, i.e., cube sharing. To understand the latter, recall that each node of a D-dimensional hypercube can have a D-bit address $(d_{D-1}d_{D-2} \cdots d_1 d_0)_2$ and is composed of two logically disjoint subcubes with addresses $(1 d_{D-2} \cdots d_1 d_0)_2$ and $(0 d_{D-2} \cdots d_1 d_0)_2$, where d_i can assume the values 0 or 1. Although these two subcubes are physically connected, they are logically disjoint. Moreover, on the Ametek System/14, each subcube has an independent DMA interface to the host. Hence, the host can partition a D-dimensional cube into two $(D-1)$ dimensional cubes. This partitioning enables two users to simultaneously use a smaller hypercube for software development and debugging. Finally, a parent process executing on the host interacts with node processes via calls to the host application library.

Unlike the Intel iPSC, the System/14 nodes do not contain an operating system as such. When the parent process of an application program begins execution on the host, it downloads the object file constituting the child program to the hypercube nodes. The PROM-based monitors on the hypercube insure that the downloaded code is disseminated to all nodes. Before the download, the child object file was linked with the node library routines necessary to realize internode and node-to-host communication. Thus, the user application runs stand alone on each node; there is no multiprogramming, process creation, or operating system interface.

The node application library, collectively known as XOS, supports internode communication. Because internode communication is solely synchronous, several variations of standard send and receive primitives are necessary. These variations provide message routing and forwarding in restricted circumstances; see table 8.4 and [Amet86] for complete details. The channels of table 8.4 are *not* logical channels similar to those provided by the Intel iPSC NX operating system; rather, they are physical channel addresses. Thus, a channel value of $(00010)_2$ corresponds to the node whose binary address differs from that of the current node in the second bit position.

All communication routines in table 8.4 are expansions of the basic **rdELT** and **wtELT**[7] primitives. These synchronous primitives read 8 bytes of data from the adjacent node specified by the channel. Each endpoint of a **rdELT/wtELT** pair blocks until the other completes; no buffering is possible. **Pass, pipe, shift, exchELT, brELT,** and **cmELT** all exist to compensate for the absence of message routing. Consider, for example, the **pipe** routine. It accepts input from an adjacent node and forwards it to another adjacent node. If a sequence of nodes execute **pipe** routines, the data will be forwarded to the final node in the sequence. This is equivalent to an operating system forwarding the message from a source to some destination - with one exception. If any intermediate node fails to execute the **pipe,** the transmission fails. More importantly, **pipe** requires all intervening nodes to "know" about the message, even if it is logically unrelated to the computation on the intervening nodes.

The primary advantage of the Ametek crystalline communication mode is efficiency. Because there is neither operating system overhead nor message buffering, the application program executes as efficiently as the programmer's expertise permits. The price paid for this efficiency is programmer overhead. The communication routines are low level, and each application program becomes a *de facto* operating system, scheduling message transmissions and avoiding deadlock.

The communication routines of table 8.4 interact with both the 80286, 80186, and the DMA controllers on each node. When an application program executes **rdELT,** the 80286 issues a command to the 80186 communication co-processor via a command buffer in their shared 1 megabyte memory. The 80186 directs the DMA controller corresponding to the appropriate channel to synchronize with its counterpart on the adjacent node. After an indeterminate interval, during which the recipient node executes a **wtELT,** the two DMA controllers have synchronized. They then transfer the data from the source program's data buffer to the destination program's data buffer via direct memory access to the dual ported dynamic RAM on each node. After the transmission completes, the sending DMA controller interrupts the 80186, and the 80186 writes a command completion signal in the command buffer shared with the 80286. Similarly, the receiving DMA controller interrupts its 80186, which signals the

---

[7]read ELemenT and write ELemenT.

Table 8.4

Ametek System/14 node communication library

Procedure	Invocation	Function
wtELT	wtELT (&data, channel);	Sends eight bytes of data on the specified channel to an adjacent node. wtELT does not return until the recipient node has received the data.
rdELT	rdELT (&data, channel);	Receives eight bytes of data on the specified channel from an adjacent node. rdELT does not return until a corresponding wrELT has been issued.
PASS	pass (&data, input_channel, output_channel, count);	Reads count 8-byte packets of data from the input channel and writes them to the output channel. A copy of all packets is saved at the address specified by &data.
PIPE	pipe (input_channel, output_channel, count);	Identical to PASS except the data are not saved as they are forwarded.
SHIFT	shift (&input_data, input_channel, &output_data, output_channel, count);	Transfers count 8-byte packets by writing the data in output_data on the output channel while reading the data from the input channel.
exchELT	exchELT (&input_buffer, input_channel, input_count, &output_buffer, output_channel, output_count);	Reads 8-byte packets from the input channel and places them in the input buffer while writing packets from the output buffer.
brELT	brELT (&buffer, source_node, channel_mask, count);	Sends count packets from the buffer to all nodes of a subcube specified by the channel mask.

Table 8.4 (continued)
Ametek System/14 node communication library

Procedure	Invocation	Function
cmELT	cmELT (&buffer, function, count);	Combines count packets of data from all nodes using the combining function.
rdrdy	rdrdy (channel);	Returns true if data are available on the channel.
wtrdy	wtrdy (channel);	Returns true if data can be written on the channel.

receiving 80286 that the read is complete. There is no overlap of computation on the 80286 and communication via the 80186. While the 80286 is computing, the 80186 is halted; while the 80186 is directing a communication, the 80286 is halted. Only one of the two processors is ever active.[8]

8.1.3. JPL Mark-III

The Mark-III is the latest in a series of hypercubes developed by the Concurrent Computation Project at JPL and CalTech [FoOt84, FoOt86]. Unlike the earlier Mark-I and Mark-II, based on the Intel 8086/8087 chip set, the Mark-III is based on the Motorola 68020 microprocessor. The synchronous, **crystalline** programming paradigm supported on the earlier Mark-II has been reimplemented in the CrOS-III operating system. In addition, asynchronous communication and message routing are supported in **Mercury**, a new operating system developed at JPL.

The Mark-III was designed as an extensible architecture. Like the Intel iPSC, it is possible to add additional functionality such as faster floating point support via daughter boards. As we shall see, however, the primary evolutionary emphasis is on increased communication performance.

---

[8]Why are there two processors? The System/14 hardware was designed to support both the crystalline and asynchronous communication paradigms. Ametek only recently announced an operating system that supports asynchronous communication.

8.1.3.1. Hardware Organization

As figure 8.8 shows, each Mark-III node contains a 16 MHz Motorola 68020 microprocessor with associated 68881 floating point co-processor, another 68020 for communication support, 4 megabytes of dynamic RAM, and up to seven communication links. Although the figure also shows an 68851 memory management unit with the computation processor, this was removed from the nodes after fabrication. JPL designers felt that the additional functionality did not warrant the associated memory wait state performance penalty. Finally, the Mark-III nodes are individually clocked, and the communication co-processor can potentially execute independently of the computation processor.

In addition to the 4 megabyte dynamic RAM that is shared by both the computation and communication processors, both processors have private, static memories - 64K bytes of static RAM for the communication processor and 128K bytes for the computation processor. These memories are accessible with no wait states, unlike the four wait states and two bus accesses required for the dynamic RAM. By placing frequently executed code and data structures in the static memories, bus contention and access times are reduced.

The 68020 communication co-processor manages, via a channel controller, seven 8-bit parallel link drivers on an I/O bus attached to the processor's communication bus. Each link has an associated FIFO (first-in-first-out) buffer that temporarily stores message packets.

Figure 8.8 shows optional daughter boards connected to the computation, communication, and system buses. These boards can provide extended functionality similar to that obtainable via the iLBX connectors on the Intel iPSC.

Several 32 node Mark-III systems are currently operational at JPL and CalTech and work is in progress on a successor, the Mark-IIIe. The Mark-IIIe nodes will contain ten *serial* communication channels (in contrast to the parallel channels on the Mark-III), 8 megabytes of dynamic RAM, and operate with a 25 MHz clock. The serial communication channels will boost the single link communication rate from 13.5 Mbits/second[9] to 29 Mbits/second. The 68881 floating point co-processor will be augmented with an accelerator based on the Weitek floating point chip set. These additions to the Mark-III are largely evolutionary and present no serious engineering obstacles. Other proposals for vastly improved communication, however, are considerably riskier.

---

[9]This is the sustained rate, verified experimentally.

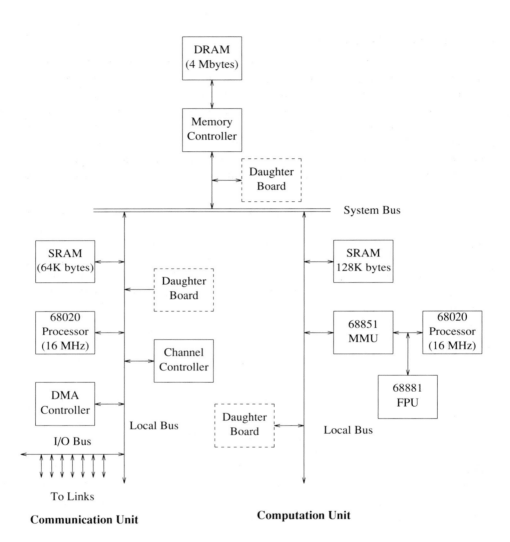

Figure 8.8
Mark-III node organization.

As discussed in chapter three, there are two primary approaches to internode communication: packet and circuit switching. The former minimizes resource utilization at the expense of store-and-forward delays. In contrast, circuit switching simultaneously holds a series of links from the message source to its destination. This profligate resource use minimizes message delay, after circuit setup, at the expense of increased network utilization. JPL currently plans to replace the Mark-IIIe communication subsystem with a circuit switched mechanism that can pass messages at 100 Mbits/second. A custom chip design, the **hyperswitch**, will control message passing and routing. As just noted, circuit switching is known to increase link utilization. Moreover, all current hypercubes use fixed path routing, even though the hypercube topology provides several (disjoint) alternate source to destination paths. To compensate for the increased link utilization and to decrease the probability of blocking during circuit setup, the hyperswitch also uses adaptive routing [ChBN81, Sega77]. The efficacy of the routing heuristics and their performance as a function of workload is a subject of current research [Mada87, GrRe87b].

Improving the performance of a system bottleneck, e.g., internode communication, always exposes another [DeBu78]. If circuits can be quickly established and messages rapidly transmitted, then the overheads for message buffering and preparation become more significant. Indeed, the cost for packetization, checksum computation, and buffering can dominate transmission time. Hence, the final component of the proposed Mark-IIIe message passing support is a **dispatch processor** designed for this purpose. There is no software intervention from the time an application processor issues a message transmission request until the message is buffered at the destination. While the JPL design differs from that presented in chapter four, its goals are similar: hardware support for message passing that obviates the need for software control.

8.1.3.2. Software Organization

As noted earlier, the Mark-III supports both synchronous (crystalline) and asynchronous communication modes. CrOS-III, the synchronous communication system, is a direct outgrowth of CrOS-II, the operating system for the JPL Mark-II, and the differences are minor and largely syntactic. The communication routines for the Mark-II CrOS-II and the Ametek System/14 XOS (shown in table 8.4) are identical. The CrOS-III communication routines are similar.

The Mercury operating system supports asynchronous communication.[10] Interestingly, it also provides *synchronous* communication support [JPL86]. That is, it

---

[10]Because Mercury is still developing, our discussion is necessarily brief.

is possible to switch between communication modes *during* an application. For example, to switch from synchronous to asynchronous mode, all nodes execute an **async_comm** command. This call advises Mercury that it must now manage buffers and route messages between non-adjacent nodes.

8.1.4. Ncube/ten

Unlike the Intel iPSC and the Ametek System/14 that are based on standard microprocessors, augmented with communication support hardware, the Ncube/ten [HMSC86, Ncub86b] contains a single-chip processor designed expressly for a multicomputer. Taking node design to its logical limit, each node consists solely of a single processor chip and six memory chips. This compactness permits construction of systems with up to ten dimensions: 1024 nodes on 16 boards of 64 nodes each, all housed in a single cabinet and connected via the system backplane. As we shall see, however, this design is not without limitations.

8.1.4.1. Hardware Organization

As figure 8.9 shows, each Ncube processor contains on-chip support for IEEE standard floating support and communication. The 32-bit instruction set is reminiscent of the DEC VAX-11™. With a 10 MHz clock, Ncube claims the processor executes at 2 MIPS (millions of instructions per second) for register-to-register, non-arithmetic instructions, 0.5 MFLOPS (millions of floating point operations per second) for single precision floating point operations, and 0.3 MFLOPS for double precision floating point. The processor chip contains approximately 160K transistors and is housed in a pin-grid-array package with 68 pins.

Although memory addresses are 32 bits long, the current node implementation only supports a 17-bit physical address space. This limitation arises from two sources: pin limitations[11] and memory chip density. To achieve compactness, maximizing the number of nodes per board, each node has only six memory chips. With six 256K dynamic RAMs, each organized as 64K X 4 bits, each node has 128K bytes of single-error correction and double-error detection (SECDED) memory.[12] Because of the pin limitation, each node must load 32-bit data as successive 16-bit half-words.

---

[11]Unlike conventional microprocessors, the Ncube chip must also support internode communication. This requires pins in addition to those for power and memory access and limits the number available for memory addresses.

[12]Ncube will shortly upgrade their systems to 1 Mbit dynamic RAMs.

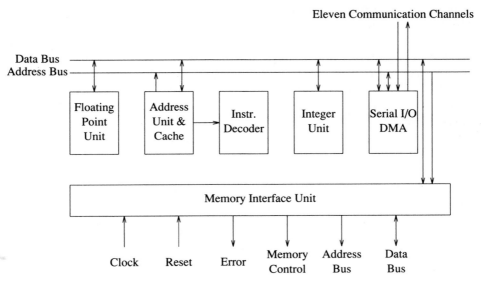

Figure 8.9
Ncube/ten node processor organization.

Special instructions are provided to support communication between neighboring nodes. The load pointer and load counter instructions initiate internode data transfers. The processor communication hardware includes 22-bit serial lines for communication with other nodes via asynchronous DMA transfer. These lines are paired as 11 bi-directional channels allowing a ten-dimensional hypercube with one additional connection to an I/O board (discussed below). Each internode channel operates at 10 MHz with parity, giving a transfer rate of roughly 1 megabyte/second in each direction. Associated with each channel are two registers that contain the start address and byte count for the DMA transfer; these are loaded by the aforementioned load pointer and load counter instructions. After the processor has initiated a message transfer, it is free to continue execution; the DMA transfer is autonomous.

External input-output and control are provided via up to eight I/O boards. These include graphics boards and open systems boards than can be configured for custom designs [HMSC86]. Any combination of I/O boards is permissible. However, at least one of these I/O boards must serve as the system host[13]. This board contains an Intel 80286 microprocessor and 80287 floating point co-processor with 4 megabytes of memory and supports up to four disk drives and eight terminals. All I/O boards each have 128 bi-directional channels directly connected to a portion of the hypercube. These channels are provided by 16 Ncube processor chips, each connected to 8 nodes in the hypercube via the eleventh channel of each node. The 16 Ncube processors function as I/O processors, and their 128K byte address spaces are mapped into the address space of the 80286. After reading data from a disk into the address space of the 80286, an Ncube processor functioning as an I/O processor can then transfer the data directly to the desired node in the hypercube.

8.1.4.2. Software Organization

Like the Ametek System/14 and Intel iPSC, the Ncube/ten programming model is one of a host processor connected to a hypercube. Unlike the other two systems, the connectivity of the host and the hypercube nodes is considerably richer, providing increased flexibility and greater I/O.

As noted earlier, the host I/O boards each contain an 80286 microprocessor. These processors execute a variant of Unix, called Axis™ [Ncub86a], developed by Ncube. Axis is a combination and extension of System V™ and Berkeley 4.3bsd and is completely compatible with neither. All application program development is done under Axis. Because there can be up to eight host I/O boards, each running Axis and managing a file system, the potential for data inconsistency and conflict exists. To avoid this, Axis supports a unified, distributed file system and hypercube partitioning. The latter is similar to Ametek's cube sharing; users can partition the hypercube into several smaller sub-cubes and work concurrently.

Compared to NX on the iPSC and XOS on the System/14, the Ncube node operating system, Vertex™, is extremely small, approximately 4K bytes. Vertex provides little other than internode communication support and message routing (see table 8.5). Message passing primitives are similar to those on the Intel iPSC. Messages have associated types, and message transmissions block until the message has been transmitted from the sender's buffer.

8.1.5. FPS T Series

The three machines just discussed are primarily educational and research machines. Their performance, with the possible exception of the Ncube/ten, is not sufficient to

---

[13]A system can contain multiple hosts, up to the maximum of eight.

Table 8.5

Ncube/ten node communication library

Procedure	Invocation	Function
NREAD	error = nread (&buffer, buffer_length, &source_node, &type, &status);	Receives a message of the specified type from the given node.
NTEST	length = ntest (&source_node, &type);	Checks for the presence of a message with the specified type from the source node and returns its length.
NWRITE	error = nwrite (&buffer, buffer_length, destination_node, type, &status);	Sends a message of the specified type, given by the contents of the buffer, to the destination node. The status flag indicates when the message buffer is free (i.e., the message has been sent).

challenge the traditional domain of supercomputers such as the Cray X-MP [LuMM85]. In contrast, Floating Point Systems (FPS) clearly designed the FPS T Series [GuHS86] with the supercomputer market as its primary target. System sizes range from a minimum of sixteen nodes up to a maximum size of 16384 nodes, a 14-dimensional hypercube.

8.1.5.1. Hardware Organization

The heart of each FPS T Series node is an Inmos Transputer [Whit85] microprocessor chip. A transputer is a 32-bit processor with a byte addressable, 32-bit address space. There are 2K bytes of memory with a single cycle access time on each Transputer chip. Additional, off chip memory can be accessed in three cycles. Each transputer contains four bi-directional serial communications links. Clearly, four communications links per node do not suffice to create a 14-dimensional hypercube. The techniques used to augment these links will be clear shortly.

As figure 8.10 shows, the transputer functions as the *control processor* for each T Series node. The control processor executes system and application code, including all integer operations, manages the internode communication, and configures operands for the attached vector processor. The control processor programming language is Occam [Inmo84], a process oriented language similar to Hoare's CSP [Hoar78] that provides communication primitives in the language. Occam is the *only* language supported on the Transputer and the FPS T Series; compilers for procedural languages such as C and Fortran do not yet exist.

The primary memory of the T Series is organized in a somewhat unusual way. In addition to the 2K bytes of static RAM on each Transputer chip, each node contains 1 megabyte of dual-ported dynamic RAM. From the Transputer control processor's perspective, this memory is a conventional memory of 256K 32-bit words with a 400 nanosecond access time. Thus, the two banks of memory shown in figure 8.10 are, from the control processor's perspective, only one bank. However, the vector processor sees the memory as two banks of vectors. The first bank contains 256 vectors that are 256 32-bit words long or 128 64-bit words long. The second contains 768 vectors of equivalent length. Simple arithmetic shows that all vectors must be aligned on 1K byte boundaries and have unit stride.

The division of the memory into two vector banks permits two vector operands to enter the vector floating point unit each 125 nanoseconds; giving a peak performance of 16 MFLOPS per node. As figure 8.10 shows, the vector floating point unit, based on the Weitek floating point chip set, contains a six stage, addition pipeline and a five stage (32 bit) or seven stage (64 bit) multiplication pipeline. These two pipelines are managed by a microprogrammed vector arithmetic controller with a 4K by 64-bit microcode store. The entire vector floating point unit can operate independently of the control processor, interrupting it when a vector operation has completed.

A major liability of the T Series floating point hardware is the absence of scalar floating point. The Transputer control processor does only integer arithmetic. On the surface, this is not disastrous; the vector floating point unit can process scalars as single element vectors. Unfortunately, the organization of the vector memory makes this very expensive. Specifically, the result of any vector operation destroys the previous contents of an entire 256 word block of memory, even if the specified vector is shorter than 256 words. Thus, scalar floating point operations are as expensive as vector operations. The overhead for scalar floating point and the need to process vectors shorter than 256 words mean that the control processor spends a significant portion of its time configuring data for the vector processor. The configuration overhead is exacerbated by the requirement that vectors have unit stride, i.e., they must occupy contiguous memory locations. A matrix, whether stored by rows or columns, has unit

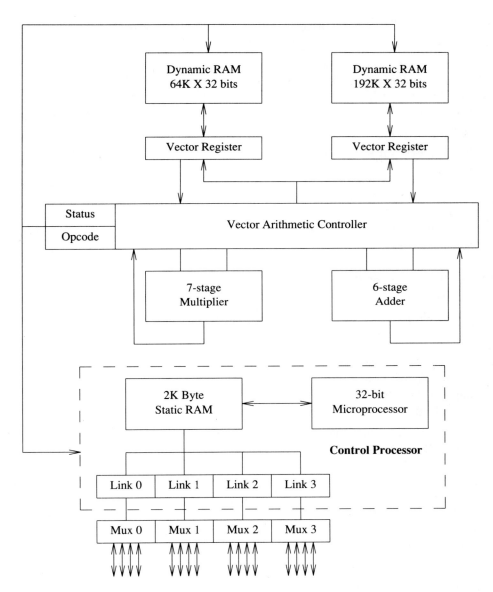

Figure 8.10
FPS T Series node organization.

stride in one dimension and constant stride equal to the matrix dimension in the other. The matrix must be transposed to permit unit stride in the offending dimension.

The Transputer control processor can drive each of its four serial communication links at a maximum rate of 7.5 Mbits/second. Each link is multiplexed four ways to provide 16 total links per node. Two of the 16 links are used for system communication and two others can be used for external I/O.

A T Series hypercube is organized using *modules*. Each module contains eight node boards, a system board, and disk storage. The system board provides I/O and other management functions and is connected to the eight nodes via a ring, formed using two of the 16 communication links on each node. Larger systems are configured by connecting modules. Multiple module systems connect their system boards via a system ring that is independent of the hypercube topology. This permits system communication without interfering with application message traffic on the hypercube communication links.

8.1.5.2. Software Organization

As mentioned earlier, the FPS T Series is programmed solely in Occam,[14] a process oriented language similar to Hoare's CSP [Hoar78] that contains synchronous message passing primitives. Processes execute at one of two priorities. High priority processes are not time sliced; they execute until they are blocked or they complete. If a high priority process becomes unblocked while a normal priority process is executing, it will preempt the normal priority process. Thus, high priority processes are preemptive but non-preemptable. In contrast, normal priority processes are time sliced every 1 millisecond.

The multiplexing of the Transputer's four communication links to increase the fanout of each node *is* user visible. Before two nodes can communicate, they must each execute a **set.links** procedure.[15] The procedure enables from one to four links on the executing node. Only after nodes connected by the specified links have all executed **set.links** will the procedure return; this synchronizes the communicating nodes. With the implicit synchronization of **set.links** and its associated overhead, the FPS T Series does not implement message routing in its system software.

---

[14]The Cornell University Center for Theory and Simulation in Science and Engineering is currently developing a C compiler for the FPS T Series.

[15]**Set.links** is not an Occam feature. It is a library routine added by Floating Point Systems.

Before a different set of links can be enabled, a **release.links** procedure must be invoked. Experiments show that the **set.links/release.links** combination is expensive, requiring between 0.5 and 1 millisecond [BFHP87, HePo87]. This suggests that it is inappropriate to view the T Series as a hypercube. Instead, it should be viewed as a reconfigurable network with a maximal internode connectivity of four. Computations move through phases, where a phase is a computation interval delimited by network reconfigurations.

8.2. Hypercube Performance Analysis

The Intel iPSC, Ametek System/14, JPL Mark-III, Ncube/ten, and FPS T Series differ greatly in architecture and system software. These differences are reflected in both the programming paradigm and the realizable computation and communication performances. All hypercube computations combine both communication and computation [Heat86]; hence, a single number such as MIPS, MFLOPS, or bits/sec will not accurately reflect either the interplay between communication and computation or the performance for differing applications. Moreover, computation speeds and message transmission rates both have hardware and software components; for example, a fast processor can be coupled with a poor compiler, or slow communication hardware can be coupled with efficient communication software. The goals of a performance analysis determine the relative importance of hardware and software components and, in turn, the composition of the benchmark set.

Ideally, one should evaluate all hypercubes using a single benchmark set. A uniform comparison would provide confidence in the equivalence of the measurement methodology and the associated results. As with most benchmark studies, resource availability is the primary limitation; no single site has simultaneous access to all machines. Moreover, machine differences such as the Intel iPSC vector processor and Occam on the FPS T Series make universal benchmarks difficult. Given these constraints, we present the results of three performance studies: a comparison of the Intel iPSC, Ametek System/14, and JPL Mark-III [GrRe87]; measurements of the Intel iPSC vector processor [Inte86c]; and an evaluation of the FPS T Series [BFHP87, HePo87].

8.2.1. Performance Study I (Intel, Ametek, JPL)

To isolate the effects of hardware and software, and to explore their interaction, Grunwald and Reed [GrRe87] developed a hypercube benchmark set and associated methodology for the Intel iPSC, Ametek System/14, and JPL Mark-III. This benchmark set includes four components:

- simple processor benchmarks,

- synthetic processor benchmarks,

- simple communication benchmarks, and

- synthetic communication benchmarks.

The simple processor benchmarks are, as the name implies, simple enough to highlight the interaction between processor and compiler, including the quality of generated code. In turn, the synthetic processor benchmarks reflect the typical behavior of computations and provide a ready comparison with similar benchmarks on sequential machines.

Communication performance is closely tied to system software. Some hypercubes support only synchronous communication between directly connected nodes; others provide asynchronous transmission with routing. In both cases the simple communication benchmarks measure both the message latency as a function of message size and the number of links on which each node can simultaneously send or receive. For systems that support routing and asynchronous transmission, the synthetic communication benchmarks reflect communication patterns in both time *and* space.

8.2.1.1. Test Environment

Although the Intel iPSC, Ametek System/14, and JPL Mark-III were described earlier, system software configurations change. In fairness, one must understand the hardware and software configurations used during the benchmark study. For convenience, these characteristics are summarized below and in table 8.6.

JPL Mark-III

During benchmarking, a four-node prototype of the Mark-III, running the CrOS-III operating system, was used. CrOS-III provides synchronous, single-hop communication primitives. The communication primitives used during benchmarking included: **cwrite** to send a message to adjacent nodes, **cread** to read a message from an adjacent node, **exchange** to implement an indivisible read and write operation pair, and **broadcast** to send a message to all other nodes. All benchmark programs were compiled using the Motorola 68020 C compiler provided on the CounterPoint System 19™ (CP) host processor.

Intel iPSC

All benchmarks used a 32-node iPSC running NX Beta Version 3.0. The communication primitives used during benchmarking were: **send** to asynchronously send a message to any node while program execution continues, **sendw** to send a

Table 8.6

Hypercube characteristics

Characteristic	JPL Mark-III	Intel iPSC	Ametek System/14	Ametek System/14 beta
Processor	16 MHz 68020	8 MHz 80286	8 MHz 80286	6 MHz 80286
Floating Point	16 MHz 68881	6 MHz 80287	8 MHz 20287	6 MHz 80287
I/O Processor	16 MHz 68020	none	10 MHz 80186	8 MHz 80186
Minimum Memory	4 Mbytes	0.5 Mbytes	1 Mbyte	1 Mbyte
Maximum Memory	4 Mbytes	4.5 Mbytes	1 Mbyte	1 Mbyte
Channels per Node	8	7	8	8
Peak Bandwidth	13.5 Mbits/s	10 Mbits/s	3 Mbits/s	3 Mbits/s

message to any node and wait for message transmission to complete, **recv** to asynchronously receive a message while program execution continues, **recvw** to receive a message and wait for it to arrive. Operations equivalent to **exchange** were composed from **send** and **recv** operations. The **broadcast** operation was performed by specifying a special destination address in a **send** operation. Programs were compiled using the L-model of the Microsoft C compiler provided with XENIX, the operating system on the hypercube host.

Ametek System/14

All benchmarks used a 32-node System/14 system running XOS Version D [Amet86]. The message primitives used during benchmarking were: **wtELT** to send a message to an adjacent node, **rdELT** to receive a message from an adjacent node, **exchELT** to indivisibly exchange messages between two nodes, and **brELT** to broadcast a message to all other nodes in the system. All programs were compiled using the L-model of the Lattice C V3.1 compiler.

Ametek System/14 β

A beta-test version of the System/14 system was used. This machine is functionally equivalent to the System/14, although the processor clocks are slower, and XOS Version 1.1 was used. Programs were compiled using the D-model of Lattice C V2.14 compiler.

8.2.1.2. Processor Benchmarks

The simple processor benchmarks have been used to evaluate other microprocessors [PaSe82]. The synthetic benchmarks, Dhrystone [Weic84] and Whetstone [CuWi76], were designed to represent typical systems programs and test floating point speeds, respectively. All the benchmarks were written in the C programming language, the only language available during the benchmark study. Unfortunately, this precluded using such standard numerical benchmarks as Linpack [DBMS79]. Table 8.7 describes the benchmarks, their characteristics, and the features they were each designed to test. Table 8.8, in turn, shows the results of the benchmarks.

For both variations of the *Dhrystone* benchmark, the results are given in *Dhrystones*, a normalized measure of Dhrystone performance. Likewise, the *Whetstone* benchmark results are given in *Whetstones*, the normalized measure of Whetstone performance. Larger values for Dhrystones and Whetstones indicate greater performance. All other results are in seconds.

For those benchmarks involving many procedure calls, in particular the *Fibonacci*, *Sieve* and *Hanoi* tests, the Ametek System/14 is faster than the Intel iPSC. However, all other benchmarks, even the highly recursive *Sort* test, favor the Intel iPSC. Most notably, the Intel iPSC is 4.4 times faster on the Dhrystone synthetic benchmark.

Because the processor architectures for the Intel iPSC and the Ametek System/14 are identical, these dramatic differences must be due to software. To investigate these differences, the *Loops* program was compiled using both the Microsoft and Lattice C compilers and then disassembled. The Intel 80286 provides a 16-bit ALU, while the innermost loop bound in *Loops* requires a 32-bit integer. The Lattice C V2.14 compiler used with the Ametek System/14 β release invokes a subroutine for 32-bit comparison on each loop iteration. In contrast, the Lattice C V3.1 compiler for the production Ametek System/14 expanded the procedure call in-line, providing better performance. Finally, the Microsoft C compiler for the Intel iPSC transformed the innermost loop into two loops, each of which tested a 16-bit integer. The outer loop tested the high-order 16-bits of the loop counter, and the inner loop tested the low-order 16-bits.

To further corroborate the view that compiler technology was the dominant performance determinant, the *Dhrystone* benchmark was compiled and disassembled using both the C compiler provided with the Ametek System/14 β system and an Intel 80286 compiler developed by AT&T. Although lines of generated code is a dubious performance predictor, smaller code is *usually* faster code. The number of disassembled instructions, shown in table 8.9, supports the theory that quality of

Table 8.7

Hypercube processor benchmarks

Simple Benchmarks	
Loops	10 repetitions of a 1,000,000 iteration null loop. Tests loop overhead
Sieve	100 repetitions that each calculate the primes from 1 to 8190. Tests loops, integer comparison, assignment.
Fibonacci	20 repetitions that each calculate Fibonacci (24). Tests recursion, integer addition, parameter return.
Hanoi	Solve the Towers of Hanoi problem with 18 disks. Tests recursion, integer comparison.
Sort	14 repetitions of quicksorting a 1000-element array of random elements. Tests recursion, comparisons, array references, multiplication and modulus.
Puzzle (subscript)	10 repetitions of Baskett's Puzzle program with subscripts. Tests explicit array subscript calculations and procedure calls.
Puzzle (pointer)	10 repetitions of Baskett's Puzzle program with pointers. Tests use of pointer versus explicit array subscripts.
Synthetic Benchmarks	
Whetstone	The Whetstone synthetic benchmark. General test of floating point performance, including trigonometric functions, multiplications and divisions.
Dhrystone (no registers)	The Dhrystone synthetic benchmark without register optimization. Tests integer scalar performance with a 'typical' instruction mix.
Dhrystone (registers)	The Dhrystone synthetic benchmark with register optimization. Tests the availability and effects of register variables

Table 8.8

Hypercube processor comparison

Benchmark	JPL Mark-III	Intel iPSC	Ametek System/14	Ametek System/14 beta
Loops	8.8	65.6	164.3	263.8
Fibonacci	10.0	39.2	21.3	32.7
Sieve	6.4	21.5	19.3	35.0
Sort	11.8	42.3	83.0	†
Hanoi	4.4	12.5	6.9	†
Puzzle (subscript)	45.5	87.6	97.9	164.3
Puzzle (pointer)	20.2	112.5	491.7	792.4
Whetstone[‡]	684,463	102,637	185,874	7367
Dhrystone (registers)[‡]	3472	724	165	107
Dhrystone (no registers)[‡]	3322	717	167	108

[†]These tests could not be run due to stack size limitations.
[‡]Performance figures in Whetstones or Dhrystones.

generated code is the major contributing factor to the performance differences observed.

Additional conclusions can be drawn from table 8.8. The *Puzzle* benchmark exists in two variations. The first variation uses arrays; the second was "optimized" by using explicit pointers and pointer arithmetic rather than implicit array subscript calculations. On processors with 32-bit integers and pointers, the pointer version typically executes faster because the compiler can more easily optimize the code. On the JPL Mark-III this is the case. With the Intel 80286-based systems, pointer arithmetic is more expensive than array subscript calculations because the former requires 32-bit operations. In contrast, array indexing in the 80286 "small memory model" requires only 16-bit quantities.

Similarly, the two variations of the *Dhrystone* benchmark show that, for the 80286-based systems, "optimizing" the program by using register variables does not improve performance. Precisely the opposite statements can be made for the JPL Mark-III.

The floating point performance of the Ametek System/14 is greater than that of the Intel iPSC, primarily due to the faster floating point unit. The Lattice C compiler for

Table 8.9

Intel 80286 compiler comparison (*Dhrystone* benchmark)

Compiler	Lines of Assembly Code
Lattice C V2.14	751
AT&T System V C (unoptimized)	467
AT&T System V C (optimized)	360

the Ametek System/14 β system uses procedures to implement floating point operations, hence the dramatic performance reduction.

Finally, table 8.8 shows that the JPL Mark-III is clearly superior to both systems based on the Intel 80286 microprocessor.[16] Based on the *Dhrystone* tests, a Mark-III node is approximately five times faster than a node based on the Intel 80286. Although identical benchmark programs were used on all machines, the benchmarks are *not* identical. The Mark-III, based on the Motorola 68020, always manipulates 32-bit quantities; the Intel 80286 operates on both 16-bit and 32-bit items. Those benchmarks that can be executed using only 16-bit quantities are unfairly biased toward the Intel 80286-based hypercubes.

Despite the differences in processor architecture, two points are clear. First, the quality of generated code varies greatly across compilers and can change the performance of otherwise identical systems by factors of four or more. Secondly, the performance superiority of the 68020 over the 80286 is significant and striking.

8.2.1.3. Simple Communication Benchmarks

To provide a small set of benchmarks that tests all link-level characteristics, Grunwald and Reed derived five operations that reflect a broad range of common single-link communications. In all of the simple communication benchmarks, the programs were structured to provide maximal communication concurrency, using the appropriate idiom in each hypercube operating system. In particular, the Intel iPSC versions use the asynchronous **send** and **recv** operations wherever possible, and the CrOS-III and XOS implementations use such special operations as **exchange** or **exchELT**. As with the processor benchmarks, all results are the means of 95 percent confidence intervals, and all intervals are less than 5 percent of the corresponding mean. Figure 8.11

---

[16]Informal benchmarks suggest that a single Mark-III node is comparable to a Sun-3/52™ workstation.

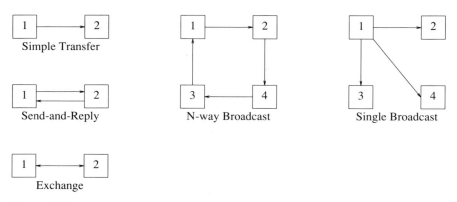

Figure 8.11
Simple communication benchmarks.

illustrates the communication patterns tested by each of the simple communication benchmarks.

Simple Transfer

The first test measures transmission speeds across a single link between two processors. Figure 8.12 compares the four different hypercubes. As with the simple processor benchmarks, the JPL Mark-III is significantly faster than any of the systems based on the Intel 80286. In addition, the Intel iPSC transmission time for small messages is much smaller than that for earlier versions of the iPSC operating system [SaNN87].

If the messages transmitted between nodes are not broken into packets, message transmission time t can be modeled as

$$t = t_l + Nt_c, \tag{8.1}$$

where t_l is the communication latency, i.e., the startup time for a transmission, t_c is the transmission time per byte, and N is the number of bytes in the message. Statistically, the linear model is a good fit to experimental data obtained for single link transmissions on the hypercubes tested, even though some systems do packetize large messages. Table 8.10 shows the result of a least-squares fit of the data to this linear model. Although the measured bandwidth for the JPL Mark-III is higher than the rated peak bandwidth (see table 8.6), this anomaly is likely due to the use of a prototype system. The Ametek System/14 has a lower latency than the Intel iPSC, but the higher bandwidth of the Intel iPSC yielded smaller total communication time for messages of more than 150 bytes.

Average Delay (seconds)

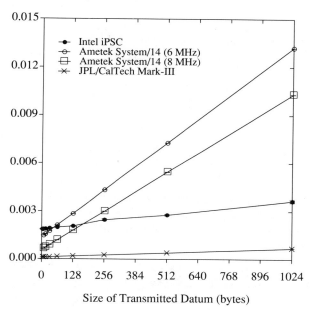

Figure 8.12
Simple transfer.

We emphasize that extrapolating general communication performance from single link tests is fallacious. Such simple tests highlight only link-level characteristics. More general benchmarks are needed to investigate routing and buffering behavior; this is the motivation for the synthetic communication benchmarks presented in the sequel.

Send-and-Reply and Exchange

In the second test, a message was sent, and the sender awaited a reply, analogous to a remote procedure call. This benchmark was designed to test the minimum response time of a node as a function of message size.

The third test was an *exchange* of data values, similar to that in many numerical computations, notably iterative solution of partial differential equations. If full-duplex transmission links were available, this test would measure their effective use.

Comparing the first test, figure 8.12, with the second test, figure 8.13, shows that for both the JPL Mark-III and Ametek System/14 the time to complete the send-and-reply

Table 8.10

Hypercube communication comparison

Feature	Mark-III	Intel iPSC	Ametek S/14	Ametek S/14 β
Latency (seconds)	9.5×10^{-5}	1.7×10^{-3}	5.5×10^{-4}	1.3×10^{-3}
Transmission time (sec/byte)	5.63×10^{-7}	2.83×10^{-6}	9.53×10^{-6}	1.17×10^{-5}
Bandwidth (Mbits/s)	14.3	2.8	0.84	0.69

is roughly twice that for the simple send operation. However, for the Intel iPSC, the time for the send-with-reply is less than twice the cost of a simple send. Because all four hypercubes provide only simplex communication channels, this differential cannot be attributed to communication overlap.

In the first test, the Intel iPSC benchmark executes a **(sendw)/(recvw)** communication sequence, i.e., one processor executes a **sendw** and the other executes a **recvw** primitive. In the send-and-reply test, the call sequence is **(send;recvw)/(recvw;sendw)**. Here, the processor executing the **send** has completed most of the overhead associated with a **recvw** call by the time the second processor has initiated the **sendw** operation, allowing the operating system to write the message directly into the user's buffer rather than a system buffer.

This is more evident in the exchange operation in the third test (see figure 8.14). Here, the Intel iPSC executes a **(send;recvw)/(recv;sendw)** sequence. The overlap afforded by the asynchronous **send** and **recv** calls allows the processor to establish where a message is to be placed before it arrives, eliminating buffer copies. Also, the processor is able to execute the setup code for the next message transmission while the communication is in progress. When the data for the third test on the Intel iPSC was fitted to (8.1), and the results are divided by two to compare them to a simple transfer, the transmission latency drops to 1.4 milliseconds, a 20 percent improvement. This reduction is the *ex post facto* motivation for asynchronous message transmission primitives on the Intel iPSC. In contrast, the JPL Mark-III provides no equivalent improvement because the CrOS-III operating system permits no asynchrony and executes little code during communication operations.

Average Delay (seconds)

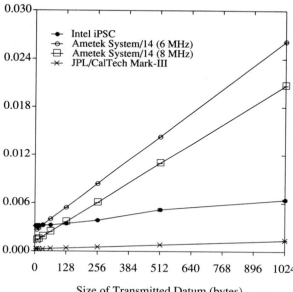

Size of Transmitted Datum (bytes)

Figure 8.13
Send-and-reply.

N-way Broadcast

The fourth test is an *N*-way broadcast, used when every processor must disseminate a message to all other processors. Because multiple communication links connected to each node can potentially be simultaneously active, this benchmark tests link simultaneity.

The intuitive implementation of this benchmark would use *N* broadcast operations. However, a more efficient approach for existing hypercubes uses a *ring broadcast* where node *i* receives messages from node *i* − 1 and sends messages to node *i* + 1. This requires only *O* (*N*) time.

With simplex communication links, the time for a ring broadcast on a four-node hypercube should be approximately six times that for a transmission across a single link, i.e., three link crossings with a send and receive for each. As figure 8.15 shows, both the JPL Mark-III and Ametek System/14 exhibit this behavior. In contrast, the performance of the Intel iPSC is non-intuitive. One tenable explanation for the Intel

Average Delay (seconds)

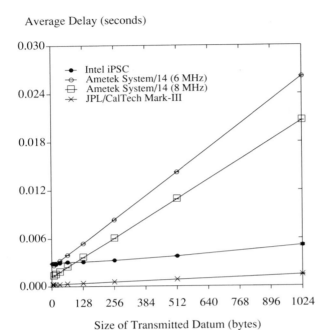

Size of Transmitted Datum (bytes)

Figure 8.14
Exchange.

iPSC is that the increased interrupt processing required to service two channels causes a significant amount of time to be spent context switching. Because an Intel iPSC node does not have an I/O processor, the 80286 processor must context switch to prepare an in-coming message, switch back to the user program, and switch twice more when the message has completely arrived. For small messages, context switching overhead is a large proportion of the total transmission time. As the message size increases, this cost is amortized over each byte of the message, and the Intel iPSC broadcast time is smaller than that for the Ametek System/14 when the message length becomes large.

Single Node Broadcast

The fifth and final test, shown in figure 8.16, exercised the broadcast mechanism provided by all the operating systems. Since only a four-node version of the Mark-III was available at the time of the study, the test was restricted to a four-node cube in all cases. As can be seen, the Intel iPSC performance is significantly better, relative to the other hypercubes, than for the N-way broadcast. This improvement is due to reduced link contention and context switching overhead.

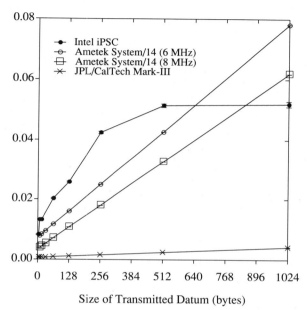

Figure 8.15
N-way broadcast.

8.2.1.4. Synthetic Communication Benchmarks

Application programs can be used to study hypercube communication performance, but because each program occupies only a small portion of the space of potential communication behaviors, many application programs are needed to achieve adequate coverage. Moreover, it is difficult to separate computation from communication. To study hypercube performance under a variety of communication traffic patterns, Grunwald and Reed developed a model of communication behavior. Each hypercube node executes a copy of the model, generating network traffic that reflects some pattern of both *temporal* and *spatial* locality. Intuitively, temporal locality defines the pattern of internode communication in time. An application with high temporal locality would exhibit communication affinity among a subset of network nodes. However, these nodes need not be near one another in the network. Physical proximity is determined by spatial locality.

Average Delay (seconds)

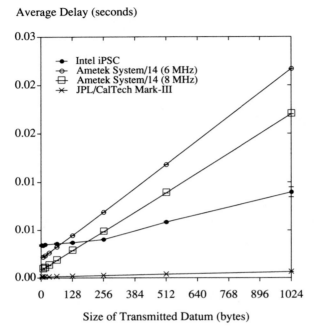

Size of Transmitted Datum (bytes)

Figure 8.16
Single broadcast.

8.2.1.5. Temporal Locality

The implementation of *temporal* locality is based on a Least Recently Used Stack Model (LRUSM), originally used to study management schemes for paged virtual memory [Denn80]. When used in the memory management context, the *stack* after memory reference $r(t)$ (the reference at time t) contains the n most recently accessed pages ordered by decreasing recency of reference. The stack distance $d(t)$ associated with reference $r(t)$ is the position of $r(t)$ in the stack defined just after memory reference $r(t-1)$ occurs. These distances are assumed to be independent random variables such that *Probability* $[d(t) = i] = b_i$ for all t. For example, if $b_1 = 0.5$, there is a 50 percent chance the next page referenced will be the same as the last.

In the adaptation of LRUSM to network traffic, each node has its own stack containing the n nodes that were most recently sent messages. In other words, destination nodes in the network are analogous to pages in address space of a process for the LRUSM model of memory reference patterns. Parameters to the model include the stack reference probabilities b_i and the stack size n.

We emphasize that the sum of the probabilities, $\sum\limits_{i=0}^{n} b_i$ is normally less than 1. Consequently, it is possible for the condition $d(t) > n$ to occur. In this case, a stack *miss* occurs. This corresponds to a page fault in the virtual memory context. In the model, a stack miss means that a new node not currently in the stack is chosen as the destination of the next transmission. This selection is based on a *spatial* locality model.

8.2.1.6. Spatial Locality

The communication model provides three types of spatial locality:

- *Uniform.* Any network node can be chosen to be the destination with equal probability. The uniform routing distribution is appealing because it makes *no* assumptions about the type of computation generating the messages; this is also its largest liability. However, because most computations should exhibit some measure of locality, it provides what is likely to be an upper bound on the mean internode message distance.

- *Sphere of Locality.* Each node is viewed as the center of a sphere of radius L, measured in hops. A node sends messages to the other nodes inside its sphere of locality with some (usually high) probability ϕ, and to nodes outside the sphere with probability $1 - \phi$. This model reflects the communication locality typical of many programs, e.g., the nearest neighbor communication typical of iterative partial differential equations solvers coupled with global communication for convergence checking.

- *Decreasing Probability.* The probability of sending a message to a node decreases as the distance from the source to the node increases. Specifically, the probability of sending a message l hops is

$$\Phi(l) = Decay(d, lmax) \cdot d^l, \qquad 0 < d < 1$$

where $lmax$ is the diameter of the network, d is a selected decay factor, and $Decay(d, lmax)$ is a normalizing constant chosen such that

$$Decay(d, lmax) \cdot \sum_{i=1}^{lmax} d^l = 1.$$

This model reflects the diffusion of work from areas of high utilization to areas of lower utilization.

More detailed descriptions of sphere of locality and decreasing probability routing can be found in chapter two. By pairing parameters for temporal locality with parameters for spatial locality, a wide variety of traffic distributions can easily be

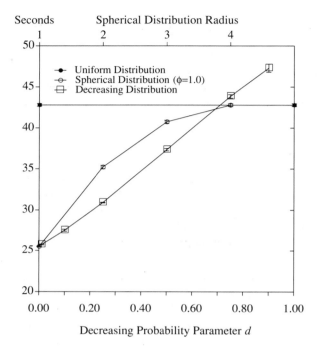

Figure 8.17
Spatial communication locality.

generated. By flushing the temporal stack periodically, a new set of destinations is selected; this can be used to simulate multiprogramming at individual nodes. Finally, additional input parameters control the frequency of message generation and the distribution of message lengths.

8.2.1.7. Experimental Results

Figure 8.17 shows the mean time for a 16 node Intel iPSC to transmit 3000 messages whose lengths follow an exponential distribution with a mean of 512 bytes. The horizontal line denotes the uniform message routing distribution. This provides a point of reference for the decreasing probability and sphere of locality distributions.

In figure 8.17, $\phi = 1$ for the sphere of locality distribution. This means that all messages generated will be sent to destinations within the radius. Thus, the expected execution time approaches that of the uniform routing distribution as the radius approaches the network diameter. With the decreasing probability distribution, increasing d means that a larger fraction of all messages are sent to distant nodes. For large enough values of d, the decreasing probability distribution is *anti-local*. Specifically, the mean internode distance is larger than that of the uniform routing distribution.

As figure 8.17 shows, approximately 43 seconds are required to send 3000 messages when the traffic distribution is uniform. For a 16 node hypercube, the average message crosses $\frac{32}{15} = 2.1\overline{33}$ communication links, assuming messages must cross at least one link. Hence, the average time to transmit a 512 byte message across a single link is approximately

$$\frac{43}{2.1\overline{33} \times 3000} = 6.7 \text{ milliseconds.}$$

This transmission time is over twice that for an idle link and greater than the N-way broadcast of figure 8.15. The overhead is directly attributable to link and memory contention, illustrating the need for enhanced communication hardware on the Intel iPSC.

Figure 8.18 shows the effect of varying the temporal locality of the three spatial locality distributions, using the same number and types of messages as in figure 8.17. In the figure, the temporal stack has depth one. This means that the number of messages sent to the node in the stack is the mean of a binomial distribution with parameter p, the probability of referencing the stack. Intuitively, there are "runs" of consecutive messages sent to a single destination node. Figure 8.19 illustrates these runs for one of the spatial distributions.

The most striking feature of figure 8.18 is the small variation in time to complete the suite of message transmissions. One would expect the temporal locality and its associated message runs to induce transient queues of outstanding messages on one link of each iPSC node. This phenomenon should manifest itself as increased delays when the probability of a stack reference increases. However, the variations shown in figure 8.18 are not statistically significant. Why? Suppose the rate each node generated messages were perfectly balanced with the transmission capacity of each of the node's communications links. In this case, no message queues would form. Now suppose temporal locality were introduced. The presence of stack runs would induce an imbalance, a queue would form for at least one link, and messages would be delayed. This phenomenon does *not* occur in figure 8.18, due to an imbalance of computation and communication speeds on the Intel iPSC. Nodes can generate messages faster than they can be transmitted by the communication links. Thus, queues develop for *all* links, masking the effects of temporal locality.

Time (seconds)

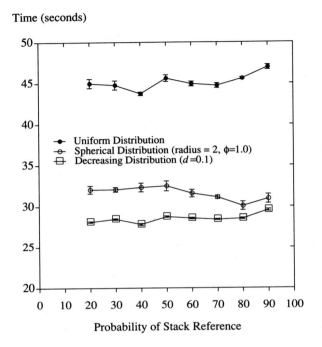

Probability of Stack Reference

Figure 8.18
Temporal communication locality.

Computation speeds, communication capacity, and communication patterns, both in time and space, interact in subtle ways. By using a synthetic benchmark that provides a broad spectrum of communication patterns, coupled with an understanding of the underlying analytic models, one can systematically and formally explore these interactions. This knowledge can be used to guide system design.

8.2.2. Performance Study II (FPS T Series)

Using the models developed by Grunwald and Reed [GrRe87], Helminen and Poplawski [HePo87] extended an earlier study [BFHP87] of the FPS T Series to include similar benchmarks. This later study examined a 32 node T Series hypercube running the A02 release of the FPS software [FPS86a, FPS86b].

Run Length

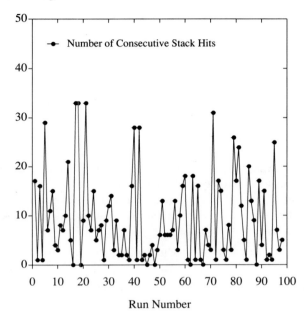

Figure 8.19
Temporal locality run lengths.

8.2.2.1. Processor Benchmarks

Figure 8.10 shows that the FPS T Series processors do not contain scalar floating point hardware. With scalar floating point operations performed in software, the T Series performance is but a few *kiloflops* [HePo87]. Hence, obtaining good vector performance is crucial; this was the subject of the Helminen and Poplawski study.

On the FPS T Series, there are two sets of vector routines. One is a low-level set of subroutine calls, or **parameter blocks** in FPS terminology, that requires careful attention to both the size of vectors and their placement and alignment in memory. This attention to detail is necessary to maximize vector performance.

The subroutines in **generic mathematics library** also support vector processing. These subroutines are more flexible than parameter blocks, allowing vector placement in arbitrary memory locations. However, the overhead for this flexibility is substantial, ranging from 200 percent for 128 element vectors to 25 percent for 4096 element vectors [HePo87].

Helminen and Poplawski selected two members of the generic library for analysis, double precision vector addition and DAXPY[17] [DBMS79]. If X, Y, and Z are vectors and a is a scalar, the library routines compute

$$Z_i = X_i + Y_i$$

and

$$Z_i = aX_i + Y_i$$

respectively. Although deceptively similar, these two routines are quite different. Vector addition uses only the addition pipeline of the FPS vector unit (see figure 8.10). In contrast, DAXPY simultaneously uses both the addition and multiplication pipelines. Figure 8.20 shows the performance of these two routines as a function of the vector length for double precision (64 bit) operands. For comparison, the parameter block equivalent of vector addition is also included.

Because the vector memory is organized as 64-bit vectors of length 128^{18}, the vector pipelines must process vectors of length less than 128 as if they were exactly 128 elements long. Consequently, the performance for short vectors is independent of their length, and the curves in figure 8.20 are flat over this interval. Longer vectors are processed as sequences of 128 element vectors.

With a 125 nanosecond clock, each of the FPS T Series' vector pipelines is theoretically capable of 8 megaflops. As figure 8.20 shows, vector addition achieves only 3.5 megaflops for vectors of length 32,768, and does not reach one half of this maximum until the vector length exceeds 256 elements. Because DAXPY drives both the addition and multiplication pipelines, it should approach an asymptote of 16 megaflops for long vectors. Instead, the asymptote is less than 5 megaflops, and 512 element vectors are needed to achieve one half of this maximum.

The limitations of the vector memory organization are painfully apparent in the performance asymptotes of vector addition and DAXPY. Of greater concern, however, is the large vector length needed to achieve one half the reduced asymptotes. Repeated studies show that well-designed vector processors achieve a large fraction of their asymptotic performance even for small vectors [HoJe81]. Moreover, the performance in figure 8.20 was obtained with vectors in contiguous memory locations, i.e., unit

---

[17]**D**ouble precision **a** times **X** Plus **Y**.

[18]Or equivalently, 32-bit single precision vectors of length 256.

Megaflops

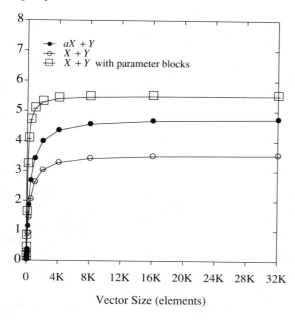

Vector Size (elements)

Figure 8.20
FPS T Series vector performance.

stride. Because the vector unit can only process unit stride vectors, data must be **gathered** prior to vector operations. Gather operations are extremely time consuming, requiring approximately 9 microseconds per data element. Consequently, a 128 element, non-contiguous vector can be processed at roughly

$$\frac{1}{\text{vector arithmetic time + data movement time}} =$$

$$\frac{1}{(1.12 + 9 \times 128) \times 10^{-6} \text{ seconds}} = 0.00087 \text{ megaflops.}$$

If the power of the FPS T Series nodes is to be realized, it is clear that vectors must be contiguous and of substantial length. Unfortunately, these conditions are frequently not met in practice.

Table 8.11

FPS T Series set.links timing

Number of Links	Time (milliseconds)
1	0.450
2	0.625
3	0.850
4	1.100

8.2.2.2. Communication Benchmarks

As figure 8.10 shows, there are only four physical links on each T Series node. The sixteen logical links are mapped onto the physical links such that logical link L corresponds to physical link L *mod* 4. Two logical links that are congruent modulo four cannot be simultaneously active. A program activates a set of four logical links via a **set.links** procedure. As table 8.11 shows, **set.links** is expensive, making it realistic to view the FPS T Series nodes as four-connected. Dynamic reconfiguration to realize the complete hypercube connectivity is too expensive to be practical. To appreciate the expense of link reconfiguration, one must understand the communication speed of configured links. To investigate this behavior, Helminen and Poplawski [HePo87] used the Grunwald and Reed simple transfer and exchange benchmarks. These benchmarks are discussed below.

Simple Transfer

The simplest test of communication performance is the transmission rate of data across a single link connecting two processors. Using the linear model of §8.2.1.3, Helminen and Poplawski measured the transmission time of an N byte message as

$$t = 8 + 1.468N$$

microseconds. Comparing this with table 8.10 reveals that the FPS T Series transmission latency is an order of magnitude smaller than that of the JPL Mark-III and two orders of magnitude lower than either of the Intel 80286 hypercubes. Moreover, the per byte transmission time is smaller than all but the JPL Mark-III. The FPS T Series does not route messages and all communication is synchronous, so there are no message headers and messages need not be buffered. These characteristics, coupled with the integrated communication support on the Transputer control processor, are the reasons for the low transmission latency and small per byte transmission time.

Link Speed (Kbytes/second)

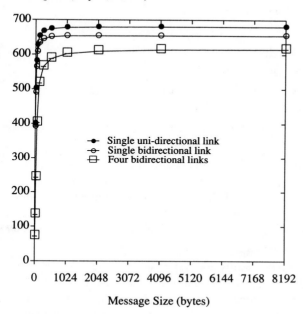

Message Size (bytes)

Figure 8.21
FPS T Series synchronous communication.

Exchange

Rarely do nodes transmit data on a single link. The typical communications paradigm has nodes simultaneously exchanging data on one or more links. Figure 8.21 shows the transfer rate *as seen by a single node in one direction* when data is exchanged with an adjacent node and with four adjacent nodes. The transfer rate for a uni-directional communication is also shown to facilitate comparison. As figure 8.21 shows, when the nodes at both endpoints of an FPS T Series communication link simultaneously transmit data, the aggregate bandwidth of the link is nearly doubled. This is in striking contrast to figures 8.12 and 8.14 which showed that most other hypercubes cannot effectively support bi-directional communication. Even when a node simultaneously exchanges data with its four neighbors, the degradation from eight-fold speedup is relatively minor, approximately eleven percent for messages containing 1024 bytes.

Context switching on the Transputer is the source of degradation for data exchanges. Communication on each link in each direction is managed by a different Occam process. Each time a process blocks while awaiting completion of a transmission, that process's context is replaced with that of an executable process. When the transmission completes, the context must be restored.

Routing Behavior

The absence of complete hypercube connectivity forces the programmer of the FPS T Series to adopt one of two programming paradigms:

- Invoke the **set.links** procedure each time a message must be sent to an adjacent node that is not a member of the "active set."

- Initially select a topology that connects all nodes, even if the topology is not optimal for the application program.

Given the communication speed of connected nodes and the large reconfiguration overhead, the first solution is acceptable only if reconfiguration occurs infrequently. With four active links per node, the FPS T Series can be configured as a torus. Although this configuration increases the network diameter from $O(log_2 N)$ to $O(N^{1/2})$, fixing the connectivity avoids the reconfiguration overhead and permits implementation of message routing software.

The current FPS T Series system software supports only nearest neighbor communication. To implement routing in the general hypercube topology, both endpoints of each link must establish a connection before the data can be transmitted. Because there is no internode signaling mechanism, the nodes must poll one another by establishing connections via **set.links** in a predetermined cycle. Given the overhead for **set.links**, it is more efficient to adopt a torus interconnection and route messages using its fixed connectivity.

Helminen and Poplawski have implemented a message routing library using the torus topology of the FPS T Series. Eight communication processes are created on each node, a sender and a receiver process for each of the four torus links. The semantics of the communication primitives are similar to the **send/recv** primitives of the Intel iPSC. Sends are non-blocking, and messages are not copied from the user buffer. Similarly, message receives provide a receipt buffer to the receiving process associated with the appropriate communication link.

The measured overhead for message transmission across a single link, using the routing package, shows that the transmission time for an N byte message takes the form

$$t = 139 + 1.449N$$

microseconds. The transmission latency is substantially higher than for synchronous transmission. The primary sources of this overhead are routing decisions and the

Link Speed (Kbytes/second)

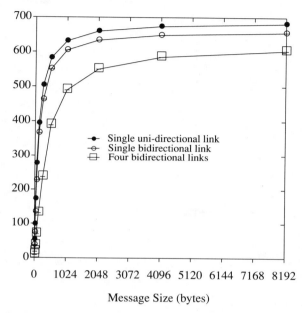

Message Size (bytes)

Figure 8.22
FPS T Series asynchronous communication.

construction of message headers. With nearest neighbor **crystalline** computations, the synchronous communication mode provided by the FPS T Series system software is clearly preferable. Figure 8.22 shows the performance degradation, compared to figure 8.21, when the routing software is used to repeat the data exchange experiments. The two figures converge to similar asymptotes. However, in figure 8.22 the higher latency of the routing software manifests itself as larger delays for small messages.

8.2.2.3. FPS T Series System Balance

The true measure of a multicomputer network is the balance of computation and communication speeds. A balanced system has no single bottleneck and both nodes and communication links operate near peak capacity. Figure 8.23 shows the per element time to compute a vector result and to send or receive a single datum. In scalar mode, the FPS T Series computation and communication speeds are well matched; the time to compute a single element is roughly equal to the time to transmit one datum. As the vector length increases, the vector unit approaches its asymptotic rate. In

Time/Element (microseconds)

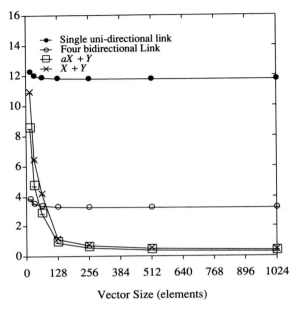

Figure 8.23
FPS T Series performance balance.

contrast, the transmission time per datum is constant. Thus, the system becomes highly communication bound when the processors operate in vector mode. To maintain communication balance in vector processing mode, the communication hardware of the T Series would need a ten-fold increase in transmission speed.

The limitations of the FPS T Series hypercube are many and varied. The vector memory organization is the most striking. Constant stride access to vector operands is imperative if the vector unit is to reach its peak performance. Similarly, the large overhead for reconfiguring the network interconnections pragmatically limit the topology to a 2-dimensional torus. The associated routing costs for large tori leave the performance of large T Series systems in doubt. Finally, the imbalance of computation and communication speeds make the system severely communication limited when operating in vector mode.

Table 8.12

Intel iPSC/VX performance specifications

Operation	Megaflops	
	32-bit	64-bit
Add/Sub/Mult[†]	2.6/6.2	1.3/3.2
Divide	0.52/0.52	0.28/0.28
Sin/Cos	0.47/0.47	0.24/0.24
DAXPY	8.8	8.8
Dot Product	9.1/18.2	3.3/6.7

[†]Dynamic and static memory

8.2.3. Performance Study III (Intel iPSC/VX)

The Intel iPSC Vector eXtension, shown in figure 8.3, contains pipelined addition and multiplication units with a 100 nanosecond cycle time for 32-bit operations. Hence, each node has a theoretical maximum computation rate of 20 megaflops for 32-bit operands and 6.67 megaflops for 64-bit operands. Table 8.12 shows the performance specifications published by Intel [Inte86c]. Intel does not state the vector lengths used to obtain these measurements. However, with both vector operands and the vector result stored in the 4K byte, scratch pad static RAM, the maximum vector length is 170 64-bit words.

Moler recently reported initial measurements of a vectorized linear systems solver based on LU decomposition with partial pivoting [Inte86d]. LU decomposition solves the linear system $Ax = b$ by reducing it to the equivalent linear system $LUx = b$ where $LU = A$. This system is then solved by evaluating $Ly = b$ and $Ux = y$ using forward and back substitution, respectively. The i-th reduction step selects the maximum element in the i-th column, exchanges the i-th row and the row containing the pivot element, and adds a multiple of the row containing the pivot element (now the i-th row) to each other row in the matrix. A physical row interchange can be avoided by careful indexing.

Because this benchmark takes into account the interaction of computation and communication, it is a better measure of the realizable vector performance on the iPSC/VX. The distributed version of this Linpack [DBMS79] algorithm places column j of a matrix A in node $(j - 1) \, mod \, P$, where P is the number of nodes in the hypercube. Because the matrix is distributed across the hypercube by columns, identifying pivot elements is straightforward [Heat86]. The identified pivot element is then broadcast to all other nodes, and used to reduce the rows below the row containing the pivot element. After N iterations, a matrix A of dimension N is reduced to the product LU, where L and U are respectively lower triangular and upper triangular factors of A.

Although the reduction step represents the most significant computational cost of the LU decomposition program, it is easily vectorized. Why? The pivot element is a scalar value that must be multiplied by the elements of the pivot row in each node and added to the rows below the one containing the pivot element.[19] This operation is simply a DAXPY.

Moler reports that a scalar implementation of this algorithm on the iPSC executes at approximately 2.2 megaflops on a 128 node system when solving a 64-bit linear system of size 1024. A vector implementation on a 16 node iPSC/VX executes at approximately 15 megaflops for a linear system of size 1024. By comparison with table 8.12, this suggests that each node of the iPSC/VX is operating at approximately 25 percent of its asymptotic DAXPY rate. Given the internode communication during each iteration of LU decomposition, this rate is quite impressive. As the size of the linear system decreases, the vector performance falls precipitously, however. Why? For small linear systems, the computation time is dominated by communication costs.

8.3. Hypercube System Comparisons

We have discussed the hardware and software organization of existing hypercubes and the associated performance of the machines. However, the design choices and the commercial success of any computer system are determined by social and economic pressures as well as technical issues. Of the machines we have discussed, some were marketed quickly, others had a longer gestation period; some were custom designs, others were not; most used standard programming languages, at least one did not. The motivations for and effects of these decisions are our next topic.

---

[19]Recall that each node contains $\left\lfloor \dfrac{N}{P} \right\rfloor$ columns of each row, where N is the order of the matrix and P is the number of nodes.

8.3.1. Hardware

Of the commercial hypercubes, the Intel iPSC and Ametek System/14 are clearly "learning machines" designed to test the market for message-based parallel processors and to provide machines for the university research environment. In this regard, Intel has been far more successful than Ametek, with an installed base of over 100 systems. In contrast, Ametek has installed less than 10 systems. Both machines were marketed after short development cycles to capitalize on the research interest stirred by Seitz's Cosmic Cube [Seit85]. This goal is reflected in the simple hardware designs of both machines. The use of standard microprocessors and communication components simplified design at the expense of performance.

Although the computing capabilities of both the iPSC and System/14 are limited, the relative performance of the associated communication subsystems is even more limited. The ratio of times for atomic operations, e.g., simple arithmetic, to transmission of small messages is unacceptably large. The addition of vector processors to the Intel iPSC exacerbates this situation by pushing the ratio of computation to communication times near that of networked workstations. It does, however, raise the computing performance of the iPSC to competitive levels. Both Intel and Ametek have announced second generation systems that should provide both a better balance of computing and communication speeds and greater absolute performance.

Although it may seem unfair to compare a research machine, the JPL Mark-III, to commercial products, the Mark-III typifies what can be expected from second generation hypercubes. The communication performance is significantly better than either the iPSC or System/14, and JPL has outlined a set of evolutionary performance improvements that should make the Mark-III competitive with future commercial offerings.

Unlike the iPSC, System/14, or Mark-III, which were based on existing hardware components, the Ncube/ten was designed expressly for a message passing environment. Consequently, the hardware support for message passing is excellent, and the small chip count of each node makes large systems cost-effective. However, the limited chip count is a mixed blessing. Because there are only six memory chips for each node, the node memory is limited by the density of dynamic RAM (DRAM) chips. Although the recent availability of 1 Mbit DRAMs enabled Ncube to increase the node memory from 128K bytes to 512K bytes, there is widespread agreement that additional memory is necessary. Indeed, Intel added the expansion memory option to the iPSC to permit execution of large Lisp programs. Despite the memory limitations of the Ncube/ten, it has been successfully used in oil reservoir modeling, where one group has reported performance with a 256 processor system greater than that of a Cray X-MP [Moor87]. Moreover, the installed base is growing, second only to that for the iPSC.

Of the commercial hypercubes, the FPS T Series is clearly the most unusual and commercially daring. Although the T Series raw hardware performance is impressive, idiosyncrasies caused by the Inmos Transputer and vector processor juxtaposition, coupled with the pseudo-hypercube connectivity provided by the multiplexing of communication links, make efficient use of the hardware difficult. Thus, the effective performance is considerably less than that potentially available.

The extraordinarily high purchase price of the T Series, compared to other hypercubes, has limited its acceptance. Only a small number of machines have been installed. Skepticism about parallel computing in general and message passing specifically has made potential users understandably chary about investing heavily in unproven computing paradigms. This is reflected in the willingness to purchase low-cost "learning machines" rather than more expensive, and more powerful machines.

8.3.2. Software

Because the Intel iPSC, Ametek System/14, Ncube/ten, and JPL Mark-III are all programmable in traditional languages such as C and Fortran, existing libraries of standard software, e.g., Linpack [DBMS79], and application programs can be readily ported. For the FPS T Series, programmable only in Occam, such is not the case. Regardless of the claimed superiority of Occam, the absence of other languages on the FPS T Series is both a marketing and a programming liability. As noted earlier, the Cornell University Center for Theory and Simulation in Science and Engineering is developing a C compiler for the FPS T Series. In addition, the Department of Computer Science at Michigan Technological University has developed a library of Occam routines that provide message passing. Together, these two developments should significantly expand the available software for the FPS T Series.

All machines contain an application host,[20] and because all hosts run either a variant of Unix or VMS,™ the software development environments are similar. Undoubtedly the largest difference among the systems is the node programming paradigm; synchronous on the Ametek System/14, the Ncube/ten and the FPS T Series; asynchronous on the Intel iPSC; and user selectable on the JPL Mark-III.

As an example of the software differences, consider a set of P processors, each containing a vector of length N. If V_i denotes the vector contained in processor i, we wish to compute the sum

---

[20]An Intel 310 for the Intel iPSC, a VAX-11 or MicroVAX-II for the Ametek System/14, a Counterpoint System 19 for the JPL Mark-III, an 80286 system for the Ncube/ten, and a MicroVAX-II for the FPS T Series.

```
/*********************************************************************/
/*                                                                 */
/*        Intel iPSC - computes the element by element sum of      */
/*        (P-1) vectors, where P is the number of processors.      */
/*                                                                 */
/*********************************************************************/

#define HOST              0x8000              /* host address (-32768)      */
#define VECTOR_LENGTH 1024                    /* maximum vector length      */
#define PROCESS_ID        1                   /* user defined process id    */
#define   SCALAR_TYPE     1                   /* message types              */
#define VECTOR_TYPE       2

main()
{
        int     Left, LeftChannel;            /* channel identifiers        */
        int     Right, RightChannel;
        int     Channel;

        int     FromNode, FromPid;            /* message parameters         */
        int     InBytes;

        int     j, k;                         /* loop counters              */
        int     N;                            /* vector length              */

        float   V [VECTOR_LENGTH];            /* vector sum at current node  */
        float   Vleft [VECTOR_LENGTH];        /* vector sum from left neighbor */

        Channel = copen (PROCESS_ID);         /* communication channel      */
        LeftRight ((1 << cubedim()),          /* find left & right neighbors */
                  mynode(), &Left, &LeftChannel,   /* code not shown        */
                  &Right, &RightChannel);

        recvw (Channel, SCALAR_TYPE, &N,      /* read vector length         */
               sizeof (int), &InBytes,        /* from host                  */
               &FromNode, &FromPid);
```

Figure 8.24
Intel iPSC node program.

```
for (j = 0; j < N; j++)                              /* create vector              */
    V [j] = 1.0 / ((float) mynode () + (float) j + 1.0);

for (k = 1; k < N; k++) {
    while (status (Channel)) flick();                /*wait for previous send      */

    send (Channel, VECTOR_TYPE,                      /* send data to right ring node */
          V, N * sizeof (float), Right, PROCESS_ID);

    recvw (Channel, VECTOR_TYPE,                      /* get data from left ring node */
           Vleft, N * sizeof (float),
           &InBytes, &FromNode, &FromPid);

    for (j = 0; j < N; j++)                           /* update current vector      */
        V [j] += Vleft [j];
}
}
```

Figure 8.24 (continued)
Intel iPSC node program.

$$W_i = \sum_{\substack{j=1 \\ i \neq j}}^{N} V_{ij}$$

in each processor i, where V_{ij} denotes the j-th element of the vector V_i. If V_i denotes the i-th column of a matrix, processor i wishes the element by element sum of all other other columns. A simple implementation of this algorithm has each node broadcasting its vector to all other nodes. Unfortunately, this requires $O(P^2)$ messages, each of length N, that must compete for communication resources. In principle the broadcasts could complete in $O(log_2 P)$ time by using the hypercube topology. In practice, it is more efficient to use a ring. Each node receives a vector V_k from its left ring neighbor, adds its own vector V_i, and sends the resultant vector to its right ring neighbor. After $O(P)$ communications, each processor will have the desired sum.

Figures 8.24-8.28 illustrate the implementation of this algorithm for the Intel iPSC, Ametek System/14, JPL Mark-III, Ncube/ten, and FPS T Series respectively. The iPSC program uses asynchronous sends to provide buffers and partially overlap message transmission and receipt. Even if the iPSC hardware included bi-directional communication links, this would still be the implementation of choice. In contrast, the synchronous communication of the Ametek System/14 requires even and odd numbered nodes to execute their send and receive operations in opposite order, or

```
/*********************************************************************/
/*                                                                 */
/*        Ametek System/14 - computes the element by element        */
/*        sum of (P-1) vectors, where P is the number of processors. */
/*                                                                 */
/*********************************************************************/

#include "userELT.h"

#define VECTOR_LENGTH 1024              /* maximum vector length        */

#define  PACKET_SIZE   8                /* Ametek sends 8 byte packets  */

x_main()
{
        char    Buffer [PACKET_SIZE];         /* buffer for message from host  */

        int     Left, LeftChannel;            /* adjacent node identifiers     */
        int     Right, RightChannel;

        int     j, k;                         /* loop counters                 */

        int     N;                            /* vector length                 */

        int     PacketCount;                  /* number of packets/message     */

        float   V [VECTOR_LENGTH];            /* vector sum at current node    */
        float   Vleft [VECTOR_LENGTH];        /* vector sum from left neighbor */

        LeftRight ((1 << doc), procnum,       /* find left & right neighbors   */
                  &Left, &LeftChannel, &Right, &RightChannel);

        rdsig (Buffer, 1);                    /* read vector length from host  */

        N = atoi (Buffer);

                                              /* number of 8 byte packets      */
        PacketCount = (sizeof (float) * (float) N)
                        / (float) PACKET_SIZE + 0.5;
```

Figure 8.25
Ametek System/14 node program.

```
    for (j = 0; j < N; j++)                          /* create vector                  */
        V [j] = 1.0 / ((float) procnum + (float) j + 1.0);

    for (k = 1; k < N; k++) {
        if (evennode) {                              /* synchronous data transfer      */
            pass (V, NULLCHAN,                       /* send data to right ring node   */
                RightChannel, PacketCount);

            pass (Vleft, LeftChannel,                /* get data from left ring node   */
                NULLCHAN, PacketCount);
        } else {
            pass (Vleft, LeftChannel,                /* get data from left ring node   */
                NULLCHAN, PacketCount);

            pass (V, NULLCHAN,                       /* send data to right ring node   */
                RightChannel, PacketCount);
        }

        for (j = 0; j < N; j++)                      /* update current vector          */
            V [j] += Vleft [j];
    }
}
```

Figure 8.25 (continued)
Ametek System/14 node program.

deadlock results (see figure 8.25). The Mark-III Mercury communication primitives (figure 8.26), are similar to those for the iPSC. Unlike the iPSC, Mercury packages all parameters as members of a C structure. The Ncube primitives are the simplest of all, providing message routing with synchronous transmission.

Finally, figure 8.28 shows the Occam equivalent of this algorithm for the FPS T Series. Given the differences between Occam and C, it is difficult to write an analogous program for the FPS T Series. The initial program declarations explicitly specify vector memory addresses to maximize performance. In the initialization section, the **recip** routine, not shown, computes the reciprocal of a floating point value.[21] Finally, the **vvo** call in the body of the program computes the vector sum.

---

[21]Due to Occam idiosyncrasies, **recip** is more difficult to write than the other routines.

```
/********************************************************************/
/*                                                                  */
/*      JPL Mark-III (Mercury) - computes the element by element    */
/*      sum of (P-1) vectors, where P is the number of processors.  */
/*                                                                  */
/********************************************************************/

#define   VECTOR_LENGTH        1024          /* maximum vector length     */

#define   SCALAR_TYPE   1                    /* message types             */
#define   VECTOR_TYPE   2

main()
{
        int     Left, LeftChannel;           /* adjacent node identifiers */
        int     Right, RightChannel;

        int     j, k;                        /* loop counters             */

        int     N;                           /* vector length             */

        float   V [VECTOR_LENGTH];           /* vector sum at current node */
        float   *Vleft;                      /* vector sum from left neighbor */

        struct  MSG_STRUCT rptr;             /* message structure         */

        init_merc();                         /* initialize Mercury OS     */

        async_comm (INF);                    /* switch from the CrOS-III  */
                                             /* paradigm to Mercury's     */

        LeftRight ((1 << cubedim()),         /* find left & right neighbors */
                mynode(), &Left,
                &LeftChannel, &Right, &RightChannel);

        for (j = 0; j < N; j++)              /* create vector             */
           V [j] = 1.0 / ((float) mynode () + (float) j + 1.0);
```

Figure 8.26
JPL Mark-III node program.

```
rptr -> source = CP;                          /* read vector length from host    */
rptr -> type = SCALAR_TYPE;                   /* (the control processor CP)      */
while ((status = get_buf (rptr)) != OK);

for (k = 1; k < N; k++) {
   rptr -> source = Left;                     /* get data from left ring node    */
   rptr -> type = VECTOR_TYPE;
   while ((status = get_buf(rptr)) != OK);

   Vleft = (float *) rptr -> buf;

   for (j = 0; j < N; j++)                     /* update current vector           */
      V [j] += Vleft [j];

   rptr -> source = Right;                     /* send data to right ring node    */
   rptr -> buf = V;
   send_msg_w (rptr, &Status);
   }
}
```

Figure 8.26 (continued)
JPL Mark-III node program.

8.3.3. Summary

Of the existing hypercubes, Intel has by far the largest customer base. The associated user group has fostered software exchange and improvements to Intel's software. Most message passing experiments are now conducted on the Intel iPSC. In contrast, the Ncube/ten currently provides the maximum configuration flexibility and is the largest threat to Intel's dominance. Ametek's hardware does not distinguish it from Intel, and its software does not have the support of a large user community. In contrast, the FPS hardware is fast, but its high price and the absence of standard programming languages have limited its acceptance.

8.4. Future Directions

What is the future of commercial message passing systems? Processor and communication performance will continue to improve, both with technology advances and engineering improvements. Low latency communication via hardware circuit switching is being explored and will likely appear in at least one second generation system. Circuit switched systems will lessen the dependence on the hypercube

```
/********************************************************************/
/*                                                                  */
/*        Ncube/ten - computes the element by element sum of        */
/*        (P-1) vectors, where P is the number of processors.       */
/*                                                                  */
/********************************************************************/

#define VECTOR_LENGTH 1024                    /* maximum vector length        */

#define  ANYNODE                -1

#define  SCALAR_TYPE    1                     /* message types                */
#define  VECTOR_TYPE    2

main()
{
        int       Left, LeftChannel;          /* adjacent node identifiers    */
        int       Right, RightChannel;

        int       Node;                       /* node number                  */
        int       ProcessId;                  /* process number               */
        int       NodeOnHost;                 /* host identifier              */
        int       CubeSize;                   /* hypercube dimension          */
        char      Status;                     /* transmission status          */

        int       j, k;                       /* loop counters                */

        int       N;                          /* vector length                */

        float     V [VECTOR_LENGTH];          /* vector sum at current node   */
        float     Vleft [VECTOR_LENGTH];      /* vector sum from left neighbor */

        whoami (&Node, &ProcessId,            /* determine node identity and  */
                &NodeOnHost, &CubeSize);      /* cube dimension               */

        LeftRight ((1 << CubeSize),           /* find left & right neighbors  */
                Node, &Left, &LeftChannel, &Right, &RightChannel);
```

Figure 8.27
Ncube/ten node program.

```
nread (N, sizeof (int), ANYNODE,            /* read vector length from host    */
    SCALAR_TYPE, Status);

for (j = 0; j < N; j++)                      /* create vector                   */
    V [j] = 1.0 / ((float) Node + (float) j + 1.0);

for (k = 1; k < N; k++) {
                                            /* send data to right ring node    */
    nwrite (V, N * sizeof (float), Right, VECTOR_TYPE, Status);

                                            /* get data from left ring node    */
    nread (Vleft, N * sizeof (float), Left, VECTOR_TYPE, Status);

    for (j = 0; j < N; j++)
        V [j] += Vleft [j];
}
}
```

Figure 8.27 (continued)
Ncube/ten node program.

topology in algorithm design. Although communication locality will still be important to minimize circuit blocking, alternate topologies will likely emerge [DaSe86].

Improved input/output capabilities are crucial. With the possible exception of the Ncube/ten, all current hypercubes are input/output limited. Generally, there exists only a single channel to secondary storage. To support database, artificial intelligence, and graphics applications, concurrent input/output is mandatory. Second generation hypercubes should provide both small (20-40 megabyte) disks at each node and an input/output network linking the nodes to external storage. The input/output network should be separate from the message passing network because the latency and bandwidth requirements for input/output are different from those for message passing.

Groups of heterogeneous nodes are also likely in second generation systems. Such groups would permit computations requiring dissimilar resources. Consider a task that included symbolic integration of a function, followed by its numerical evaluation, and a graphical display of the results. Rather than having large amounts of memory for the symbolic evaluation and a vector processor for the numerical evaluation at *each* node, the computation could be partitioned and assigned to those nodes with the resources suited to that portion of the computation. Intel and Ncube currently provide the hardware support for this computing mode and Intel has released (unsupported) prototype software to support heterogeneous nodes.

```
--
--          FPS T-Series - computes the element by element sum of
--          (P-1) vectors, where P is the number of processors.
--

value VADDR = #80000,                       -- address of V (bank b2)
      VleftADDR = #c0000,                   -- address of Vleft (bank a)
      TADDR = #f0000:                       -- temporary workspace (bank a)

var N,                                      -- vector length
    RightChannel, LeftChannel,              -- channel identifiers
    STATUS:                                 -- vector unit status response


SEQ
  -- read vector length from host
  read.int (N, portA, release)

  -- create vector
  SEQ j = [0 FOR N]
    SEQ
      -- temp1 := nodenumber + j + 1
      PUTWORD (processor+(j+1), TADDR+8>>2);
      -- temp2 := float (temp1)
      GN.SO (TADDR+8, AF.Xfloat, TADDR, 0, VP.64, STATUS)
      -- V[j] := 1.0 / temp2
      recip(VADDR+(j*2), TADDR)


  -- find left and right neighbors
  torus.1d (LeftChannel, RightChannel)

  -- set links for ring communication
  set.links (RightChannel, LeftChannel, -1, -1)
```

Figure 8.28
FPS T Series node program.

```
-- exchange vectors and compute
SEQ k = [1 FOR N-1]
  SEQ
    PAR
      -- send data to right ring node
      byte.slice.output (VADDR, N * 8, RightChannel)
      -- get data from left ring node
      byte.slice.input (VleftADDR, N * 8, LeftChannel)

    -- update current vector
    vvo (VADDR, VleftADDR, AF.XYadd, VADDR, NULL, N, STATUS)
```

Figure 8.28 (continued)
FPS T Series node program.

Finally, second generation systems should have vastly improved operating system software. Developing a message passing application can currently be likened to writing an operating system. The user must partition his or her computation and assign the tasks to individual nodes in a way that balances the computational load while attempting to minimize communication costs. Conventional operating systems do not encourage or even permit users to provide page replacement algorithms on virtual memory systems; it is unreasonable to expect users to assign tasks to processors in a message passing system. Dynamic load balancing will permit applications to create new tasks as they execute. The operating system will assign these tasks to nodes as appropriate. Similarly, adaptive routing algorithms will avoid congested areas of the network.

The future of multicomputer networks is bright. Many pragmatic lessons have been learned since the first generation hypercubes appeared; many other issues remain to be explored. Nevertheless, if the experience already obtained is incorporated in the design of second generation systems, the promise of multicomputer networks may finally be realized.

References

[Amet86]   *Ametek System 14 User's Guide: C Edition.* Ametek Computer Research Division, Arcadia, California, 1986.

[ArBG85]   M. Arango, H. Badr and D. Gelernter, "Staged Circuit Switching," *IEEE Transactions on Computers* (February 1985), Vol. C-34, No. 2, pp. 174-180.

[BFHP87] D. Bergmark, J. M. Francioni, B. K. Helminen and D. A. Poplawski, "On the Performance of the FPS T-Series Hypercube," In: *Hypercube Multiprocessors 1987*, M. T. Heath, ed. Society for Industrial and Applied Mathematics, Philadelphia, PA, 1987.

[ChBN81] W. Chou, A. W. Bragg and A. A. Nilsson, "The Need for Adaptive Routing in the Chaotic and Unbalanced Traffic Environment," *IEEE Transactions on Communications* (April 1981), Vol. COM-29, No. 4, pp. 481-490.

[CuWi76] H. J. Curnow and B. A. Wichman, "A Synthetic Benchmark," *Computer Journal* (February 1976), Vol. 19, No. 1, pp. 43-49.

[DaSe86] W. J. Dally and C. L. Seitz, "The Torus Routing Chip," *Journal of Distributed Computing* (1986), Vol. 1, No. 3.

[DBMS79] J. J. Dongarra, J. R. Bunch, C. B. Moler and G. W. Stewart, *Linpack Users' Guide*. Society for Industrial and Applied Mathematics, 1979.

[DeBu78] P. J. Denning and J. P. Buzen, "The Operational Analysis of Queueing Network Models," *ACM Computing Surveys* (September 1978), Vol. 10, No. 3, pp. 225-261.

[Denn80] P. J. Denning, "Working Sets Past and Present," *IEEE Transaction on Software Engineering* (January 1980), Vol. SE-6, No. 1, pp. 64-84.

[FoOt84] G. C. Fox and S. W. Otto, "Algorithms for Concurrent Processors," *Physics Today* (May 1984), Vol. 37, pp. 50-59.

[FoOt86] G. C. Fox and S. W. Otto, "Concurrent Computation and the Theory of Complex Systems," In: *Hypercube Multiprocessors 1986*, M. T. Heath, ed. Society for Industrial and Applied Mathematics, Philadelphia, PA, 1986, pp. 244-275.

[FPS86a] *T-Series User Guide 860-0002-004B*. Floating Point Systems, Beaverton, Oregon, 1986.

[FPS86b] *Programming the FPS T-Series: Math Library Manual*. Floating Point Systems, Beaverton, Oregon, 1986.

[Fuji83] R. M. Fujimoto, *VLSI Communication Components for Multicomputer Networks*. Ph.D. Dissertation, Electronics Research Laboratory Report No. UCB/CSD 83/136, University of California, Berkeley, California, 1983.

[GrRe87] D. C. Grunwald and D. A. Reed, "Benchmarking Hypercube Hardware and Software," In: *Hypercube Multiprocessors 1987*, M. T. Heath, ed. Society for Industrial and Applied Mathematics, Philadelphia, PA, 1987.

[GrRe87b] D. C. Grunwald and D. A. Reed, "An Analysis of Hypercube Circuit Switching," *in preparation*.

[GuHS86] H. L. Gustafson, S. Hawkinson and K. Scott, "The Architecture of a Homogeneous Vector Supercomputer," *Proceedings of the 1986 International Conference on Parallel Processing* (August 1986), pp. 649-652.

[Heat86] M. T. Heath, *Hypercube Multiprocessors 1986*. Society for Industrial and Applied Mathematics, Philadelphia, PA, 1986.

[HePo87] B. K. Helminen and D. A. Poplawski, "A Performance Characterization of the FPS T-Series Hypercube", Computer Science Technical Report CS-TR 87-6, Michigan Technological University, Houghton, Michigan, February 1987.

[HMSC86] J. P. Hayes, T. Mudge, Q. F. Stout, S. Colley, et al., "A Microprocessor-based Hypercube Supercomputer," *IEEE Micro* (October 1986), Vol. 6, No. 5, pp. 6-17.

[Hoar78]   C. A. R. Hoare, "Communicating Sequential Processes," *Communications of the ACM* (August 1978), Vol. 21, No. 8, pp. 666-677.

[HoJe81]   R. W. Hockney and C. R. Jesshope, *Parallel Computing.* Adam Hilger, Limited, Bristol, 1981.

[Inmo84]   *Occam Programming Manual.* Prentice-Hall International, London, 1984.

[Inte86a]   *Intel iPSC System Overview, Order Number 310610-001.* Intel Scientific Computers, 1986.

[Inte86b]   *Intel iPSC Programmer's Reference Manual, Order Number 310612-001.* Intel Scientific Computers, 1986.

[Inte86c]   "Intel iPSC/VX Product Summary," Intel Scientific Computers, (1986).

[Inte86d]   "Matrix Computation on Intel Hypercubes," Intel Scientific Computers, (September 1986).

[Inte87]   *Intel Microprocessor and Peripheral Handbook, Volume I - Microprocessors.* Intel Corporation, 1987.

[Jord78]   H. F. Jordan, "A Special Purpose Architecture for Finite Element Analysis," *Proceedings of the 1978 International Conference on Parallel Processing* (August 1978), pp. 263-266.

[JPL86]   *Mercury I/O Library User's Guide: C Language Edition.* Jet Propulsion Laboratory, Pasadena, CA, 1986.

[KuWR82]   T. Kushner, A. Y. Wu and A. Rosenfeld, "Image Processing on ZMOB," *IEEE Transactions on Computers* (October 1982), Vol. C-31, No. 10, pp. 943-951.

[LuMM85]   O. Lubeck, J. Moore and R. Mendez, "A Benchmark Comparison of Three Supercomputers: Fujitsu VP-200, Hitachi S-810/20, and Cray X-MP/2," *IEEE Computer* (December 1985), Vol. 18, No. 12, pp. 10-23.

[Mada87]   H. Madan, "private communication," *Jet Propulsion Laboratory* (April 1987).

[Moor87]   W. D. Moorhead, "private communication," *Shell Development Corporation* (April 1987).

[Ncub86a]   *C Guide for Use on Ncube Axis Systems.* Caine, Farber, and Gordon, Inc., 1986.

[Ncub86b]   *Ncube/ten Handbook,* Ncube Corporation., 1986.

[PaSe82]   D. A. Patterson and C. H. Séquin, "A VLSI RISC," *IEEE Computer* (September 1982), Vol. 15, No. 9.

[PTLP85]   J. C. Peterson, J. O. Tuazon, D. Lieberman and M. Pniel, "The Mark III Hypercube-Ensemble Concurrent Computer," *Proceedings of the 1985 International Conference on Parallel Processing* (August 1985), pp. 71-73.

[Ratt85]   J. Rattner, "Concurrent Processing: A New Direction in Scientific Computing," *Conference Proceedings of the 1985 National Computer Conference* (1985), Vol. 54, pp. 157-166.

[SaNN87]   J. H. Saltz, V. K. Naik and D. M. Nicol, "Reduction of the Effects of the Communication Delays in Scientific Algorithms on Message Passing MIMD Architectures," *SIAM Journal of Scientific and Statistical Computing.* (January 1987), Vol. 8, No. 1, pp. 118-134.

[SeFu82]   C. H. Séquin and R. M. Fujimoto, "X-Tree and Y-Components," In: *Proceedings of the Advanced Course on VLSI Architecture,* P. Treleaven, ed. Prentice Hall, Englewood Cliffs, New Jersey, 1982.

[Sega77]   A. Segall, "The Modeling of Adaptive Routing in Data-Communication Networks," *IEEE Transactions on Communications* (January 1977), Vol. COM-25, No. 1, pp. 85-95.

[Seit85]   C. L. Seitz, "The Cosmic Cube," *Communications of the ACM* (January 1985), Vol. 28, No. 1, pp. 22-33.

[Stee84]   G. N. Steele, *Common Lisp: The Language*. Digital Press, 1984.

[Weic84]   R. Weicker, "Dhrystone: A Synthetic Systems Programming Benchmark," *Communications of the ACM* (October 1984), Vol. 27, No. 10, pp. 1013-1030.

[Whit85]   C. Whitby-Strevens, "The Transputer," *Proceedings of the 12th International Symposium on Computer Architecture, Boston, Mass.* (June 1985), Vol. 13, No. 3, pp. 292-300.

[Witt80]   L. D. Wittie, "MICROS: A Distributed Operating System for MICRONET, A Reconfigurable Network Computer," *IEEE Transactions on Computers* (December 1980), Vol. C-29, No. 12, pp. 1133-1144.

Index

The MIT Press, with Peter Denning, general consulting editor, and Brian Randell, European consulting editor, publishes computer science books in the following series:

ACM Doctoral Dissertation Award and Distinguished Dissertation Series

Artificial Intelligence, Patrick Winston and Michael Brady, editors

Charles Babbage Institute Reprint Series for the History of Computing, Martin Campbell-Kelly, editor

Computer Systems, Herb Schwetman, editor

Exploring with Logo, E. Paul Goldenberg, editor

Foundations of Computing, Michael Garey, editor

History of Computing, I. Bernard Cohen and William Aspray, editors

Information Systems, Michael Lesk, editor

Logic Programming, Ehud Shapiro, editor; Fernando Pereira, Koichi Furukawa, and D. H. D. Warren, associate editors

The MIT Electrical Engineering and Computer Science Series

Scientific Computation, Dennis Gannon, editor